LONGMAN CLASSICS *in* POLITICAL SCIENCE

Party Politics in America

FOURTEENTH EDITION

MARJORIE RANDON HERSHEY

Indiana University

Foreword by

FRANK J. SORAUF

University of Minnesota

Longman

New York   San Francisco   Boston
London   Toronto   Sydney   Tokyo   Singapore   Madrid
Mexico City   Munich   Paris   Cape Town   Hong Kong   Montreal

Editor-in-Chief: Eric Stano
Editorial Assistant: Elizabeth Alimena
Supplements Editor: Donna Garnier
Marketing Manager: Lindsey Prudhomme
Project Coordination, Text Design, and Electronic
    Page Makeup: Sadagoban Balaji / Integra Software Services Pvt. Ltd.,
Cover Design Manager: Jayne Conte
Production Manager: Fran Russello
Printer and Binder: Courier Companies, Inc.

Library of Congress Cataloging-in-Publication Data
Hershey, Marjorie Randon.
    Party politics in America/Marjorie Randon Hershey: foreword by
Frank J. Sorauf.—Fourteenth ed.
        p. cm.—(Longman classics in political science)
    Includes bibliographical references and index.
    ISBN-13: 978-0-205-79319-8 (alk. paper)
    ISBN-10: 0-205-79319-3 (alk. paper)
    1. Political parties—United States.   I. Title.
JK2265.H477 2011
324.273—dc22

                                                    2004001983

1 2 3 4 5 6 7 8 9 10—CRS—13 12 11 10

Longman
is an imprint of

www.pearsonhighered.com   ISBN 13: 978-0-205-79319-8
                           ISBN 10:   0-205-79319-3

Brief Contents

Contents

Figures and Tables

Figures

Tables

Foreword

RAISING A COLLEGE TEXTBOOK

If you have already noticed that you are reading the fourteenth edition of this book, you know that it has a long history. The first edition, indeed, was published in 1968, but the decisions and hard work of producing the book began years before that. So, let me begin with the early 1960s.

But first, who am I? I was the first author of this textbook and its author through its first five editions. My name is Frank Sorauf, and I retired from the political science department of the University of Minnesota in 1996. You may think of me as the father or grandfather of this enterprise—and a living authority on its early history.

The publisher of the first edition was Little, Brown, and Co., an old and storied publisher of serious books in Boston. For most of its history it had not published college textbooks, but it created a "college division" after World War II when the GIs were pouring into the nation's colleges and universities. Its management also made the decision to begin with just a few fields of knowledge, one of them political science. The editors in political science set about identifying young scholars who were establishing themselves and becoming more and more visible in the profession, even if they were inexperienced in textbook writing. I remember talking with Little, Brown editors about a textbook in American political parties as early as 1960 or so.

At this point, Little, Brown made a strategic decision to explore an alternative to the large, single textbook, and to publish a series of short paperback books that would be the brief "core" book for a course, which the instructor could supplement with paperbacks of more popular books on the subject.

I agreed to write such a core book, and it was published as *Political Parties in the American System.*

It had only 186 smallish pages, and as a paperback, it had the mandatory soft binding. It did well in sales and got good reviews, as did some of its paperback siblings. Alas, not all of the siblings did.

The marketplace also delivered a broader verdict: many college teachers were not ready to abandon the thick, single volume textbook.

The summer of writing was not wasted, however. I thought a great deal about organizing a book on the subject, and I had a splendid, experienced copyeditor at Little, Brown who taught me lessons on the theme "Write a book for students, not a piece for your scholarly peers." He, along with my teacher in an "advanced placement" section of the freshman course in writing nonfiction were the two best teachers of writing good English prose that I ever had.

Just a few years later, the marketplace intervened in another way. The author of the best-selling textbook on American parties, V. O. Key of Harvard, died in October of 1963. Key was a scholar of towering reputation, and his book had become a reference book as well as a textbook for college students. It did have one vulnerability in the marketplace, however. It covered American interest groups as well as political parties at a time when the two topics were being divided into separate courses in many political science departments. There was also the possibility that the Key book might not sell in the next version since it would not be by Key himself. However, the point became moot when Key's widow decided that V. O.'s great book should not be revised. And so it died with its author. Shortly thereafter, Little, Brown decided to publish a full-length text on American political parties, and I was asked to write it. Obviously I agreed. I submitted an outline for the book that reflected a balance between theory and description not unlike that of Key's book. But unlike Key, I would not deal with interest groups, nor would I include his lengthy material on the history of the American parties.

I also would represent a political science divided between old historical, descriptive traditions and the "new" political science (aka "behavioralism") that was more theoretical and analytical, more in search of empirical explanation. At about 400 pages, the book was planned to be shorter than Key's.

As I recall, the book was initially scheduled to appear in 1967, a target we missed by a year. The fault was largely mine. I was offered a Fulbright professorship to teach (in English) in Bologna, Italy, at the European Center of Johns Hopkins School of Advanced International Studies. Its student body at the time was graduates of American and European universities, and I was to teach courses in American elections and parties and American courts and constitutional law for Europe's brightest students curious about our ways. How could I turn down that challenge and the great food of Italy's culinary capital?

I promised my editor at Little, Brown that I would make progress on the manuscript in Italy since I was teaching courses I had already prepared. But I had not reckoned with the charms of Italy, and the fact that my rented apartment was only three short blocks from one of Italy's most important railroad stations. But I did do some writing, largely writing the prose shell of some chapters, leaving until later the "plugging in" of specific data, references to books and articles, etc. Indeed, one of the chapters was sketched out on a rainy day in Venice as I sat nibbling and sipping under the umbrellas of a restaurant on the Piazza San Marco. The prose was, of course, inspired.

So, I returned home with more than half of the book in skeletal form. But Minneapolis had its distractions, too. In 1966, I was appointed by the mayor of Minneapolis to the Board governing the city's library system. (It was the only time I ever held public office.) And later in the year, my colleagues and the dean asked me to take a three-year term as chair of the department of political science, those three years being ones of campus troubles over the war in Vietnam. Moreover, in 1966, I was only 38 years old and struggling at a research university to find time for my research agenda. So, more than a little of the book was written after nine at night. The miracle is that it appeared in 1968, only one year late.

In all of this—the paperback book, my other delays, and the editing of the book's manuscript itself—Little, Brown was wonderfully supportive. It was my first major book with a publishing house, and I soon realized as a beginner in producing a book how fortunate I was. My good fortune continued once the book appeared, and some of my fellow political scientists pointed out errors in the text. The great majority of the errors and the critics (all very polite and understanding) came from specialists in state politics. I had erred in not being aware of recent changes in state practices, especially in election law. Neither the Twin Cities newspapers nor the *New York Times* proved to be interested in recording the changes states make from an open to a closed primary, for instance, unless the state is New York or in its region.

From the beginning, I was also committed to writing an accurate, authoritative book, in good and lucid English prose. That commitment is central to my personality and self-image. I always liked writing, and initially was a beginning journalist. I edited my high school newspaper, worked as a freelance writer to earn spending money, and spent my first two years in college as a journalism major, shifting to political science only in my junior year. That experience made me a fluent, quick writer, but hardly a very elegant one. Style and genuine respect for the expressiveness of the English language came in college in the composition course I mentioned. The instructor, with the unforgettable name of Gracia Torinus, was a true believer in the beauty and expressiveness of the language. From her, I learned to respect the musicality of good English. It must scan—must have a regular rhythm, she insisted. Reading one's prose out loud to test the scan was one of her major mantras. And the search for the enemies of smoothly rolling prose—such as clusters of nouns—became our obsession. Until the day I retired, I never stopped noting clusters of three or more nouns in student term papers. ("Senate committee chairperson" does not sing.)

Once in Little, Brown's hands, the manuscript moved quickly through production. In that process, it also received its formal title, *Party Politics in America*, the same title it carries in this edition. Exactly when it appeared for sale in 1968, I am not sure. If I am vague about such matters, it is because I never kept records, and that was because I never imagined writing an essay such as this. I do remember that Little, Brown was pleased with early sales and that the pleasure never let up. And the sales rose with new editions every four years. Those were years, I might add, in which the used book industry was a largely unorganized, largely local competitor with the new books of the publisher. That distinction is important to an author, since the author receives royalties only on the new books the publisher sells. For me, the success of the book meant unanticipated royalties and the prospect of preparing a new edition in four years. The royalties I largely turned into an acquisition fund for my art collecting, in particular the art of Native Americans, and especially the pottery of the Pueblos.

Fortunately, my terms in the departmental chairmanship and on the Library Board both expired in 1969, although there were still students to teach, as well as a research project to keep moving forward. So, I began assembling new data and new references for the next edition. Little, Brown wanted to publish a new edition every four years, and the next one would appear in 1972. I began by drawing up a list of the items that would require updating—election outcomes, major changes in the regulation of elections and political parties, the voting behavior of Americans at the previous presidential elections, and so on. Once again, the greatest problems were in identifying the changes the states made in their regulations of elections and parties. I also had to review the scholarly journals and books to make sure that I knew of all the new scholarship on the American parties. Since I had been hiring undergraduate research assistants for some time, I sometimes diverted their work from my research project for some scanning of the abstracts and indexes to recent scholarly work.

My chief role in revision, however, was a careful review of the text to catch the sentences that might be improved, to carve up paragraphs that were too long, and generally to reconsider both the prose and the strategies of making sense out of complex subjects (such as American campaign finance). I also became aware that some of the pages in the first edition were composed too exclusively of my paragraphs. So illustrative materials—some visual and some textual—were added. I especially looked for material to put in "boxes" to break up gray pages. The result was a lighter, more inviting look on many pages. I even splurged on a cartoon from the *New Yorker*—splurged, I say, because rights to it did not come cheaply. Fortunately, the two cartoons of late nineteenth century bosses were in the public domain and thus without charge.

I am confident that the four revisions I put the book through improved it and its appearance. And I am proud to say they were accomplished without greatly inflating the book: the first edition had 430 pages of text, the fifth had only 446. As much as I was happy to tend the garden I had planted, eventually the gardening began to wear. Moreover, I came to believe the book needed a fresher rethinking than I could give it. At some point, one becomes the prisoner of one's own prose. Furthermore, I wanted time to write a book on American campaign finance. I had been immersed in the subject while working with a committee of prominent citizens assembled by the Twentieth Century Fund to weigh the new importance of political action committees (PACs). I doubted that I could find time to write that book while revising the textbook for the fifth time. So, I approached Little, Brown, explained my dilemma, and we began the process of finding a new author for the book. I made a list of five people I thought would be great successors, and we agreed easily on Paul Allen Beck. He was a recognized scholar in the field, he was younger than I, and had better ties to the younger generation than I. He also had a great reputation as a colleague and an accomplisher. Both the publisher and I were delighted when he agreed to sign on.

Once Paul agreed to take over for the sixth edition, I stopped all participation as an author, even though my name appeared on the sixth (Sorauf and Beck) and seventh editions (Beck and Sorauf). The publisher wanted my name in order to reassure the market (i.e., the professors who decide which book or books their students will buy) that it would be a book with roots in the earlier editions. I think I made it clear to Paul that I was not going to second-guess him and that he should not hesitate to make changes where he thought necessary. He did consult me on several questions, and I replied as briefly and helpfully as I could, but he was free to make the book his, and over several editions he did.

So, I bowed out of the enterprise in 1984 or 1985. I do admit that I retain a residual pride in it. That is why I am so pleased that two very talented political scientists have continued the quality and the professional reputation of the book. College textbooks must change in order to stay abreast of both new knowledge in political science and new trends and events in the American political parties and the campaigns they dominate. It is often a process that requires both change and continuity, but without change textbooks do not survive.

Frank Sorauf
PROFESSOR EMERITUS
UNIVERSITY OF MINNESOTA

Preface

WHY SHOULD YOU ASSIGN THE NEW EDITION?

Publishing a new edition of a book about party politics every two years is costly—for the students who will buy it, the instructors who will assign it, and even the person who researches and writes it! So why do it? American federal elections take place every two years, and each election tells us something new about the American parties. The edition of this book published in 2005 critically evaluated the argument, made frequently after George W. Bush's reelection, that the Republicans were on the verge of becoming the majority party. By 2007, popular analysis had taken a 180-degree turn; the Democratic takeover of Congress in 2006 was hailed as evidence of a Democratic resurgence. Again, the 2007 edition of *Party Politics* presented the evidence and considered the probabilities.

The new fourteenth edition comes at a time when the American political winds have shifted yet again. But this current edition of the book does much more than completely update the election results, campaign finance data, voter turnout, and public opinion findings through the 2008 elections. It also analyzes a number of the events that have changed our views about modern politics, such as the nomination of the first Latino justice of the U.S. Supreme Court, the comparative campaign strategies of Barack Obama and Hillary Clinton, and the application of texting, Twitter, and other new communication techniques to campaigns.

You'll find many other new features as well. The reconfigured chapter on voter turnout focuses on the parties' efforts to broaden or limit access to the polls, including controversial state laws requiring voter ID and proof of citizenship in order to vote. Chapters 7 and 8 devote more attention to the participation and views of young voters. Innovations in the national party organizations' fund-raising and voter contact programs are detailed in Chapter 4, along with consideration of the likely fate of the Democratic National Committee's "50-state strategy." The Obama fund-raising phenomenon is detailed in Chapter 12, as is the rise in campaign activity by 501(c) groups. Chapters 11 and 16 assess the pathways the Republican Party could choose to regain the momentum it has recently lost, and Chapter 7 examines the impact of the 2008 election on the remarkable regional shifts in the two parties' bases of support. Chapter 13 makes use of the "conditional party government" and "cartel" theories of legislative party leadership. Why did a highly front-loaded schedule of presidential primaries result in the longest nomination battle in decades? See Chapter 10!

Even with all these changes, however, the aims of the book are the same as they have always been. Frank J. Sorauf, a pioneer of modern political science, had the vision to create *Party Politics in America* in 1968, and Paul Allen Beck brought the book into the late 1980s and 1990s, with the intellectual mastery and comparative perspective that has marked his work on voting. Their goal for each new edition was to provide students with the clearest, most comprehensive and engaging understanding of political parties and partisanship, which in turn are key to understanding the workings of elections, public opinion, policy-making, and leadership. They succeeded so well that *Party Politics in America* has long been known as the "gold standard" of political parties texts.

This edition contains new and updated versions of the features that have been so well received in recent editions. The boxes titled "A Day in the Life" tell the personal stories of individuals whose experiences help to illustrate recent changes in the parties. Many of my students see political parties as remote, abstract, and a bit underhanded— something that might interest elderly people, but not teens and twenty-somethings. I hope these compelling stories—for instance, that of a college student striving to win votes for Obama in the rural areas and small towns of Appalachia—can show readers why studying party politics is worth their time.

In other chapters, the feature titled "Which Would You Choose?" presents students with major debates about party politics: for instance, whether encouraging greater voter turnout would help or harm American democracy (see Chapter 8). These summaries, using the point–counterpoint format with which undergraduates are familiar, could serve as the basis for classroom debate on these and many other fundamental concerns.

As in previous editions, I've tried to make the reader's job easier by putting important terms in boldface and clearly defining them, emphasizing the central points even more, and making some of the long tables into figures or shorter, clearer tables. And for instructors, I have worked to make sure that each chapter can stand alone, so that teachers can assign chapters in any order they choose without leaving their students puzzled because relevant concepts were explained elsewhere.

Like political parties and elected officials, textbooks have constituents. However, as elected officials know, being accountable to a constituency requires getting information about its preferences. It isn't easy for textbook writers to find detailed information as to what readers like and don't like about a book. I have been very lucky to get reactions from some users of *Party Politics in America*, but I would like to receive many more— including yours! You can reach me at hershey@indiana.edu; I'll be happy to respond.

ACKNOWLEDGMENTS AND THANKS

I have received a generous amount of help in researching and writing editions of the book: from my graduate and undergraduate students; present and former colleagues at Indiana University, particularly Bob Huckfeldt, Bill Bianco, Eileen Braman, Ted Carmines, Mike Ensley, Leroy Rieselbach, John Williams, and Jerry Wright; and departmental staff members Fern Bennett, Steve Flinn, Marsha Franklin, Sara Huntsman, Sharon LaRoche, Amanda Perry, Jan Peterson, James Russell, and Deb Speer.

Austin Ranney, Leon Epstein, Jack Dennis, and Murray Edelman were most responsible for my interest in party politics and for my training in political science. Murray Edelman deserves special mention in that group, not only as a mentor and model for so many of us but also as a much-beloved friend. John Aldrich and Frank Sorauf, two of the most insightful and systematic analysts of political parties, have been kind enough to write the Foreword that accompanied several editions of the book. I've learned so much as well from Bruce Oppenheimer, Gerry Pomper, Tony Broh, Jennifer Hochschild, Burdett Loomis, Richard Fenno, Anthony King, John Kingdon, Mike Kirn,

Brian Silver, Jim Stimson, and Brian Vargus. Many others provided valuable help with this edition, including Alan Abramowitz, Rachel Bloom, John Cranford, Christian Hilland, Ray La Raja, John Orman, Richard Rubin, Megan Trusnik, Brad Warren, Darrell West, Richard Winger, Joshua Young, and especially my terrific research assistant, Nate Birkhead.

The political scientists who reviewed the previous edition—Craig Brians of Virginia Tech, David Darmofal of the University of South Carolina–Columbia, Scott McClurg of Southern Illinois University, and John McGlennon of the College of William and Mary—offered lots of useful comments, which helped me continue adapting the book to meet students' and instructors' needs. And it remains a pleasure to work with the people at Pearson Longman: Editor-in-Chief Eric Stano, Editorial Assistant Elizabeth Alimena, and members of the production team.

Most of all, I am very grateful to my family: my husband, Howard, and our daughters, Katie, Lissa, Lani, and Hannah. Everything I do has been made possible by their love and support.

MARJORIE RANDON HERSHEY

Part One

PARTIES AND PARTY SYSTEMS

S nack food lovers were hit hard in early 2009. Little Debbie products, peanut butter sandwich crackers, brownies, and 167 brands of candy were all recalled because of a salmonella outbreak. The salmonella contamination, traced to a peanut paste factory in Georgia, killed eight people and sickened hundreds more.

Who is responsible for protecting you from tainted snack foods? Who determines whether a peanut factory or the kitchen of your favorite pizza place is sanitary, and what "sanitary" means? Who decides how old you must be to drive a car or to drink beer legally?

It's government that makes these decisions and thousands more that affect your life every day. In fact, you would have to look very hard to find an aspect of your life that is *not* affected by government action. The federal government determines whether the lettuce in your salad needs to be tested for contamination and whether schools are allowed to serve irradiated beef. State governments have decided which sex acts can be prosecuted. Local governments choose when to fill potholes and how aggressively to prosecute drug and alcohol crimes. It is the political system that plays the most important role in deciding, as a famous political scientist put it, "who gets what, when, how."[1]

Because government decisions affect almost everything we do, large numbers of groups have mobilized to try to influence these decisions, as well as the selection of the men and women who will make them. In a democracy, the political party is one of the oldest and most important of these groups. Parties have a lot of competition, however. Organized interests such as the National Rifle Association and the National Gay and Lesbian Task Force also work to get the government policies they want, as do pro-life groups, NORML (National Organization for the Reform of Marijuana Laws), and People for the Ethical Treatment of Animals. Even organizations whose main purpose is nonpolitical, such as universities, Wal-Mart, and MTV, try to influence the government decisions that affect them.

All these groups serve as *intermediaries*—links between citizens and the people in government who make the decisions that affect our lives (Figure I.1). They raise issues that they want government to address. By bringing together people with shared interests, they amplify these people's voices in speaking to government. They tell people what government is doing. They keep an eye on one another's behavior as well as on the actions of public officials.

1

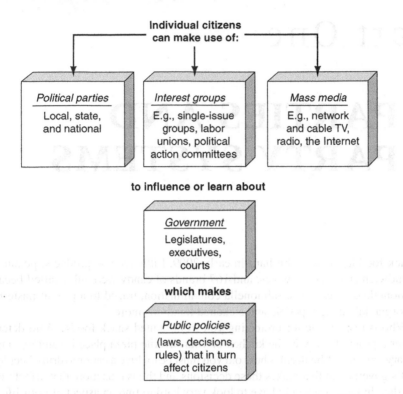

FIGURE I.1   Parties and Other Intermediaries Between Citizens and Government.

Different intermediaries specialize in different political activities. Parties focus on nominating candidates, helping to elect them, and organizing those who win. Most organized interests represent narrower groups; they are not likely to win majority support so they try instead to influence the views of candidates who do win office—and of appointed officials, such as bureaucrats and judges. Groups like these in other democracies may play different roles. The American parties, for example, tend to concentrate on election activities, whereas many parties in Europe have been more committed to spreading ideologies and keeping their elected officials faithful to the party's program.

The competition among these intermediary groups is fierce. Parties, of course, compete with one another. They vie with interest groups for money, expertise, and volunteer help and then, with those resources in hand, for the support of individual citizens and elected officials. Getting people's attention and support is difficult in an age when TV and Web-surfing soak up the free time of so many prospective activists and voters. Parties must even fight for a major role in political campaigns; the American parties are not nearly as dominant in the business of campaigning as they were a century ago. In many newer democracies, such as those of post-Communist nations, parties face even greater competition from "party substitutes" such as governors' nonpartisan political machines, which also provide money and services to candidates.[2]

Adding to their burden, the American parties fight for power in a culture that claims to hate partisanship. Even though many writers have celebrated political parties as the tools with which we build and repair our democracy and as the "distinguishing marks" of a modern government,[3] parties have been the targets of suspicion and ridicule since the nation began. James Madison and the other founders were very wary of organized factions in their new republic. A century later, the Progressive movement—reformers intent on rooting out political corruption and returning power to middle-class people like themselves—targeted the parties' "boss rule" and worked to combat it. Disgust with party power in the 1960s and 1970s led to another series of party reforms that has helped to reshape current politics. Many Americans today remain skeptical and even hostile to the idea of political parties.[4]

Public hostility has led state legislatures to pass waves of restrictions on how parties can organize and what they can do. Parties have tried to adapt to these rules over time by changing their organizations and activities. The political parties of the 2010s would hardly be recognizable to politicians of a century ago, and the parties that we know today may change dramatically in the coming decades.

The aim of this book is to explore the American parties: how they have developed, how they affect us, and what they are capable of contributing to a democratic politics. Given the rise of the Internet, the growth of single-issue groups, and the many other ways in which we can learn about and affect government, are political parties really as essential to the survival of a democracy as many have assumed? Are they a benefit to both candidates and voters, or do they deserve the distrust with which so many Americans— and probably you yourself—view them?

CHAPTER 1

What Are Political Parties?

<hr />

Before Barack Obama could become President of the United States, he had to become the candidate of his party. Why did Obama, a charismatic personality with an excited following among young people, need the help of a political party? Couldn't he have been elected without it?

Probably not. His party affiliation signaled to tens of millions of his party's supporters that despite his relatively brief political resumé, he shared their views on some important issues. After winning his party's nomination, he could count on the active efforts of Democratic Party activists, fund-raisers, and organizations in a variety of states to work on his behalf. His status as his party's nominee put his name on the ballot throughout the country, a feat that would have taken his supporters many months of work and millions of dollars if he had run independent of party.

Why, then, do so many Americans see political parties as meaningless, or even as self-serving and underhanded, if they think of them at all? Their suspicion of parties has long roots; George Washington declared in his Farewell Address that "the spirit of party" was the "worst enemy" of popular government. Parties, he feared, would encourage people to pursue their narrow self-interest at other people's expense, seek domination over others, and engender jealousy, division, and revenge. Without parties, in this view, we'd be more likely to get noble and uncorrupted leaders who could speak for the nation as a whole, in a spirit of unity and mutual benefit.

Washington was expressing a widely shared dream but one difficult to put into practice. Without parties, how would we choose a president? Without party primaries and caucuses, who would be able to trim down the thousands of presidential wannabes to the very few who will run in the general election? Could members of Congress make that decision? Not in a system designed to separate legislative from executive powers. How about nomination by the nation's mayors and other elected officials, as happens in France? A special edition of the television series *American Idol*? The answer is not obvious, though it is obviously vital to the nation's future.

Strong party organizations help bring voters to the polls. Without any political parties, would voter turnout, already lower in the United States than in most other industrialized democracies, decrease even further? Most people are not very interested in politics, so how would they decide on a candidate without the guidance that party labels provide? Will they spend hours researching each candidate's experience and stands on the issues, or will they choose the candidate with the most attractive personality, at least as seen on TV? When the new president takes office, how would he or she gain majority support for new programs from a Congress elected as individuals, with no party loyalties to unite them?

What is this political organization that is so necessary and yet so distrusted? Does the concept of party include only the politicians who share a party label when running for and holding public office? Does it also include the activists who work on the campaigns and the citizens who vote for a party's candidates? Or is a party any group that chooses to call itself a party, whether Republican or Boston Tea?

THE THREE PARTS OF PARTIES

Most scholars would agree that *a party is a group organized to nominate candidates, to try to win political power through elections, and to promote ideas about public policies.* To the analysts quoted in "What Is a Political Party?" on page 7, the central figures in a political party are the candidates and elected officials who share a party's label (see, for example, Edmund Burke's and Anthony Downs's definitions). Many parties in democratic nations, including the United States, began as groups of political leaders who organized to advance certain policies.

Most observers, however, see the American parties as including more than just candidates and officeholders. As John Aldrich's definition (see "What Is a Political Party?") reminds us, parties are organizations; they are institutions that have a life and a set of rules of their own, beyond that of their candidates. Interested individuals can become active in them and help set their goals and strategies, just as one would do in a sports team or a church youth group. They can link the party to a network of "policy demanders" in organized interests such as pro-life, pro-choice, business, or labor groups.[1] These activists and organizations are central parts of the party, too.

It is tempting to close our definition at this point and to view the American parties solely as teams of political specialists—elected officials, candidates, party leaders, activists, and organizations—who compete for power and then exercise it. That leaves the rest of the population on the outside of the parties, a position that many citizens may well prefer. Yet this would ignore an important reality: Parties are rooted in the lives and feelings of citizens as well as candidates and activists. Even though the American parties do not have formal, dues-paying "members," many voters develop such strong and enduring attachments to a particular party that they are willing to tell a pollster, "I'm a Democrat" or "I'm a Republican." Further, when writers refer to a "Democratic surge" or a "Republican suburb," they see parties that include voters and other supporters as well as officeholders, office seekers, and activists.

The Progressive movement of the late 1800s and early 1900s, which promoted voter registration and the practice of nominating candidates in direct primary elections, strengthened the case for including a citizen base in a definition of American parties. Voters in primary elections make the single most important decision for their party: who its candidates will be. In most other democracies, only the party leaders and activists have the power to make this choice.

WHAT IS A POLITICAL PARTY?

A party aims to promote certain policies:

> [A] party is a body of men united, for promoting by their joint endeavors the national interest, upon some particular principle in which they are all agreed.
>
> *Edmund Burke (1770)*

It works to gain power in government:

> In the broadest sense, a political party is a coalition of men seeking to control the governing apparatus by legal means . . . [through] duly constituted elections or legitimate influence.
>
> *Anthony Downs (1957)*

It is an organization with rules and durability:

> Political parties can be seen as coalitions of elites to capture and use political office . . . . (But) a political party is . . . more than a coalition. A major political party is an institutionalized coalition, one that has adopted rules, norms, and procedures.
>
> *John H. Aldrich (1995)*

It inspires loyalty among voters:

> [A] political party in the modern sense may be thought of as a relatively durable social formation which seeks offices or power in government, exhibits a structure or organization which links leaders at the centers of government to a significant popular following in the political arena and its local enclaves, and generates in-group perspectives or at least symbols of identification or loyalty.
>
> *William Nisbet Chambers (1967)*

A political party is all of the above:

> Within the body of voters as a whole, groups are formed of persons who regard themselves as party members . . . . In another sense the term party may refer to the group of more or less professional political workers . . . . At times party denotes groups within the government . . . . Often it refers to an entity which rolls into one the party-in-the-electorate, the professional political group, the party-in-the-legislature, and the party-in-the-government . . . . In truth, this all-encompassing usage has its legitimate applications for all the types of groups called party interact more or less closely and at times may be as one.
>
> *V. O. Key, Jr. (1958)*

Because American voters have the right to nominate the parties' candidates, the line that separates party leaders from followers in most other nations becomes blurred in the United States. American voters are not only consumers who choose among the parties' "products" (candidates) in the political marketplace but also managers who decide which products will be introduced in the first place. Making consumers into

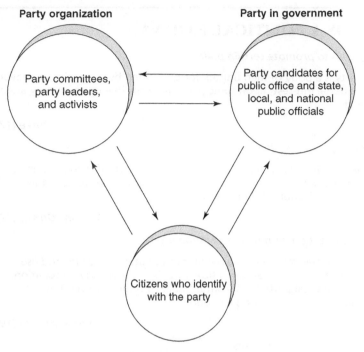

Party organization

Party in government

Party committees, party leaders, and activists

Party candidates for public office and state, local, and national public officials

Citizens who identify with the party

Party in the electorate

FIGURE 1.1   The Three Parts of American Political Parties.

managers has transformed political parties, just as it would revolutionize the market economy. Taking this into account in our definition of parties, as do the Chambers and Key definitions in the box on page 7, makes for a messier concept of political party, but a more realistic one in the American political environment.[2]

In short, the major American parties are composed of three interacting parts. These are the ***party organization***, which includes party leaders and the activists who work for party causes and candidates; the ***party in government***, composed of the men and women who run for and hold public office on the party's label; and the ***party in the electorate***, or those citizens who express an attachment to the party (see Figure 1.1).[3] We explore each of these parts separately, keeping in mind that the character of the American parties is defined by the ways in which they interact.[4]

The Party Organization

Party organizations are made up of people who hold party jobs with titles—the national and state party chairs and other officers; the county, city, ward, and precinct leaders and committee people (see Chapters 3 and 4)—and other supporters who are devoted enough to volunteer their time, money, and skills to the party (see Chapter 5). These groups are charged with promoting *all* of the party's candidates and its stands on major issues, not just an individual candidate or two. Some party leaders or activists may be waiting for the right time to run for public office (and thus cross over into the party in government); others have been pressed into service as candidates for Congress or city clerk when nobody else wants the job. Many party activists prefer the tasks of meeting volunteers and making phone calls from the party headquarters, however, rather than the frenzied days and anxious nights that are the life of a political candidate.

The Party in Government

The party in government consists of the candidates for public office and those who hold office, whether elected or appointed, who share a party label (see Chapters 13 and 14). The major figures here are presidents, governors, judges, Congress members, state legislators, bureaucrats, mayors, and other local officials who hold the same party affiliation.

Members of the party in government do not always have smooth relationships with people in the party organization. They regularly work together to meet shared goals, but they may have different priorities in reaching those goals. A senator, for example, may be trying to raise as much campaign money as possible in order to win a big victory that will boost her chances of running for president later. At the same time, the party organization's leaders may be hoping to convince the same campaign contributors to support other, more vulnerable party candidates instead, in the hope of keeping a party majority in Congress.

These two parts of the parties also contend for leadership of the party as a whole. When reporters want to get a "Republican view" on an issue, they will often interview a source in the White House, if the president is Republican, or a Republican leader in Congress; these members of the party in government are often assumed to speak for the party. Leaders of the party's organization, such as the chair of the New York Republican State Committee, might want to put a different spin on the issue. But presidents and congressional party leaders do not have to clear their pronouncements with the party organization, nor can they be controlled by it. These tensions, and the competition for scarce resources, show why it is helpful to treat the party organization and the party in government as separate parts of the party.

The Party in the Electorate

The party in the electorate consists of the women and men who *see themselves* as Democrats or Republicans: citizens who feel some degree of loyalty to the party, even if they have never set foot in the party's headquarters or met its candidates. We call them *partisans* or *party identifiers.* Many of these partisans declared themselves to be a Democrat or Republican when they registered to vote; more than half of the states require citizens to register by party. Others see themselves as partisans even if they do not register to vote under a party label or even if they do not vote at all.

Partisans are usually inclined to support their party's candidates and issue stands, but nothing forces them to do so. In general elections, they may vote for one of their party's candidates and reject another; in primaries, they may decide to saddle the party with a candidate that the organization can't stand. However, they are vitally important as the core of the party's electoral support; without this base, the party would have to work much harder to win and keep power.

This relationship between the party organization and the party in government, on the one hand, and the electoral party, on the other, is one of the most striking characteristics of the major American parties. Other political organizations—interest groups such as teachers' unions and oil companies—try to attract supporters in addition to their members, but these supporters remain outside the group's organization. In contrast, in the American parties, the party in the electorate is not just an external group to be mobilized. In addition to its power to choose the parties' candidates by voting in primaries, in many states the electoral party selects local party officials, such as precinct committee leaders. So the major American party is an open, inclusive organization. The extent to which citizens can affect the choice of its leaders and candidates sets it apart from parties in most other democracies.

WHAT PARTIES DO

Political parties in every democracy engage in three sets of activities to at least some degree. They select candidates and contest elections; they try to educate citizens about issues important to the party; and they work to influence government to provide certain policies and other benefits.[5] Parties and party systems differ in the degree to which they emphasize each of these activities, but no party can completely ignore any of them.

Electing Candidates

Parties often seem completely absorbed by their efforts to elect candidates. The activity of the American party follows the cycles of the electoral calendar, with activity reaching a peak at election time and falling off between elections. Parties are goal-oriented, and in American politics, achieving one's goals depends on winning elections. The need to elect candidates is the main link connecting the three parts of the parties. Party leaders and activists committed to a particular elected official often join with other members of the party in government and with party identifiers to return that official to office. When the election is won or lost, they will frequently drift apart again. These groups of individuals from different parts of a party, drawn together to elect a particular candidate, are like the nuclei of the party.[6]

Educating (or Propagandizing) Citizens

Parties also try to teach or propagandize citizens. (If you like their message, you might call it "voter education." If not, it may sound like propaganda.) The Democrats and Republicans do not promote all-inclusive ideologies like those of a fundamentalist Islamic party. They do, however, represent the beliefs and interests of the groups that identify with and support them. In this sense, the Republicans have often been regarded as the party of business and conservatives, and Democrats are often seen as the party of labor and the disadvantaged. (More on this can be found later in the chapter.) Party positions on issues have become clearer and more polarized since the 1960s.

Governing

Almost all American national and state elected officials ran for office as either Democrats or Republicans, and their partisan perspectives affect every aspect of the way government works. The legislatures of 49 states[7] and the U.S. Congress are organized along party lines. On some issues, party cohesion may break down. Yet, in general, there is a surprising degree of party discipline in voting on legislation. In executive branches, presidents and governors usually choose cabinet officers and agency heads of their own party. Even the courts show evidence of the guiding hand of parties, though in more subtle ways.

The American parties, however, do not have a monopoly on educating citizens, working to elect candidates, or governing. They compete regularly with interest groups, other political organizations, and even the media in all these areas. Although the parties organize state legislatures and Congress, they vie with interest-group lobbyists and legislators' own beliefs to influence legislators' votes. In elections, especially at the local level, other groups—those backing or opposing a new sports stadium or a smoking ban, for instance—also try to influence primaries or urge candidates to run. Single-issue groups may champion an issue more than the parties do.

Because the American parties' activities center on electing candidates, the party in government dominates the party to a degree unusual among Western democracies. In parties more strongly committed to educating citizens about the party's ideology— European Marxist parties, for instance—party organizations are more likely to be able to dictate to the legislative parties, telling them what to emphasize and holding them accountable for their votes.

THE EFFECTS OF PARTY ACTIVITY

How do these party activities affect American politics? First, parties help people make sense of the complexities of politics. Most of us don't pay much attention to government. Parties simplify issues and elections for us; thus, people can make sensible choices in politics, by using their party attachment as a guide for evaluating candidates and issues, even when they don't have a lot of political information. By making it easier for citizens to form political judgments, parties ease the way for people to become politically active. They educate Americans by transmitting political information and values to large numbers of current and future voters.

Second, the American parties help aggregate and organize political power. They put together individuals and groups into blocs that are powerful enough to govern. So in the political world as well as within the individual, parties help to focus political loyalties on a small number of alternatives and then to build support for them. Parties also provide an organized opposition. That is not a popular role to play; the behavior of a constant adversary may seem like that of a sore loser. But an organized opposition is vital to a democracy because it has a natural incentive—its own ambition—to serve as a watchdog on a powerful government. Few of us would be willing to devote the time and effort to play this important role on our own.

Third, because they are so focused on contesting elections, the parties dominate the recruitment of political leaders. Large numbers of legislators, political executives, and even judges entered public service through party activity. Because the parties work at all levels of government from local to national, they can encourage the movement of leaders from one level to another. Further, because they are constants in the election process, parties help to make changes in government leadership more routine and orderly. In nations where parties are not stable from one election to the next, leadership changes can be much more disruptive.

Finally, the parties help pull together a divided American political system. The U.S. government was designed to fragment political power, to make sure that no single group could gain enough of it to become a tyrant. The division between the national government and the states, multiplied by the separation of powers at each level, does an impressive job of fragmenting power. The challenge is to make these fragmented units work together to solve problems. The two major national parties are a unifying force in American politics. Their ability to bridge the separation of powers has limits, but the major parties can provide a basis for cooperation in a government marked by decentralization and division.

HOW DO PARTIES DIFFER FROM OTHER POLITICAL GROUPS?

We have seen that parties have a lot of competition as intermediaries in politics. *All* political organizations, not just parties, try to educate at least some citizens and mobilize their supporters either to win public office or to influence those who do win. How, then, do parties differ from these other political organizations?

Parties are Paramount in Elections

Above all, a party can be distinguished from other political organizations by its role in structuring elections. In most elections, candidates are listed on the ballot as "Democrat" or "Republican"; they are not listed as "Microsoft lobbyist" or "gay rights activist." It is the major parties that normally recruit the election clerks and the poll watchers, not the Chamber of Commerce. The parties are paramount among political groups in contesting elections.

They Have a Full-Time Commitment to Political Activity

The major American parties are fully committed to political activity; it is the sole purpose of their existence. Interest groups and other political organizations, in contrast, move freely and frequently from political to nonpolitical activities and back again. The Steelworkers' Union, for example, is fundamentally concerned with collective bargaining for better pay and working conditions. It may turn to political action to support sympathetic candidates or to lobby Congress for favorable legislation, but its interests are rooted in the workplace. Parties live entirely in the political world.

They Mobilize Large Numbers

An interest group, such as an organization that lobbies on behalf of investment banks, does not need millions of supporters to persuade Congress to bail out failing banks; it may be able to succeed with only a few strategists and a small, well-mobilized clientele. Because winning elections is so vital to parties' goals, however, parties must mobilize an enormous range of supporters to win large numbers of races. The result is that in a system such as that of the United States, a major party cannot afford to represent only a narrow range of concerns.

They Endure

The American parties are unusually stable and long-lived. Most business, environmental, and single-issue groups are mere juveniles by comparison. Both major American parties can trace their histories for more than 150 years, and the major parties of other Western democracies also have impressive life spans. This remarkable endurance adds to their value for voters. The parties are there as points of reference, year after year, election after election, and candidate after candidate, giving continuity to the choices Americans face and the issues they debate.

They Serve as Political Symbols

Finally, political parties differ from other political organizations in the extent to which they operate as symbols, or emotion-laden objects of loyalty. For tens of millions of Americans, the party label is a social identity, like that of an ethnic or religious group. It is the chief cue for their decisions about candidates or issues; it relates their values to the real options of American politics.

Remember, however, that the differences between parties and other political organizations are differences of degree. Interest groups do become involved in elections, and the larger organized interests serve as political symbols, too. Groups such as the AARP can recruit candidates, promote their endorsed candidates to their members and friends, and get their supporters to the polls on Election Day. Other nonparty groups may do the same. Interest groups also promote issue positions, try to influence officeholders, and give money to campaigns. But candidates are listed on the ballot as representatives of a party, not of an interest group.

In some respects, the major parties have more in common with some of the larger interest groups, such as the Chamber of Commerce and the AARP, than they do with minor or third parties. Most minor parties are electoral organizations in name only (see, for example, the box on page 14 "A Party of One?"). Most of their candidates are in no danger of needing a victory speech on election night. They may have few or no local organizations. Their membership base, often dependent on a single issue, may be just as narrow as that of most interest groups. However, minor parties may qualify to be listed on the ballot, and their candidates can receive public funding where it is available and where they can meet the criteria for it. In these ways (and sometimes *only* in these ways), they can be more like the major parties than the large interest groups.

HOW THE AMERICAN PARTIES DEVELOPED

The world's first political parties developed in the United States. For more than 200 years, the development of the American parties has been closely interrelated with the expansion of popular democracy. At times during their history, the party in government, then the party organizations, and then both the parties in government and in the electorate have taken the dominant role within the parties.[8]

The Founding of American Parties

Although the founders of the American government despised the idea of factions, they nevertheless began taking sides and moving in the direction of creating rudimentary

A PARTY OF ONE?

Joe Lieberman was one of the few Democratic senators who remained a staunch supporter of the U.S. war in Iraq. That did not endear him to more liberal Democrats in his home state of Connecticut. In 2005, a professor of politics at Fairfield University, John Orman, announced that he would run against Lieberman in the August 2006 Democratic primary. Orman pulled out of the race six months later because of a lack of campaign money, but Ned Lamont, a wealthy cable TV entrepreneur who also opposed the war, stepped in to oppose Lieberman in the primary. Fearing a loss, Lieberman had a Plan B. He filed petitions to create a new party, Connecticut for Lieberman (CFL). When he did lose the Democratic nomination to Lamont, Lieberman ran in the general election as the CFL Party's only candidate and won the seat, calling himself an "Independent Democrat."

Orman objected that CFL was a sham—a fake party created only to give Lieberman an end run around the Democratic Party's selection process. Orman discovered that according to the secretary of state, the CFL Party had no members at all; not even Lieberman had joined. So in November, Orman changed his party registration to the CFL Party. He called a meeting of all registered party members—that is, himself—and nominated himself to be party chair. As he describes it, "I seconded my own nomination and then I voted for myself. I was selected unanimously as Chair of Connecticut for Lieberman on November 15, 2006," and then adopted a set of party rules, with tongue firmly in cheek. The secretary of state's office accepted Orman's filing of party rules in January 2007.

Controversy erupted. A Lieberman supporter claimed that *he* had joined the CFL Party in July and was its chairman. Although each state makes its own rules as to what constitutes a political party, the Connecticut secretary of state's office sidestepped the challenge. The CFL Party remains active, with a new chair and more members (though still not Joe Lieberman), and plans to nominate a candidate to oppose Lieberman in 2012 when the senator's current term is up. If Lieberman decides to run for reelection, then he might need to create another new party or to run for a major party's nomination. Given that he supported Republican John McCain for President in 2008 and gave a speech critical of the Democrats at the Republican National Convention, it is not clear which major party that might be.

political parties soon after the new government began its work. Groups within the Congress disagreed about how much power the new national government should have, relative to the states. The dominant group came to be called *Federalists*; led by the ambitious young treasury secretary, Alexander Hamilton, they championed centralized (federal government) control over the economy, a central banking system, and high tariffs to protect fledgling American industries (see the box on page 15).

The opposition rallied around Thomas Jefferson and James Madison, who wanted to uphold the states' rights against national government interference. Each group gathered in meetings, called "caucuses," to plan ways to get their ideas adopted. During the 1790s, these alignments took a more enduring form. Their differences, as is the case now, were both principled and personal; as historian David McCullough reports, the animosity between Hamilton and Jefferson "had reached the point where they could hardly bear to be in the same room. Each was certain the other was a dangerous man intent on dominating the government."[9]

THE AMERICAN MAJOR PARTIES

There have been only five major political parties in more than two centuries of American history:

1. **The Federalist Party, 1788–1816.** The champion of the new Constitution and strong national (federal) government, it was the first American political institution to resemble a political party, although it was not a full-fledged party. Its strength was rooted in the Northeast and the Atlantic Seaboard, where it attracted the support of shopkeepers, manufacturers, financiers, landowners, and other established families of wealth and status. Limited by its narrow electoral base, compared with that of the Democratic-Republicans, it soon faded.

2. **The Democratic-Republican Party, 1800–1832.** Many of its leaders had been strong proponents of the Constitution but opposed the extreme nationalism of the Federalists. It was a party of small farmers, workers, and less-privileged citizens, plus southern planters, who preferred the authority of the state governments and opposed centralizing power in the national government. Like its leader, Thomas Jefferson, it shared many of the ideals of the French Revolution, especially the extension of the right to vote and the notion of direct popular self-government.

3. **The Democratic Party, 1832–Present.** Growing out of the Jacksonian wing of the Democratic-Republicans, it was the first really broad-based, popular party in the United States. On behalf of a coalition of less-privileged voters, it opposed such business-friendly policies as national banking and high tariffs. It also welcomed the new immigrants (and sought their votes) and opposed nativist (anti-immigrant) sentiment.

4. **The Whig Party, 1834–1856.** This party, too, had roots in the old Democratic-Republican Party, but in a faction that opposed the Jacksonians. Its greatest leaders, Henry Clay and Daniel Webster, stood for legislative supremacy and protested the strong presidency of Andrew Jackson. For its short life, the Whig Party was an unstable coalition of many interests, among them nativism, property, and business and commerce.

5. **The Republican Party, 1854–Present.** The Republicans were formed largely to oppose slavery. As the Civil War approached, the new party came to stand for the Union, the North, Lincoln, the freeing of slaves, victory in the Civil War, and the imposition of Reconstruction on the South. From the Whigs it also inherited a concern for business and industrial expansion.

These early parties, then, were formed "from the top" by their party in government, as well as by activists at the grassroots. They focused at first on issues that concerned the national leaders who formed them—not surprisingly at a time when most Americans played only an indirect role in politics. At this time, in almost every state the vote was restricted to those free men who could meet property-owning or taxpaying requirements. Even these relatively small numbers of voters had limited power, as the writers of the Constitution intended. The president was chosen not directly by the voters, but indirectly by the Electoral College. Although members of the House of Representatives were selected by a direct popular vote, state legislatures were given the right to choose their state's U.S. senators. This cautious start for democratic self-government produced very limited political parties.

The party groupings in Congress made some efforts to reach out to the activists and other voters at home. Each side established a newspaper to propagandize for its cause. Party organization at the grassroots level began as "committees of correspondence" between national and local leaders. And public sentiment found its way to the Capitol. Organized public protest against some unpopular administration measures was directed at the party in Congress, and fights broke out occasionally between rival party mobs.

One of these two incipient parties, the **Democratic-Republicans** (led by Jefferson), began organizing in the states and local communities in time for the 1800 elections. The more elitist Federalists, who had earlier dominated the Congress, failed to keep up; splits arose within their caucus, and the Federalists began to disappear in most states soon after the defeat of their last president, John Adams, in 1800. In short, the pressures for democratization were already powerful enough by the early 1800s to scuttle an infant party whose leaders in the government could not adapt to the need to organize a mass electorate, especially in the new states of the frontier. Yet the Federalists gave a historic gift to American democracy. They accepted Adams's defeat in 1800 and handed control of the presidency to their Democratic-Republican rivals.[10]

The Democratic-Republicans, who were the party of agrarian interests, the less-privileged, and the frontier, quickly established their electoral superiority and held a one-party monopoly for 20 years. They dominated American politics so thoroughly by the time of James Monroe's election in 1816 that the absence of party and political conflict was called the "Era of Good Feelings." Despite the decline of one party and the rise of another, however, the nature of party politics did not change much during this period. It was a time when government and politics were the business of an elite group of well-known, well-established men, and the parties reflected the politics of the time. Without party competition, leaders felt no need to establish larger grassroots organizations, so the parties' further development was stalled.

American politics began to change sharply in the 1820s. By then, most states had eliminated the requirement that only landowners could vote; the suffrage was extended to all white males, at least in state and federal elections. The growing pressure for democratization also led governments to make more and more public officials popularly elected rather than appointed.[11]

The most obvious change in the 1820s was the emergence of the presidential election process that has lasted to this day. The framers of the Constitution had crafted an unusual arrangement for selecting the president, known as the Electoral College. Each state, in a manner selected by its legislature, would choose a number of presidential voters (electors) equal to the size of its congressional delegation. These electors would meet in the state to cast their votes for president; the candidate who received a majority of the states' electoral votes was the national winner. If no candidate received a majority, the president was to be selected by the House of Representatives, with each state casting one vote.

This Electoral College was an ingenious invention. By leaving the choice of electors to the state legislatures, the framers avoided having to set uniform election methods and voting requirements, issues on which they strongly disagreed (and which involved, of course, the explosive question of whether and how to count slaves). This also eliminated the need for federal intervention in a question on which the states had previously made their own decisions, and which might have produced state opposition. Requiring electors to meet simultaneously in their respective states helped prevent a conspiracy among electors from different states to put forward their own choice for president. At first, states used a variety of methods for selecting presidential electors, but by the 1820s, popular election was the most common method.[12]

This growing enthusiasm for popular control also raised doubts about whether the party's congressional caucus should have the power to nominate a presidential candidate. Some criticized caucus nominations as the actions of a small and self-appointed elite. At the same time, the caucus system began to fall apart from within. In 1824, the Democratic-Republicans' attempt to nominate a presidential candidate ended in chaos. No candidate won a majority in the Electoral College, so the House of Representatives had to choose among John Quincy Adams, William H. Crawford, and Andrew Jackson. Although Jackson was the front-runner in both the popular and electoral votes, the House chose Adams. Jackson, in turn, defeated Adams in 1828. The congressional party caucus, then, was losing its role as the predominant force within the parties as the nation entered a new phase of party politics.

A NATIONAL TWO-PARTY SYSTEM EMERGES

The Era of Good Feelings gave way to a two-party system that has prevailed ever since. The Democratic-Republicans had developed factions that chose divorce rather than reconciliation. Andrew Jackson led the frontier and agrarian wing of the Democratic-Republicans, the inheritors of the Jeffersonian tradition, into what is now called the **Democratic Party**. The National Republicans, another faction of the old Democratic-Republicans who had earlier promoted Adams for president, merged with the **Whigs** (an old English term referring to those who opposed the dominance of the king, by whom they meant Jackson). That created two-party politics in the United States.

Just as important, the parties developed even more of a nationwide grassroots (citizen) base. The Jacksonian Democrats held the first national nominating convention in 1832 that, not surprisingly, nominated Jackson himself for a second term. (The small Anti-Masonic Party had held a more limited convention a year earlier.) Larger numbers of citizens were now eligible to vote, so the presidential campaign became more concerned with reaching out to the public; new campaign organizations and tactics brought the contest to many more people. Party organization in the states also expanded. Candidates for state and local office were increasingly nominated by conventions of state and local leaders, rather than by the narrower legislative caucuses. By 1840, the Whigs and the Democrats were established in the first truly national party system and were competitive in all the states.

During the 1840s and 1850s, the bitter issue of slavery increasingly affected both parties. The Whigs fractured on the issue and then collapsed. Antislavery activists created the **Republican Party** to demand that slavery be abolished. The Republicans then adopted the Whigs' commitment to protect American businesses with high tariffs and to levy high taxes in order to subsidize industrial development—roads, railroads, and settlement of the frontier. The party organized throughout the nation, except in the South and the Border States, which were Democratic strongholds, and won the presidency in 1860. The party system and the nation broke into North and South.

In short, modern political parties similar to those we know today, with their characteristic organizational structures, bases of loyal voters, and lasting alliances among governmental leaders, had developed by the mid-1800s.[13] The American parties grew hand in hand with the early expansion of the electorate in the United States. Comparable parties did not develop in Great Britain until the 1870s, after laws were passed to further expand the adult male electorate.

The Golden Age of the Parties

As the parties were developing, they received another massive infusion of voters from a new source: European immigrants. Hundreds of thousands of Europeans, the majority from Ireland and Germany, immigrated to the United States before the Civil War. The newcomers were welcomed by the Democratic Party, which sought their votes. But their large numbers worried others, and an anti-immigrant minor party, the American Party (the so-called Know-Nothing Party), sprang up in response in the 1850s.

The tide of immigration was halted only temporarily by the Civil War. After the war ended, new nationalities came in an almost constant flow from 1870 until Congress closed the door to mass immigration in the 1920s. More than five million immigrants arrived in the 1880s (equal to one-tenth of the 1880 resident population), and 10 million more came between 1905 and 1914 (one-eighth of the 1900 resident population).

The political parties played an important role in assimilating these huge waves of immigrants. The newcomers gravitated toward the big cities where industrial jobs were available. It was in the cities that a new kind of party organization, the city "machine," developed in response to the immigrants' needs and vulnerabilities. These party machines were like social service systems that helped the new arrivals cope with the challenges of an urban industrial society. They softened the hard edge of poverty by helping needy families with food and funds, smoothed the way with government and the police, and taught immigrants the customs of their new home—all in exchange for the immigrants' votes for the party's candidates at election time.

The political machine in a city was often indistinguishable from the city's government; this was the classic case of "party government" in the American experience (see Chapter 15). The machines also were the means by which the new urban working class won control of the cities from the largely Anglo-Saxon, Protestant elites who had governed for so long. As the parties again embodied the hopes of new citizens, they reached their high point of power and influence in American history.

The period of the late 1800s and the early 1900s was the "golden age" of the American parties. Party organizations, now the dominant segment of the party, existed in all the states and localities and flourished in the industrial cities. Party discipline was at a record high in Congress and most state legislatures. Parties ran the candidates' campaigns for public office; they held rallies and torchlight parades, canvassed door-to-door, and brought voters to the polls. They controlled access to many government jobs, ranging from street inspectors to members of the U.S. Senate. They were an important source of information and guidance for a largely uneducated and often illiterate electorate. As a result, the highest voter turnouts in American presidential history were recorded during the latter half of the 1800s. The parties suited the needs and limitations of the new voters and met the need for creating majorities in the rapidly industrializing nation.[14]

The Progressive Reforms and Beyond

The drive to democratize American politics continued into the 1900s. Passage of the Seventeenth Amendment gave voters, rather than state legislatures, the right to elect U.S. senators. Women and then blacks finally gained the right to vote. As popular democracy expanded, a movement arose that would impose important changes on the parties.

The period that parties saw as their "golden age" did not seem so golden to groups of reformers. To Progressive crusaders, party control of politics had led to rampant corruption and inefficient government.[15] Because the Progressives saw party power as the culprit, they tried to weaken the control that the parties, and especially the party organizations, had achieved by the late 1800s. The reformers attacked party "boss rule" by pressing for primary elections (see Chapters 9 and 10), which took the power to choose the parties' candidates out of the hands of party leaders and gave it to voters instead. Presidential nominations were made more open to the public by establishing presidential primaries in the states. Many state legislatures wrote laws to define and limit party organizations.

The reforms succeeded in weakening the party organizations and their power in elections. But success had its price. When citizens gained the right to nominate the parties' candidates, they took away the most important function of party organizations and party leaders. Candidates, who could now appeal directly to primary voters, became more independent of the party organizations. The effect of the Progressive reforms, then, was to undercut the dominance of the party organization within the party as a whole. So the expectations of a democratic society, which first made the parties more public, more decentralized, and more active at the grassroots level, later turned on the party organization, leaving it less capable of the important role that it once played in American politics.[16]

More recently, however, the party organizations and their leaders have created new sources of power for themselves. Beginning in the 1970s, first the Republicans and then the Democrats expanded the fund-raising capacity of their national party organizations and used their new money to provide more services to candidates and to increase the capabilities of state party organizations. In the past three decades the Democratic Party, through its national committee and convention, has created rules for state Democratic Parties to follow in nominating a presidential candidate. Both of these changes have strengthened the national party organizations; in fact, the national organizations probably have more of a presence within the two major parties, relative to the state and local party organizations, now than at any other time in American history. (Chapters 3 and 4 say more about these changes.)

In short, the parties have changed dramatically and continue to change. Yet they remain the leading organizations of popular democracy. They grew with the expansion of the right to vote and the increasing role of citizens in electoral politics. They are the channel through which voters come together to choose representatives and ambitious people gain positions of power. They help to clarify the alternatives on such challenging issues as abortion, taxes, and terrorism. They amplify the voices of some groups in making demands on public policy and dampen the voices of others.

WHAT DO THE PARTIES STAND FOR?

There have been many changes over time in the parties' positions on issues as well, even major issues. The national Democratic and Republican Parties, for example, have shifted their positions dramatically over the years on the question of civil rights for black Americans. The traditional decentralization of the American parties (discussed in the next chapter) has meant that party organizations in some states or local communities have taken stands different from organizations of the same party in other areas.

Yet there have been times of clear party differences on big policy questions. The current period is one of those times. Although some would argue that the parties' issue stands are simply a means to attract votes, the ongoing competition between the Democrats and Republicans, and party politics in general, has always been more than just a story of raw ambition. Ever since the parties began, they have organized to gain power in order to achieve particular policy goals. Changes in the electorate and the growing strength of the national party organizations in the past three decades have encouraged *party polarization*: greater agreement on policy stands *within* each party and sharper policy differences *between* the Democrats and Republicans.

If you explore the Republican National Committee's Web site, the party platform, or the votes of Republicans in Congress, you will find that the Republican Party has long believed in a strong business sector and distrusted the power of government to remedy individual inequalities by creating welfare programs or redistributing income. Former president George W. Bush referred to the Republican vision as an "ownership society," in which individuals will have more opportunities to build up their own wealth and to free themselves from the heavy yoke of government intervention.

These principles can be seen in the party's stands on many current issues (see Table 1.1). Tax cuts for individuals and businesses are high on the party's agenda in the early 2000s; lower taxes shrink the government's revenue and, therefore, its ability to create new programs—a strategy that some conservatives call "starving the beast" (government).[17] The tax cuts should favor those who are better off, many Republicans would argue, because that helps the economy grow. The party has traditionally argued for protecting property rights, which also limits the government's ability to interfere in the economic decisions of its citizens.

Republican positions on other issues also demonstrate these commitments to private rather than governmental solutions to problems and to state and local rather than national and international authority. On the environment, for example, the party argues for greater flexibility for businesses in complying with environmental laws. In defense, the Republican tradition defines a strong national defense as requiring a powerful military rather than as giving priority to international agreements on arms control and other matters.

Over time, Republicans have been more likely than Democrats to draw their party leaders and candidates from the business sector. Consistent with that, the party's relationship with labor unions has long been somewhere between strained and nonexistent. Core groups of Republican supporters include conservatives (conservative Christians in particular), white southerners, and people living in rural and exurban areas.

The Democratic Party represents a different tradition. To Democratic activists, government is a valuable means of redressing the inequalities that the marketplace can cause. These activists believe that needed social services should be provided by

TABLE 1.1 Party Differences in the Early 2000s, Issues and Core Supporters

Democrats	Republicans
Core belief	
A strong government provides needed services and remedies inequalities	A strong government interferes with business and threatens freedom
Biggest exception	
Government should stay out of people's decisions on such issues as abortion and homosexuality	Government should regulate people's decisions on such issues as abortion and homosexuality
Issue agenda	
Education, health, social services	Strong military, tax cuts
Environmental protection	Property rights
Emphasizes	
Fairness, especially for disadvantaged groups	Individual success, not group rights
Relations with labor unions	
Close and supportive	Distant and hostile
Core supporters	
Northeast, West Coast	South
Minority groups	Caucasians
Secular individuals	Conservative Christians
Teachers, trial lawyers	Business people

Source: Compiled by the author from materials including the 2008 party platforms and the American National Election Studies *Guide to Public Opinion and Electoral Behavior*, at http://www.electionstudies.org.

government rather than be privatized. Tax cuts, they argue, limit the ability of government to provide these services. Any tax cuts, they say, should be directed toward helping the needy rather than those who are more affluent. Whereas Republicans believe that the purpose of government is to promote greater individual economic achievement, even at the cost of economic inequality, Democrats feel that fairness requires reducing economic inequality, and that it is government's job to offer a safety net to those who need it.

During the past half-century, the national Democratic Party has favored using government to enforce civil rights for black Americans, and during the past 30 years has been the party of abortion rights and environmental action. If property rights get in the way of environmental protection, Democratic activists contend, then property rights must usually give way. The party's stand on education, similarly, stresses the need for investment in public schools and equality of opportunity. That is one reason why the Democrats are more likely to draw their candidates and activists from among teachers and trial lawyers. The core of Democratic support comes from lower-income people, those living in the Northeast and West Coasts, minorities, and labor unions.

These party differences were crystal clear in the parties' responses to the economic crisis that began in 2007. Characteristically, Democrats moved to fix the economy through massive government intervention. Early in Democratic President Barack Obama's administration in 2009, he and the Democratic-controlled Congress promoted almost $800 billion in government spending to stimulate the economy as well as measures that increased government involvement in failing industries. Many Republican leaders, just as characteristically, opposed the stimulus as a dangerous step toward government control of the economy. A poll in early 2009 showed that 72 percent of Democratic identifiers said they trust government more than they trust businesses to solve the nation's economic problems; 64 percent of Republicans said they placed greater trust in businesses.[18]

Yet, even today, neither party is a model of consistency on issues. In particular, as Table 1.1 shows, the parties seem to switch core beliefs on some issues of individual morality. The Republican Party, which usually opposes government interference, asks for government action to limit abortions and homosexual behavior and to support conservative family values. And the Democrats, the party that sees government as an ally for the needy, often wants government to stay out of individuals' lives on issues such as abortion and homosexuality.

This party switch on traditional values could be seen in a dramatic series of events in 2005. Terri Schiavo, a seriously brain-damaged woman in a persistent vegetative state, had been kept alive by a feeding tube for 15 years. Her husband wanted to have the feeding tube disconnected, saying that his wife had expressed a desire not to be kept alive by extraordinary means. Her parents disagreed and, with the support of pro-life groups, sought to have her feeding tube reconnected. After several state judges sided with the husband, national Republican leaders pushed hard for federal authority to override the state courts, citing the need for a "culture of life." The Republican efforts failed and Schiavo died, but the scenario of Republicans arguing for federal intervention and Democrats opposing it brought this inconsistency in the parties' stands into sharp relief.

These twists and turns in party principles can sometimes stem from a party's efforts to pick up additional support. In the case of traditional values, for example, some conservative Republicans in the 1970s became aware that the pro-life and antigay rights stands of the Christian Right were much more engaging to swing groups of voters than were some of the conservative wing's economic proposals and moved to attract these voters by adopting their causes. Over time, as more of these voters became enthusiastic Republican activists, their issues rose to a leading place on the party's agenda.

These changes also grow out of the powerful impact of their environment on the parties' development. The Republican Party could begin life as a party of both business interests and big government because the expanding businesses of the 1800s needed government help. The building of roads and other means of transporting products, large-scale communications networks, and high tariffs to protect American-made goods could be done much more efficiently by the national government than by the states or the businesses themselves. Once American business became well established and the needed infrastructure was in place, however, a strong national government could become a threat to businesses—as it did in responding to the Depression of the 1930s—because it could regulate their operations and raise their taxes to help fund social programs.

PARTIES ARE SHAPED BY THEIR ENVIRONMENT

Throughout their history, then, the nature of the parties' activities, their issue positions, and even their organizational form have been influenced by forces in their environment, and they have affected that environment in return. A major task of this book is to explain those impacts. One of the most important of these forces has been the nature of the electorate: who has the right to vote?

Voters and Elections

As we have seen, the expansion of the right to vote has helped shape the parties' development. Each new group of voters entering the electorate challenges the parties to readjust their appeals as they vie for the group's support. Parties in states where black citizens finally gained the right to vote, for example, learned to campaign differently from the days when they needed to appeal to an all-white clientele. The increasing numbers of Latino voters are affecting the strategies of both parties now.

The parties' fortunes are also bound up with the *nature* of American elections. The move from indirect to direct election of U.S. senators, for instance, transformed both the contesting of these elections and the parties that contested them. If the Electoral College is ever abolished and American presidents are chosen by direct popular vote, that change, too, would affect the parties.

A state's election rules influence the parties' activities as well. If you were a party leader in a state where conventions of party activists used to nominate candidates for governor, imagine how your work would change when your state switched to the direct primary and voters gained the power to choose these candidates. Even relatively minor differences in primary laws from state to state—for instance, whether a state's primary is held early or late in the nomination season—affect the parties. These electoral institutions set the rules within which the parties compete for votes, and thus influence parties' efforts and organization.

Political Institutions

The two main "rules" of American politics, federalism and the separation of powers, affect the parties profoundly. Consider, for example, the impact of the separation of powers. Nationally and in the states, American legislators and executives are elected independently of one another. That makes it possible and, in recent decades very likely, for the legislature and the governorship or the presidency to be controlled by different parties. Most other democracies, in contrast, have parliamentary systems in which the legislative majority chooses the officials of the executive branch from among its own members. When that parliamentary majority can no longer hold, a new government must be formed. In contrast, in the American system of separated powers, legislators can vote against a president or governor of their party on key issues without fearing that they will bring down the entire government and force new elections. As a result, American legislative parties can rarely achieve the degree of party discipline and cohesion that is common in parliamentary systems.

The federal system, in which states have a number of independent powers (rather than being "branch offices" of the national government), has also left an imprint on the

American parties. It has permitted the survival of local political loyalties and traditions. It has spawned an awesome range of public offices to fill, creating a system of elections that dwarfs that of all other democracies in size and diversity. These local traditions and loyalties have nurtured a large set of semi-independent local parties within the two national parties.

Laws Governing Parties

No other parties among the world's democracies are as entangled in legal regulations as are the American parties. It was not always this way. Before the Progressive reforms a century ago, American parties were self-governing organizations, almost unrestrained by state or federal law. For most of the 1800s, for example, the parties made their own rules for nominating candidates and also printed, distributed, and often—with a wary eye on one another—even counted the ballots. Since then, the "Australian" (or secret) ballot gave the responsibility for running elections to government. The arrival of the direct primary in the early 1900s and recent reforms of the presidential nominating process have also severely limited the parties' freedom to govern themselves.

The existence of 50 different sets of state laws governing the parties has produced 50 different varieties of political parties. State laws control the forms of their organization and even define the parties themselves, often by defining the right to place candidates on the ballot. Most states try to regulate party activities; many, for example, regulate party finances, and most place some limits on their campaign practices. More recently, the federal government has added burdens of its own, including regulating parties' campaign finances.[19]

Political Culture

A nation's political culture is the set of political values and expectations held by its people. One of the most persistent components of the American political culture is the feeling that party politics is an underhanded, dirty business. A 2008 survey, for example, showed such limited enthusiasm for the two parties that, when given a "feeling thermometer" ranging from 0 to 100 degrees on which to indicate their level of positive feeling, the modal respondent chose a rating of between 40 and 60 for both the Democrats and Republicans—a chilly temperature to live in.[20]

These and other elements of the political culture help shape what the parties can do. Public distrust of parties encourages candidates to campaign as individuals rather than as members of a party team. The widespread view that legislators ought to vote based on their local district's interests can make it harder to achieve party discipline in Congress and state legislatures. Even the question of what we regard as fair campaigning simply reflects the values of large numbers of Americans. Whether a strongly worded campaign ad—for instance, "Congressman X has taken thousands in pay raises for himself while refusing to support our troops"—is seen as "mudslinging" or as "hard-hitting and informative" depends on cultural values, not on some set of universal standards. These cultural values affect the parties' appeals to voters, their fund-raising, and their selection of leaders.

The Broader Environment

Parties' environment is broader than their *political* environment. Changes in the nature of the mass media have profoundly affected the parties' development. With increasing media use, people no longer had to depend on the parties to get information about candidates and issues. Candidates can contact voters directly as individuals through the Internet, and in larger audiences through TV, rather than having to depend on the parties to carry the message for them. That has weakened party control over candidates' campaigns. To add insult to injury, media coverage tends not to pay much attention to the parties themselves. Television attaches great importance to visual images, of course, so it is much more likely to cover individuals—candidates and public officials—than to cover institutions, such as parties, that do not have a "face."

Economic trends in the nation as a whole can greatly affect the parties. The severe economic downturn that began in 2007 produced a new set of issues for the parties to address. It has challenged party organizations' ability to raise money, and it contributed to the Democratic victories for president and congressional seats in the 2008 elections.

In this chapter, we have explored the nature of parties, what they do, and how they have developed in and been shaped by their environment. These themes will continue to guide us throughout the book. The next chapter tackles one of the biggest puzzles that students of parties face when comparing the American parties with those in other nations: Why does the United States have two major parties, rather than several, or only one?

CHAPTER 2

The American Two-Party System

Most Americans believe that party politics comes in twos: two parties, two candidates for each office, two sides of an issue. A two-party system has been in place for almost two centuries of American history, so it seems as though all democracies must work that way.

Except that they don't. The United States is one of the few democracies with a two-party system. Some democratic nations, such as Mexico, have had extended periods of one-party rule. Many more democracies, including most of those in Europe, have long supported multiparty systems with three, four, or even more parties. (Nepal currently has 22.) In these nations, it often happens that one single party cannot win a majority of the votes, so two or more parties put together a coalition in order to govern.[1]

In the United States as well, some states and cities have had a long tradition of one-party rule; in other areas, several parties have flourished at certain times. Minor ("third") parties and independent candidates continue to affect elections on occasion. Green Party candidate Ralph Nader took just enough votes in key states from the Democrats in 2000 to tip the presidential election to Republican George W. Bush.[2] Ross Perot's independent presidential campaign in 1992 won the votes of almost 20 million Americans—the third highest percentage of the popular vote for a minor-party candidate in U.S. history. At the state level, comic country singer Kinky Friedman ran for governor of Texas as an independent candidate in 2006 with the campaign slogan, "Kinky: Why the Hell Not?" (After a well-publicized start, he lost, with 13 percent of the vote.)

These campaigns are fun to watch; Friedman, for instance, may have been the only candidate to support both school prayer and gay marriage and had written a book titled, *Kill Two Birds and Get Stoned.* And in 2009, it was probably hard to ignore the write-in candidate for mayor of New York who called himself, nearly accurately, the "Naked Cowboy." Minor-party and independent candidacies are rare, however. For most of American history, ever since the Era of Good Feelings ended in the 1820s, only two parties have had a realistic chance of winning any given national election and of governing. Even the rapid rise of the most successful third party in American history, the

Republican Party, shows the power of two-party politics in the United States. The party was founded in 1854, but instead of competing with the existing Democrats and Whigs, it replaced the Whig Party within two short years.

Why has American politics remained a two-party system for so long, when most other democracies have more than two competitive national parties? In this chapter, we look at the level of competition between the parties, the major theories as to how the two-party system developed, and the efforts by third parties and independent candidates to break the two-party mold.

THE NATIONAL PARTY SYSTEM

Over this remarkably long period of two-party politics, the two major parties have been close competitors, at least at the national level. Since 1868, the great majority of presidential elections have been decided by less than 10 percent of the vote. It has been a quarter of a century since a presidential candidate—Ronald Reagan in 1984—won by more than 10 percentage points in the popular vote. Some of the closest presidential contests in American history have taken place in the past decade. The 2000 election was a virtual tie, and in 2004 President Bush's margin of victory was the smallest ever achieved by an incumbent president.

Currently, the Democratic Party dominates in Congress; after two Democratic "wave" elections in 2006 and 2008, the party holds about 60 percent of the seats in both the U.S. House of Representatives and the Senate. At other times, the Republicans have had runs of congressional victories, most recently from 1994 to 2006. Averaging by decade during the past 70 years, however, the percentage of the two-party vote cast for all Democratic candidates has not differed much from the percentage cast for Republicans (see Table 2.1). Both parties have a voice at the state level as well. In 2009, 23 states had divided party

TABLE 2.1 Percentage of the Two-Party Vote Won by Republican Candidates for President and House of Representatives, 1940–2008

	Presidential Elections		House Elections	
Decade Average	Percentage Republican of Two-Party Vote	Percentage Difference Between Republican and Democratic Vote	Percentage Republican of Two-Party Vote	Percentage Difference Between Republican and Democratic Vote
1940s	46.3	7.3	49.8	5.9
1950s	56.6	13.1	48.1	4.2
1960s	46.3	7.8	46.7	6.7
1970s	55.4	12.6	44.5	10.7
1980s	56.1	11.9	46.1	7.6
1990s	45.9	7.1	49.5	4.3
2000s	49.1	3.4	48.6	5.8

Sources: Calculated from Harold W. Stanley and Richard G. Niemi, *Vital Statistics on American Politics 1999–2000* (Washington, DC: CQ Press, 2000), Tables 1–7 and 1–12, and Dave Leip's "Atlas of U.S. Presidential Elections," at http://www.uselectionatlas.org (accessed March 16, 2009).

control (as opposed to unified control, in which one party controls the governorship and both houses of the state legislature), 17 were fully Democratic-controlled, and 9 were Republican-controlled. (The remaining state legislature, Nebraska's, is nonpartisan.)

In short, the two major parties have shown a great deal of resilience over time. Media coverage may suggest otherwise because it trumpets the events of the moment. But whenever one party has had a string of big wins, in the long term, the other party has been able to restore the balance. Although the Democrats seemed to be on the ropes after the Reagan victories of the 1980s and the Republican congressional sweep of 1994, they recovered quickly enough to keep the presidency in 1996. After the Republican successes in 2004, Democrats won back both houses of Congress in 2006 and gained a total of 55 House and 14 Senate seats in the 2006 and 2008 elections, even at a time when safer House seats have limited the opportunities for sweeping gains by either party. Similarly, the GOP (or Grand Old Party, a nickname the Republican Party developed in the late 1800s) was able to rebound from the Roosevelt victories of the 1930s, landslide defeat in 1964, and the Watergate-related losses of the mid-1970s. Unless there is a major political upheaval, it should recover from its current setbacks as well.

THE 50 STATE PARTY SYSTEMS

Interestingly, however, this pattern of close competition at the national level has coexisted for a long time with one-party dominance in many states and localities. Georgia, for example, chose Democratic governors in 50 consecutive gubernatorial elections, starting before the end of Reconstruction, until finally electing a Republican in 2002.[3]

How can we measure the level of competition in the 50 state party systems? There are many questions to answer in building an index. Which offices should we look at: the vote for president, governor, senator, statewide officials, state legislators, or some combination of these? The competitiveness of a state's U.S. Senate seats may be strikingly different from that of its state legislative races. Should we count the candidates' vote totals, the number of offices that each party wins, or something else?

Measuring State Party Competition

The approach used most often to measure interparty competition at the state level is an index originated by Austin Ranney.[4] The Ranney index averages three indicators of party success during a particular time period: the percentage of the popular vote for the parties' gubernatorial candidates, the percentage of seats held by the parties in each house of the legislature, and the length of time plus the percentage of the time that the parties held both the governorship and a majority in the state legislature.

Like any other summary measure, the Ranney index picks up some trends more fully than others. One reason is that it is based wholly on state elections. This protects the measure from being distorted by landslide victories and other unusual events at the national level. Yet those national events may foreshadow what will happen in voting for state offices. In the South, for example, growing GOP strength appeared first in competition for national offices and only later worked its way down to the state and local levels. In these states, for a time the Ranney index showed less interparty competition than really existed. Nevertheless, its findings provide a valuable picture of state party competition.

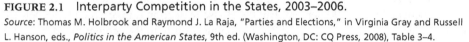

FIGURE 2.1   Interparty Competition in the States, 2003–2006.

Source: Thomas M. Holbrook and Raymond J. La Raja, "Parties and Elections," in Virginia Gray and Russell L. Hanson, eds., *Politics in the American States,* 9th ed. (Washington, DC: CQ Press, 2008), Table 3–4.

Figure 2.1 presents the calculations for the Ranney index for the period 2003–2006. It shows what appears to be more balanced party competition at the state level than had appeared in these calculations earlier in the years since World War II. Note especially that no states are classified as fully one party. The driving force in this change has been a regional transition in party strength, especially in the South and New England. For years a solid Democratic region, southern states began moving toward Republican dominance in recent decades, with the tipping point occurring in 1994 (see Chapter 7). As this Republican trend has continued, we have recently seen states such as Georgia and South Carolina moving from "competitive" to "modified one-party Republican." The New England region has shifted dramatically in the opposite direction; although moderate Republicans won most congressional elections in these states until fairly recently, not a single Republican was elected to the U.S. House from a New England state in 2008. So although the Ranney index shows greater two-party competitiveness in the first decade of the 2000s, this seems to reflect the movement from one pattern of regional party strength to a different, but even more polarized, pattern.

Limits on Competitiveness: Incumbency

Below the statewide level, the decline in party competition is more apparent. For example, although the House of Representatives as a whole has often been closely divided, most House candidates are elected with a comfortable margin of victory. In 2008, more than two-thirds of House candidates won with relative ease, getting at least 60 percent of the total vote. In fact, in 56 of these House races, one of the major parties (in 40 cases, the Republicans) did not even field a candidate. At the state legislative level, in recent years, fewer than two-thirds of the races had both a Democratic and a Republican candidate.[5]

What keeps the relatively close party competition at the national level from infiltrating congressional districts to as great an extent? One brake on competition in these districts has been the electoral value of incumbency. Although there was a lot of party turnover during the 1800s, and the fates of candidates from politically competitive areas depended on the national or statewide forces affecting the parties, members of Congress have had greater electoral security in the past half-century. From 1954 through 1988, for example, the average success rates for incumbents seeking reelection were 93 percent in the U.S. House of Representatives and 81 percent in the Senate. These rates peaked in 1988 for the House when more than 98 percent of the incumbents who ran for reelection won, and in 1990 when all but one of the senators running for reelection won. (A congressional incumbent in these years probably stood a greater chance of being hit by an SUV in Washington, DC, traffic than of losing reelection.)

That job security seemed to be at risk in the early 1990s. A well-reported scandal and a resulting crop of especially strong challengers, followed by an effective national Republican House campaign in 1994, dropped the success rate of House incumbents to "only" between 88 and 90 percent. But the House reelection rate returned to 98 percent in each election between 1998 and 2004, dipping slightly to 94 percent in 2006 and 95 percent in 2008.[6] Incumbents in most state legislatures were just as likely to keep their jobs.[7] In fact, the incumbency advantage has increased in elections for all types of executive and legislative offices.[8]

There are many reasons why incumbency came to be such a valuable resource in congressional elections. Incumbents learned how to benefit from the "perks" of holding office—their name recognition and the attention they receive from the media, the services they can provide to constituents, the greater ease with which they can raise campaign money, as well as their experience in having run previous successful campaigns, all of which discourage potentially effective candidates from running against them. These add up to what can be called the *personal* incumbency advantage.[9]

... and Other Reasons for Declining Competitiveness

Researchers have found, however, that although there are more safe House seats now than in the early 1990s, the *size* of the average House incumbent's advantage in winning reelection has declined since that time. So the personal incumbency advantage can't fully explain why congressional races are getting less competitive.

Another possible explanation is that during the past decade, state legislators have been able to use sophisticated computer programs to redraw legislative district lines for themselves and for U.S. House members. Thus they make their districts safer by "choosing their own voters." Redistricting after the 2000 census reduced the number of competitive House seats by making three-fourths of these districts safer for one party.[10] Yet redistricting can't be the only reason for safer districts because incumbents are also doing better in elections for offices that are not redistricted, such as local and statewide offices.

Bruce Oppenheimer has suggested an alternative: that new patterns of residential mobility are a major cause of declining party competition. As people have become more mobile, they are more able, and likely, to move to areas where like-minded people live. As a result, areas become more homogeneous—and, thus, congressional districts are more likely to be dominated by one party.[11] This ideological "sorting" has added to the growing geographic divergence in party loyalties. An analyst found that although the 2000 and 1976 presidential elections were both won by narrow margins, almost twice as many of the voters in 2000 lived in counties where one candidate or the other won by a landslide, and suggested that there has been a "voluntary political segregation" in the United States.[12] Alan Abramowitz and others show that the declining ability of challengers to raise campaign money also helps explain why House elections have become less competitive.[13]

At times, as in 2008, national conditions favor one party to the extent that candidates will be elected in districts that would normally support the other party. But the trend has been toward an increasing proportion of House districts that are relatively safe for one party. The result is that in recent decades, when we have seen lively party competition in the nation as a whole, it has been built not on large numbers of highly competitive House, state legislative, and other districts, but rather on the fact that the large number of fairly safe districts for one party has been closely matched, over time, by the number of fairly safe districts for the other party.

Political competition is vital in a democracy. To the extent that incumbents continue to be reelected because they work hard to serve their districts, then their constituents may be well-represented.[14] But when an officeholder expects to win reelection easily, he or she has less incentive to pay close attention to voters' needs. In particular, the needs of disadvantaged citizens are more likely to be ignored (because advantaged citizens have other means, in addition to voting, to make their voices heard in government). The increase in safe seats, then, is a cause for concern.

WHAT CAUSES A TWO-PARTY SYSTEM?

We have seen that the American parties are durable and that, at least at the aggregate level, when one party has had a run of dominance, the other party has been able to bounce back. Why have we had a two-party system for so long, when most other democracies do not? There are several possible explanations.

Institutional Forces

The most frequent explanation of the two-party system ties it to the nature of American electoral institutions. Called *Duverger's law*,[15] it argues that single-member districts with plurality elections tend to produce two-party systems. A *single-member district* means simply that one candidate is elected to each office, and a *plurality election* is one in which the candidate with the largest number of votes, even if not a majority, wins. Finishing a close second, or third or fourth, brings no rewards. The American election system is, for most offices, a single-member district system with plurality election; it offers the reward of winning an office only to the one candidate who gets the most votes. So the theory suggests that minor parties will see no point in running candidates if they don't have a shot at winning.

The flip side of Duverger's law is that multimember constituencies and proportional representation result in multiparty systems. A system with multimember constituencies is one in which a particular legislative district will be represented by, say, three or four elected legislators.[16] In proportional representation (PR), each party prepares a slate of candidates for these positions, and the number of party candidates

PLURALITY VERSUS PROPORTIONAL REPRESENTATION: HOW IT WORKS IN PRACTICE

Does it matter whether an election uses plurality or proportional representation rules to count the votes? To find out, let us compare the results of one type of American election in which both rules are used. In presidential primaries—the elections in which party voters choose delegates to the national parties' presidential conventions—the Democrats use PR to select delegates (with at least 15 percent of the vote needed for a candidate to win delegates) and the Republicans generally use some form of plurality election (also called winner-take-all).

Imagine a congressional district that will send four delegates to the national convention, in which candidates A, B, C, and D get the following percentages of the vote. The candidates would win the following numbers of delegates, depending on whether the plurality or PR rule was used:

	% of vote	Delegates Won Plurality	PR
Candidate A	40	4	2
Candidate B	30	0	1
Candidate C	20	0	1
Candidate D	10	0	0

With the *plurality* (winner-take-all) rule, candidate A, who has gotten the most votes, wins all the delegates at stake in that district. So in a typical Republican primary, using the plurality rule, only the leading candidate will emerge with delegates; the other candidates win nothing. Under most circumstances, the less successful candidates will find it hard to stay in the race very long when they are winning no delegates in return for their efforts. In 2008, for example, all of John McCain's rivals for the Republican presidential nomination had left the field within the first two months of the five-month primary season, after a series of narrow McCain victories gave him an overwhelming lead in delegates. Under *PR* rules, in contrast, *three* candidates win delegates in rough proportion to their popular support. So in a typical Democratic primary, the less successful candidates are encouraged to stay in the race longer because the PR rules permit them to keep winning at least a few delegates.

The contrast is even clearer when we compare British elections with the multimember district systems of most European legislative elections. The use of PR in the European elections promotes multiparty politics and coalition governments in which two or more different parties often share control of the executive. In the British parliamentary system, on the other hand, single-member districts operating under plurality rules typically produce a parliamentary majority for one party, giving it sole control of the executive, even if it does not win a majority of the popular vote.

who win is proportional to the overall percentage of the vote won by the party slate (see box on this page). Because a party may be able to elect a candidate with only 15 or 20 percent of the votes, depending on the system's rules, smaller parties are encouraged to keep competing.

However, a puzzle remains. Single-member district systems with plurality elections exist in some other democracies that support more than two parties. Shouldn't the United States, with its great diversity, do the same? To some analysts, the nature of the American presidency helps to sustain Duverger's law. The presidency is the most visible single-member district in the United States. It is the main prize of American politics, and only one person is elected to that office at a time. Many other democracies, using a parliamentary system, have a governing "cabinet" as the executive authority. This cabinet is made up of a number of officeholders, so it can be a coalition that includes representatives of several parties, including smaller parties.

In a system with a single executive, minor parties will be weakened because they do not have a realistic chance to compete for the presidency.[17] Even the minor parties strong enough to elect candidates in their own localities typically find it unrealistic to run a candidate for president. That denies a minor party the national attention that major parties get. Add to that the uniquely American institution of the Electoral College. To win, a presidential candidate must get an absolute majority of electoral votes—so far, at least, an impossible task for a minor-party candidate. Because the presidency is so prominent in American politics, the argument goes, it shapes the politics of the system as a whole. Because third parties have no chance of winning the presidency, they will not thrive.[18]

Of course, some minor parties try for the presidency anyway. In 1996, the Reform Party focused primarily on the presidential race. But its candidate, Ross Perot, a billionaire willing to spend tens of millions on his campaign, is clearly not typical of most minor parties, no matter how much they may dream of such an opportunity. So the importance of the single, indivisible executive office in the American system strengthens the tendency toward two-party politics.

Political scientist Leon Epstein has identified another institutional factor, the direct primary, as a force that prevented the development of third parties in areas dominated by one party.[19] Primaries, which allow voters to choose the parties' nominees, have become the main method of selecting party candidates. When disgruntled groups have the opportunity to make their voices heard within the dominant party through a primary and may even succeed in getting a candidate nominated, the resulting taste of power will probably discourage them from breaking away to form a third party. Thus, in the one-party Democratic South of an earlier era, where traditional animosities kept most people from voting Republican, factional disputes that under other conditions would have produced one or more third parties were contained within the Democratic Party by the existence of primary elections.

"Dualist" Theories

Some theorists believe that there is a basic duality of interests in American society that has sustained the two-party system. V. O. Key, Jr., argued that tension between the eastern financial and commercial interests and the western frontiersmen stamped itself on the parties as they were forming and fostered two-party competition. Later, the dualism shifted to North–South conflict over the issue of slavery and the Civil War and then to urban–rural and socioeconomic divisions.[20]

We can see tendencies toward dualism even in multiparty systems, in that some parties will join together to construct a governing coalition and the other parties will find themselves in opposition. In the 2007 French presidential race, for example, the Socialists and other leftist parties, and the various conservative and rightist parties, all competed against one another in the election's first round, but then came together along largely ideological lines to contest the runoff election. So, the argument suggests, there is a natural dualism within democratic institutions: government versus opposition, those favoring and opposing the status quo. What distinguishes two-party from multiparty systems, in short, may be whether this basic tendency toward dualism is expressed in every aspect of the electoral process or only in the creation and functioning of a government.

Social Consensus Theories

Another possible explanation for the American two-party system is that it reflects a broad consensus on values in American society. Despite their very diverse social and cultural heritage, Americans reached an early consensus on many of the fundamentals that divide other societies. Almost all Americans have traditionally accepted the prevailing social, economic, and political institutions: the Constitution and its governmental structure, a regulated but free enterprise economy, and (perhaps to a lesser extent) American patterns of social class and status.

In traditional multiparty countries, such as France and Italy, noticeable segments of the public have favored radical changes in those and other basic institutions. They have supported fundamental constitutional change, the socialization of the economy, or the disestablishment of the national church. Perhaps American politics escaped these divisions on the essentials because Americans did not have a history of the rigid class structure of feudalism. Perhaps the early expansion of the right to vote in the United States made it unnecessary for workers and other economically disadvantaged citizens to organize in order to gain some political power. Perhaps it was the expanding economic and geographic frontiers that allowed Americans to concentrate on claiming a piece of a growing pie rather than on battling one another. Because the matters that divide Americans are secondary, the argument goes, the compromises needed to bring them into one of two major parties are easier to make.[21]

Party Self-Protection (The Best Defense Is a Good Offense)

Once a two-party system has developed, the two dominant parties are highly motivated to protect it. The two major parties will support election systems (such as single-member districts and plurality elections) that make it hard for minor parties to do well. Through their control of Congress and state legislatures, the Democrats and Republicans have manipulated the rules to keep third parties from qualifying for the ballot and third-party candidates from getting public funding. The major parties have no interest in leveling the playing field so that their minor-party competitors can take a shot at replacing them.[22] Further, after the two-party system was launched, it created deep loyalties within the American public to one party or the other and attachments to the two-party system itself.

The two parties' openness to new groups and adaptability to changing conditions—qualities rare among democratic parties—have also undermined the development of strong third parties. Just when a third party rides the crest of a new issue to the point where it can challenge the two-party monopoly, one or both of the major parties is likely to absorb the new movement. In the 2004 campaign, for example, the Democrats worked hard to appeal to the nearly 3 million voters who supported Ralph Nader's Green Party candidacy in 2000.[23]

The most important of these explanations for a two-party system is the institutional arrangement of American electoral politics. Without single-member districts, plurality elections, the Electoral College, and an indivisible executive, it would have been much easier for third parties to break the near-monopoly enjoyed by the Republicans and Democrats. Other Anglo-American democracies such as Britain and Canada, which share many of the American institutional arrangements, also tend to be dominated by two parties, although third parties are more successful in these nations than in the United States.

EXCEPTIONS TO THE TWO-PARTY PATTERN

As we have seen, there are pockets of one-party politics in states and localities within the American two-party system. Some areas have even developed a uniquely American brand of no-party (nonpartisan) politics. Third parties or independent candidates have occasionally made their presence felt. Where do we find these exceptions to two-party politics?

Nonpartisan Elections

One of the Progressive movement's most treasured achievements was to restrict the role of parties by removing party labels from many ballots, mostly in local elections. About three-quarters of American cities and towns, including Los Angeles, Chicago, Miami, and Atlanta, conduct their local elections on a nonpartisan basis. Many states elect judges using a nonpartisan ballot. Nonpartisanship adds to the parties' burdens; even the strongest local parties have to work much harder to let voters know which candidates are affiliated with their party.

Removing party labels from the ballot has not usually removed partisan influences where parties are already strong. A resourceful party organization can still select its candidates and persuade voters when party labels are not on the ballot. Even where local elections are nonpartisan, local voters are still affected by the partisan content of state and national elections. Typically, however, the reform took root in cities and towns that already had weak parties and for offices, such as judgeships and school boards, where the traditional American dislike of party politics is most pronounced. Most northeastern cities, where strong party machines were the main targets of the Progressives, were able to resist the reforms and to continue holding partisan local elections.

Beyond adding to the difficulties faced by party organizations, what difference does it make if an election is nonpartisan? Researchers had long believed that nonpartisan elections gave an advantage to Republican candidates, who were more likely to have the financial resources to attract voter attention in the absence of party labels. More recent research suggests, however, that it is the minority party in an area that benefits, because the nonpartisan ballot takes away the party cue that would otherwise remind the majority's voters to choose the majority party's candidates.[24] Nonpartisan elections have also been found to reduce voter turnout. The party label is an important and low-cost shortcut for voters to use in elections; without it, fewer people make the effort to vote.[25]

In an ingenious experiment, one group of researchers compared the behavior of state legislators in Nebraska, who are selected in nonpartisan elections, with those in partisan Kansas. They found that legislators' votes on bills were not as clearly structured in Nebraska as they were in Kansas; that made it harder for voters to predict how their representatives will behave and to hold them accountable.[26] So nonpartisan elections can weaken the policy links between voters and their legislators—a result that would have greatly disappointed the Progressives.

Areas of One-Party Monopoly

In the past, the states of the Deep South were the country's best-known examples of one-party domination. Today, traces of one-party politics can still be found in thousands of cities, towns, and counties in which a mention of the other party can produce anything from raised eyebrows to raised tempers.

Where do we find these one-party areas? For most of their history, the major parties, especially in national elections, have divided the American voters roughly along social-demographic lines. (More about this can be found in Chapter 7.) A local constituency may be too small to contain the social diversity that supports both Democratic and Republican politics. Thus, we can find "safe" Democratic congressional districts in the poorer, older, and black neighborhoods of large cities and "safe" Republican districts in small town and rural, heavily white, Christian and southern areas. The less diverse its people are, at least in terms of the demographic characteristics that typically divide Republican from Democratic voters, the more likely the district is to foster one-party politics.

Alternatively, there may be some local basis of party loyalty so powerful that it overrides the relationship between socioeconomic status and partisanship. In the classic one-party politics of the American South until the last quarter of the 1900s, racial fears, white hatred of Republicans as the party of abolition and Reconstruction, and laws and practices preventing blacks from voting long outweighed the factors that were dividing Americans into two parties in most of the rest of the country.

Once one party has established dominance in an area, the weaker party may have a hard time overcoming the dominant party's advantages. These advantages begin with stubborn party loyalties. Many voters are not easily moved from their attachments to a party, even though the reasons for the original attachment are long past. A party trying to become competitive may find itself caught in a vicious circle. Its inability to win elections limits its ability to raise money and recruit attractive candidates because, as a chronic loser, it offers so little chance of achieving political goals. The Republican Party in the South, for example, found for many years that the Democrats had recruited the region's most promising politicians and claimed its most powerful appeals. Now, in many parts of the South, it is the Democrats who face this same disadvantage.

The weaker party's ability to attract voters locally is also affected by media coverage of its national party's stance. If the Democratic Party is identified nationally with the hopes of the poor and minority groups, its appeal in an affluent suburb may be limited, no matter how attractive its candidates are. So a nationalized politics may rob the local party organization of the chance to develop strength based on its own issues and candidates. To the extent that party loyalties grow out of national politics, as

Democrats in the South have learned, competitiveness may be beyond the reach of some local party organizations.

And as noted earlier in this chapter, redistricting can make it harder for the weaker party to bounce back. Majority parties have found effective ways to redraw legislative district lines that preserve their advantage, so the minority party in an area must compete in districts drawn by the stronger party. This is why parties are especially concerned with winning state legislative majorities in years ending in zero, when district lines must be redrawn.

Third Parties

Minor parties, often called "third" parties, have a long history in American politics, but they rarely win elections. Only seven minor parties in all of American history have carried even a single state in a presidential election. The recent high point of third-party strength was Ross Perot's run as the Reform Party candidate for president in 1996, when he won just over 8 million votes. In 2008, all third-party presidential candidates combined won less than a quarter of that number.

Third-party successes below the presidential level are as uncommon as they are fascinating. Of more than a thousand governors elected since 1875, fewer than 20 ran solely on a third-party ticket and another handful ran as independents.[27] The successful candidacy of former professional wrestler Jesse "The Body" Ventura for governor of Minnesota in 1998 got enormous media attention precisely because it was so unusual, but Ventura stepped down from the governorship in 2002 after having been largely ignored by the state legislature, and the next candidate of his party attracted only 16 percent of the vote.[28] Third-party and independent candidates won more than four million votes for governor in 2006, plus another 400,000 in 2008, but they were too widely spread to elect any candidate.

The Libertarian Party has been the strongest vote-getter of any minor party in the past quarter century. Libertarian candidates received a total of more than a million votes for U.S. House seats in 2008 (see Table 2.2), though no Libertarian candidate won. A handful of other minor-party and independent candidates were elected to state legislatures that year, and a few were successful in local races; in 2009, there was a Green Party county commissioner in Colorado, a Green township clerk in Michigan, a Libertarian county attorney in Kansas, and a Working Families Party voter registrar in Connecticut. One Green elected official, the mayor of tiny New Paltz, New York, stepped out of third-party obscurity in 2004 when he conducted weddings for hundreds of same-sex couples. (He lost his bid for reelection.)

More significantly, a third party has sometimes shifted the balance in an important race. In 2006, Democrats regained control of the U.S. Senate thanks to a shift of two seats, and in both elections a minor party candidate got more votes than the Democrat's margin of victory. In 2008, the Democrats won their 60th vote in the Senate when the Democratic candidate was finally declared the winner of a virtually tied race. An Independence Party candidate took 15 percent of the vote in that election. If only a tiny proportion of the minor-party voters had supported the Republican candidate instead, he would have won the seat. However, for every example of third-party success in local elections, there are thousands of races with no minor-party candidate. The two major

COMPETING AGAINST THE "BIG GUYS"

The Democrats and the Republicans, Brad Warren says, have a "death grip" on the American political process. Warren, a tax attorney in Indianapolis, is a Libertarian Party activist who ran for the U.S. Senate under that party's banner. "If I need a new pair of socks," he points out, "I can go to dozens of stores and pick from several different brands and dozens of colors—for something as insignificant as socks. But when it comes to politics, which has a monopoly on the lawful use of force in our society, we have only two choices. That is tremendously scary! How do you hold them accountable? If you get angry with the incumbents, you can throw them out, only to reelect the nasty incumbents you had thrown out in the previous election. Four years from now, you'll be throwing out the incumbents you elected today. There's no choice."

Third-party activists, such as Warren, must compete against the "big guys"—the two major parties—on an uneven playing field. A major problem for a third party, Warren says, is simply to get its candidates' names on the ballot. The Indiana state legislature used to require any minor party to win just half of 1 percent of the vote for secretary of state in order to qualify its candidates to get on the state ballot automatically in later elections. The Libertarians met that goal in 1982. The result? The legislature raised the hurdle to 2 percent. Ballot access requirements differ from state to state, making it difficult for a minor party to appear on the ballot in all 50 states.

"Even once you have ballot access," Warren argues, "you will still be excluded from any *meaningful* participation in the election. In practice, we run elections on money, not on votes, and in presidential elections, the Republicans and Democrats divide up hundreds of millions of federal dollars among themselves."

The worst problem for third parties, Warren feels, is getting noticed after the major primaries hold primary elections. "I got pretty good media coverage up to the primary election. After the primary, I was nobody. Even though the primary doesn't elect anybody to any office, it *seems to*. Primaries are a government-funded means of anointing the two major parties' candidates as the "real" candidates and de-legitimizing all the others. The media say we have no chance to win, so they won't cover any candidates except the [major] party-anointed ones. The debates typically don't include third-party candidates. Why? Because the commissions that decide who's going to be allowed to participate in debates are 'bipartisan' commissions, made up entirely of Republicans and Democrats, just like the legislatures that write the ballot access laws and the judges who interpret them. A party that has gotten on the ballot in all 50 states, like the Libertarians, deserves to be heard."

"The two major parties won't give you any choice," Warren contends, and "if you continually vote for the lesser of two evils, what you get is evil." So what is the role of a third party? To Warren, "It's like that of a bee: You rise up, you sting, and then you die."

parties have monopolized elections even more fully in the states and cities than at the national level (see "A Day in the Life" on this page.)

Third parties in the United States vary greatly in their purposes, origins, and levels of activity:[29]

TABLE 2.2 Voting for Independent and Minor-Party Candidates for U.S. House, 2008

Party	Votes
Libertarian (127 candidates in 27 states)	1,078,179
Green (58 candidates in 19 states)	596,964
Working Families (Connecticut, New York)	293,435
Conservative Party (New York only)	194,841
Constitution (41 candidates in 10 states)	186,177
Independence Party of New York	157,831
Independence Party (Minnesota)	116,835
Independence Party of Oregon	65,109
Peace and Freedom (California only)	47,659
Alaskan Independence Party (Alaska only)	14,274
Other minor parties	69,471
Total votes for minor-party candidates	2,820,755
Total votes for independent (nonparty) candidates	973,251

Note: Democratic U.S. House candidates received a total of 65.2 million votes in 2008, and Republican U.S. House candidates received 52 million votes.

Source: Richard L. Winger, *Ballot Access News*, November 1, 2008, p. 3 and January 1, 2009, p. 4.

Differences in Ideology   Most minor parties are driven by issues and ideologies, but they differ in the nature and scope of that commitment. The New York State Right to Life and the Independent American Party are very specific and targeted: the former in wanting to ban all abortions and the latter in favoring Christian principles in politics. At the other extreme are socialist parties whose programs demand sweeping changes, including an end to capitalism and class privilege. The Libertarian Party wants government to involve itself only in national defense and criminal law and to turn over all other programs, from Social Security to education, to private efforts.[30] In sharp contrast, Green Parties argue for extensive government programs on behalf of the environment, peace, and social justice.

Difference of Origins   Minor parties differ, too, in their origin. Some were literally imported into the United States. Much of the early Socialist Party strength in the United States came from the freethinkers and radicals who fled Europe after the failed revolutions of 1848. Socialist candidates did well in cities such as Milwaukee, New York, and Cincinnati because of the concentrations of liberal German immigrants there. Other parties, especially the Granger and Populist Parties, were homegrown channels of social protest, born of social inequality and economic hardship in the marginal farmlands of America.

Some minor parties began as splinters or factions of one of the major parties. For example, the Progressives (the Bull Moose Party) of 1912 and the Dixiecrats of 1948 objected so strenuously to the platforms and candidates of their parent parties that they ran their own slates and presented their own programs in presidential elections. In fact, the Dixiecrats, an anti-civil rights faction within the Democratic Party, substituted their own candidate for the one chosen by the party's national convention as the official Democratic presidential candidate in several southern states.

Differing Purposes   Finally, third parties differ in their intentions. Some of these parties aim to educate citizens about their issues; getting votes is merely a sideline. They run candidates because their presence on the ballot brings media attention that they could not otherwise hope to get. Many of these parties serenely accept their election losses because they have chosen not to compromise their principles to win office. The Prohibition Party, for example, has run candidates in most presidential elections since 1872 with unflagging devotion to the cause of banning the sale of alcoholic beverages but without apparent concern for the fact that its highest proportion of the popular vote was 2 percent, and that came in 1892.

Other minor parties are serious about trying to win office. Often, their goal is local, although today they find it difficult to control an American city, as the Socialists once did, or an entire state, like the Progressives. More realistically, they may hope to hold a balance of power in a close election between the major parties, as Ralph Nader did in the 2000 presidential election. Ross Perot even claimed to be looking for an outright victory in both 1992 (as an independent) and 1996.

What Difference Do They Make?   Some argue that minor parties deserve the credit for a number of public policies—programs that were first suggested by a minor party and then adopted by a major party when they became politically popular. A possible example is the minimum wage, which was advocated by the Socialist Party for more than two decades before the minimum wage law was enacted in the 1930s by a Democratic Congress. Did the Democrats steal the Socialist Party's idea, or would they have proposed a minimum wage for workers even if there had been no Socialist Party? There is no way to be sure. Major parties usually propose a new policy once a large number of Americans has accepted the idea, so the party can gain votes. However, the major party might have picked up the new proposal from any of a number of sources in addition to the Socialists.

If the impact of third parties is so limited, then what attracts some voters to them? There aren't many such voters; the self-fulfilling prophecy that a vote for a third party is a wasted vote is very powerful in American politics.[31] Yet some voters do cast third-party ballots. To Steven Rosenstone and his colleagues, this results from the failure of major parties "to do what the electorate expects of them—reflect the issue preferences of voters, manage the economy, select attractive and acceptable candidates, and build voter loyalty to the parties and the political system."[32] So third parties tend to gain support when they promote attractive ideas that the major parties have ignored, or because of public dissatisfaction with the major party candidates, rather than because many voters believe in a multiparty system as a matter of principle.

The Rise of Independent Candidates

In recent elections, dissatisfaction with the two major parties has also produced several notable independent candidacies—those who run as individuals, independent of any party organization. The most successful was Ross Perot, who mounted a well-funded independent candidacy for president in 1992 before running as the Reform Party candidate in 1996. The story of Perot's two candidacies, one as an independent and the other as a third-party candidate, helps us understand some of the advantages and disadvantages of each choice.

In his race as an independent candidate in 1992, Perot and his supporters built a remarkably strong national organization. Through its efforts, Perot got on the ballot in all 50 states. He ended the race with 19.7 million votes—a larger share of the popular vote than any "third" candidate in history who was not a former president. In fact, he outdrew the combined total of all his third-party opponents in that race by more than 19 million ballots. The key ingredient in his success was money; Perot invested more than $65 million of his own funds in his campaign. That financed organizational efforts at the grassroots level and bought large blocks of expensive television time. Even so, Perot failed to win a single state, and much of his support came from voters who were more dissatisfied with the major-party candidates than they were attracted to a long-lasting commitment to another party or candidate.[33]

Three years later, Perot organized the new Reform Party and sought to qualify it for the ballot in all 50 states. That was harder than qualifying to run as an independent. In California, his toughest challenge, Perot had to get at least 890,000 signatures on a petition by October 1995 to win a place on the state's ballot 13 months later. He failed. Using a different mechanism, Perot finally qualified in California and in all other states but found it difficult to recruit acceptable Reform candidates for other offices. On Election Day, Perot got less than half as many votes as a Reform Party candidate than he had four years earlier as an independent.

Why was his third-party effort less successful? Many factors were at work. One may have been simple familiarity; at times, a candidate does not benefit from letting voters get to know him or her better. Perot spent much less of his own money in 1996 than he had four years earlier. In addition, it is harder for an organization to support many candidates rather than just one. In the 2000 presidential campaign, for example, conflicts among Reform Party activists became so intense that the party's national convention disintegrated into a fistfight and the party split.

Ralph Nader's experience as a presidential candidate in 2000 and 2004 was very different from Perot's. In 2000, Nader won access to 43 state ballots fairly easily because he ran as the Green Party candidate, which had already qualified for ballot access in those states. In 2004, Nader struggled to get on those same ballots as an independent candidate. Democratic activists filed lawsuits to try to keep Nader off state ballots; Republicans often supported Nader's efforts, because his candidacy was expected to hurt Democrat John Kerry more than Republican George W. Bush.

Even when a third party meets the difficult challenge of maintaining its line on the ballot, it will still face the enormous hurdle of recruiting candidates for thousands of state legislative seats and county offices as well as for president. The Greens and the Libertarians have made real efforts since 2000 to establish themselves as organizations that extend beyond a relatively small number of candidates. If history is any guide, however, that is a battle they are likely to lose. The result is that when voters consider alternatives to the major parties, independent candidates (especially if they happen to be billionaires, such as New York mayor Michael Bloomberg, who considered running for president as an independent in 2008) will continue to have advantages over those who try to form fully elaborated third parties.

WANT TO RUN AS AN INDEPENDENT? GOOD LUCK!

If you want to run for the U.S. House of Representatives as an independent (nonparty) candidate in some districts in California, Georgia, Illinois, or North or South Carolina, you will have to get more than 10,000 people to sign a petition for you. (As a result, no independent candidate for the House has ever appeared on a government-printed ballot in either North or South Carolina.)

If you want to run as an independent candidate for president, then you must get a total of about 650,000 valid signatures on petitions. Each state has its own requirements, which you will have to unearth and follow. In Texas alone, you need to get 74,000 signatures from registered voters during a 75-day period, which ends in May of an election year, and none of the signers can have voted in the most recent party primaries. In Florida, you must have 104,338 signatures from registered voters by July 15 of the election year.

Paid signature-gatherers usually earn about $2 for each signature collected, so unless you are able to recruit a small army of volunteers, you'd pay at least $1.3 million just to get the petitions signed and much more for the lawyers in each state who will be needed to defend your petitions against legal challenges from other candidates or parties. These are examples of ways in which the state legislatures, made up almost entirely of Democrats and Republicans, have protected the two major parties by passing laws making it much tougher for minor-party and independent candidates to get on the ballot.

Sources: Richard L. Winger, *Ballot Access News,* September 1, 2007, p. 3 (on House rules); Ken Belson and Serge F. Kovaleski, "Bloomberg in '08?" *New York Times,* January 1, 2008, p. B1 (on presidential candidacies).

WILL THE TWO-PARTY SYSTEM CONTINUE?

This look at two-party politics and its alternatives leads to two main conclusions. First, in important respects, the two-party system is secure in the United States. Third parties are not gaining ground. Third-party members of Congress, common in the early decades of the two-party system, have been very rare throughout the 1900s and especially in recent years. Since 1952, only three members of Congress have been elected on a third-party ticket. Four have recently served as independents, but all have aligned themselves with one of the major parties' caucuses. Minor-party candidates have also fared poorly in state legislative contests during this period.

The barriers to ballot access for minor-party and independent candidates are not as high now as they once were. And quirks in local election laws continue to support a few local third parties. The classic instance is New York's minor parties, notably the Conservatives and the Working Families Party. They survive because they can nominate candidates of a major party to run under their own parties' labels as well.[34] But in most cases, candidates other than Republicans and Democrats must still jump substantial hurdles to get on state ballots and satisfy a patchwork of different state laws to qualify for the ballot nationwide. Even when courts have overturned laws that discriminate against these candidates, the decisions have been limited, requiring petitioners to mount a challenge in each state.[35]

In addition, independent and third-party candidates still face huge financial disadvantages. Although candidates don't need to be Democrats or Republicans in order to reach voters throughout the United States with television and the Internet, the enormous cost of modern campaigns probably restricts this opportunity to only a few highly visible or personally wealthy individuals. Third-party presidential candidates can receive public funding for their campaign if they win at least 5 percent of the popular vote. But in 30 years, the only campaign to qualify was Perot's Reform Party in 1996. That assured the Reform Party's 2000 presidential candidate of receiving $12 million in federal funds for his campaign. The money no doubt increased the attractiveness of the party's presidential nomination; yet the eventual nominee, Patrick Buchanan, earned less than half of 1 percent of the popular vote.

Independent candidates for president and governor have made some elections less predictable. But running by themselves, with no other candidates on their "tickets," they are not likely to create a lasting challenge to the Democrats and Republicans. To make a sustained challenge that could fundamentally transform the American parties, these independents would need to organize to confront the major parties from the top to the bottom of the ballot. Those who try soon realize that the two-party system may not be greatly beloved, but it is very well entrenched.

How would a multiparty system change American politics? Proponents could cite a number of benefits. Voters would have more choices. A greater variety of views would be able to find expression through a party platform. Smaller parties, speaking for identifiable segments of society, might give citizens in these groups more confidence that their voices are being heard by government.

On the other hand, when the threshold for ballot access is lowered, extremist parties are better able to compete. In a system where the government will probably be a coalition of several parties, voters need to anticipate the compromises that their preferred party will make in order to form a government and perhaps, in order to influence that compromise, vote for a party whose views are more extreme than their own.[36] Votes are more directly translated into leadership in a majoritarian two-party system, though American politics, with its separation of powers, limits that direct translation now. Coalition governments can be unstable. And a multiparty system would likely require major changes in American electoral institutions, such as the single-member presidency and plurality elections. But these advantages and disadvantages are a moot point, because of the durability of American two-party politics.

The second major trend that we have seen in this chapter is an especially intriguing one. The Democratic and Republican Parties are highly competitive at the national level; presidential elections are won by relatively small margins, and both parties have had recent runs of dominance in Congress. When we look beneath the aggregate level at individual House and state legislative districts, however, the close competition vanishes. The intense party competition at the national level is often built on the backs of fairly equal numbers of safe Democratic and safe Republican congressional and lower-level seats.[37]

Officeholders elected in districts that are relatively safe for their party may not feel as great a need to appeal to voters of the other party as they would if the district were more competitive. Incumbents in safe districts face more of a threat from within their own party, in the primary election, than from the other party. These primary threats usually come from the ideological extremes of their party. As Chapter 13 shows, then, the increasing number of safe incumbents can take more partisan stands in order to ward off a primary challenger, knowing that they are not likely to suffer for it in the general election. Party polarization in Congress, state legislatures, and among politically involved citizens has accompanied this process. Even in a relatively stable two-party system such as that in the United States, moderation in political debate can be in short supply.

Part Two

THE POLITICAL PARTY AS AN ORGANIZATION

Two of the three parts of the American parties are easy enough to see. We all have friends or relatives who are passionate Democrats or dedicated Republicans; they belong to the *party in the electorate*. News stories mention members of the *party in government* daily when they refer to presidents, the Democratic Speaker of the House, or the Republican Minority Leader in the Senate. The third part of the parties is less visible. It is the *party organization*, or the party committees and volunteers who work at all the levels at which Americans elect public officials: precincts, townships, wards, cities, counties, congressional districts, states, and the federal government. The next three chapters examine these organizations and the activists and leaders who give them life. How do the party organizations work, and how have they changed over time? What kinds of people become party activists? These internal characteristics influence the party's ability to act effectively in the larger political system.

American party organizations vary tremendously, from powerful and elaborate structures to empty shells. Compared with those of other Western democracies, however, most American party organizations would be considered fairly weak. Shackled by state laws, the party organizations have rarely been able to exercise much influence over the party's candidates and officeholders (the party in government) and the party in the electorate.

The three parts of any party differ in their goals. In an election, for instance, the party organization hopes to support as many of its candidates as possible, whereas each individual candidate wants as much of the party's money as he or she can get, and party voters are concerned instead with taxes or same-sex marriage or cheaper college tuition. Each seeks control of the party to achieve its own ends. In the American system, the party organizations find it difficult to hold their own in this competition and to get the resources they need to influence elections and promote policies. American party organizations can't translate their platform planks into law; they must depend on the members of their party in government to do that. Party organizations must work hard to court and mobilize the party electorate, who may be loyal party voters at some times but more fickle at others.

This lack of integration among the party's component parts is typical of *cadre parties*—one of two terms often used to describe the nature of party organizations. Imagine that party organizations are arranged along a continuum. At one end of this continuum is the cadre party, in which the organization is run by a relatively small number of leaders and activists with little or no broader public participation. These officials and activists make the organization's decisions, choose its candidates, and select the strategies they believe voters will find appealing. They focus mainly on electing party candidates rather than on issues. Thus the party becomes active mainly during campaigns, when candidates need their party organization's help the most. The cadre party, then, is a coalition of people and interests brought together temporarily to win elections, only to shrink to a smaller core once the elections are over.

At the other end of this scale is the ***mass-membership party***, a highly participatory organization in which all three parts of the party are closely intertwined. In this type of party, large numbers of voters become dues-paying members of the party organization and participate in its activities year-round, not just during campaigns. A mass-membership party concentrates on promoting an ideology and educating the public as well as on winning elections. Its members decide what the party's policies should be as well as choose its organizational leaders. Members of the party in the electorate are so integral to the party organization that the party may even provide them with such nonpolitical benefits as insurance and leisure-time activities. Because the membership-based party organization has great power over candidate selection (it does not need to give less involved voters the right to choose party candidates, as happens in a primary election), it can also exercise much greater control over the party in government.

In important ways, the major American parties can be considered cadre parties. Most local and state party leaders and activists are not paid professionals but volunteers, whose party activities ramp up around election time. These organization leaders do not try hard to control the party's candidates and elected officials, nor are they likely to succeed. Most party identifiers in the United States are not involved at all in the party organization.

They do not fit the cadre mold perfectly; in practice, parties have a tendency to slip out of precise definitions.[1] For example, party leaders contact their supporters in the electorate more frequently now than they did a few decades ago, and the state and national party organizations are active year-round. Nevertheless, these changes have not made the major American parties into mass-membership organizations. The major parties concentrate on electing candidates more than on educating voters on issues. Also, in contrast to mass-membership parties, the American parties do not monopolize the organization of political interests in the nation; rather, they compete in a political system in which voters are also mobilized by large numbers of interest groups and other organizations.

Why does it matter whether party organizations are strong or weak, cadre or mass membership? Because party organizations are at the very core of the political parties. They are the sector of the parties that can provide continuity, even as the party's candidates, elected officials, and identifiers come and go. A strong party organization can hunt for the resources needed for long-term election success and can present a united, persuasive approach to issues. So the development of a stronger party organization can change the character of politics and elections. In fact, as American party organizations have become more robust in recent years, they have altered our politics in ways ranging from campaign fund-raising to the nature of political debate. Chapter 3 begins by exploring the party organizations closest to home: state and local parties.

CHAPTER 3

The State and Local Party Organizations

Party organizations in the United States have transformed themselves in the past century. During the late 1800s and early 1900s, local parties were often described as "machines," with the power to control city governments and mobilize vast armies of activists. Even so, many American local parties at this time were not very machine-like. By the mid-1900s, most party organizations at the state and local levels were thought to be weak and inactive. That has changed as well.

What difference does it make if a party organization is vibrant or weak? As the Introduction noted, in many ways, the party organization is the foundation of a political party. It gives the party a way to endure, despite a changing cast of candidates and elected officeholders. More than the party in government or the party identifiers, the party organizations are the keepers of the parties' symbols—the unifying labels or ideas that give candidates a shortcut in identifying themselves to voters and that give voters a means to choose among candidates. Without this organization, a party becomes only an unstable alliance of convenience among candidates, and between candidates and groups of voters—too changeable to accomplish the important work that parties can perform in a democracy.

In this chapter, after considering how to measure "party strength," we will explore the reality of state and local party organizations by viewing them in their environment. Next, we will turn to the local party organizations, tracing their path from the fabled "political machines" that dominated a number of eastern and Midwestern cities beginning in the last half of the 1800s to the fall and rise of local parties more recently. Finally, we will see how the state parties grew from weakness to greater strength in the closing decades of the twentieth century.

WHAT IS A "STRONG" PARTY?

How can a "strong" party be defined? Many researchers measure a party's vigor by examining its organizational features. Stronger parties would have larger budgets and more full-time, paid staff members. That can be termed *party organizational strength*.

There are other ways to measure party strength. A strong party would work effectively to register voters, tell them about party candidates, and get them to the polls on Election Day. It would be successful in filling its ticket with attractive candidates. Its candidates would win more races than they lose. We could even measure whether the party is able to get its platform enacted into law (and we will, but not until Chapter 15).

In order for a party to do these things, especially to register voters, canvass, and get out the vote, it needs money, staff, and other forms of organizational strength. We will look at most of these measures of party strength in this chapter but focus mainly on party organizational strength.

STATE REGULATION OF THE PARTIES

Americans' traditional suspicion of political parties has led most states, especially during the Progressive Era of the late 1800s and early 1900s, to pass large numbers of laws intended to control their party organizations. Party committees are regulated "lightly" in only about a third of the states, most of them in the South, Plains states, and upper Midwest.[1] At the other extreme, in 15 states—including California, New Jersey, and Ohio—lawmakers have thought it necessary to control even the smallest details of state party activity, such as the types of public buildings in which parties must hold their conventions.

These extensive state rules have not necessarily weakened the parties; some of the strongest party organizations in the nation are also the most tightly regulated. In fact, all these state laws help prop up the Democratic and Republican Parties against competition from third parties. However, they do give state governments a set of tools for keeping an eye on their parties. They also indicate that state law does not view the parties simply as private groups. As Leon Epstein argued, the parties are seen as public utilities that can be subject to a great deal of state direction.[2] And federal campaign finance laws since the 1970s have built a substantial body of national law that affects party organizations and candidates.

States do not have complete freedom to decide how to regulate the parties. Federal courts have frequently stepped in to protect citizens' voting rights (see Chapter 8), to keep the states from unreasonably limiting third-party and independent candidates' ballot access (see Chapter 2), and to acknowledge the parties' right to control their internal affairs. In the 1980s, for example, the Supreme Court ruled that the state of Connecticut could not prevent the Republican Party from opening up its primary to independents if it wanted to. Soon after, the Court threw out a California law saying, among other things, that parties could not endorse candidates in primary elections. A 2000 Supreme Court decision overturned a California state initiative setting up a "blanket primary" on the ground that it violated the party organization's First Amendment right to decide who votes in its primaries.[3] Even so, American party organizations are more heavily regulated than are their counterparts in other democracies.

LEVELS OF PARTY ORGANIZATION

The party organizations created by the states follow a common pattern. Their structure corresponds to the levels of government at which voters elect officeholders. This structure

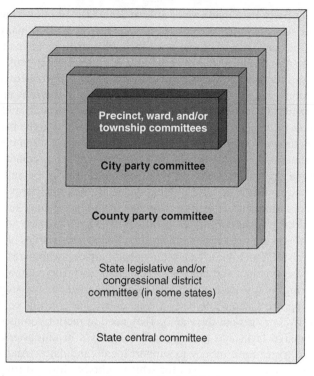

Precinct, ward, and/or
township committees

City party committee

County party committee

State legislative and/or
congressional district
committee (in some states)

State central committee

FIGURE 3.1 The Party Organizations in a Typical State.

is often pictured as a pyramid based in the grassroots and stretching up to the statewide organization. A pyramid, however, gives the misleading impression that the layer at the top can give orders to the layers below. So picture these party organizations, instead, as they fit into a geographic map (Figure 3.1).

Local Party Committees

The county is the main unit of local party organization in most states, because so many important local officials are elected at the county level, and usually in partisan elections: sheriffs, prosecutors, county attorneys, judges, commissioners and council members, county clerks, treasurers, assessors, auditors, surveyors, coroners, and more. These officials control vital functions ranging from policing the area and prosecuting those accused of crime to assessing and collecting property taxes. Party organizations exist in almost all of the nation's counties to at least some degree. These are the parties' "grassroots," where a lot of the activity of party volunteers takes place.

In most areas, counties are divided into smaller units called precincts. Each precinct (or town, township, or ward, in some areas) in theory has a party leader—a committeeman and/or committeewoman—to conduct the party's activities in that area. Because there are about 193,000 precincts in the United States, it would be easy to imagine a vibrant party base made up of at least 200,000 committed men and women. However, this exists only in the dreams of party leaders; in reality, many of these local committee positions are vacant because nobody volunteers to serve in them.

When these (unpaid) positions do get filled, it generally happens in one of three ways. Most committeemen and women are chosen at local party caucuses (meetings) or in primary elections, but in a few instances, higher party authorities appoint them. In states that use caucuses, parties hold local caucuses in the precincts and wards that are open to any voters of the area who declare themselves attached to the party. These local party supporters then elect the precinct committee leaders and often elect delegates to county and/or state conventions as well. In states that choose precinct committeemen and women in the primaries, any voter may nominate him- or herself for the job by filing a petition signed by a handful of local voters. If, as often happens, there are no nominees, the committeeman or woman may be elected by an even smaller handful of write-in votes. These local committee positions, in short, are not normally in great demand, especially in the weaker party in an area. So the local parties are far from being exclusive clubs; their "front doors" are often open to anyone who cares to walk in.

What do these precinct and county party leaders do? Their three most important jobs are registering new voters, going door-to-door (called "canvassing" or "d2d") to tell potential supporters about the party's candidates, and getting voters to the polls (known as "GOTV," or "get out the vote"). They need to recruit volunteers to help with these labor-intensive tasks and to help staff the party's headquarters. County party leaders may also try to raise money to support local candidates. And when there are vacancies on the party ticket—offices for which nobody chose to run in the primary election and for which the party has not been able to recruit candidates—then the local party committees are responsible for appointing a candidate to run. In the less active local parties, the committeemen and women may do little more than show up at an occasional meeting and campaign for a party candidate or two.

The precinct committeemen and women usually come together to make up the next level of local party organization, or they elect the delegates who do. In some states, the next level is the city party committee; in others, it may be the town, county, or state legislative and congressional district committees. Usually, however, there is greater activity at the county level than in any other layer of the local party.

State Central Committees

At the state level, the party organization is usually called the state central committee. The state parties typically help to recruit candidates for statewide offices (for instance, state treasurer or attorney general) and state legislative seats, assist in training them, and raise money to support their campaigns. Increasingly they also work with local parties on the crucial tasks of voter registration, canvassing, and GOTV.

State law usually gives party central committees a number of other important powers: the responsibility for calling and organizing party conventions, drafting party platforms, supervising the spending of party campaign funds, and selecting the party's presidential electors, representatives to the national committee, and some of the national convention delegates and alternates. Some other states give these powers to the party's statewide convention instead. In a few states, such as Indiana, the party's state convention actually nominates candidates for some statewide offices, a reminder of the power that party conventions had in the days before primary elections.

These are the formal organizational structures that state law creates for the state and local parties. From them, we can draw three important conclusions. First, the levels of party organization have been set up to correspond to the voting districts in which citizens choose public officials in that state (for example, county and congressional districts), and the main responsibility of these organizations under state law is to contest elections. State laws, then, see the party organizations as helpers in the state's task of conducting nominations and elections—tasks that before the turn of the twentieth century belonged almost entirely to the parties alone.

Second, the laws indicate that state legislators are ambivalent about what constitutes a party organization. Many of these laws treat the parties as cadre organizations (see pages 45–46) run by a small number of party officials. Yet when they specify that the party's own officials, including local committeemen and women, must be chosen in a primary election, this gives party voters—and potentially, any voters—a vital, quasi-membership role in the party organization. So state laws help to create a party that is semipublic, rather than a genuinely private group whose active members choose its leaders and set its direction.

Finally, the relationships among these state and local party organizations are not those of a hierarchy, in which the lower levels take their orders from the higher levels. Instead, through much of their history, the parties were best described as "a system of layers of organization,"[4] or as a "stratarchy,"[5] in which each of the levels has some independent power. In fact, power has traditionally flowed from bottom to top in the local and state parties, as opposed to a hierarchy, where power would be centralized at the top.[6] Party organization is a system of party committees growing from the political grassroots. Thus, the party organizations remain fairly decentralized and rooted in local politics, even in the face of recent trends toward stronger state and national committees.

THE LEGENDARY PARTY MACHINES

The high point of local party organizational strength in the United States occurred in the late 1800s and early 1900s, when the urban political "machine" reached its peak of power. At this time, by some accounts, a large majority of American cities were governed by machines.[7] The party machine was a disciplined organization that controlled the nominations to elective office. It had the hierarchical structure that today's local parties lack. It relied on material incentives—giving out jobs and favors—to build support among voters. Above all, it controlled the government in a city or county.[8]

Yet, for all their power in shaping how we think of party organizations, the great urban machines were not found in all cities, and, like the dinosaurs, they have disappeared. The last of the great urban machines was Chicago's, and it declined after the death of Mayor Richard J. Daley (the father of the current mayor) in 1976. These dinosaurs were brought down by a number of forces. Some party machines, such as those in Pittsburgh and New York, never recovered from election upsets by middle-class reformers. Others, including those in Philadelphia and Gary, Indiana, lost power when racial tensions overshadowed the old ethnic politics.[9]

How the Party Machines Developed

In the late 1800s, large numbers of the immigrants arriving in major American cities had urgent economic and social needs. These newcomers were poor, often spoke no English, and faced a difficult adjustment to their new urban environment. Party leaders in many of these cities—usually Democrats, reflecting that party's history of openness to immigrants—saw the opportunity for a mutually profitable exchange. The immigrants needed jobs, social services, and other benefits that a city government could provide. The party leaders needed large numbers of votes in order to gain control of city government. If the party could register these new arrivals to vote, their votes could put the party in power. In return, the party would then control the many resources that the government had available and could give the new voters the help they needed so desperately.

Jobs ranked high among the newcomers' needs. So the most visible of the benefits offered by party machines were *patronage* jobs in the city government—those awarded on the basis of party loyalty rather than other qualifications. During the glory days of the machine, thousands of these patronage positions were at the machines' disposal. By giving patronage jobs to party supporters, the party's leaders could be assured that city workers would remain loyal to the machine and would work to help it win elections by delivering not only their own votes but those of their family, friends, and neighbors as well. After all, if the party lost the election, then the city workers would lose their jobs.

For example, in its prime, the Chicago Democratic machine controlled an estimated 35,000 patronage jobs in government and influenced hiring for another 10,000 jobs in the private economy. Adding the families and friends of these jobholders, the party machine could deliver 350,000 motivated voters at election time. Local party workers also won voter loyalties by finding social welfare agencies for the troubled or by providing Christmas baskets or deliveries of coal for the poor. Machine leaders, called "bosses," attended weddings and wakes, listened to job seekers and business executives, bailed out drunks, and helped the hungry and homeless.

The machine had favors to offer local businesses as well. Governments purchase many goods and services from the private sector. If a bank wanted to win the city's deposits, it could expect to compete more effectively for the city's business if it were willing to contribute to the party machine. Insurance agents and lawyers who wanted city contracts, newspapers that printed city notices, even suppliers of soap to city bathrooms were motivated to donate money or services to the party machine. In addition, city governments regularly make decisions that affect individuals' and businesses' economic standing, such as building permits and health inspections. If you were helped by one of these decisions, you could expect the machine to ask for your thanks in the form of contributions and votes. A political leadership intent on winning support in exchange for these so-called "preferments" can use them ruthlessly and effectively to build its political power.

How Machines Held On to Power

The classic urban machine, then, was not just a party organization but also an "informal government," a social service agency, and a ladder for upward social and economic mobility. In some ways, it looked like the local organization of a European mass-membership party, except that the American machine had little or no concern with ideology. Its world was the city; it focused on the immediate needs of its constituents, and its politics were almost completely divorced from the issues that animated national politics.

An important source of the machines' strength was their ability to appeal to ethnic loyalties. The rise and fall of the American political machine is closely linked to changes in ethnic-group migration to the big cities. The machine was a method by which ethnic groups, especially the Irish, gained a foothold in American politics.[10]

Machines were capable of creating a "designer electorate" by using force and intimidation to keep their opponents from voting. Because the party machines controlled the election process, it was possible, in a pinch, to change the election rules and even to count the votes in a creative manner. One of the indispensable tools of rival party workers in Indianapolis, for example, was a flashlight—to locate ballots that did not support the dominant party's candidates and happened to fly out of the window at vote-counting headquarters in the dark of night.

Machine politics was most likely to flourish in the big cities, but American party machines took root in other areas as well. The conditions that led to the development of machines, especially a large, parochially oriented population with short-term economic needs, were also found in small southern and one-company towns. Even some well-to-do suburbs have spawned strong machine-style party organizations. In the affluent Long Island suburbs of New York City, for example, a Republican Nassau County political machine controlled local government "with a local party operation that in terms of patronage and party loyalty rival[ed] the machine of the famed Democratic mayor of Chicago, Richard J. Daley."[11] The Nassau machine, which was generations old, was dominated by Italian Americans and provided jobs just like the big-city machines of old, before losing its dominance in the 1990s. But in nearby Queens, the local Democratic organization rebounded from scandal and continued to elect candidates, fill judgeships, and control primaries. And Americans were reminded of the old machine days in 2009, when Illinois governor Rod Blagojevich sought to use his power to appoint a Senate replacement for newly elected President Barack Obama by trading the appointment for cash or a new job for himself. In contrast with the old machine days, however, Blagojevich soon found himself out of office.

We cannot be sure how powerful the party machines really were, even at their strongest. A Chicago study found, for example, that in 1967 and 1977, the party machine distributed public services mainly on the basis of historical factors and bureaucratic decision rules rather than to reward its political supporters.[12] In New Haven, researchers reported that ethnic loyalties seemed more important to a party machine than even its own maintenance and expansion. The machine, led by Italian Americans, distributed summer jobs disproportionately to Italian kids from nonmachine wards, who rarely took part in later political work, and not to kids from strong machine areas.[13]

Regardless of how well they functioned, there is no doubt that the conditions that helped sustain party machines have been undercut. Economic change and political reform took away the machine's most important resources. Most city jobs are now covered by civil service protection, so the number of patronage jobs that can be used to reward the party faithful has been greatly reduced. Federal entitlement programs, such as welfare and Social Security, have reduced the need for the favors that party machines could provide. Economic growth has boosted many Americans' income levels and reduced the attractiveness of the remaining patronage jobs; the chance to work in the sewer system or on garbage pickup just doesn't have the allure that it once may have had. Higher education levels have increased people's ability to fend for themselves in a complex bureaucratic society. And in many areas, racial divisions have overwhelmed the machine's ability to balance competing ethnic groups.

LOCAL PARTY ORGANIZATIONS DECLINED AND THEN REBUILT

After the machines failed, local parties' organizational strength dropped dramatically in many areas. By the mid-1900s, many city and county parties were starved for leadership, money, and volunteers. Then the rebuilding began.

Local Parties in the 1970s

We got the first comprehensive look at the nature of local party organizations in a 1979–1980 survey of several thousand county leaders (see Table 3.1).[14] The results showed the distinctive fingerprints of cadre parties, and fairly weak ones at that. The researchers found that most county organizations were headed by a volunteer party chair and executive committee; almost none received salaries for their efforts, and only a few had a paid staff to assist them. Not many of these local party leaders had even the most basic forms of organizational support, such as a regular budget, a year-round office, or a listing in the phone book. Most did meet regularly, had formal rules to govern their work, and, together with a few other activists, raised funds and sought out and screened candidates. However, their activity was not constant; it peaked during campaigns.

Democratic local parties didn't differ much from Republican local parties in terms of the overall strength of their organizations during the 1970s. States differed a great deal, however, in the organizational strength of their local parties. Some states in the East and Midwest had relatively strong local organizations in both parties, while others—Louisiana, Georgia, Alabama, Kentucky, Texas, and Nebraska— had weak parties at the county level. In a few states, such as Arizona and Florida, one party was considerably stronger than the other party at the local level. Most often, strong organizations of one party were matched with strong organizations in the other party.[15]

There is persuasive evidence, however, that the county party organizations in 1980 were in the middle of a growth spurt. In a 1980 survey, by asking county party chairs about the changes in their parties since 1964, researchers found that, on average, local parties had become much more involved in the nuts-and-bolts activities of registering voters, raising money, and publicizing candidates. When the researchers checked in again with these county organizations in 1984, they saw further development, and a national survey in 1988 indicated even higher levels of local party activity. Similar trends were reported in studies over time of local party organizations in Detroit and Los Angeles.[16]

TABLE 3.1 Changes in Local Parties' Organizational Strength, 1980s–2000s

The local party organization has (in percent)	Democrats			Republicans		
	1980	1996	2003*	1980	1996	2003*
A complete or nearly complete set of officers	90	95		81	96	
A year-round office	12	17	35	14	25	42
A telephone listing	11	27		16	30	
Some paid staff members			6			9
Full-time	3	4		4	4	
Part-time	5	6		6	7	
A regular annual budget	20	26		31	34	
A campaign headquarters	55	60	63	60	60	61
Average yearly budget			$37K			$41K
Campaign activities						
Door-to-door canvassing	49	55		48	57	
Organized campaign events	68	81		65	82	
Arranged fund-raising events	71	74		68	76	
Contributed money to candidates	62	75		70	78	
Distributed posters or lawn signs	59	93		62	93	
Used public opinion polls	11	13		16	15	

Note: 1979–1980 figures are based on responses from 2,021 Democratic and 1,980 Republican organizations to a mail survey; 1996 figures are from mail surveys of all county party chairs in nine states (Ariz., Col., Fla., Ill., Mo., Oh., S. C., Wash., and Wis.), with responses from 340 Democrats and 335 Republicans; 2003 data are from telephone surveys of a random sample of local parties in the thousand most populated counties in the United States, with 403 Democratic and 402 Republican responses.

* The 2003 survey asked only some of the same questions as the earlier studies; therefore, several cells are blank.

Sources: John Frendreis and Alan R. Gitelson, "Local Parties in the 1990s," in John C. Green and Daniel M. Shea, eds., *The State of the Parties*, 3rd ed. (Lanham, MD: Rowman & Littlefield, 1999), pp. 138–139, and Daniel M. Shea and John C. Green, "Local Parties and Mobilizing the Vote," in John C. Green and Daniel J. Coffey, eds., *The State of the Parties*, 5th ed. (Lanham, MD: Rowman & Littlefield, 2007), p. 221.

Local Parties Today: Richer and More Active

Currently, although local parties continue to depend on unpaid volunteers, they are enjoying more of the benefits that money can buy. At least in urban areas, more county parties had the basic ingredients for a viable party organization (a permanent office, a budget, a telephone listing, a staff) in 2003 than had been the case in 1980.[17] Most of these county parties organize campaign activities, run GOTV drives, arrange fund-raising events, donate money to candidates, send out mailings, call voters to urge them to support the party ticket, and distribute yard signs; and again, more local parties report conducting these activities now than they did in 1980.

Other forms of campaigning, such as using public opinion polls and buying radio or TV time for candidates, are less common. A third of the parties in 2003 reported none of the organizational features listed in Table 3.1, and not very many put a priority on mobilizing young voters.[18] Relatively few county parties are active year-round, raising funds and holding events at times when no campaigns are going on. But it seems clear that as more money has been flowing to local party organizations in recent years, more local parties have been energized.

Michigan's Democratic Party provides an example of this increase in party organizational strength. Michigan Democrats, long the minority party, were in sorry shape for the first half of the 1900s, after machine politics had faded. By the end of the 1940s, more than half of the state's counties had no Democratic county committees. Then, labor unions, led by the United Auto Workers, stepped in to bring volunteer and financial support to the Democrats. Within two years, there was a Democratic Party organization in almost every county in the state. After internal conflicts took their toll in both parties during the 1960s and 1970s, organized labor moved again to rebuild the Democratic organization. By the late 1990s, the great majority of local Democratic Parties were raising money and contributing to candidates, buying ads, and distributing literature. The county organizations have now become the backbone of the state Democratic Party.[19]

Local party leaders in many areas of the country have recently stepped up their efforts regarding absentee and early voting. By 2008, most states had relaxed their requirements for casting an absentee ballot. Large numbers of registered voters can now vote by mail or in person before Election Day. To take advantage of these changes, many local parties—those in Washington state, for example—now mail absentee ballot requests to all known party voters. By working to "bank" as many loyalists' votes as possible, the party organization can protect itself against last-minute campaign surprises or Election Day thunderstorms that might depress the party vote. Local parties can spread their GOTV efforts over several weeks and then focus their Election Day activities on mobilizing less involved voters. The downside is that because absentee voting is much harder to monitor than voting at the polls, parties need to find ways to keep the other party from delivering absentee ballots that have been filled out illegally or with "help" from overzealous party workers.

Local parties are also expanding their efforts to recruit candidates.[20] One study found that more than a third of people regarded as potentially strong candidates for Congress in 1998 had, in fact, been contacted by local party leaders and that those contacted were more likely to run.[21] In another study, almost half of all state legislative candidates reported that local party leaders had encouraged them to run.[22] County party leaders can improve their chances of recruiting candidates when, as in Ohio, they can endorse candidates in primaries and fill vacancies in elections. Keep in mind, however, that it is not yet clear whether being recruited by a local party organization, as opposed to being a "self-starter," helps a candidate win the general election.

In sum, we have good evidence that county party organizations are stronger and more active now than they were a generation ago. It is harder to determine whether county parties now are as effective organizationally as were the old city machines, because there are so few reliable records prior to the 1960s. But it is possible that many counties now have more robust party organizations than they have ever had.

What accounts for the growing strength of the county parties? The short answer is money. Party organizations at all levels have developed more effective tools for raising money than they have had for some time. Local parties have benefited from the willingness of the increasingly well-heeled state parties to share the wealth. At the same time, however, the nature of the local parties has changed. From organizations that once were at the very center of election activity, county parties have become service providers to candidates who often have several other sources of help. So the challenge for the local parties is this: In an age of largely candidate-centered campaigns, does this growing county organizational presence matter as much as it would have a few decades ago?[23]

THE STATE PARTIES: GAINING MONEY AND SERVICES

State parties have been the poor relations of American party politics. Throughout the parties' history, the state committees rarely had significant power within the party organizations. There have been exceptions; some powerful, patronage-rich state party organizations developed in the industrial heartland in the late 1800s.[24] But in most states, most of the time, the state committee was traditionally the weak link in the party organization.

In recent years, however, state parties have grown in importance. They are richer, more professional, and more active now than they have ever been before. There has been some centralization of activity throughout the party structure. Let us start the story in the years before this change began.

Traditional Weakness

State party organizations were traditionally weak for several reasons. They began as loose federations of semi-independent local party chairs. These local parties within a state differed from one another in many ways: rural/urban, regional, ethnic, and religious differences, loyalties to local leaders, and, especially, conflicts between more liberal and more conservative interests. If one of these factions gained control over the state party organization, the others would be seriously threatened. So this threat was often avoided, in the past, by keeping most of the party's resources out of the hands of the state organization. Power was decentralized, collecting in the most effective of the local organizations.

Progressive reforms in the early 1900s also weakened the state party organizations. In particular, the introduction of the direct primary (see Chapters 9 and 10) limited the influence of state parties on campaigns for state offices. Candidates could win party nominations in primary elections without party organization support, raise money for their own campaigns and, thus, run them without party help. Even today, relatively weak state party organizations are still found in the states where the Progressives and Populists had greatest strength—the western states, especially the more rural ones.[25]

Beginning in the late 1960s, the national Democratic Party adopted reforms that greatly increased the number of primaries in the presidential nominating process. That reduced the state party's role in selecting a presidential candidate. The voters, rather than the state party organization, choose most convention delegates now, and most of the delegates come to the convention pledged to a particular candidate rather than controlled by state party leaders. Further, extensions of civil service protections and unionization eroded the patronage base for many state parties. In what may have been the final indignity for patronage politics, some courts have even prevented the firing of patronage workers when the governing party changes.

One-party dominance in several states during the first half of the 1900s also kept a number of state parties weak and conflict-ridden. Southern Democratic Parties were a notable example. When a single party dominates a state's politics, the diverse forces within the state are likely to compete as factions within that party; the state party organization has neither the incentive nor the ability to unify, as it might if it faced a threat from a viable opposition party. For all these reasons, many state party organizations were described as "empty shells" in the 1940s and 1950s.[26]

Increasing Strength in Recent Years

Since the 1960s, however, state party organizations have become stronger and more active. The state parties began to institutionalize—to become enduring, specialized, well-bounded organizations—during the 1960s and 1970s. In the early 1960s, for example, only half of a sample of state organizations had permanent state headquarters; two decades later, by 1980, that was true of 91 percent. The number of full-time, paid state party chairs doubled during this time, as did the number of full-time staff employed by the parties in nonelection years. These resources—full-time leaders and a stable location—are vital to the development of parties as organizations.[27]

As with local parties, the state organizations have continued to expand since then. More than half of the state parties surveyed in a 1999 study had full-time party chairs, research staff, and public relations directors. Three-quarters had a field staff, and 91 percent employed a full-time executive director, perhaps the most crucial position in a state party organization. A number of state parties have created internship programs for college students; the Mississippi Republican Party is a good example. In California, the Republican Party set up a task force in 2009 to apply leading-edge technologies, including the next generation of computer applications that will come after Facebook, Twitter, and YouTube, to all aspects of party work. The empty shells are being filled.

Fund-raising   State parties have put special effort into developing fund-raising capabilities. By 2000, according to two research studies (see Table 3.2), almost all of the state parties surveyed raised money at events and by direct mail. They used the money to support a variety of races; party candidates for governor, state legislature, and the U.S. Senate and House received contributions from more than four-fifths of these parties. Over 90 percent of the parties made efforts to recruit candidates for state races; the parties' new fund-raising skills can be very useful in convincing attractive prospects to run for an office.[28]

The parties are especially active in recruiting and helping fund candidates for the state legislature.[29] These state legislative candidates rely on different levels of party committees for different kinds of help. State legislative parties' campaign committees[30] often provide fund-raising support and advice on consultants, whereas the local parties are thought to be more helpful in traditional grassroots activities such as GOTV drives.[31]

The increase in state parties' election-year fund-raising since 1980 fairly leaps off the page in Table 3.2. National party committees played an important role by transferring increasing amounts to the state parties and candidates. The transfers peaked in 2000, when the national party organizations gave a whopping $430 million to parties and candidates at the state level, many times the amounts that the national parties had infused into the state organizations just a few years earlier.[32] Collectively, the state

TABLE 3.2 Increasing Organizational Strength Among the State Parties

Party Strength and Activity	1979–1980	1999–2000	Difference
Typical election-year budget	$340 K	$2.8 million	+$2.46 million
Typical election-year full-time staff	7.7	9.2	+1.5
Off-year budget	$337 K	$812 K*	+$475 K
Off-year staff	7.2	7.6*	+0.4
Conducted campaign seminars	89%	95%	+6%
Recruited a full slate of candidates	—	91%	—
Operated voter ID programs	70%	94%	+24%
Conducted public opinion polls	32%	78%	+46%
Held fund-raising event	19%	98%	+79%
Contributed to governor candidate	47%	89%	+42%
Contributed to state legislator	47%	92%	+45%
Contributed to state senator	25%	85%	+60%
Contributed to U.S. congressional	48%	85%	+37%
Contributed to local candidate	—	70%	—

Note: Data for 1979–1980 are from a mail survey of state parties. Data for 1999 come from a mail survey by John H. Aldrich and associates of 65 state party chairs (39 Democrats, 26 Republicans), and data for 2000 come from a mail survey by Raymond La Raja of 37 Republican and 37 Democratic state party executive directors.

*Data from La Raja's 2000 survey.

Sources: For the 1999 data, see John H Aldrich's "Southern Parties in State and Nation," *Journal of Politics* 62 (2000): 659. For 2000, see Raymond J. La Raja, "State Parties and Soft Money," in John C. Green and Rick Farmer, eds., *The State of the Parties*, 4th ed. (Lanham, MD: Rowman & Littlefield, 2003), p. 141. The 1979–1980 data are from James L. Gibson, Cornelius P. Cotter, and John F. Bibby, "Assessing Party Organizational Strength," *American Journal of Political Science* 27 (1983): 193–222.

parties were able to spend $53 million raised in large sums, called "soft money" (see Chapter 12), on voter mobilization and GOTV activity in the 2000 campaigns.[33]

Just as important for the development of strong party organizations, fund-raising during nonelection years was growing as well. The nonelection-year budgets of the state parties climbed from an average (in absolute dollars) of under $200,000 in 1960–1964 to more than $800,000 by 2000. The result is that now, "most state parties are multimillion-dollar organizations with experienced executive directors and knowledgeable staffs."[34]

Passage of new campaign finance legislation in 2002 (the Bipartisan Campaign Reform Act, or BCRA, discussed in Chapter 12) took away the national parties' ability to transfer soft money to the state parties. Although that raised worries about their financial future, BCRA did allow state parties to spend federally regulated money (which the national parties could transfer to states without limits) on federal campaign activities and to raise a certain amount of soft money themselves (up to $10,000 per donor) for grassroots mobilization and party-building. These, added to the high stakes of polarized politics, helped the state parties to expand their fund-raising further; in 2003, right after the end of the soft-money transfers, state Democratic and Republican Parties raised a total of $189 million—more than they had in 2001.[35] Since that time, collective state party receipts and media buys by state parties have not matched their pre-BCRA levels, but party spending in some states, including Missouri and Indiana, has gone up considerably. State parties, then, have become effective fund-raisers and most have learned to cope with the BCRA reform rules.

Campaign Services   To run a competitive campaign, state legislative and statewide candidates need consultants, voter lists, and computers, and they turn to the state party organizations to provide these expensive services. With their increased organizational and financial resources, the state parties have been able to comply. All the parties surveyed in a study by John H. Aldrich operated voter identification programs to determine which voters were most likely to support their party's candidates. They also took part in GOTV drives, as well as joint fund-raising with county party organizations. Most provided campaign training seminars, and almost four-fifths conducted public opinion polls in the late 1990s.[36] Coordinated campaigns (called "victory plans" by the Republicans), emphasizing the sharing of campaign services among a variety of candidates, could be run through the state party organizations, though the BCRA rules have limited these shared efforts since 2002.

Republican Advantage   Unlike the situation at the county level, Republican state organizations are stronger than their Democratic counterparts. The Republican parties surveyed by Aldrich had much larger budgets and bigger and more specialized staffs. Because they are bigger and richer, they can provide more services to their candidates and local parties. For example, Republican state parties are more likely to conduct polls, employ field staff and researchers, and contribute to local parties than the Democrats are.[37] This GOP advantage comes in part from the money the national party provides to all the state parties.

But Democratic state parties are catching up. Howard Dean was elected Democratic National Chairman in 2005 by promising state party chairs that he would give every state, not just the closely fought "battleground states," enough resources to hire at least three or four field organizers and access to a party database of voters. Many of the party's Washington-based consultants opposed this "50-state strategy," asking why an increase in the Alaska Democratic Party's staff would help Democrats nationally. But after major Democratic gains in the 2006 and 2008 elections, Dean's expensive efforts to build strong state parties were acclaimed by some as "visionary."[38]

Allied Groups   Labor unions, especially teachers' and government employees' unions, have worked closely with their state Democratic Party organizations to provide money, volunteers, and other services to party candidates, though this, too, has become more difficult since BCRA was passed. In states such as Alabama and Indiana, the state teachers' union is so closely connected with the state party that critics might find it hard to tell where one stops and the other begins. State Republican Parties have close ties to allied groups as well. Small business groups, manufacturing associations, pro-life groups, and Christian conservative organizations often provide services to Republican candidates. As the state parties gain strength, these constituency groups often try to increase their influence on, or even take over, state party organizations. Christian Right groups, in particular, have come to dominate or have substantial influence on a majority of state Republican Parties.[39]

Because of the close association between parties and these allied groups, it is possible to think of the parties as networks of organizations, which include the interest groups, consulting firms, and "think tanks" (research groups) that offer their resources and expertise to a party.[40] For party leaders, these allied groups can be a mixed blessing, of course; labor unions and religious groups have their own agendas, and they can be as likely to try to push the party into locally unpopular stands as to help elect party candidates.

PARTY FACTIONAL FIGHTS: THE VIRGINIA REPUBLICANS

Several state Republican Party organizations have suffered bitter splits in recent years between social conservatives, whose primary concerns are abortion, same-sex marriage, and related issues, and economic conservatives. In 2008, Jeffrey Frederick, a young state representative in Virginia fiercely committed to pro-life policies and home schooling, defeated the moderate Republican state party chair. Intense controversy soon followed among party activists. Frederick was criticized for telling canvassers in the 2008 presidential race to emphasize that Barack Obama and Osama bin Laden "both have friends who bombed the Pentagon." Many Republican loyalists complained that Frederick refused to work closely with the campaign staff of the Republican presidential candidate, John McCain. Frederick really riled party activists by giving party business to a company he owned. In March of 2009, most of the party's state central committee members signed a letter calling for his ouster. Frederick was voted out in April, leaving his party deeply divided. "There's going to be a backlash," predicted one social conservative; "You'd better believe it." The venomous dispute did not help the party's effort to elect a Republican governor in 2009. So even in these polarized times, when the various state and local organizations of a party tend to unite on issues to a greater extent than they had in past decades, party organizations still split over deeply felt disagreements on policy, as well as over personal, strategic, and financial disputes.

Sources: Tim Craig, "GOP Chairman Fires Back as Party Leaders Seek His Ouster," *Washington Post*, March 18, 2009, p. B1; quotes from Anita Kumar, "Va. GOP Ousts Chairman Who Ignored Call to Resign," *Washington Post*, April 5, 2009, p. A1.

It is not easy to build a powerful state party organization. It requires having to overcome the localism of American politics, widespread hostility toward party discipline, and antagonisms among party supporters (see box on this page). Strong and skillful personal leadership by a governor, a senator, or a state chairman helps.[41] So does a state tradition that accepts the notion of a unified and effective party. State law makes a difference as well. More centralized party organization has flourished in states that make less use of primary elections, so the party organization has more control over who the statewide and congressional candidates will be. Good examples include both Pennsylvania parties, the Indiana Republican Party, and the North Dakota Democratic organization.

The Special Case of the South   The most striking instances of party organizational development have occurred in the formerly one-party Democratic South. As the national Democratic Party showed greater concern for the rights of African Americans in the 1960s and 1970s, and particularly as the Voting Rights Acts greatly increased the proportion of African American voters in southern states, conservative southern Democrats became increasingly estranged from their national party. Southern support for Republican candidates grew, first in presidential elections, later in statewide and U.S. Senate races (as you will see in Chapter 7).

In the 1980s, state legislative candidates could sense the opportunity to run and win as Republicans. By 1994, Republicans were contesting almost one-third of the state legislative seats in the South and winning two-thirds of those seats. Since 1994, Republicans have won the governorship of all but one southern state at least once, as well as a majority in at least one house of the state legislature in most of these states. Republicans are now surpassing Democrats in state elections—this in a region where, just a few decades before, it was often more socially acceptable to admit to having an alcoholic than a Republican in the family.[42]

Along with these electoral gains, southern Republican Parties grew stronger organizationally. North Carolina's state Republican Party, for example, was only minimally organized in the early 1970s. It started in earnest to recruit state legislative candidates during the mid-1980s. By the 1990s, with a much expanded budget and staff, the party focused on attracting experienced candidates for targeted districts, producing direct mail and radio ads, and helping candidates with training and research. Even the Florida Republicans, still not very strong organizationally, have come a long way since the years when state party chairs had "portable offices" in their homes or businesses.[43] Democrats have had to respond, so the strength of both parties' organizations has been increasing since the 1990s.[44] Southern parties, long among the weakest and most faction-ridden, have become some of the strongest state party organizations in the past two decades.[45]

National Party Money   An important ingredient in strengthening the state party organizations has been the national parties' party-building efforts. The full story of these efforts is told in Chapter 4, but the central point is that the national parties, with more energetic leadership and more lavish financial resources than ever before, have infused a great deal of money into the state parties, and at least some of the money has been directed toward helping build the state parties' organizational capacity. State parties have also become major fund-raisers in their own right, raising money for both state and federal campaigns, and the BCRA rules have spurred them into even greater activity. Thus the state parties, so recently the poor relations of the party organizations, have come into money.

SUMMING UP: HOW THE STATE AND LOCAL PARTY ORGANIZATIONS HAVE TRANSFORMED

There have been dramatic changes in party organizational strength at the state and local levels. The high point of *local* party organizations may have been reached a hundred years ago, when some parties could be described as "armies drawn up for combat" with an "elaborate, well-staffed, and strongly motivated organizational structure."[46] Although this description did not apply to party organizations throughout the nation even then, it would be hard to find a local party organization that could be described in these terms today.

Local parties were buffeted by a variety of forces since then. Progressive reforms adopted in the early 1900s undermined party organizations by limiting their control over nominations and general elections as well as their valued patronage resources.

A number of other factors—federal social service programs, economic growth, a more educated electorate, and even racial conflict—also undercut the effectiveness of the local parties.[47]

Yet local parties have come a long way toward adapting to these changes. County parties have moved to fill at least some of the void created by the decline of the urban machines. New sources of funding are enabling these county parties to expand their activities. Local party organizations, in short, are demonstrating again their ability to meet the new challenges posed by a changing environment—a resilience that has kept them alive throughout most of American history.

The state party organizations have followed a different route. Traditionally weak in all but a handful of states, state party organizations have grown much more robust and professional in recent years. They are providing campaign and organizational services to local parties and candidates who, in an earlier era, would not have dreamed of looking to their state headquarters for help. In fact, the recent flow of money, resources, and leadership from the national party to the state party, and in turn from the state to the local parties, has helped to modify the traditional flow of party power. Through most of their lives, the American parties have been highly decentralized, with power and influence lodged at the grassroots. The parties were hollow at the top, depending on the base for whatever influence and resources they had. Because of the death of urban machines and the birth of vigorous state and national party organizations, we no longer see this extreme form of decentralization. The nationalization of American society and politics has affected the party organizations as well, leading to more of a balance of power among party organizations at different levels.

Yet ironically, even though they are much stronger now, the state and local party organizations probably have less impact on our politics than they once did. One reason is that they have much more competition for the attention of voters, candidates, and the media. The campaign communications sent out by the parties merge into a flood of direct mail fund-raising and advertising by citizen groups, corporate and labor political action committees, and nonprofit groups, all of whom try to influence voters' choices. Many of these groups encourage individuals to run for office. They can offer candidates money and a means to reach voters independent of the party organization. They have campaign expertise rivaling that of the party's experts.

Second, although most state parties have become much better able to raise funds, the party's resources are still dwarfed by those of other actors in elections. In state legislative campaigns, for example, this new party money has accounted for only about 5–10 percent of the funds received by most candidates. Campaigners are happy for every dollar, of course, but these relatively small sums, even with the helpful services that accompany them, may not be enough to entice candidates to listen carefully to the party on legislative matters or any other concerns.

So the increasing organizational strength of the state and local parties has helped them adopt modern campaign skills and recapture a role in candidates' campaigns. However, it is not a *dominant* role—not in the way it could have been if party organizations, rather than voters in primaries, selected party candidates. Party organizations rarely *run* the campaigns; instead, their new resources give them more of a chance to compete for the attention of those who do—the candidates—at a time when other competitors (organized interests, consultants, and others) have become more effective as well.

Does this mean that the increases in party organizational strength are unimportant? Not at all. In a very competitive political environment, there is little doubt that it is better to have a stronger organization than a weaker one and to have more resources rather than fewer. In the end, however, despite all the changes in party organization during the past few decades, their most basic structural features have not changed. The American state and local parties remain cadre organizations run by a small number of activists; they involve the bulk of their supporters mainly at election time. By the standards of parties in other democratic nations, American state and local party organizations are still weaker—more limited in their activities and authority and more easily dominated by a handful of activists and elected officials. But by the standards of American politics, the state and local organizations are more visible and active than they have been in some time.

CHAPTER 4

The Parties' National Organizations

A few decades ago, the national organizations of both major parties were like many college students: chronically short of cash and searching for new housing. Their small staffs moved back and forth between New York and Washington, and their activity was visible mainly during presidential campaigns. Leading students of the national committees could accurately describe them as "politics without power."[1] The real power in the party system was decentralized, collected in the local party organizations.

There is good reason why the parties have long been decentralized, as Chapter 3 indicated. Almost all American public officials are chosen in state and local elections; even the voting for president is conducted mainly under state election laws. In years past, most of the incentives parties had to offer, such as patronage jobs, were available at the state and local levels, and the state governments have been the chief regulators of parties. All these forces have given the parties a powerful state and local focus that can restrain any centralization within the party organizations. So state and local party organizations have chosen their own officers, taken their own stands on issues, and raised and spent their own funds, usually without much interference from the national party.

In recent years, however, both parties have responded to the powerful nationalizing forces that have affected most other aspects of American politics. Since the 1970s, the two parties have reacted to a series of crises by strengthening their national committees. Their resources and staffs have grown; both the Democratic National Committee (DNC) and the Republican National Committee (RNC) are now multimillion-dollar fund-raising and candidate-support operations. They have taken on new activities and influence, and the Democrats have limited the independence of state and local organizations in selecting delegates to the parties' national conventions.

The change has been remarkable. Only in the earliest years of the American parties, when presidential candidates were nominated by congressional caucuses, were the national parties as important in American politics. Although the local pull remains strong, the distribution of power among the national, state, and local parties is now more balanced than ever before. This chapter will examine the effects of this expansion of national party power.

THE NATIONAL PARTIES

What is the national party? Officially, each major party's supreme national authority is the *national convention* it holds every four years to nominate a candidate for the presidency. But the convention rarely does more than select the presidential and vice-presidential candidates and approve the party's platform and rules. Between conventions, the two parties' main governing bodies are their national committees.

The National Committees

Each party's *national committee* is a gathering of representatives from all its state parties; its leaders run the national party on a daily basis. Their main focus is to help elect the party's presidential candidate; they also promote the party's issue agenda, help state parties, and assist in some other races, such as major gubernatorial campaigns. Both national committees have a long history: the Democrats created theirs in 1848 and the Republicans in 1856. For years, every state (and some territories, such as Samoa and Guam) was represented equally on both national committees, regardless of the size of its voting population or the extent of its party support. California and Wyoming, then, had equal-sized delegations to the national party committees, just as they do in the U.S. Senate, even though California has a population of about 37 million and Wyoming's is about 550,000. That system overrepresented the smaller states and also gave roughly equal weight in the national committees to the winning and the losing parts of the party. In practice, this strengthened the southern and western segments of each party, which tended to be more conservative.

Since 1972, when the Democrats revised the makeup of their national committee, the parties have structured their committees differently. After briefly experimenting with unequal state representation in the 1950s, the Republicans have kept their traditional confederational structure by giving each of the state and territorial parties three seats on the RNC. In contrast, the DNC, now almost three times the size of its Republican counterpart, gives weight both to population and to party support in representing the states. California, for example, has 21 seats on the DNC, and Wyoming has 4. This change reduced the influence of conservatives and moderates within the DNC.

The two national committees also differ in that the Democrats give national committee seats to representatives of groups especially likely to support Democratic candidates, such as blacks, women, and labor unions—a decision that shows the importance of these groups to the party—as well as to associations of elected officials, such as the National Conference of Democratic Mayors. National committee members in both parties are chosen by the state parties and, for the Democrats, by these other groups as well.

National Party Chairs

The national committee's chair and the staff he or she chooses are the heart of the national party organization. Members of the full national committees come together only two or three times a year, mainly to call media attention to the party and its candidates. Officially, the national committees have the power to select their own leaders. By tradition, however, a party's presidential candidate can name his or her party's national chair for the duration of the presidential campaign, and the committee ratifies this choice without question. The national chair chosen by the winning presidential candidate usually keeps his or her job after the election, at least until the president picks someone else. So in practice, only the "out" party's national committee actually selects its own chair (see box on this page).[2]

Presidents and Their National Parties

Presidents came to dominate their national committees early in the twentieth century and especially since the 1960s and 1970s. In the president's party, then, the national committee's role is whatever the president wants it to be. James W. Ceaser cites the example of Robert Dole, RNC chair from 1971 to 1973, who was quickly fired by the president when Dole tried to put a little distance between the party and the president's involvement in the Watergate scandal: "I had a nice chat with the President . . . while the other fellows went out to get the rope."[3] Some presidents have turned their

---

CHAIRING A NATIONAL PARTY IN A TIME OF CHANGE

Democratic National Committee Chair Howard Dean's "50-state strategy" was an effort to build his party's long-term prospects by investing DNC funds in every state, even in solidly Republican states such as South Carolina and Texas. The strategy seemed to pay off in 2006 and 2008 with big Democratic victories. But Dean's effort to expand the playing field cost his party a lot of money, and in 2007–2008 the DNC raised only about 60 percent as much money as its Republican counterpart. Although Dean's strategy was very popular with state party chairs, fund-raising remains the primary basis on which a national party chair is judged. As a result, after the 2008 presidential election, Barack Obama replaced Dean with Virginia governor Tim Kaine, a close ally of Obama's, and suspended the 50-state strategy. Obama's national grassroots campaign organization, "Obama for America," was renamed "Organizing for America" and became a new focus for the DNC.

The national Republicans faced an even bigger challenge in choosing a new party chair in 2009. After Republicans suffered big defeats in 2006 and 2008, the RNC was buffeted with criticisms about the direction of the party. Why wasn't it more high-tech? Why was the fund-raising sluggish? And who bore the responsibility for the jarring Republican defeats? After a long public battle, former Maryland lieutenant governor Michael Steele won the chair's job. Steele, the first black RNC chair, had a rocky start. He questioned party orthodoxy in some media interviews and raised fears among some party loyalists that he wasn't conservative enough. But these concerns would take second place to Steele's success or failure in raising money for the party.

Sources: See Tim Craig, "Juggling 2 Roles is Kaine's Third Job," *Washington Post*, January 25, 2009, p. C1; Perry Bacon, Jr., "Steele's Focus Turns to Nuts and Bolts," *Washington Post*, March 15, 2009, p. A5.

national committees into little more than managers of the president's campaigns and builders of the president's political support between campaigns. Other presidents, such as George W. Bush, have used their control to build up the national committee to achieve party, not just presidential, goals.

When their party does not hold the presidency, the national party chair and committee have the freedom to play a more independent role in national politics. At these times, the "out" party's national chair becomes one of several people (including past presidential nominees and even media commentators, such as Rush Limbaugh after the 2008 election) who may speak for the party and its policies. He or she will also need to help pay any debts from the losing presidential campaign, energize the party organization around the country, and—always of prime importance—raise as much new money as possible for the party.

Because of changes in campaign finance rules (see Chapter 12), the national committee has had to work separately from the presidential candidate's own campaign organization in presidential elections. To play this more autonomous role, national chairs have recruited staffers with extensive experience in raising money, managing databases, and mobilizing organizers and grassroots supporters.

OTHER NATIONAL PARTY GROUPS

Several other party organizations are normally included in the term "the national party," even though they work independently of one another and often compete for donors, resources, and other sources of power.

Congressional Campaign ("Hill") Committees

The most important of these related groups are each party's *House and Senate campaign committees*, called the *"Hill committees"* (because Congress is located on Capitol Hill) or the CCCs (Congressional Campaign Committees). The House committees were founded in the immediate aftermath of the Civil War; the Senate committees came into being when senators began to be popularly elected in 1913. The Democratic Congressional Campaign Committee (DCCC) and the National Republican Congressional Committee (NRCC) are concerned entirely with House elections, and the Democratic Senatorial Campaign Committee (DSCC) and the National Republican Senatorial Committee (NRSC) fund Senate races.

Although incumbent House and Senate members control these committees, they have resisted the pressures to work only on behalf of incumbents' campaigns; they also support their party's candidates for open seats and challengers who have a good chance of winning. In short, they concentrate their money where they think they are likely to get the biggest payoff in increasing their party's representation in Congress. During the past three decades, the Hill committees have developed major fund-raising and service functions, independent of the DNC and RNC. They provide party candidates with a wide range of campaign help, from get-out-the-vote (GOTV) efforts to hard cash (see box on page 70). For House and Senate candidates, the Hill committees are more influential than their parties' national committees.

Women's and Youth Groups

For a long time, both the Democrats and Republicans have had women's divisions associated with their national committees.[4] The importance of these women's divisions has declined markedly in the past 30 years as women have entered regular leadership positions in the parties.

On campuses, the College Republican National Committee (the CRs) and the College Democrats (whose Web log or "blog" was named Smart Ass, in honor of the party's donkey mascot) have experienced big increases in membership and numbers of chapters in the 2000s. Both these groups train field representatives to recruit volunteers for campaigns at all levels. The CRs have been closely associated with a number of conservative nonparty groups. The Young Democrats of America and the Young Republican National Federation also work actively among high school and college students as well as other young adults.

Democratic and Republican Governors' Associations

State governors have long had a powerful voice in their national parties, for several reasons. They hold prestigious offices, earned by winning statewide elections. Many lead or, at least, are supported by their state party organization, and some will be considered potential candidates for president; examples are former Governor George W. Bush of Texas, Governor Bill Clinton of Arkansas, Governor Sarah Palin of Alaska, and Governor Ronald Reagan of California. By the early 1980s, the governors of both parties had Washington offices and staffs. They frequently lobby their congressional colleagues on the special concerns of state governments, such as the high cost of health care to state taxpayers. Governors' organizational influence in the national parties tends to be greatest, like that of the national committee chair, in the power vacuum that occurs when the other party holds the presidency.

State legislators and local officials are formally represented on the DNC, but they do not have much influence on either party's national operations. Several other groups outside of the formal party structure serve as "idea factories" for the party in government. For the Democrats, the leftist Center for American Progress and the more moderate Progressive Policy Institute and Democratic Leadership Council (DLC) serve this function. On the Republican side, groups such as the conservative Heritage Foundation and the more libertarian Republican Liberty Caucus also try to affect party policy.

TWO PATHS TO POWER

The two national parties have traveled two different roads to reach these new levels of effectiveness. The Republicans have followed a service path by building a muscular fund-raising operation that pays for needed services to their candidates and state parties. The Democrats, in contrast, first followed a procedural path, strengthening their national party's authority over the state parties in the selection of a presidential nominee. The central element in both national parties' continued development, however, was their ability to attract thousands of small contributions through mass mailings to likely party supporters. This gave the national parties, which formerly depended on assessments provided by the state parties, an independent financial base.

HOW TO TARGET A CONGRESSIONAL CAMPAIGN

The parties' Hill committees hope to support all their congressional candidates to at least some degree, but they target a few candidates for much more intensive help. The most important criteria for choosing which campaigns to target are the competitiveness of the district and candidate quality, as measured by the amount of money the candidate has been able to raise (or contribute to his or her own campaign) by midsummer of the election year. Candidates, then, raise money not only to run their campaigns but to leverage even more money by impressing the party operatives. In giving money directly to candidates, Hill committee targeters also ask: Is the candidate's organization capable of spending the money effectively? Has he/she effectively generated media coverage? How expensive are the district's media? Targeting decisions can change daily as the election approaches, depending on movement in the candidates' poll numbers and on the parties' finances. The Hill committees can offer these services to targeted candidates:

- Help with hiring and training campaign staff, choosing consultants, and making strategic decisions
- Information about issues and "oppo" research on the opponent's strengths and weaknesses—a function ramped up dramatically in recent elections
- Advice and facilities to help candidates make effective television and radio ads at low cost (though the production is done mainly by party-related private consultants)
- Poll data to gauge the campaign's progress and measure responses to particular issues and messages
- Contributor lists given to selected candidates on the condition that these candidates give their own contributor lists to the party after the election
- Fund-raising events in Washington and party leaders' visits to candidate events, live and via satellite, to help candidates raise money and attract votes
- "Hard-money" direct contributions to campaigns*
- "Coordinated spending" to buy polls, media ads, or research for a candidate*
- Independent spending on ads in the candidate's district* and help in raising money from political action committees (PACs), other political groups, and individuals

---

*Explained in Chapter 12.
Sources: Paul S. Herrnson, *Congressional Elections*, 5th ed. (Washington, DC: CQ Press, 2008), pp. 90–131, and Victoria A. Farrar-Myers and Diana Dwyre, "Parties and Campaign Finance," in Jeffrey E. Cohen, Richard Fleisher, and Paul Kantor, eds., *American Political Parties: Decline or Resurgence?* (Washington, DC: CQ Press, 2001), pp. 143–146.

Ironically, then, at a time when some were warning that the parties were in decline, the national party organizations were reaching levels of strength that had never been seen before in American politics.

The Service Party Path

A *service party* is a party organization that supports campaigns with money and other help, as opposed to running the campaigns itself. The service party was born during the 1960s, when RNC Chair Ray Bliss involved the committee to a much greater degree in helping state and local parties with the practical aspects of party organizational work. Chair William Brock continued this effort in the mid- to late 1970s as a means of reviving the party's election prospects after the Republican losses of the post-Watergate years. Under Brock, the RNC helped to provide salaries for the executive directors of all 50 state Republican Parties; offered expert assistance to the state parties in organizing, strategizing, and fund-raising; and contributed to more than 4,000 state legislative candidates. Bliss and Brock fashioned a new role for the RNC by making it into an exceptionally effective service organization for the state and local parties.[5]

There were two keys to success in performing this new service role: money and campaign technologies. Using a marketing innovation of that time, computer-generated mailing lists, the Republicans began a program of direct mail appeals that brought in ever-higher levels of income. The RNC's fund-raising jumped from $29 million in 1975–1976 to $105.9 million in "hard money" (contributions regulated by federal law; these terms are explained in Chapter 12) in 1983–1984—a record for national committee fund-raising that wasn't broken until 1995 (see Table A.1 in the Appendix). The RNC used the money, as Bliss and Brock had, to offer a broad array of services to candidates and state and local party organizations, including candidate recruitment and training, research, public opinion polling, data processing, computer networking and software development, production of radio and television ads, direct mailing, and legal services. State party leaders were glad to accept the help; as the party more closely identified with the business community, Republicans felt comfortable with these marketing techniques.

The Democrats' Procedural-Reform Path

At about the same time, the national Democrats expanded the power of the national party organization for other reasons. Reformers supporting the civil rights movement and opposing American involvement in the Vietnam War pressed for change in the Democratic Party's positions on these issues. The reformers focused on changing the rules for selecting presidential candidates. Their aim was to make the nominating process more open and democratic and, in particular, more representative of the concerns of people like themselves: blacks, women, and young people.

The reforms started in the mid-1960s with efforts to keep southern Democratic Parties from sending all-white delegations to the national convention and excluding blacks from participation. After the 1968 election, the first of a series of reform commissions overhauled the party's rules for nominating presidential candidates. (This story is told in more detail in Chapter 10.) In doing so, the Democrats limited the autonomy of the state parties and the authority of state law in determining how convention delegates were to be selected, thus giving the national party the authority over the presidential nominating process.[6] Key court decisions upheld these actions, further solidifying the newfound power of the national party.

Why would the state party leaders have been willing to go along with this erosion of their independence? The reforms were probably due to the unusual politics of that time and the existence of a power vacuum at the top of the Democratic Party in the late 1960s. This change was limited to the Democrats, however. Republican leaders, consistent with their party's commitment to states' rights, did not want to centralize power in their own party organization.[7] Yet the GOP was still affected by the tide of Democratic Party reform because the bills passed by state legislatures to implement the reforms usually applied to both parties.

In the early 1980s, the Democrats took stock of the reforms and did not like what they saw. The newly centralized authority in nominating a presidential candidate and increased grassroots participation in the nominating process had done little to win elections. Further, it had divided the party and alienated much of the Democratic Party in government, many of whom stayed home from party conventions in the 1970s. So the national Democrats decided to soft-pedal procedural reforms and move toward the Republican service model. The party rushed to broaden the base of its fund-raising and to help recruit candidates and revitalize state and local party organizations. When the dust from all this effort settled, authority over party rules had become more nationalized, and what had been two models for strengthening the national party were rapidly converging into one.[8]

Both Parties Take the Service Path

The good news for the Democrats in the 1980s was that they were dramatically improving their fund-raising, reducing their long-standing debt, and increasing their activities in the states and localities. The bad news was that the Republicans were far ahead of them to begin with and were continuing to break new ground. The national Democrats made no secret of their effort to imitate the Republican success in raising money and using it to buy services. Slowly, they began to catch up; what began as a three-to-one and even five-to-one financial advantage for the Republicans was reduced over time (see Figure 4.1).

One reason was the Democratic Party's increasing reliance on "soft money" (see Chapter 12)—funds donated to party organizations in unlimited amounts, most often by labor unions, businesses, and wealthy individuals, and exempted from federal campaign finance rules. Big contributions from labor unions made it easier for the Democrats to compete with Republicans in soft money than they could in raising hard money. Both national parties' committees began major efforts to solicit soft money in the early 1990s. In 2000, the national Republicans established the "Republican Regents" program for individuals and corporations who gave at least $250,000 in soft money to the party during a two-year period, which helped produce record soft-money donations. The Democratic "Jefferson Trust" honored givers of at least

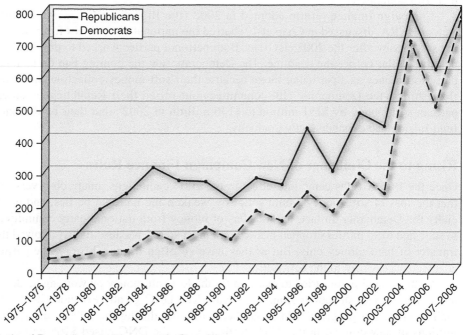

Republicans Lead in Fund-Raising: 1975–2008

Ratio of Republican to Democratic Receipts:
2.9   3.2   4.6   5.5   3.0   3.9   2.1   2.4   1.5   1.8   1.9   1.8   1.7   2.0   1.1   1.2   1.0

FIGURE 4.1   Democratic and Republican Fund-Raising, 1975–1976 to 2007–2008.
Note: The data points are total party receipts (including state/local, House, Senate, and national committees) in millions of dollars. Soft money is not included, nor is money (after 1987) transferred among committees. Table A.1 in the Appendix provides a breakdown of these totals by type of party committee within each party.
Source: Federal Election Commission at www.fec.gov/press/press2009/05282009Party/20090528Party.shtml (accessed May 29, 2009).

$100,000. By that year, almost half of the national parties' fund-raising came in the form of soft money.

Some of the money went into building up the state and even the local parties. In the 2002 election cycle, for example, the RNC and the Republican Hill committees transferred $145.6 million to their state and local organizations, and the three Democratic committees transferred $158.6 million.[9] Most of this was soft money, which could be used for campaign advertising as long as it did not use words such as "elect" or "defeat" in connection with a candidate. But at least some of the money went into voter mobilization drives that could help the state party more generally.

A much larger portion of the national parties' money has gone into races for the U.S. House and Senate. Since the mid-1980s, both parties have provided increasing amounts of aid to selected candidates. The Republican committees opened an early lead; the stunning success of GOP candidates in the 1994 congressional elections, for example, was due in part to aggressive fund-raising as well as candidate recruitment by their Hill committees.

Campaign finance reform adopted in 2002 (the Bipartisan Campaign Reform Act, or BCRA, discussed in Chapter 12) barred the national committees from collecting soft money after the 2002 elections. Both national parties worked to pull in every possible dollar before the deadline. The Democrats saw the coming ban on national party soft money as a particular threat because their soft-money collections had been flourishing—the Democratic Hill committees out-raised their Republican counterparts in soft money by $151 million to $136 million in 2002—but their hard-money fund-raising had expanded only gradually.

Rising to the Challenge of New Campaign Finance Rules

Once the BCRA rules came into effect in the 2004 campaigns, many observers felt that the loss of soft money would seriously weaken the national parties, and especially the Democrats. In fact, the transfers of money from national party committees to state and local parties dropped markedly in most states, because BCRA allowed the transfer of hard money only. But as they have so often in their history, the parties adapted successfully to the new rules.

Both national parties tried to make up for the lost soft money by working harder to attract hard-money donations from individuals. The DNC greatly expanded its direct-mail fund-raising program, which had been minimal during the 1990s, and reaped millions of new donors. In the 2004 election cycle, the DNC raised $166 million in contributions of less than $200—more than 40 percent of its total fund-raising. In all, the DNC collected almost five times as much hard money in 2004 as it had in 2002—$312 million compared with $67 million. The DCCC and the RNC both doubled their hard-money fund-raising in 2004, and the DSCC came close. BCRA made it easier for the party committees to raise hard money by setting the cap on an individual's aggregate donations to party and political action committees (which reached $65,500 in 2008) higher than the aggregate cap on donations to candidates. Both parties encouraged big hard-money donors to solicit similar contributions from their friends and colleagues and to "bundle" these donations to reach totals of $100,000 or $200,000 or more, in return for recognition from the party.

With all these incentives, the national parties broke all fund-raising records in the 2000s. In the 2002 campaigns, the six national party committees collectively raised almost $1 *billion*—substantially more than in any previous midterm race and almost as much as the two parties had raised in the 2000 general election, when they had a presidential candidate to support. Even after the BCRA reforms, the two parties' national and Hill committees came up with an eye-popping $1.2 billion in 2004 and again in 2008. Remarkably, the Democrats almost matched the Republican Party's fund-raising during the 2008 election cycle for the first time in at least 30 years.

Party Money and Activism in the 2008 Elections

Although the biggest portion of party fund-raising comes from individuals, an increasing proportion of the contributors to party committees and candidates were members of Congress. In the early 1990s, some Republican House leaders, fed up with their long-time

WHO GOT THE MOST NATIONAL PARTY MONEY IN 2005–2006 AND 2007–2008?

State parties

2005–2006	2007–2008
Missouri Democratic Party $6.1 million	Ohio Democratic Party $10.3 million
New Jersey Democratic Party $5.6 million	Florida Democratic Party $10.1 million
Virginia Democratic Party $5 million	Florida Republican Party $9.9 million
Ohio Democratic Party $4.9 million	Pennsylvania Democratic Party $7.4 million

Senate candidates (including party direct contributions, coordinated spending, and party independent spending)

James Talent, Missouri Republican (incumbent—lost) $10.8 million	Jeff Merkley, Oregon Democrat (challenger—won) $12.5 million
Claire McCaskill, Missouri Democrat (challenger—won) $10.5 million	Kay Hagan, North Carolina Democrat (challenger—won) $11.7 million
Mike DeWine, Ohio Republican (incumbent—lost) $8.2 million	Jeanne Shaheen, New Hampshire Democrat (challenger—won) $9.6 million
Sherrod Brown, Ohio Democrat (challenger—won) $7.8 million	Al Franken, Minnesota Democrat (challenger—won) $9.5 million

House candidates (including party direct contributions, coordinated spending, and party independent spending)

Jim Gerlach, Pennsylvania Republican (incumbent—won) $4 million	Travis Childers, Mississippi Democrat (incumbent—won) $3.1 million
Curt Weldon, Pennsylvania Republican (incumbent—lost) $3.6 million	Carol Shea Porter, New Hampshire Democrat (incumbent—won) $2.5 million

Note: National party money includes money spent or transferred by all six national party committees (DNC, RNC, NRSC, DSCC, NRCC, DCCC).
Source: Federal Election Commission data, at www.fec.gov/press/press2009/05282009Party/20090528Party.shtml (accessed May 29, 2009).

minority status, pressed party colleagues to donate some of their campaign war chests to Republicans in more competitive races. The aim was to redirect campaign money from those who could most easily raise it to those who most needed it, and therefore to increase the number of Republicans in the House. Winning a majority of seats would give all House Republicans the power to achieve their policy goals, given that the flow of legislation in the House is controlled by the majority party. In fact, Republicans did capture control of both the House and Senate in 1994; soon after, the new Democratic minority saw the value of spreading the wealth to help vulnerable incumbents and promising challengers.

Since then, both parties' Hill committees have urged, and even required, their members to channel money to the party committee, not just to particular candidates. This gives the party the opportunity to target the races it considers the most winnable, rather than leaving the decisions to individual incumbents. House members can donate funds from their personal campaign committees and their "leadership PACs" (see Chapter 12) and also ask their own contributors to give to the party's Hill committee. In 2008, for instance, each House Democrat was expected to give $125,000 to the DCCC and raise $75,000 more for the party. Committee and subcommittee chairs were asked to give between $150,000 and $500,000, depending on their positions and committees, and raise between $100,000 and $1 million for the party. House Speaker Nancy Pelosi had to contribute $800,000 and raise an additional $25 million. Each member's contributions were tracked by party leaders, just as party whips track legislative votes.[10]

Getting members of Congress to give to their parties can be a difficult sell, especially for incumbents of the weaker party, who are understandably worried about holding their own seats. As a result, the House and Senate Republican committees raised only $27 million from federal candidates in 2008, compared with the Democratic committees' $68 million.[11] But the parties' success in getting incumbents to hand over these impressive sums and to put their fund-raising skill in the service of other party candidates demonstrates the extent to which the congressional parties have become important instruments of collective power for their members.

With this big increase in fund-raising, the Democratic committees had the money to take a page or two from the Republicans' playbook. Starting in 2000, the national GOP had created a massive databank of voter information gleaned from party canvassers and commercial databases—individuals' past voting records, their opinions and consumer preferences—so that, just as businesses do, party strategists can make predictions as to how particular types of people are likely to behave. This "micro-targeting" helped the Republicans focus their persuasive efforts and GOTV activities on the individuals most likely to support Republican candidates. The resulting database, called Voter Vault, required funding and computer facilities on a scale that the national Republicans were capable of providing. It was widely heralded as a major reason for the Republican victories in 2002 and 2004.

Democrats were slow to respond, but later created two separate national databases. One, maintained by the DNC, was made available to Democratic candidates at all levels. The other, a huge dataset managed by Catalist, an organization headed by Democratic political operative Harold Ickes, was used extensively by the Obama campaign and liberal groups supporting Obama. Voter contact programs ("field operations") based on these datasets were field-tested in some congressional special elections in 2008, all of which resulted in Democratic wins. The DCCC and DSCC then applied these programs nationally, beginning well in advance of the presidential election.

By early September, the DCCC had four times more money to spend on House races as the NRCC did and embarked on a lavish independent spending drive. As you'll see in Chapter 12, court cases have allowed party organizations to run unlimited amounts of advertising in House and Senate campaigns as long as the party spends its money independently of the candidate it intends to help ("independent spending"). This produces the odd picture of two groups of partisans from the same party—those helping the candidate and those doing independent spending—working to elect the same candidate but officially ignorant of one another's activities. The great majority of party funds in 2008 House and Senate races, as in recent elections, came in the form of independent spending (see Figures 4.2 and 4.3). Although the Republican committees' independent spending fell dramatically in 2008, in tandem with their election prospects, Democratic spending reached unprecedented levels. The DCCC put $1 million or more into each of 38 House races, largely open seats and challengers' campaigns, and won most of them. In the 12 most competitive Senate races, the DSCC's independent spending made up for Republican candidates' edge in fund-raising.

Freshman Democratic legislators were among the biggest beneficiaries of these programs. Freshmen, especially those elected in districts that normally vote for the other party's candidates, tend to be most vulnerable in their first reelection race. To protect their freshmen, Democratic House leaders had focused on giving helpful committee assignments to Democrats elected in 2006 and useful advice in raising money for 2008. The two Democratic Hill committees followed up with careful targeting of funds and other services. With this help, only four of the freshman Democrats lost. Flush with money, the DCCC also aggressively went after Republican-held seats, recruiting experienced challengers and backing them with party funds. The NRCC was forced to use most of its independent spending to defend embattled incumbents.[12] Strategic efforts by the two parties' Hill committees resembled a game of chess, with the moves changing day by day toward the end of the race as each group worked to outflank the other.

Since the mid-1980s, then, both national parties have become institutionalized as active, well-staffed "service parties" working to support party candidates and state and local organizations, not only through direct contributions and independent spending, but also through investments in voter identification and database management.[13]

WHAT IS THE IMPACT OF THESE STRONGER NATIONAL PARTIES?

These dramatic changes in the national party organizations have helped to beef up the parties' roles in nominating and electing candidates, roles that had been seriously undercut a century ago with the advent of the direct primary. To an important degree, the national and state parties are now actively involved in the campaign support functions that private campaign consultants and other political groups had monopolized

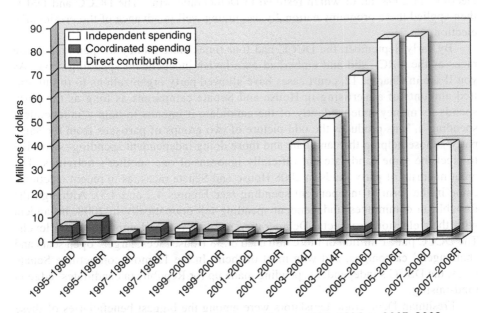

FIGURE 4.2   National Party Money in House Races, 1995–1996 to 2007–2008.

Source: Federal Election Commission, at www.fec.gov/press/press2009/05282009Party/20090528Party.shtml (accessed May 29, 2009).

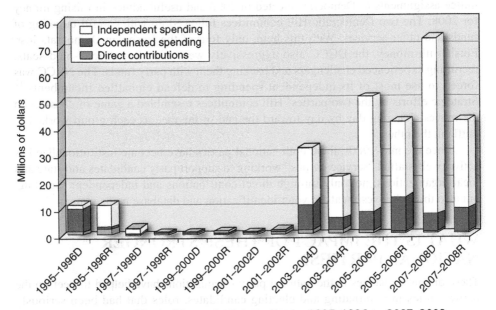

FIGURE 4.3   National Party Money in Senate Races, 1995–1996 to 2007–2008.

Source: Federal Election Commission, at www.fec.gov/press/press2009/05282009Party/20090528Party.shtml (accessed May 29, 2009).

until recently. The money and services provided by the national parties have helped to raise their profiles in the eyes of candidates. The increasing strength of the national parties has also altered the relationships within the parties.

Effects on Candidates' Campaigns

The strengthened national parties perform a number of vital functions in presidential campaigns. Both national committees research issues, study the opponent's record and background, and search for their own candidate's weak points and ways to thwart attacks. They train state party staff and field directors and maintain relationships with important groups in the party's constituency: organized labor, minority groups, women, and environmentalists for the Democrats; evangelical and other conservative Christian groups, and business organizations for the Republicans.

In Senate and House campaigns, however, there have been some marked recent changes in the national parties' decisions as to where to deploy their newfound strength. In the 1980s and 1990s, the national party committees had supported a wide range of viable candidates. The committees tended to protect their incumbents when they expected a lean election year and to invest in challengers and open seats when a big victory looked likely. But by the 2000s, the House and Senate were so closely divided by party and the number of truly competitive seats had shrunk so much that both parties' congressional committees were pouring the great majority of their money and help into those competitive races.[14] That remained true in 2006, though the number of Democratic opportunities grew as the campaign progressed. But in 2008, the Democratic Hill committees felt secure enough in their chances, and successful enough in their fund-raising, to expand the playing field substantially.

There was so much party money and field staff coming into these competitive campaigns that at least in those targeted races, party money at times outweighed candidate spending. The national party committees' money and other resources have given them real power over the targeted campaigns. For instance, in 2002, the national parties spent more in a closely fought Colorado congressional race than the candidates' own campaigns did, and the national party committees specified exactly what the campaigns had to do with the party money. The Democratic candidate's campaign manager probably spoke for both candidates in his exasperation at the national party's micromanaging: "They crawl up our ass on a daily basis."[15]

Sometimes the candidate balks at all this "help." In 2008, Republican House candidate Woody Jenkins learned that he would have to meet certain financial benchmarks before the NRCC would support him financially. Jenkins simply decided to ignore the NRCC's suggestions (though he did receive aid in the end) and narrowly lost his race. Party staffers often believe that they know more about campaigning than the candidate does. A DCCC staffer, for instance, complained that candidates want the national party's money but don't want to take its valuable campaign advice. He had hoped that Democratic campaigns looked on the DCCC "as a sort of bank of knowledge and support. I found out they perceived us only as a bank."[16]

The competitive races are unusual, however. In most congressional races, the national party committees have not put in enough money or other resources to attract even some attention from, much less power over, the candidates and their staffs. That can result in a great deal of frustration for the less competitive candidates and, in some cases, missed opportunities. As Gary Jacobson points out, nine Democratic House challengers lost narrowly in 2008, each receiving more than 45 percent of the vote, but did not receive substantial help from the DCCC. Some of these candidates might have won if they had received party money.[17]

Effects on State and Local Parties

More generally, have the increasing visibility and resources of the national parties led to a transfer of power from the state and local to the national party organizations—to centralization rather than decentralization of the parties? Probably not. The forces that encourage a state and local party focus remain strong.

But it is clear that the national parties' new strength has lessened the *de*centralization of the party organizations. When the national parties have a lot of money and services to give, their power and influence grow. In a number of cases, as in the Colorado campaign mentioned above, national party committees have made their funding or other help contingent on the campaign's or state party's acceptance of certain requirements: that they hire particular staffers or consultants or use particular campaign techniques. The result can be more of a national imprint on the issues discussed in state and even local campaigns, the kinds of candidates recruited, and the ways in which the parties are organized. Is this a good thing for American politics? "Which Would You Choose?" (on page 81) provides arguments on both sides of this question.

The Dean 50-State Strategy   At times, this national involvement has been welcomed by state parties. One of the more successful examples of national and state party cooperation was DNC Chair Howard Dean's *"50-state strategy"* in the 2006 and 2008 elections. Dean used DNC money to pay field organizers to work with each of the state parties. Colorado, for instance, had been a Republican state for several decades, but had experienced an influx of younger, more liberal voters in the early 2000s. So starting in 2005, the DNC provided money for the state party to fund field directors in rural areas and to purchase a new database of voter information. One study found that these DNC staffers improved the candidates' vote totals in these races, even beyond the other advantages that Democrats had in 2006.[18] The DNC investment also invigorated several other state parties in areas that the national Democrats had previously written off as Republican-dominated. Dean and his supporters argued that this was the foundation on which the Obama campaign's successful national strategy was built in 2008.[19] The Obama campaign felt differently, noting that it had relied almost entirely on its own staff and money in these "red" states; it contended that the candidate's own strengths and the Bush administration's weaknesses were at least as important.[20]

Under other conditions, the increased national influence can strain the relationships among party organizations at different levels, just as it has produced strains between the parties and some candidates. One of the areas of greatest conflict between the national parties and their state and local brethren centers on national party involvement in primaries. It is always a temptation for national party officials to try to select and groom the candidate they think will have the best odds of winning in a district. The House and Senate campaign committees, whose chance for a majority in Congress depends on the

WHICH WOULD YOU CHOOSE?

COULD A STRONGER NATIONAL PARTY HELP YOU?

YES! Political parties offer you a valuable shortcut. Government decisions affect almost everything you do, but you may not have time to research dozens of complicated issues (health care, energy prices) and candidates in order to vote for those who will act in your interest. A party can do the research for you. If you generally agree with, say, the Republican Party, it can offer you a set of recommended candidates with no effort on your part. But if each state and local Republican organization can act independently, and if some of these organizations are moderate and others are conservative, then how can you be sure that your state and local Republican candidates will support the positions that drew you to the party? A strong national party could help recruit candidates whose views are consistent with the party's philosophy and help them get elected. Besides, who would you rather have raising campaign money: the national party or the individual candidates who will soon be voting on bills affecting the donors' interests?

NO! The United States is very diverse; the concerns of Democrats in Omaha may well be different from those in San Francisco, New Hampshire, and the Florida Panhandle. If a national party is strong enough to promote a clear set of ideas on what government should be doing, then whose ideas should it promote: those of the Omaha Democrats or the San Francisco Democrats? If a national party is strong enough to elect its candidates, wouldn't it be capable of telling them how to vote in Congress, whether or not their constituents agree? Even if a national party organization confines itself to raising money and giving it to candidates, doesn't that give the national organization a great deal of influence over state and even local candidates? In a nation with a tradition of hostility to "boss rule," couldn't a strong national party raise those fears again?

effectiveness of candidates in competitive races, dread the possibility that a less capable candidate will win their party's primary and go on to run a less-than-professional campaign for the seat.

Yet there are big risks involved when a national party organization tries to endorse a candidate in a primary. If the party organization backs a candidate who later loses the primary, then the party alienates the winning candidate, perhaps splits the state party in the process, and makes itself look weak to boot. The DCCC provided a textbook example of these hazards when it decided to endorse four congressional candidates in the 2000 primaries. Two of the four lost, and the resulting intraparty fighting became a public embarrassment to the national Democrats.

National Democratic committees stayed out of party primaries in the 2002 election, but the national Republicans chose to wade boldly into this thicket and came out relatively unscathed. Anxious to regain control of the Senate in 2002, the NRSC focused early on ten states that it considered winnable for a strong Republican candidate. Using public opinion polls to measure the favorability ratings of various possible candidates,

NRSC strategists identified the strongest prospective contenders and, with President Bush, worked to persuade these people to run. The NRCC did the same in some key House races. All three national Republican committees then raised record amounts of money to pour into the closest races.[21]

The Republican Hill committees were able to recruit many of those on their wish list and to win enough races to capture the Senate. Yet this national intervention, according to one reporter, "infuriated" several state Republican Party leaders when the NRCC chair campaigned in their states for the national party's preferred candidates.[22] The Democrats had the same experience in 2006, when DCCC Chair Rahm Emanuel bulldozed more than a few local party chairs to get moderate candidates nominated in socially conservative areas and thus increase the party's likelihood of winning.[23] When the national party committees use their money to affect the choice of candidates or the direction of a campaign, it is likely that there will be ruffled feathers within the state party and the campaign, who feel that they are better judges of what works in the district.

Effects on the Presidency

Is a stronger national party likely to compete with the president's power or to add to it? Clearly, the increasing resources of the national committees give them the opportunity for a more independent political role. Federal funding of presidential campaigns, with its strict limits on party spending for presidential races, freed the national committees from their traditional concentration on presidential elections and allowed them to dedicate at least some of their resources to party-building at the state and local level. At the same time, the party committees carved out new roles in raising money for use in federal campaigns.

On the other hand, these new capabilities make the national committee an even more attractive resource for presidents. Naturally, presidents want the new party power to be at their service, and every president in recent memory has kept his party's national committee on a short leash. RNC Chair Jim Gilmore was edged out in late 2001, for example, because he clashed with the White House over control of the committee. Presidents will certainly want the party committees to mobilize all those members of Congress whom they recruited, trained, financed, and helped elect to support the president's program. Presidents in their first term will want to draw on the assets of the national party for their reelection campaigns, as much as campaign finance rules permit. So there is considerable pressure on these stronger national parties to put their capabilities at the service of presidential goals.

Effects on Congress

At around the time that the Hill committees have become much more active in recruiting and supporting party candidates, Congress members have been more likely to cast legislative votes with the majority of their party (as Chapter 13 shows). Did these new campaign resources help convince Congress members to vote for their party's positions on bills? To this point, the party committees have not given out campaign money and services on the basis of a candidate's support for the party's program. In two special elections in 2008, for instance, the DCCC poured money into the campaigns of conservative southern Democratic candidates whose positions on issues put them out of the mainstream of congressional Democrats. Party funds usually go to competitive races rather than to candidates who are ideologically "pure."[24]

Yet the committees have not been bashful in reminding members, especially newly elected members, that the party played some role in their election success. Party campaign help is only one part of the story of party support in Congress, but the remarkable cohesion of the Republican majority in the House from 1995 to 2007 was surely bolstered by the party leadership's financial and other support for Republican candidates. Constituency pressures will always come first in Congress. The more that senators and representatives can count on campaign help from the congressional party, however, the more open they will be to party-based appeals.

Relationships within the National Party

The three national committees of each party—the DNC or RNC and the party's Hill committees—have good reasons to cooperate with one another. When the party's presidential candidate does well, most of the voters he or she attracts will also vote for the Senate and House candidates of the president's party. Similarly, an effectively run Senate campaign can bring out voters for party colleagues running for president and House seats.

But the party's resources are not unlimited, and each of the party's national committees would prefer the biggest share. Although the DNC's 50-state strategy was popular with state Democratic Parties, the House and Senate campaign committees initially saw it as a threat. The Democratic Hill committee chairs feared that unless DNC money went into the most competitive races, rather than into state party-building, Democrats in these competitive elections would be overrun by the Republican "turnout machine." Conflicts arose on the Republican side as well. The RNC, unimpressed with the efforts of the NRSC, set up its own independent spending division to run ads in some closely fought Senate races. The party committees have long competed with one another in raising as well as spending money. They seek financial support from the same contributors (and jealously guard their contributor lists) and recruit political talent from the same limited pool.

THE LIMITS OF PARTY ORGANIZATION

In sum, the national party organizations have recently generated remarkable amounts of new money and other resources. They have used these resources, expertise, and energy to become major players relative to the state and local parties and major influences on the lives of many federal and even state-level candidates. Organizations capable of raising and spending a billion dollars during a two-year period are not easily ignored.

This impressive increase in strength has not come at the expense of the state and local parties; in fact, the national parties have used at least some of their resources to build the capabilities of these party organizations. Nor has the national parties' new strength made the local and state party organizations into branch offices of their national parties, following their orders in developing campaign strategy and taking stands on public policy. There are still too many forces in American politics encouraging independence, especially in the local parties, to permit the two major parties to centralize their organization and power. The federal system, in which most public officials are elected at the local level, the separation of powers, variations among states and local areas in public attitudes and regulation of the parties, and the new BCRA rules that discourage cooperative campaigns between federal and nonfederal candidates all work against a centralized party system.

So as resource-rich as they have become, the American party organizations remain fairly decentralized by international standards. At a time when Americans can be assured of getting the same Big Mac in Cincinnati as they can in San Diego, the American parties lack the top-down control and efficiency, the unified setting of priorities, and the central responsibility that we often find in other nations' parties. Where the party organizations of many other Western democracies have had permanent, highly professional leadership and large party bureaucracies, most American party organizations, especially at the local level, are still in the hands of part-time activists.[25]

The parties have increased their emphasis on grassroots campaigning through canvassing and phone banks and have used the information to develop micro-targeting, aiming specific messages at individuals known to be receptive to those messages. Yet even this greater reach into the grassroots may not be enough to make the party organizations more prominent in the public's mind. The parties' messages focus on the candidates rather than on the party itself. More professional, service-oriented parties may be better at helping candidates run for office than in expanding the role of the party organization in citizens' political thinking.[26] American political values do not welcome stronger and more centralized party organizations with more power in American political life.

The American party organizations are fundamentally flexible and election-oriented. Their purpose is to support candidates for office and to make the adjustments needed to do well in a pragmatic political system. As a result, they have long been led by candidates and officeholders, not by career party bureaucrats. As the political system grows more polarized, the party organizations have taken the opportunity to expand their roles and to add to the polarization. But at least to this point, even though the national party committees now have unprecedented levels of funding and activity, they remain candidate-centered organizations in a candidate-centered political world.

CHAPTER 5

Party Activists

If the presidential election in 2012 is like that of 2008, hundreds of thousands of Americans—maybe even you—will devote hours or even months of their time to working for a political party or its candidates. Why would people spend their precious free time knocking on doors or making phone calls for a political party? Most likely because they feel that they get something in return. People who become active in a party organization have some reasons—seek some payoffs—for devoting their time to the party rather than to relaxing in front of MTV with their beverage of choice. The party organization has to be able to work toward its aims—winning elections, educating the public, and governing—while also allowing its volunteers and leaders to achieve theirs. How it meets this tricky challenge (and whether it does) is determined by the ways it recruits party activists and mobilizes them for action.

WHAT DRAWS PEOPLE INTO PARTY ACTIVITY?

People become involved in organizations of all kinds, from party organizations to dance marathons, for three types of reasons. *Material incentives* are tangible rewards for activity—direct cash payments or other concrete rewards for one's work. *Solidary incentives* are the intangible, social benefits that people can gain from associating with others, networking, and being part of a group. *Purposive incentives* are intangible as well, referring to the sense of satisfaction people feel when promoting an issue or principle that matters to them.[1] Although the American parties once offered a lot of material incentives for party work, now individuals are attracted to party organizations and campaigns mainly for the purposive and solidary benefits they provide.

Material Incentives

For many years, the main material, or tangible, reason why people became involved in party activity was to share in the "spoils" gained when a party controlled the government. These "spoils" came in the form of patronage and preferments. *Patronage* is the appointment of an individual to a government job as a reward for party work. Although patronage is very limited today, the party can still provide loyal workers with a base of support if they seek elected office. *Preferments* are other favors a governing party can grant to party supporters, such as contracts or preferred treatment in enforcing laws. Patronage, access to elected office, and preferments have all played important roles in building and sustaining the American party organizations.

Patronage   Early in the life of the Republic and for more than a century afterward, Americans were attracted to party work by the prospect of being rewarded with government jobs if the party won. Patronage has been used in other nations as well, but no other party system has relied on patronage as fully and for as long as the American system. When party "machines" controlled many cities, city governments were staffed almost entirely by loyalists of the party in power.[2] As the price to be paid for their jobs, patronage appointees traditionally "volunteered" their time, energy, and often even a part of their salary to the party organization. Campaign help was especially expected; American party politics is rich with tales of the entire staff of certain government departments being put to work in support of their boss's reelection. Even now, when such practices are usually frowned on and sometimes illegal, government employees can still face a lot of pressure to contribute time or money to their party.

As the number of government jobs grew, however, the number of patronage jobs available to the parties was shrinking dramatically. Most government employees are now hired under civil service and merit systems, in which applicants get jobs based on their scores on competitive exams. The number of full-time federal positions filled by political appointees has dwindled over the years to fewer than 10,000 today, many of them high-level policy-making positions. States and cities have followed the same path, though more slowly.

The Supreme Court has helped to dismantle patronage at the state and local levels. In 1976 and 1980, the Court ruled that some county political employees could not be fired simply because the party in power changed. The Court went further in a 1990 Illinois case, determining that politically based hiring and promotion violated the First Amendment freedoms of speech and association. In each case, the Court agreed that party affiliation might be a relevant qualification in filling policy-making positions, but not in lower-level offices.[3] Even where patronage jobs remain, they are usually under the control of elected executives—mayors, governors, and others—who are more interested in using patronage to build their own political followings than to reward loyal service to the party itself.

Yet some patronage still survives. Mayors, governors, and presidents continue to reserve top policy-making positions for their trusted supporters. Legislatures often resist bringing their staff members under the protection of civil service systems. Civil service rules for governmental employees can be bypassed by hiring politically loyal, "temporary" workers outside of the civil service system or by channeling party loyalists into jobs in private firms that depend on government business. A few big campaign contributors will continue to be named ambassadors to small and peaceful nations. Wherever political leaders have some discretion in hiring people, in short, they will find a way to award jobs to their supporters, who usually share their party affiliation, so these opportunities will attract at least some people to party activity.

Keep in mind that some observers are sorry to lose the practice of patronage. Its use was promoted by President Andrew Jackson as a means of encouraging a more democratic and less elitist government.[4] When government jobs are filled (and then protected) only by civil service procedures, it becomes almost impossible for reform-minded leaders to replace a sluggish or ineffective bureaucrat with a more efficient worker. Patronage was also thought to keep party organizations strong as instruments of democracy. Material incentives can be very effective in attracting workers. Those who participate for reasons other than material rewards may make other demands, for example, for the party to take an ideological stand that might alienate moderate voters. That could undermine the ability of a party organization to act pragmatically and inclusively.

Patronage jobs in government are not the only employment opportunities a party can offer. State and national party organizations now hire hundreds of professional campaign workers, as do consulting firms associated with the parties. To provide services to their candidates, party organizations need computer specialists, pollsters, media production experts, field organizers, researchers, fund-raisers, strategists, webmasters, direct mail specialists, and other experts in campaign techniques. Some activists are drawn to party work by the chance of landing these jobs, but in general, patronage is no longer an important force in motivating activists.

Elected Office   Some women and men become party activists because they see party work as a first step toward running for office. This has been true for a long time; about 40 percent of the county chairs interviewed in a 1979–1980 national survey hoped to hold public office, and an earlier study found that one-third of all state party chairs became candidates for elective office after serving the party.[5] Because of primary elections, of course, very few party organizations can simply "give" nominations to public office to loyal party activists. It is far more common for candidates to see the party as one of the bases of support for winning votes and, in some areas, as the most important one. Candidates need advice, people (staff and volunteers), and money, and the party remains a likely source of all of these. So the lure of party support in a later campaign for elected office may bring some people into party work.

Preferments   Party activity can bring tangible rewards for some people, other than elective or appointive office. Because public officials can use at least some discretion in distributing government services and in granting government contracts, there is the potential for political favoritism. Some people contribute money or time to their party in the hope of attracting these favors. The head of a construction company might give a big campaign contribution in order to win a government contract to build a new school or library. It is no accident that leaders of the construction industry are so active politically in states and cities that spend millions every year on roads and public buildings.

There are other forms of preference as well. People may hope that in return for their activism on behalf of the party, they will get special treatment such as tolerant inspection of their restaurant by the health department, faster than usual snow removal in front of their place of business, or admission to a crowded state university. It may also involve the granting of scarce opportunities, such as liquor licenses, in return for some form of political support.

Reformers have promoted a number of safeguards to limit government's discretion in giving out benefits and buying goods and services from private firms. Examples are competitive and sealed bidding, conflict-of-interest statutes, and even affirmative action. Yet, because the potential benefits are so great for both sides, there always seem to be ways of evading even the tightest controls. In addition, many reformers don't want to eliminate *all* government discretion in the awarding of contracts just in order to stamp out *partisan* discretion. The result is that preferments may have taken the place of patronage as the main material incentive for political activity. Unfortunately for party leaders, however, now it is elected officials who grant the preferments, not the party leaders themselves.

Solidary (Social) Incentives

Many more people are drawn to party work by the social contact that it provides. In an age when some people's closest relationship is with their computer or their television, the face-to-face contact found at a party headquarters or in a campaign provides a chance to meet like-minded people and to be a part of an active group. Family traditions may lead some young adults to go to party activities looking for social life, just as others may look to a softball league or a bar. Some find it exciting to meet local officials or others who appear on the news. Researchers find that a large number of party activists cite the social life of party politics as a valuable reward for their efforts.[6]

These social contacts may produce other rewards as well. Networking has become a standard means of looking for a job. Young lawyers may find potential clients among the activists and elected officials they meet in the party organization. Realtors can learn about prospective home sellers and buyers in party activities. More generally, involvement in a party can help people feel a part of something larger than themselves—a charismatic leader, an important moment in history. The party can be a small island of excitement in a sea of routine.

Purposive (Issue-Based) Incentives

To an increasing extent, people are led to party activism by their commitment to particular issues. Someone dedicated to abortion rights, for example, might begin by working for a pro-choice Democratic candidate and then come to see the candidate's party as a vehicle for keeping abortion legal. A highly observant Christian who believes that life begins at conception might be drawn to the Republican Party as a means of stopping abortion.

Other groups compete for the attention of these activists; the abortion rights supporter, for instance, could also work effectively through organized interests, such as NARAL Pro-Choice America and Planned Parenthood. But since the parties have polarized on many issues in recent years, most of those who volunteer for party work seem to be motivated by a desire to use the party to achieve policy goals[7] (see "A Day in the Life," page 89). Although we do not have comparable data on earlier periods, there is reason to believe that this was less true of party workers earlier in the nation's history.[8] The energy and passion in party organizations come increasingly from issue-driven activists—those on the right in the Republican Party and those on the left for the Democrats.

Issue-driven party activism has played a vital role in shaping politics at all levels. The victories of Ronald Reagan in the 1980s owed a lot to the efforts of Christian fundamentalists in the Republican Party, who backed Reagan in order to legalize school

FROM CAMPUS TO THE OBAMA CAMPAIGN

Like most incoming college students, Megan Trusnik had never been involved in politics before. But when she arrived at Indiana University as a freshman, seeking her own "niche" on campus, she signed up on the Indiana Democratic Party website and offered to volunteer. That's all it took. Soon she was working in a governor's race, was offered an internship, and had the chance to make a number of political contacts on campus and off.

A dozen campaigns later, in what was supposed to be her last semester, she says, "I was browsing Facebook when I got a message from an old political acquaintance. There was a job opening in the Obama campaign in Ohio. It took a little persuasion by friends and family, because I would have to postpone graduating for a semester. But after thinking about the grand and historical opportunity this was, I e-mailed him my resume.' " Days later, Megan was hired as Obama Regional Volunteer Coordinator for nine counties in the Appalachian region of southeastern Ohio.

"I had only three days to get out to Appalachia, in which I had to pack, organize myself a car because I didn't have one, and get a root canal that was scheduled for a week later," Megan recalls. When she arrived in Ohio, she walked into the Obama office and found it almost empty. A field organizer was sitting at a desk in the back of the room. "No one was greeting people; people would walk in, look around, and go back out again!" This was not the way to attract the volunteers the campaign needed so badly.

Megan's job was to bring in those volunteers—in an area she had never visited before. Although the Obama campaign was well-funded, the staff was expected to gather most of its own resources, from food to housing, from office space to supplies. "We organized many of our resources purely from connections we made in the communities," she said. First, she tried to humanize the office by adding couches from Goodwill, having food constantly available, and covering the walls with posters. To energize volunteers, she set up competitions to motivate them to meet their quotas of campaign phone calls. She encouraged them to work independently and coached them on how to be persuasive. She became skilled in soothing personality clashes between local party leaders and East Coast volunteers with decidedly non-Appalachian lifestyles.

She also learned a lot about the rural communities that were her responsibility. "It made me more aware of the extent to which rural areas struggle with poverty—to a degree that we often think doesn't touch Americans," she said. One of "her" counties had a McDonald's and a diner but no hospital. In another, the only Internet availability in the entire county was a single Internet café with a dial-up connection. Even though many local voters were uneasy about voting for a man some termed "colored"—and in fact, an effigy of Obama was hung from a stoplight in one of the towns—many were convinced by the candidate's economic plans: to bring Internet access to rural areas, recruit more doctors, and improve health care.

And she was excited to be part of what she considered a state-of-the-art campaign. In her previous campaign experience, Megan said, she'd wonder: Why is this candidate not using Facebook? Why isn't that candidate's Web page interactive? The Obama campaign was different: Web-savvy, well-organized, and rooted in local communities. "I always knew that this is how politics *should* work."

prayer, end pornography and legal abortion, and overturn gay rights laws. Many conservative Christian groups worked for George W. Bush's reelection for the same reasons. In 2008, some antiwar activists were drawn into the Democratic Party to support Barack Obama. A party leader who is seen as taking clear and principled positions on issues can motivate people who share these principles, and who find these leaders compelling, to become more active in their party. Some issues and ideological movements have had enough power to lead activists to switch parties. The abortion and race issues, for example, induced many formerly Democratic pro-lifers and southern conservatives to join the Republican Party beginning in the 1970s, and they soon cemented a set of favored issue positions into the platform of their new party.[9]

A large proportion of these issue-based activists are convinced that their activity has made a difference; in one massive survey, three-quarters of those who said that they had volunteered in a campaign believed that their involvement had affected at least some votes.[10] So even though it might seem irrational to spend a lot of time on party activity in support of an issue that could be termed a "collective good"—one that, if achieved, will benefit the whole society rather than just the activists who worked hard to achieve it— large numbers of people become active in a party to do just that. Others become party activists out of a more general sense that citizen participation is essential in a democracy.

Mixed Incentives

Most party organizations rely on a variety of incentives. Activists who hope for a political job or some other preferment work together with those motivated by a particular issue and with those who come to party activities for social contact. That can produce conflict among party volunteers who are motivated by different incentives. Someone who became a Democratic activist to work for abortion rights, for instance, is not likely to be satisfied with a party that supports a pro-lifer running on the Democratic label. Others who participate in the party for social reasons may feel that the party ought to be a "big tent," including people who differ in their attitudes toward abortion.

The incentive that recruits people to party work may not be the incentive that keeps them there. Several studies suggest that those who become active in the party to fight for certain issues are more likely to remain in the party if they come to value the social contact it gives them. The motive that sustains their party work, in short, often shifts to solidary incentives: friendships, identification with the party itself, and other social rewards.[11] It may be that committed issue activists simply burn out or that the pragmatic American parties, in their effort to remain flexible enough to win elections, do not always provide the level of ideological dedication needed to sustain party workers whose lives are devoted to a set of uncompromising ideals.

Professionals and Amateurs

Drawing on research on these incentives for party work, scholars have classified party activists into two types, based on their beliefs about the role of parties in political life. One type of party activist is the *professional* (sometimes known as "pragmatist")—the party worker whose first loyalty is to the party itself and whose operating style is pragmatic. These are the party "regulars" who support their party in good times and bad, when it nominates candidates they approve of and even when it doesn't. A different

TABLE 5.1 Comparing Professionals and Amateurs

	Professionals	Amateurs
Political style	Pragmatic	Purist
What do they want?	Material rewards (patronage, preferments)	Purposive rewards (issues, policies)
Their loyalty is to:	Party organization	Officeholders, other political groups
They want the party to focus on:	Candidates, elections	Issues, ideology
The party should choose candidates on the basis of:	Their electability	Their principles
The style of party governance should be:	Hierarchical	Democratic
Their support of party candidates is:	Automatic	Conditional on candidates' principles
They were recruited into politics through:	Party work	Issue or candidate organizations
Their SES level is:	Average to above average	Well above average

type is the *amateur* (or "purist")—the issue-oriented activist, motivated by purposive incentives, who sees party activity as only one means of achieving important political goals.[12] (On the differences between these two types, see Table 5.1).

A party organization populated by amateurs may behave very differently from a party dominated by professionals. Above all, amateur activists are drawn into the party in order to further some issues or principles; for them, the issue is the goal and the party is the means of achieving it. If the party, or its candidates, pulls back on its commitment to their issue, they may pull back on their commitment to the party. So they tend to be less willing to compromise their positions in order to win elections. (See box on page 92 for an example of an actor who has been a longtime "amateur" Democratic activist, Ben Affleck.) Amateur activists are likely to insist on full participation within the party organization in order to put their issues at the top of the party's agenda. When they lead party organizations, they often bring a strong push for reform in both the party's internal business and in the larger political system.

For professionals or pragmatists, on the other hand, the goal is the party's success in elections; issues and candidates are the means of achieving that goal. If they believe that their party is most likely to win by downplaying an issue, moderating a position, or nominating a candidate who is popular but not in lockstep with their views, then that is the course they are likely to favor. Party leaders, then, must find a balance between the demands of the growing numbers of issue-oriented, purist activists and those of their more pragmatic colleagues. It is a common problem in modern society: whether to remain loyal to the group (or the nation) in order to keep it strong and vibrant or to give priority to the principles for which the group was formed.

This conflict may not be as troublesome as it seems; differences in attitudes between amateurs and professionals do not always show up clearly in their behavior. In the nominating process, both groups have tended to support candidates who seemed

BEN AFFLECK: "AMATEUR" PARTY ACTIVIST

To actor Ben Affleck, policy change is the goal; the Democratic Party is one means to achieve it. That makes Affleck a good example of an "amateur" party activist.

Affleck's main concerns are health care reform and achieving peace and justice in international affairs. "I would say I'm a moderately liberal guy," he told Fox News host Bill O'Reilly in 2008. As a result, he usually supports Democratic candidates. Affleck campaigned for Barack Obama in 2008, just as he had for Democratic presidential candidates John Kerry in 2004 and Al Gore in 2000. He called the George W. Bush administration "one of the worst ever." Together with Matt Damon, John Legend, the liberal group MoveOn.org and others, he sponsored an "Obama in 30 Seconds" contest to choose and air the best 30-second Obama ad submitted by supporters on the Internet in the 2008 presidential race. In fact, some Democratic activists urged him to run for the U.S. Senate from Virginia, where he owns a home.

But his support for the Democratic Party and some of its candidates reflects his agreement with their policy preferences rather than his dedication to the party itself. "There are things that I agree with the Democratic Party. There are things I don't. For example, I'm not a big gun control guy. I believe in all the Bill of Rights, including the Second Amendment. I'm not a party guy one way or another . . . it's about what your agenda is for the country. . . . I object to me getting a tax cut where we got soldiers who have to pay for their own body armor in Iraq. That's what; I don't deserve a tax cut. I believe that money ought to be spent on education."

Just as Affleck fits the definition of a political "amateur," Chris Van Hollen is a consummate party "professional." When he served as chair of the Democratic Congressional Campaign Committee in 2008, Van Hollen, a liberal, recruited moderate Democrats to run for House seats in moderate to conservative districts. For Van Hollen, the success of the party is more important than any specific candidate or issue.

Source: Excerpted from transcript of "The O'Reilly Factor," July 27, 2004, at www.foxnews.com/story/0,2933,127324,00.html (accessed April 24, 2009).

electable, especially in close elections. Although policy-driven amateurs prefer to win with a candidate "they can trust to safeguard their most intense concerns,"[13] they realize that they can't achieve their policy goals unless their candidates win office. Among county party chairs in 1972, a time when amateurs were thought to hold the upper hand in the Democratic Party, the amateurs did not differ from professionals in their effort to communicate within the party, maintain party morale, or run effective campaigns.[14]

Yet the increase in amateur activists, and the accompanying increase in party polarization on issues, can cause rifts that damage a party's chances in particular races. Consider, for example, the special election held in 2009 to fill a vacant congressional seat in New York. As state law required, the county party chairs in the district chose the two parties' nominees. The Republican county chairs selected a moderate state legislator as their candidate; their longtime Republican district had voted for Barack Obama in 2008, so they felt that a centrist nominee stood the best chance of winning. But their choice outraged local and national Republican conservatives, who termed the nominee a "flaming liberal" and accused their party of trashing conservative principles. Rather than back their party's nominee, they rallied in support of a minor-party candidate running under the Conservative Party label. Even though this Republican split permitted the Democratic candidate to win, the conservative activists claimed that their stalwart defense of conservative views was a victory of sorts, and they quickly announced their intention to challenge other moderate Republican candidates in the 2010 primaries. That unnerved party leaders who valued winning more than they valued conservative ideology.

HOW DO PARTIES RECRUIT ACTIVISTS?

Like almost all other community groups, party organizations have a difficult time attracting volunteers. Except at the national level and in some states where there has been an increase in paid positions and exciting professional opportunities, parties often have few effective means of enlisting new activists. To add to the challenge, state laws often take at least part of the recruitment process out of the party's hands. Rules requiring open party caucuses and the election of party officials in primaries limit the party's control over its personnel. This can lead to the takeover of a local (or even a state) party organization by an intense group of issue activists. At the least, it leaves a party vulnerable to shifts in its direction as some leaders and activists move on and new, self-recruited leaders take their places.

Finding Volunteers: Is Anybody Home?

In a much discussed set of writings, political scientist Robert Putnam has shown that Americans' participation in community activities has declined in recent years. Not just party organizations but also groups ranging from churches to bowling leagues have been starved for participants. Fewer people are involving themselves in the face-to-face activities of politics—attending a political speech or a meeting—even as the lonely activities of Internet surfing and check writing are on the increase. Many culprits have been identified, from the number of hours Americans spend watching television and surfing the net to the increasing numbers of dual-career families. The consequences, Putnam argues, are profound: a reduction in "social capital"—the social connections, values, and trust that enable communities to solve their problems more easily.[15]

The lack of participation in party organizations has been carefully documented. One well-designed survey found in the 1990s that only 8 percent of its national sample reported working on a campaign and just 5 percent said they were involved in a party organization, among the smallest percentages reporting activity in any type of civic organization. Much larger percentages of people say that they take part in charitable, sports, and business and professional groups.[16] Similarly grim conclusions come from the American National Election Studies, in which, in each year since 1994, only about 5 percent have reported going to any political meetings and only about 3 percent said they worked for a party—even in 2008, when the Obama campaign attracted an unusually large number of volunteers.[17] Granted, that is still a lot of people; 3 percent of the adult population would be about 6 million party activists. But although some of these activists spend a considerable amount of time on political work, mainly at the local level, others are "checkbook participants" who mail in their contributions but do not volunteer their time and energy.

Party organizations need a constant supply of activists of all kinds, so at a time when volunteers are in short supply, the parties are very likely to accept whatever help is available. The nature of that help often varies from one political period to another, depending on events in the political world at that time. The nature and direction of the Democratic Party were heavily influenced by the influx of liberals activated by the Vietnam War and the civil rights movement in the 1960s and 1970s. Tax revolts in the 1980s and efforts to limit the number of terms that incumbents could serve brought new blood into Republican Party organizations. For some time, activists from the conservative Christian community have been bringing their energies and beliefs into local and state Republican Parties. Because this recruitment process often depends on the presence of magnetic personalities and powerful issues, it tends to take place in spurts rather than continuously. It produces generational differences among party activists in which political outlooks may differ considerably, depending on the time at which individuals became active.[18]

The parties' recruitment system, then, is not very systematic, and it is closely linked to the movements and passions in the larger society at the time. Yet, although the parties have only limited control over their own recruitment, it clearly affects the parties' ability to achieve their goals. A local Democratic Party whose activists come mainly from labor unions will have different concerns from a local Democratic Party dominated by environmental activists, and a Republican organization run by local business leaders can differ from one controlled by evangelical Christians. Depending on the nature of the community that these parties are trying to persuade, these local parties may have different levels of success in elections as well.

Means, Motive, and Opportunity

People are most likely to become involved in party politics if they have the resources to take part, the attitudes that support involvement, and if somebody has encouraged them to do so.[19] The resources—the means—needed to become a party activist include time, money, and civic skills. It takes free time to help plan a party's activities, canvass or call people, and attend other party events. People need money if they plan to contribute to the party organization or its candidates or go to party conventions. Their educational levels help to determine how much money and time they have available to spend.

Their attitudes toward politics are also important. People are more likely to take part if they are interested in what happens in campaigns and concerned about the workings of government, if they have a feeling of attachment to a party, and if they believe that their involvement could make a difference. Most of these attitudes are related to one's income and education levels and thus add to their impact.

The third important characteristic is simply: Has anybody asked them? The parties now have a whole arsenal of tools to contact potential activists: e-mail, regular mail, Facebook, Websites, text messaging, Twitter, telemarketing, and in-person canvassing. However, most appeals to take part in campaign work—and especially most *successful* appeals—come from friends or other people known to the potential activist. Over the years, most activists have reported that they first became involved with the party as a result of these informal, personal requests for help.[20] Being asked to participate is a powerful motivator; in a major study, almost half of those who were asked to do campaign work said yes. Most people are never asked, however; only about 12 percent of the respondents in that study reported that anyone had ever asked them to work on a campaign.[21] This helps to explain why the proportion of party activists is relatively small.

WHAT KINDS OF PEOPLE BECOME PARTY ACTIVISTS?

Who are these people who are active in party affairs? How representative are they of the rest of the American population?

People from "Political Families"

Although they differ in motivations, American party activists have several characteristics in common that set them apart from the general population. First, they often come from families with a history of party activity. Studies indicate that many party activists had an adult party activist in their immediate family when they were growing up.[22] Consider the case of George W. Bush. His grandfather was a longtime Republican Party official and U.S. senator from Connecticut. His dad, a former Republican National Committee chair, had served his party in many other posts as well before being elected president. Some of his siblings have been involved in Republican politics, including his brother Jeb, who served in the cabinet of a Republican governor and then won the governorship of Florida, and his sister, Doro Bush Koch, a delegate to the 2004 Republican National Convention. Even the father of his son-in-law was a state Republican Party chair. With such a background, politics becomes the family business.

Better Educated and Wealthier Than Average

A second distinctive characteristic of party activists is that they tend to have higher incomes, more years of formal education, and higher-status occupations than does the average American. People with incomes over $75,000 are four times more likely to do campaign work as are people whose income is at or below the poverty line. As would be expected, the gap between wealthy and poor is greater among those who contribute money to the parties, and among online activists as well. Even protest activity is more frequent among the wealthy than among the poor![23]

This tendency for party activists to be better educated and wealthier than the average citizen may seem perfectly natural; people with more money and higher education are more likely to have the means to participate in politics, the interest in political affairs, and the expectation that they would be successful at it. So we might expect this pattern to hold in other democratic nations as well. But that is not the case. Most other democracies have a viable socialist party that recruits many of its activists from within labor unions. That tends to dampen the relationship between party activism and higher education and wealth.

In fact, it was not always true of American politics either. The urban political machines tended to recruit party activists who were more representative of the populations with which they worked. The machines' jobs and favors were the main reasons for political activism at this time. When patronage and other material incentives dwindled, the social character of these parties changed. A comparison of county committee members from both Pittsburgh parties in 1971, 1976, and 1983 shows that as machine control declined, the education levels of party workers increased.[24] As issue-based incentives become more common in the American parties, the educational and income differences between party activists and the average citizen tend to grow.

The social characteristics of Democratic activists differ from those of Republicans, just as the social bases of the parties' voters do. Democratic activists are more likely than their Republican counterparts to be black, union members, or Catholic. But differences in education, income, and occupation between the parties' activists have declined in recent years. Although they may come from different backgrounds and certainly hold different political views, the leaders of both parties are drawn especially from the higher-status groups in American society, even more now than in decades past.[25] As a result, it is even more true in the United States than in many other nations that party activism and other forms of active political participation amplify the voices of privileged groups.

Different Agendas

In addition to these differences in income, education, and family background, party activists also differ from other Americans in the types of issues that they regard as important. A large study of political activists in the 1990s found that the questions of education, abortion, the economy, and human needs (including Social Security and Medicare, jobs, health care, and housing) were the main reasons for their activism. Almost one in five mentioned abortion, a larger proportion than is usually found in polls of citizens as a whole, and one in four mentioned education. International issues were close to the bottom of the list,[26] though the Iraq War may have prompted party activism in the early 2000s.

The activists' issue agendas varied according to their levels of income and education. Higher-income activists expressed greater concern about abortion and the environment, whereas lower-income activists' involvement was more likely to be motivated by a concern about basic human needs.[27] To the extent that higher-income activists are better represented in the parties, issues such as abortion may get more attention in party activities than such issues as housing and unemployment, at least in recent years.

The types of issues that most clearly divide Democratic from Republican activists have changed over time. In the early 1970s, one of the primary distinctions between the two major parties' activists was the question of social welfare—how big a role government should play in issues such as welfare and other social services. At that time, there was much greater similarity between the two parties' activists on the abortion issue. Today, in contrast, there are few issues that more clearly divide Democratic from Republican activists than their views on abortion.[28]

More Extreme Views

Most significantly, party activists (and people who take active roles in other areas of politics as well) tend to hold more extreme views on issues than does the average American. Within the last 15 years, the tendency for liberals to become more active as Democrats and for conservatives to dominate activity within the Republican Party has become more pronounced.[29] This growing gap between the two parties' issue positions is found in Congress as well, as we will see in Chapter 13.

The main reason for this widening gap has been the increasing conservatism of Republican activists.[30] Especially since 1994, when Republicans won a majority in both houses of Congress, Republican activists have been motivated by issues and principles to an even greater extent than Democratic activists have. So now, on most issues, those active in the Republican Party stand even further to the right of the average voter than Democratic activists are to the left of the average voter.

PARTY ACTIVISTS AND DEMOCRACY

In short, research tells us that the major parties attract men and women with the time and financial resources to afford political activity, the attitudes that make politics a priority to them, and the connections with others who are similarly engaged. These activists also tend to be motivated by controversial issues, hold more extreme attitudes than other citizens do, and are more polarized by party than was the case in the mid-1900s. These findings raise some important questions: Does it matter if party activists are not very representative of other Americans? What has been the impact of the increase in issue-oriented, "amateur" activists? More generally, how do the characteristics of Republican and Democratic activists affect party organizational strength?

The Problem of Representation

As we have seen, American party activists differ a great deal from other citizens—the very people these activists aim to persuade—and the gulf has been growing. Party activists are wealthier and more educated than is the average American. Activists are more concerned with some types of issues—abortion is a good example—than are other people who identify with their party. Democratic volunteers, party officials, and officeholders tend to be more liberal than the average Democrat, and Republican leaders and activists are often more conservative than other Republicans.

When party activists give the appearance of being "true believers" on contentious issues, and don't seem to share the concerns of less involved voters, then it is not surprising that many Americans think of the party organizations as alien places. There is a delicate balance to be achieved in party politics. When the two parties sound too much alike on issues, citizens may not feel that they have clear choices in politics. Democracy can be well served when the major parties take clear and distinctive stands on major policy questions. However, when Republican and Democratic activists take polarized positions, especially on questions that are not central to most Americans' daily lives, and try to marginalize anyone who disagrees, then the parties expose themselves to public distrust, an old problem in American politics.

Amateurs and Pressure for Internal Party Democracy

The increase in issue-oriented, "amateur" activists often increases the demands on the party organization itself. In the past four decades, these activists have come to demand a much louder voice in the party's organization, and their demands have been met.

Because volunteer activists are so essential to the party's success, party leaders are often willing to tolerate greater levels of internal party democracy in order to retain their volunteers' loyalty.

An internally democratic party organization might, under some circumstances, result in a stronger party, better able to fulfill its responsibilities in a democracy. Rank-and-file activists who are contributing their time and effort in the service of a strongly held principle and who feel sure that their views are taken seriously by party leaders may be even more likely to work hard on the party's behalf. They might also press the party to remain consistent in its issue stands and strive to hold the party's leaders accountable, at least to the activists themselves.

On the other hand, it is easier to imagine a strong and disciplined party organization composed of party professionals who are dedicated to the party's success above all else. Much of the discipline in the classic party machine resulted from the willingness and ability of party leaders to give or withhold material rewards. A disobedient or inefficient party worker sacrificed a patronage job or the hope of one. The newer incentives cannot be given or taken away so easily. A local Republican organization is not likely to punish an errant, ideologically motivated activist by ending the party's opposition to same-sex marriage. Even if it did, the activist could find many other organizations that may be more effective at pursuing that goal, such as religious lobbies or other organized interests. Amateurs and issue-oriented activists can complicate the lives of party leaders, though they are not necessarily a threat to strong party organizations.

Activists, Party Strength, and Democracy

Strong party organizations, however, have often been considered a threat to American politics. Since the beginning, American political culture has been dominated by a fear that a few people, responsible to no one but themselves, will control the selection of public officials and the choice of policies. The result has been a series of efforts to keep the parties from playing too powerful a role in the lives of candidates, elected officials, and voters.

Several characteristics of party activists help to keep the parties decentralized and limited in power. The shortage of volunteers means that party organizations have to pay attention to their activists' concerns; that prevents a centralization of party power (unless, of course, the party activists push for such a centralization, as they sometimes have). The demand by many activists for internally democratic parties restrains the authority of party leaders at the top. And, in turn, because power in the American parties is diffused through the various levels of party organization, precinct committee members, city leaders, county officials, and activists at all levels are free to define their own political roles and to nourish their separate bases of party power.

The traditional worry about the excesses of party power, then, is probably misplaced. There have been few occasions in American history when the parties have been able to corral the kinds of incentives and resources that they would need to develop a fully staffed, vibrant organization at all levels of government. Although the national, state, and local party organizations have all raised more money and mastered new campaign skills in the past two decades (as Chapters 3 and 4 show), the continuing challenge of putting "boots on the ground"—recruiting volunteers—remains one of the biggest challenges faced by the American parties.

Part Three

THE POLITICAL PARTY IN THE ELECTORATE

If there were a pollsters' Hall of Fame, surely the first question in it would be: Generally speaking, do you usually think of yourself as a Republican, a Democrat, an independent, or what? The question is meant to classify *party identifiers*—people who feel a sense of psychological attachment to a particular party. If you respond that you do usually think of yourself as a Democrat or a Republican, then you are categorized as belonging to the *party in the electorate*—the third major sector of the American parties. Party identifiers (also called *partisans*) make up the core of the party's support: the people who normally vote for a party's candidates and who are inclined to see politics through a partisan's eyes. They are more apt to vote in their party's primary elections and to volunteer for party candidates than are other citizens. They are, in short, the party organization's, and its candidates', closest friends in the public.

Survey researchers have measured Americans' partisanship since the 1940s. The dominant measure, just cited, has been used in polls conducted by the University of Michigan, now under the auspices of the American National Election Studies (ANES). After asking whether you consider yourself a Republican or a Democrat, the question continues:

> [If Republican or Democrat] Would you call yourself a strong [Republican or Democrat] or a not very strong [Republican or Democrat]? [If independent, no preference, or other party] Do you think of yourself as closer to the Republican Party or to the Democratic Party?

Using these answers, researchers classify people into seven categories of party identification: strong party identifiers (Democrats or Republicans), weak identifiers (Democrats or Republicans), independent "leaners" (toward the Democrats or Republicans), and pure independents.[1]

Note that this definition is based on people's attitudes, not on their actual voting behavior. Strong party identifiers usually vote for their party's candidates, but the essence of a party identification is an attachment to the idea of the party itself, distinct from feelings about particular candidates. Someone can remain a committed Republican, for example, even while choosing to vote for the Democratic candidate in a specific race. Given the large number of elective offices in the United States and the value American culture places on independence, we can often find party identifiers who vote for some candidates of the other party. In the same sense, we do not define the party electorate by the official act of registering with a party. Two-fifths of the states do not have party registration, and in states that do, some voters change their party attachments long before they change their official registration.[2]

The party electorate's relationship with the other two party sectors, the party organization and the party in government, is not always close and cooperative. Party organizations and candidates ask their party identifiers for contributions and votes during campaigns, but often don't keep in touch with partisans at other times. Party identifiers, in turn, seldom feel any obligation to the party organization other than to vote for its candidates, if they choose. Party identifiers are not party "members" in any real sense. In these ways, the American parties resemble cadre parties (see pages 45–46): top-heavy in leaders and activists without any real membership, in contrast to the mass-membership parties that have been such an important part of the European democratic experience.

Even so, party identifiers give the party organization and its candidates a continuing base of voter support; the parties, then, don't have to start from scratch in every campaign. The party in the electorate also determines most of the party's nominees for office by voting in primaries. It is a source of potential activists for the organization. Partisans help keep the party alive by transmitting party loyalties to their children. A party identification can be the most significant landmark in an individual's mental map of the political world.

A party in the electorate is not just a collection of individuals; it is a coalition of social groups. Our images of the two parties often spring from the types of people the parties have attracted as identifiers. When people speak of the Democrats as the party of minorities, or of the Republicans as the party of business, they are probably referring, at least in part, to the party in the electorate. The groups in a party's coalition help to shape its choice of nominees and its stands on issues, and in turn, those candidates and appeals help to structure elections and political debate.

The three chapters in Part Three explore the nature and importance of these parties in the electorate. Chapter 6 looks at the development of party identification and its impact on individuals' political behavior. Chapter 7 examines the parties as coalitions of social groups and traces the changes in those coalitions over time. Chapter 8 focuses on voter turnout—the challenges parties face in the vital task of getting partisans and others to the polls.

CHAPTER 6

Party Identification

B y the time you were about 10 years old, if you are like millions of other Americans, you had already begun to identify yourself as a Democrat, a Republican, or an independent. This sense of psychological attachment that most Americans develop toward a political party is called a *party identification*, or *party ID*.[1] About one-third of Americans call themselves "strong" partisans, and almost as many express some party attachment, though not a strong one. Even among those who at first claim to be independents, most admit to feeling "closer to" one party or the other and favor that party in their voting.

Researchers characterize party identification in several ways. Some look at a party attachment as a form of social identity, similar to a religious or ethnic identity. They see it as a "team loyalty" that helps people find their place in the group conflicts that characterize the political world. It often grows out of other deeply rooted loyalties; a college student, for instance, might have a long-standing sense of herself as a Republican because her parents and relatives are Republicans. Many of these researchers see party ID as a perceptual screen—a lasting picture of the political world that can filter out any conflicting information the individual may receive.

For another group of researchers, party identification is more changeable. It is like a running tally of an individual's positive or negative experiences with the party's stands or its performance in office. This assessment, constantly being updated, can be a decision-making shortcut. Politics is complicated, even for political junkies. Americans cope with more elections and longer ballots than do citizens of any other democracy. A party ID offers a useful means of cutting through the complexity. It can help him or her make efficient voting decisions without taking time to learn much about specific candidates.[2] These differing perspectives on the nature of party identification can lead to different conclusions about its stability. But the approaches are not necessarily mutually exclusive; they may each apply to some portion of the population.

Just as it can be thought of in several ways, partisanship can be measured in various ways.[3] However we measure it, people's party ID tells us more about their political perceptions and behavior than does any other single piece of information. A party ID will probably be the individual's most enduring political attachment. Where do these party identifications come from?

HOW PEOPLE DEVELOP PARTY IDENTIFICATIONS

Families are the most common source of our first party ID, as they are of so much else in our early lives. People often say that they are Democrats or Republicans because they were brought up that way, just as they may have been raised as a Baptist or a Catholic. As children become aware of politics, they absorb their family's judgments about political parties and usually come to think of themselves as sharing their family's partisanship.

Childhood Influences

Party loyalty often develops as early as the elementary grades. Although they do not usually consciously indoctrinate their children into partisanship, parents are the main teachers of political orientations in the American culture. Their casual conversations about political events are enough to convey their party loyalties to their children, just as children learn where their family "belongs" in relation to other social groups. In fact, in these polarized times, you can even find children's books titled, "Why Mommy Is a Democrat" (in which the narrator points out, "Democrats make sure we all share our toys") and "Help! Mom! There Are Liberals Under My Bed!" (in a dream, two boys set up a lemonade stand that is taxed into oblivion).[4] Family and other early influences can be powerful enough to last into adulthood, even at times when young adults are pulled toward independence.

This early party ID usually takes hold before children have much information as to what the parties stand for. It is not until the middle-school and high-school years that students begin to associate the parties with general economic interests—with business or labor, the rich or the poor—and thus to have some reasoning to support the party ID that they have already developed. Note the importance of the sequence here. Party loyalty comes first, so it can have a long-lasting impact on attitudes toward politics. Only later do people learn about political issues and events, which may then be filtered, at least to a degree, through a partisan lens.[5]

Once developed, people's party loyalties are often sustained because they tend to gravitate toward people like themselves; thus, their friends, relatives, and coworkers typically share the same partisanship.[6] Some people do leave the party of their parents. Those whose early party loyalty is weak are more likely to change. So are people whose mother and father identified with different parties or who live in a community or work in a setting where the dominant party ID differs from their own. But when parents share the same party ID, they are more likely to produce strong party identifiers among their children.

Other sources of political learning tend to support a person's inherited party loyalty or at least do not challenge the family's influence. Schools typically avoid partisan politics; they are probably more inclined to teach political independence than partisanship. During the early and mid-1900s, most American churches steered clear of partisan conflict even at a time when church-connected political parties existed in Europe. Many churches and other religious groups have become very engaged in politics recently, but they are not likely to lead young people away from their parents' partisan influence. And the American parties themselves do much less outreach than do some European parties, which maintain party youth groups, social, and recreational activities.

Influences in Adulthood

These influences on children's and teenagers' political learning are more likely to be challenged in young adulthood, when an individual moves into new environments: college, work, marriage, a new community, and the unexpected honor of paying taxes. At this time, young adults can test their childhood party loyalties against their own personal experience with politics. They can listen to others with different party preferences. Their adult experiences may reinforce their early-learned loyalties or may undermine those loyalties.[7] Or the old loyalties may exist peacefully alongside contradictory new information; people can learn more about candidates and issues, and even change their attitudes toward those political objects, without necessarily changing their party ID.[8]

The longer an individual holds a particular party ID, the more stable it normally becomes.[9] Older adults are least likely to change their party attachments. After decades of watching and taking part in politics, party ID tends to become a habit. Partisanship may grow stronger across the life cycle because it is so useful a shortcut for simplifying the political decision making of older voters,[10] or because they surround themselves increasingly with others who share their party loyalties.

There are times, however, when even committed Democrats and Republicans are driven to change their partisanship. During periods of major party change, when the issue bases of partisanship and the party coalitions themselves are being transformed, some voters switch party loyalties. (We look more fully at the idea of party coalitional change or realignment in the next chapter.) This happened in the South in the late 1900s as conservative whites moved from Democratic to Republican Party ID. Economic calamities, debates about strongly felt issues such as abortion, and even local controversies can make someone aware that she no longer feels close to the party of her earlier years. Older adults may be caught up in the excitement of the moment as well, but their partisanship, often reinforced by years of consistent partisan behavior, resists change more effectively. So, when partisan turmoil begins, young adults are more likely than older adults to embrace the change.[11]

PATTERNS OF PARTISANSHIP OVER TIME

Large-scale change in party identifications is the exception, however, and not the rule. Most Americans, once they have developed party loyalties, tend to keep them. People who do change their party ID often change only its intensity (e.g., from strong to weak identification) rather than convert to the other party.

At the national level, we can see this stability in Americans' responses to the poll question measuring party ID that has been asked in every presidential election year since 1952 by researchers for the American National Election Studies. The data

FIGURE 6.1 Party Identification by Decade, 1950s–2000s

Note: Based on surveys of the national electorate conducted immediately before each presidential and congressional elections as part of the American National Election Studies program. For each party grouping in each decade, the gray segment at the base of the bar is the percentage of respondents calling themselves strong Democrats or Republicans; in the middle are weak Democrats or Republicans, and at the top is the percentage calling themselves independents who lean toward the Democratic or the Republican Party. For the full presentation of data for presidential election years, including the "pure" independents, see Table A.2 in the Appendix.

Source: American National Election Studies, University of Michigan; data made available by the Inter-University Consortium for Political and Social Research.

are summarized by decade in Figure 6.1; the full dataset can be found in Table A.2 in the Appendix.[12] The figure shows some change in the overall partisanship of Americans: although Democrats have been in the majority throughout these years, the proportion of Republicans steadily increased from the 1950s until about 2005. In the 1950s, Democrats outnumbered Republicans by a ratio of 1.7 to 1. The gap narrowed in each decade, and especially beginning in the 1980s, until the two groups of partisans had become more equal in size by the early 2000s. This increase in Republican support, as we will see in Chapter 7, was propelled largely by the gradual movement of white southerners from Democratic to Republican identification.

Changes in overall partisanship usually happen slowly. In Figure 6.1, look, for example, at the percentage who call themselves strong Republicans (represented by the gray portion at the bottom of each Republican column). When summarized by decade, this proportion never rises above 14 percent nor drops below 9 percent. The full dataset in the Appendix shows that over more than 50 years of history, from years when the

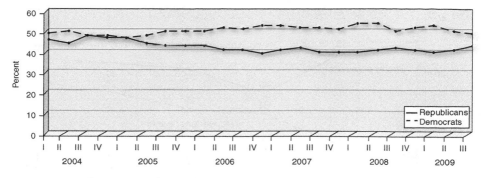

FIGURE 6.2   Short-Term Change in Party ID, 2004–2009.
Note: Roman numerals represent the three-month "quarters" of each year. Data points are the average percentages of respondents who say they identify with each party, including independent "leaners," in Gallup polls taken during each quarter.
Source: Gallup Poll, at www.gallup.com/poll/123362/Independents-Lean-GOP-Party-Gap-Smallest-Since-05.aspx# and, for 2004, at www.gallup.com/poll/26308/Democratic-Edge-Partisanship-2006-Evident-National-State-Levels.aspx (accessed October 1, 2009).

Republican Party was triumphant to years when it seemed almost dead, the proportion of strong Republicans has stayed within a 7-percentage-point range, between 9 and 16 percent of those surveyed. Overall, the percentage of respondents in each category of partisanship tends to change very little from one election year to the next; the usual difference is just 2 percent. Election campaigns can produce "bumps" in the short term, as a glance at the third and fourth quarters of 2006 and 2008 demonstrates in Figure 6.2, but these are often short-lived.

There are two exceptions to this story of fairly stable partisanship, and they appear at both the national and individual levels. During the first one, an especially turbulent period—1972 through 1976, spanning President Richard Nixon's landslide reelection, the Watergate scandals that caused Nixon to resign, his subsequent pardon by President Gerald Ford, and Ford's own 1976 defeat—researchers interviewed the same set of individuals in three successive surveys. Almost two-thirds of the respondents remained in the same broad category of party identification (44 percent were stable strong/weak Democrats or Republicans, 20 percent stable independents) throughout all three surveys. Only 3 percent changed parties.[13] People were more likely to change their evaluations of prominent politicians and issues than their party ID. The stability of party identification during these agitated times is impressive.[14]

Yet a third of the respondents did change from a party ID to independence during these three waves of surveys. And at the national level (see Figure 6.3), there had been a drop in the proportion of respondents calling themselves *strong* partisans (Democrats or Republicans) during the 1960s, and an increase in the percentage of independent "leaners." Combined with other major changes at that time—the civil rights movement, protests against American involvement in the Vietnam War, the women's movement, environmental activism—the growing number of independents suggested to many observers that partisanship was fading in the United States.

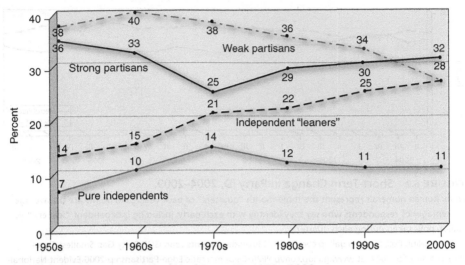

FIGURE 6.3   Change in Strength of Party ID, 1950s–2000s

Note: This is a "folded" party ID scale in which Democrats and Republicans in each category are combined (i.e., the category "strong partisans" includes strong Democrats and Republicans).

Source: Calculated from American National Election Studies, University of Michigan; data made available through the Inter-University Consortium for Political and Social Research.

Has There Been a Decline in Partisanship?

Research in other democracies bolstered the argument that partisanship was in decline. Across the Western industrialized world, analysts found a rise in the proportion of independents, a drop in confidence expressed in political parties, and an increase in *split-ticket voting* (supporting candidates of more than one party).[15] The effects of this "party decline" would have been profound.[16] What could have caused it? Education levels were rising in democracies; perhaps the better-educated voters had so much other information available that they didn't need parties as a decision shortcut any more. Maybe candidates were becoming more independent of party ties and influencing other citizens. Perhaps media coverage of politics stressed nonpartisanship or ignored parties.

These explanations provoked even more questions, however. If Americans have more information available than ever before, wouldn't they need a device, like a party ID, to help them sift through it? Even though education levels are rising, we know that most Americans are not very interested in politics, do not know very much about it, and therefore depend on shortcuts to make sense of their voting decisions.[17] Party ID, then, would probably remain a helpful tool. And among people for whom partisanship is a strong group attachment, the increase in available information would probably not lead to a decline in partisan feelings.

In fact, indicators of partisanship *have* rebounded since the 1970s. In particular, there has been a resurgence of strong partisanship (see Figure 6.3). The proportion of strong party identifiers in 2008 was only 4 percent lower than it had been in the 1950s, which was considered a very partisan time. Among those who vote, the decline in party ID has been largely reversed.[18] In fact, in some recent polls, the proportion of voters who considered themselves partisan, and the consistency between partisanship and vote choice, were the highest in more than 20 years.[19] The main changes between the 1950s and today have been a decrease in the proportion of weak partisans and a big increase in the numbers of independent "leaners," those who call themselves independents but then acknowledge, when probed by poll takers, that they lean toward one party. These "leaners," however, vote and think much more like partisans than they do like independents.[20]

The revival of party attachment in the 1980s and 1990s was prompted by greater partisanship in Congress and by more partisan political leaders such as President Ronald Reagan and former House Speaker Newt Gingrich. The increase in partisanship, then, seemed at first to benefit Republicans.

A Recent Resurgence in Democratic Party ID?

More recently, there has been another notable shift in partisanship. In tandem with a drop in President George W. Bush's approval ratings, the proportion of Republican partisans fell beginning in 2005 (see Figure 6.2). Consistent with this decline, a poll in early 2009 reported the widest gap between the two parties' favorability ratings recorded in 20 years: 62 percent favorable toward the Democrats, 40 percent toward the Republicans.[21] During the same four-year period, the numbers of voters registering as Republicans dropped, and the numbers who registered as Democrats or independents rose, especially among younger voters.

Some suggest that demographic trends should increase this Democratic edge.[22] The fastest-growing groups in the adult population are Latinos and young people who came of age politically during the declining popularity of the Bush years. Both groups leaned heavily Democratic in 2004 and 2008. But their continued enthusiasm for politics depends heavily on the Obama administration's ability to win policy battles and keep its young and minority supporters engaged. When the administration struggled with opposition to its health care and energy proposals by the second half of 2009, the expanded Democratic majority began to shrink, though the Republican Party's favorability ratings were declining as well. No matter which party is favored at the time, however, party remains an influential political attachment, and the earlier discussion of party decline is at an end.

PARTY IDENTIFICATION AND POLITICAL VIEWS

Because of their early development and stability, individuals' party loyalties can affect their views on a variety of political topics, from issues to candidates.[23] Shortly after the 2008 presidential election, for instance, party ID seemed to make a bigger difference in people's expectations about Obama's presidency than did their liberal or conservative beliefs. Even among those who called themselves conservative Democrats, fully 84 percent expressed confidence that Obama would do a good job; 94 percent of liberal Democrats agreed. Only 23 percent of conservative Republicans expressed confidence in Obama, as did 44 percent of moderate to liberal Republicans.[24]

For a more dramatic example, consider the controversial 2000 election, when the Supreme Court stopped the recount of votes in some Florida counties and decided the presidential election in favor of Bush, the Republican candidate. In a poll taken two months before the election, 70 percent of Democratic identifiers had said that they approved of the Supreme Court's job performance, and only 18 percent disapproved. A month after the Court's verdict on the presidential race, just 42 percent of Democrats now said they approved of the way the Court was handling its job, and 50 percent said they disapproved. Conversely, approval of the Court among Republicans rose from 60 percent in August 2000 to 80 percent in January 2001.[25]

Party loyalty can affect people's attitudes even when it has to compete with other valued loyalties. Democrat John Kerry was the third Catholic presidential candidate in American history. Catholics were more likely to vote for Kerry in 2004 than Protestants were. Catholic Republicans, however, were not as positive toward Kerry as were Catholic Democrats. Party ID still made a difference, even among those with the same religious affiliation. Party identification is not the only cause of political attitudes, of course, and people's reactions to particular issues or elected officials may change as a result of new information, even as their party ID remains the same. Yet party affiliation helps to condition the way people feel about issues, candidates, and public officials.[26]

PARTY IDENTIFICATION AND VOTING

The most important effect of party attachments is their influence on voting behavior. Even though partisans have to fight their way through long ballots and the culture's traditional distrust of strong parties, party identifiers tend to support their party fairly faithfully. Where partisanship is weak, as in new democracies where party ID is still developing, voting choices are more likely to be unstable and changeable.[27]

Party Voting

During the past half-century, party identifiers have voted for their party's candidates most of the time. As you can see in Figures 6.4 and 6.5, a majority in each category of partisanship has voted for their party's presidential candidate in every year, except for weak Democrats in 1972 and independent Democrats in 1980 (both GOP landslide years). As with party ID, party voting declined somewhat during the late 1960s and early 1970s. But recent studies show that the overall impact of party ID on voting behavior has been on the upswing since the mid-1970s[28] and continued to increase in the 2000s. The polarization of the major parties in recent years has probably helped some voters to clarify their political attachments and to heighten their sense of loyalty to a party and its candidates. The most faithful are the strong partisans. In the last four presidential elections, at least 94 percent of strong Democrats supported their party's candidate. Strong Republicans have been even more loyal. Only once in 50 years has their support for the GOP presidential candidate dipped below 90 percent.

These patterns appear in congressional elections as well. (The data can be found in Table A.4 in the Appendix.) A majority within each group of partisans has voted for

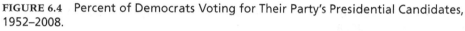

FIGURE 6.4   Percent of Democrats Voting for Their Party's Presidential Candidates, 1952–2008.

Note: The numbers for each election year can be found in Table A.3 in the Appendix. Comparable data on voting for the respondent's party's congressional candidates can be found in Table A.4.

Source: American National Election Studies, University of Michigan; data made available by the Inter-University Consortium for Political and Social Research.

their party's congressional candidates in each election, and strong partisans have been the most consistent party voters. One key to the Democrats' ability to continue winning congressional majorities in the 1970s and 1980s, at a time when their electoral base was eroding, was that they were more faithful than their GOP counterparts in voting for their party's congressional candidates. In 1994, 1996, and 1998, however, Republicans running for Congress got an extra boost in loyalty from their own partisans. This, together with the support of a clear majority of independents, helped them gain control of Congress in 1994 and to keep it in the crucial elections that followed. In mirror image, Democratic voting fidelity decreased temporarily in the mid-1990s but rebounded and, along with votes from a majority of independents, gave Democrats a House and Senate majority beginning in 2006.

Similar results appear in voting at the state and local levels. ***Straight-ticket voting***—voting for one party's candidates only—declined among all the partisan groups during the 1960s and 1970s. But most strong Democrats and strong Republicans remained straight-ticket voters. The stronger an individual's party identification, the more likely he or she was to vote a straight ticket.[29] And as with other indicators of party influence, the decline seems to have stopped and reversed. In the 2004 elections, only 59 congressional districts out of 435 (less than 14 percent) voted for a House member of one party and a presidential candidate of the other—a 50-year low. Although the number increased to 83 in 2008 (19 percent), there had been 110 such districts in 1996 and as many as 190 in 1984.

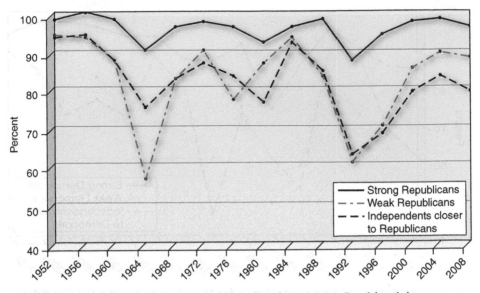

FIGURE 6.5 Percent of Republicans Voting for Their Party's Presidential Candidates, 1952–2008.

Note: The numbers for each election year can be found in Table A.3 in the Appendix. Comparable data on voting for the respondent's party's congressional candidates can be found in Table A.4.

Source: American National Election Studies, University of Michigan; data made available by the Inter-University Consortium for Political and Social Research.

Party Versus Candidates and Issues

What causes these ups and downs in the level of party voting? Individuals' voting decisions are affected by the give-and-take of two sets of forces: the strength of their enduring party loyalty (if they have one) and the power of the *short-term forces* operating in a given election, such as the attractiveness of the candidates and issues in that campaign. Usually these two sets of forces incline the voter in the same direction; as we have seen, a party ID encourages an individual to see the party's candidates and issue stands in a favorable light.

There are times, however, when an especially attractive candidate or a particularly compelling issue—an economic disaster or the threat of terrorism—may lead a voter to desert one or more of his or her party's candidates. At least by some measures, split-ticket voting has been frequent for decades.[30] Although some voters seem to split their tickets in order to create a moderate or divided government,[31] it is more common for voters to defect from their party ID because they are attracted to a very visible candidate running a well-funded campaign, most often an incumbent of the other party.[32] In 2008, for instance, Obama won the popular vote in Maine by 18 points, but incumbent Republican Senator Susan Collins was reelected as well, with a 22-point advantage over her Democratic challenger. Typically, those with the weakest party ID or the most ambivalent attitudes about the parties—for example, those who have at least some positive feelings about both parties[33]—are the most likely to defect.

Partisanship as a Two-Way Street

Which is more important in influencing people's votes: party ID, candidate characteristics, or current issues? One challenge for political scientists in answering this question is that these three forces are strongly interrelated. The early studies of party ID in the 1950s assumed that party "came first" in the causal ordering—that it affected people's feelings about candidates and issues but was not in turn influenced by them. These early studies did not have good measures of how close the voter felt to the candidates on issues.

Since then, with the use of better measures, researchers have shown that there are reciprocal relationships among these three influences. Just as an individual's party loyalty influences the way he or she views politics, feelings about candidates and issues can affect the individual's party ID. In particular, reactions to a president's management of the economy (so-called *retrospective evaluations*, in that they refer to past actions rather than hopes for the future) can feed back on party loyalties and weaken or change them. In this way, partisanship can be seen as a kind of running tally of party-related evaluations.[34] Even if party ID is usually stable enough to withstand an individual's disappointment in a particular party candidate or in the party's position on an issue or two, an accumulation of these negative experiences, especially on an issue important to him or her, can weaken or change an individual's partisanship.[35] That is what happened over several decades to the long-standing Democratic loyalties of many conservative white southerners, in response to Democratic administrations' handling of racial and other issues.

In the short run, then, issues and the candidates in a particular election can have a major impact on the outcome.[36] But party ID has continuing power to influence voters' choices and to affect their feelings about issues and candidates as well. So whether we want to explain the general trends of American voting behavior or the choices of voters in a particular election, party ID plays a prominent role.

PARTY IDENTIFICATION AND POLITICAL ACTIVITY

Another important effect of party ID is that individuals who consider themselves Democrats and Republicans are more involved in political life than are those who call themselves independents. Partisanship is emotionally engaging; it gives partisans a stake in the outcome of political events. So it is the strongest partisans who are the most likely to vote, to pay attention to politics, and to become politically active. In 2008, as in previous years, strong Democrats and Republicans were more likely than weak identifiers or independents to be interested in politics and to follow media reports about the campaign (Table 6.1).

Strong partisans are also the most active in other ways. A total of 90 and 95 percent, respectively, of the strong Democrats and Republicans reported having voted in 2008—higher than the turnout levels among weaker partisans or independents.[37] Strong identifiers were also much more likely than other citizens to try to persuade others to vote a certain way, to display bumper stickers or yard signs, and to contribute to a party or candidate. The only anomaly here is that strong partisans were less likely to seek

TABLE 6.1 Political Involvement of Partisans and Independents, 2008

	Democrats (%)		Independents (%)			Republicans (%)	
	Strong	Weak	Closer to Dem.	Closer to Neither	Closer to Rep.	Weak	Strong
Follow public affairs most of the time	33	25	26	19	34	32	32
Watched programs about campaign on TV	96	91	88	87	85	98	97
Read about campaign in newspapers	66	53	55	39	54	54	62
Used Internet to gather information about campaign	40	42	52	20	52	58	38
Voted	90	78	66	50	75	86	95
Tried to influence the vote of others	57	33	37	25	47	49	67
Displayed button, bumper sticker, sign	34	15	13	11	9	10	24
Attended rally or meeting	18	7	6	5	7	4	7
Contributed money to:							
Candidate	20	7	10	4	6	8	20
Party	14	6	7	1	5	8	15

Source: 2008 American National Election Study, University of Michigan; data made available by the Inter-University Consortium for Political and Social Research.

campaign information on the Internet, mainly because Internet use tends to be concentrated among people under the age of 50, whereas strong partisanship is much more likely among people over 50.

PARTY IDENTIFICATION AND ATTITUDES TOWARD THE PARTIES

Strong party identifiers see a greater contrast between the Republican and Democratic Parties than do weak identifiers and independents, both in general and on specific policy issues (see Figure 6.6). They are more polarized in their evaluations of the two parties' candidates as well as of the parties' ability to govern for the benefit of the nation. In the mind of the strong partisan, in short, the parties are clearly defined and highly polarized on the important dimensions of politics.

A stronger party ID, by itself, is not enough to account for greater political activism and sharper party images. Other factors, such as higher socioeconomic status, can also promote political activity. The relatively greater involvement of partisans (and, in most years, of Republicans) comes in part from their generally higher socioeconomic status as well as from their more ideological commitment to politics.[38] Even so, party ID has a major impact on people's political activity.

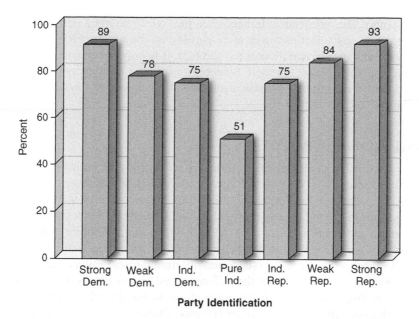

FIGURE 6.6   Percent Seeing Important Differences Between the Parties, 2008.

Note: The question was, "Do you think there are any important differences in what the Republicans and Democrats stand for?"

Source: 2008 American National Election Study, University of Michigan; data made available by the Inter-University Consortium for Political and Social Research.

THE MYTH OF THE INDEPENDENT

It is intriguing that party loyalties govern so much political behavior in a culture that so warmly celebrates the independent voter. There is clearly a disconnect between the American myth of the high-minded independent—the well-informed citizen who is moved by issues and candidates, not parties—and the reality of widespread partisanship. The problem is with the myth.

Attitudinal Independents

The definition of "independent" used so far in this chapter is someone who tells a poll taker that he or she does not identify with a political party. Studies show that these independents tend to split their tickets more often than other voters do and wait longer in the campaign to decide how to vote. In those ways, they would seem to fit the myth of the thoughtful, deliberative citizen. But they fall short of the mythical picture of the independent in most other ways. They are less well informed than party identifiers are, less concerned about specific elections, and less likely to vote. In 2008, as you saw in Table 6.1, independents stayed home from the polls at a higher rate than did party identifiers and scored lower than partisans on virtually every other indicator of political involvement.

Within this group, it is important to distinguish between independents who say they feel closer to one of the two parties (independent leaners) and those who do not ("pure" independents). The independent leaners often turn out to be more politically involved (see Table 6.1) and sometimes even more partisan in voting (especially for president) than weak partisans are (see Figures 6.4 and 6.5). It is only in comparison with strong partisans that these leaners fall short. By contrast, the pure independents typically have the most dismal record; they are less involved and less informed, on average, than are other American citizens.[39]

Behavioral Independents

We can also define independents in terms of their behavior. In his final work, the unparalleled researcher V. O. Key, Jr. explored various definitions of political independence.[40] Concerned about the picture of the American voter that was emerging from research in the 1950s and 1960s, showing an electorate much more driven by deeply ingrained party loyalties than by an understanding of major political issues, Key looked for evidence of rational behavior among voters. He focused in particular on "party switchers"—those who supported different parties in two consecutive presidential elections—rather than on the self-described independents. In practice, party switchers as discussed by Key came much closer to the flattering myth of the independent than did the self-styled independents. These party switchers, Key found, expressed at least as much political interest as did the "stand-patters" (those who voted for the same party in both elections). Above all, the switchers showed an issue-related rationality that fit the mythical picture of the independent. They agreed on policy issues with the stand-patters toward whose party they had shifted, and they disagreed with the policies of the party from which they had defected.

It is the attitudinal independents, however—those who call themselves independents, rather than those who switch parties—who are the subject of the most study. Researchers conclude that they have always been a diverse group containing some who resemble the image of the sophisticated independent but also many of the least involved and informed voters in American politics.[41] The myth that they are a carefully informed and active group of voters who operate above the party fray has withered under the glare of survey research.

Are Independents a Likely Source of Support for Third-Party Candidates?

Even if the attitudinal independents don't know or do much about politics, they still could play an important role in elections. Because they have the weakest ties to the two major parties, they could be more open to the charms of third-party and independent candidates than other citizens are.[42] That has happened on occasion. One of the biggest stories of the 1992 presidential election was the unprecedented showing of independent candidate Ross Perot. A very rich man, Perot spent millions on a campaign criticizing the two major parties as irresponsible and corrupt. Unlike most independents, Perot flourished rather than faded as the campaign came to an end. He finished with almost 20 million votes, 19 percent of those cast.

On Election Day, Perot did draw many of his votes from self-identified independents and to a lesser extent from independent leaners.[43] Fully 37 percent of pure independents said they voted for Perot, compared with only 4 percent of strong Democrats and 11 percent of strong Republicans. The same was true of Perot's third-party candidacy in 1996, although the percentages decreased by more than half. In the end, however, there were not enough independents and disgruntled partisans to make a majority for Perot. It would be difficult for any independent or third-party candidate to construct a winning coalition from a group as diverse as independent voters, who have little in common other than their dislike of the major parties. Such a candidate can serve as a "spoiler," however. Ralph Nader got enough votes as the Green Parties candidate in 2000, most of them from independents, to give the election to Bush. In the close party competition that has characterized recent elections, even a small percentage of voters has the power to determine the winner. It is a sobering thought that when an election is close, independent voters with the least interest and information about the candidates may be the ones who tip the balance.

CHANGE IN THE IMPACT OF PARTY ID

Party ID, then, is a psychological commitment that is often strong enough to guide other political beliefs and behavior. Strong partisans tend to see issues and candidates through "party-tinted" glasses. They are more likely to vote for their party's candidates and to be politically active than other citizens are. As a result, party ID is a significant force in American politics. Yet partisanship functions in a very different context now than it did a century ago.

A More Candidate-Centered Politics

Although the great majority of Americans still hold a party ID or "lean toward" the Democrats or the Republicans, the parties have faced major challenges to their influence on citizens. Early in the 1900s, states began adopting the direct primary, in which voters had to choose candidates without the useful guidance of a party label. Partisanship remains a helpful shortcut in general elections but does not distinguish one candidate from another in a party's primary. New campaign and fund-raising technologies developed that were harder for party organizations to monopolize. Candidates with enough money could use television, direct mail, and other media to reach voters directly, over the parties' heads.

During the turbulent years of the 1960s and 1970s, as we have seen, the number of self-identified independents grew, and the impact of party ID on people's voting choices declined. Candidates found it helpful to downplay their party label, running instead as individual entrepreneurs. Now, even though party loyalties have regained much of their influence, candidates still tend to downplay their partisanship as a means of attracting voter support. In addition, other elements of American politics—new and "legacy" media, organized interests, campaign consultants, candidates' characteristics, issues, and current events—have important effects on campaigns. The consequence is that elections have become less party centered and more candidate centered (see Chapter 11).[44]

The weakness of candidate-centered elections is that they make it more difficult for voters to hold government responsible. Voters may be able to hold a single candidate accountable for his or her campaign promises, but given that a typical election may include several dozen sets of candidates, it is very difficult for most busy citizens to gather the information necessary to evaluate each candidate as an individual. When elections focus on individual candidates, rather than on teams of candidates in which each team stands for an identifiable, if broad, policy orientation, elections may ask more of voters than they are willing to give.

The Continuing Significance of Party

Yet party ID remains a powerful force in American politics. Voters continue to perceive candidates, issues, and elections in partisan terms and often vote accordingly. There was a remarkably high level of party voting in the 2006 and 2008 elections—in 2006, 93 percent of Democratic identifiers supported the Democratic candidate for Congress and 91 percent of Republicans voted for the Republican,[45] and in 2008, 89 percent of Democrats voted for Obama and 90 percent of Republican partisans cast ballots for McCain.[46] Both elections mobilized strong partisans to an exceptional degree. These elections show that party-dominated contests are still very possible, even in the candidate-centered political world of the early 2000s. Will this continue, or will the instability of modern politics eat away at one or both parties' bases of support? The story continues in the next chapter, where we look more closely at the two major parties' supporting coalitions and their changes over time.

CHAPTER 7

Party Coalitions and Party Change

California governor Arnold Schwarzenegger has a mixed marriage, politically speaking. Schwarzenegger, a wealthy white man, has owned several businesses. His father was a military officer. The governor's wife, Maria Shriver, is a journalist and comes from a large Catholic family of lawyers and activists for nonprofit groups. Using just the information in this description, would you be able to tell which member of this couple is a Democrat and which is a Republican?

Party identifications are not distributed randomly among Americans. Some social groups lean heavily toward a Republican identification—business executives, Mormons, and "born-again" white Protestants, for example—and other groups—such as single mothers, African Americans, and many highly educated professionals—are more likely to consider themselves Democrats. Without any knowledge of their voting history, then, and purely on the basis of their links with certain social groups, we could predict (accurately) that Schwarzenegger is the Republican and Shriver is the Democrat.

The types of people who support a party make up what is called the party's *coalition*—the social, economic, or other groups most inclined to favor that party's candidates through good times and bad. Groups may align with a party for many reasons, but once a group has become associated with a party's coalition, its interests are very likely to affect the stands the party takes on at least some issues and the strategies it follows in campaigns.

The differences between the two parties' coalitions at a particular time are a helpful clue as to which issues dominate the nation's politics at that time. The facts that African Americans have identified overwhelmingly as Democrats in recent decades, for example, and that southern whites are now dominantly Republican remind us that racial issues continue to be powerful in American elections.[1] At various points in U.S. history, regional conflicts, ethnic and religious divisions, disputes between agriculture and industry, and differences in social class have also helped form the basis for differences between the two parties' coalitions, as they have in other Western democracies. Changes in these party coalitions, then, are closely entwined with the national political agenda. Although there are other important sources of change in the party system—for instance, times when the weaker party has gained majority support among voters,[2] and organizational changes producing "service parties" that aid candidates rather than run campaigns themselves[3] (see Chapters 3 and 4)—party researchers have lavished the most attention on coalitional changes. In much of this literature, great and enduring changes in the parties' coalitions have been called *party realignments*.[4] The concept of realignment is a controversial one, as you'll see later in the chapter. But no matter how we conceptualize them, changes in patterns of group support for the Democrats and the Republicans make a fascinating story and have made a major difference in American politics and policies over time.

In this chapter, then, we will look at party change with special attention to the parties' supporting coalitions. We'll examine the development and nature of the parties' current coalitions: from what religions, regions, educational backgrounds, occupations, and other social groups do these supporters come, and what attracts them to one party rather than the other. Finally, we will consider how best to characterize the changes in the parties' coalitions since the New Deal.

THE AMERICAN PARTY SYSTEMS

Many analysts agree that the United States has experienced at least six different electoral eras or *party systems*. Although some common themes run through all of these eras, each has had a distinctive pattern of group support for the parties. Each party system can also be distinguished by the kinds of issue concerns that dominated it and the types of public policies that the government put into effect. (See Table 7.1 for a summary of each party system.) In Chapter 1, we looked at party history to learn about the interrelationships among the three parts of the party. Now let us get a different take on these events, from the perspective of changes in social group support for the parties.

The First Party System

The initial American party system (from about 1801–1828)[5] emerged out of a serious conflict between opposing groups in George Washington's administration: How much power should the national government exercise relative to that of the states? As Chapter 1 noted, the Federalists, led by Alexander Hamilton, wanted a strong national government that would collaborate closely with business and industry to build the nation's economy. A national bank would centralize the states' banking systems. This plan would benefit business owners and wealthier citizens, who were concentrated in New England; these groups became the core support for the Federalists.

Small farmers and the less well-off, living in the southern and mid-Atlantic states, could see that the Federalists' proposals would hurt them financially; small farmers would pay taxes but businesses and speculators would reap more of the benefits. So they supported Thomas Jefferson and James Madison's demand for states' rights, limits on the national government's power, and a more egalitarian vision of the new democracy. The Jeffersonians won the debate; in the hotly contested 1800 election, these Democratic-Republicans, as they came to be called, gained the presidency. The Federalists slowly slipped into a fatal decline, and the supporters of Jefferson and Madison then enjoyed more than two decades of almost unchallenged dominance.

TABLE 7.1 Years of Partisan Control of Congress and the Presidency, 1801–2010

	House		Senate		President	
First party system	D-R	Opp.	D-R	Opp.	D-R	Opp.
(1801–1828)	26	2	26	2	28	0
Second party system	Dem.	Opp.	Dem.	Opp.	Dem.	Opp.
(1829–1860)	24	8	28	4	24	8
Third party system	Dem.	Rep.	Dem.	Rep.	Dem.	Rep.
(1861–1876)	2	14	0	16	0	16
(1877–1896)	14	6	4	16	8	12
Fourth party system						
(1897–1932)	10	26	6	30	8	28
Fifth party system						
(1933–1968)	32	4	32	4	28	8
Sixth party system						
(1969–1980)	12	0	12	0	4	8
(1981–2010)	18	12	13	17	10	20
(1969–2010)	30	12	25	17	14	28

Note: Entries for the first party system are Democratic-Republicans and their opponents; for the second party system, Democrats and their opponents (first Whigs and then Republicans); and for subsequent party systems, Democrats and Republicans. In 2001, Republicans were in the majority in the Senate for the first five months and Democrats for the last seven, so the Senate is counted as being under Democratic control.

The Second Party System

The next party system (from approximately 1829–1860) developed when the one-party rule of the Democratic-Republicans could not contain all the conflicts generated by a rapidly changing nation. The party split into two factions on the major issues of the period: not just the national government's economic powers, but also how the Union should expand and, increasingly, how to handle the explosive question of slavery. One faction continued the Jeffersonian tradition of opposition to a strong national government; it included the small farmers of the South and the western frontier, as well as the addition of urban workers and their political bosses. Led by Andrew Jackson, it would later call itself the Democratic Party or, at times, "the Democracy." The other, a more elitist and eastern faction represented by John Quincy Adams, referred to itself as the National Republicans and was eventually absorbed into the Whig Party.[6]

This second party system was just as class based as the first; wealthier voters supported the Whigs and the less privileged identified as Democrats. The Democrats dominated, growing as the franchise was extended to more and more Americans and the party system became more mass-based. Democratic rule was interrupted only twice, both times by the election of Whig war heroes to the presidency. As the issues of this period grew more disruptive, however, several minor parties developed and the Whigs began to fracture, especially over the issue of slavery.

The Third Party System

One of these new parties, an antislavery party called the Republicans, quickly gained support. Founded in 1854, it replaced the seriously divided Whigs within two years as the main opposition to the Democrats. Its rapid rise signaled the end of the second party system. The bitter conflict of the Civil War ensured that the new third party system (1861–1896) would have the most clearly defined coalitions of any party system before or since. War and Reconstruction divided the nation roughly along geographic lines: The South became a Democratic bastion after white southerners were permitted to return to the polls in 1876, and the Northeast and Midwest remained a reliable base for Republicans.[7]

The sectional division was so clear that the Democratic Party's only strongholds in the North were in the cities controlled by Democratic machines (e.g., New York City's Tammany Hall) and areas settled by southerners (such as Kentucky, Missouri, and the southern portions of Ohio, Indiana, and Illinois). In the South, GOP support came only from blacks (in response to Republican President Abraham Lincoln's freeing of the slaves) and people from mountain areas originally opposed to the southern states' secession. By 1876, there was close party competition in presidential voting and in the House of Representatives as these sectional monopolies offset one another. Competition was so intense that this period contained two of the four elections in American history in which the winner of the popular vote for President lost the vote in the Electoral College.

American industries were growing rapidly during this time, especially in the Northeast and then in the Midwest. Because the Republicans dominated the areas where these new businesses were expanding, the GOP leadership, which had long been identified with "moral Puritanism and emerging industrial capitalism,"[8] worked to support the new industries with protective tariffs (taxes) on imported goods, a railroad system that could haul products from coast to coast, efforts to develop the frontier, and high taxes to pay for these programs. In contrast, the Democrats represented groups that had been passed over by economic expansion and who were deeply suspicious of capitalism, such as farmers and the working class, as well as the white South. Economic issues, and especially attitudes toward the growth of huge industrial monopolies, were thus closely linked with the regional divisions between the parties.

The Fourth Party System

The imprint of the Civil War continued to shape southern politics for the next century. However, the Civil War party system soon began to fade elsewhere, under the weight of farm and rural protest and the economic panic of 1893. Tensions within the Democratic Party between poor whites and the more conservative party leaders erupted into a fight over the party's leadership in the 1890s. The less wealthy, more egalitarian wing won, nominated populist William Jennings Bryan as the Democratic presidential candidate in 1896, and reformed the party's issue stances. Bryan lost, however, and Republicans began a long domination of American national politics, disrupted only by their own internal split in 1912.

ximately 1897 to 1932) again reflected both
the eastern business community, which was
id southern rural "periphery," with the South
hern Democrats, out from under the heavy
itute racially discriminatory laws and to keep
'he waves of immigrants into the large cities
igh Catholic immigrants, especially from
iocratic Party.

) and the subsequent election of Democrat
..... produced the fifth, or New Deal, party system. During the 1930s, as a
means of pulling the nation out of economic ruin, Roosevelt pushed Congress to enact several large-scale welfare state programs. These Roosevelt "New Deal" programs—Social
Security, wages and hours laws, and protection for labor unions—again strengthened the
Democrats' image as the party of the disadvantaged. Even groups such as blacks, long
allied with the Republicans, were lured to the Democratic banner; socioeconomic needs
were powerful enough to keep both blacks and southern whites as wary allies in the
Roosevelt coalition. So by 1936, the new Democratic majority party had become a grand
New Deal coalition of the less privileged minorities—lower- income people, industrial
workers (especially union members), poor farmers, Catholics, Jews, blacks—plus the
South, where the Democratic loyalty imprinted by the Civil War had become all but
genetic. The costs of the New Deal and the impact of its programs heightened the stakes of
the conflict between higher- and lower-income groups and between business and labor.

It is clear from this brief tour of party history that the effects of socioeconomic,
racial, and regional divisions have waxed and waned, but all have played a major role in
shaping the parties' coalitions over time. What is the nature of the two parties' coalitions today?

THE SOCIAL BASES OF PARTY COALITIONS

Socioeconomic Status Divisions

Most democratic party systems reflect divisions along social class lines, even if those
divisions may have softened over the years.[9] James Madison, one of the most perceptive
observers of human nature among the nation's founders, wrote in the *Federalist Papers*
that economic differences are the most common source of factions.[10] The footprints of
socioeconomic status (SES) conflict are scattered throughout American history. Social
and economic status differences underlay the battle between the wealthy, aristocratic
Federalists and the less privileged Democratic-Republicans. These differences were
even sharper between the Jacksonian Democrats and the Whigs a few decades later, and
again during the fourth and fifth party systems. The connection between SES and partisanship weakened during the 1960s and 1970s but strengthened again beginning with
the Reagan years in the 1980s.

SES is still clearly related to people's partisanship, as you can see in Table 7.2.
Read across the top row of section A, for instance. You will find that among survey

TABLE 7.2 Social Characteristics and Party Identification, 2008

	Democrats (%)		Independents (%)			Republicans (%)		Dem. Minus Rep.	Cases
	Strong	Weak	Closer to Dem.	Closer to Neither	Closer to Rep.	Weak	Strong		
A. Income									
Lower third	19%	18	18	14	10	10	10	25	701
Middle third	22%	15	19	10	12	10	12	22	632
Upper third	17%	14	15	10	12	17	16	1	933
B. Education									
No high school diploma	24%	17	22	14	7	7	9	40	261
High school grad	18%	16	17	14	12	10	11	18	704
College	22%	14	14	5	10	18	17	5	581
C. Region									
South	19%	12	15	13	12	12	18	4	974
Nonsouth	19%	18	19	10	11	13	10	22	1292
D. Religion									
Jews	32%	34	15	0	0	11	8	62	30
Catholics	18%	17	16	10	13	13	12	13	411
Protestants	20%	15	13	10	11	15	17	5	1233
White Protestants*	12%	12	12	11	13	19	21	−17	937
E. Race									
Blacks	48%	23	15	8	3	1	1	81	270
Whites	14%	14	16	11	13	15	16	0	1797
F. Gender									
Female	20%	17	18	10	11	12	13	19	1251
Male	18%	13	16	13	12	14	14	7	1016

* The survey did not ask how many of these white Protestants consider themselves to be fundamentalist or "born again."

Note: Totals add up to approximately 100 percent reading across (with slight variations due to rounding). Dem. minus Rep. is the party difference calculated by subtracting the percentage of strong, weak, and leaning Republicans from the percentage of strong, weak, and leaning Democrats. Negative numbers indicate a Republican advantage in the group. The number of cases is weighted to account for the oversample of blacks and Latinos in the survey.

Source: 2008 American National Election Study, University of Michigan; data made available by the Inter-University Consortium for Political and Social Research.

respondents whose incomes are in the lower third, 19 percent call themselves strong Democrats, 18 percent can be termed weak Democrats, and 18 percent lean toward the Democratic Party but, toward the right side of the row, only 10, 10, and 10 percent, respectively, call themselves leaning, weak, or strong Republicans. The next column, titled "Dem. minus Rep.," shows that Democrats (counting strong and weak identifiers and Democratic "leaners") outnumber Republicans by 25 percentage points among these lower-income people.

Those with very limited education are even more likely to call themselves Democrats than lower-income people are (section B). Here, 24 percent of those who didn't finish high school identify as strong Democrats, 17 percent are weak Democrats, and 22 percent are Democratic leaners. On the Republican side of the table, there are only 7 percent Republican leaners, 7 percent weak Republicans, and 9 percent strong Republicans among those who didn't finish high school, for an overall Democratic edge ("Dem. minus Rep.") of 40 percentage points.

Lower-income voters have become more consistently Democratic in the past two decades as income inequality has increased.[11] Several forces help sustain the relationship between lower SES and Democratic partisanship, including the differences between the parties' stands on issues of special concern to lower-income people (such as government-insured health care and social services) and the very high Democratic identification among blacks, who are predominantly lower income.[12] The result is that, especially in congressional elections, Democrats are even more likely to win in lower-income districts now than they were 20 years ago,[13] and in 2008, Barack Obama won a greater percentage of low and lower-middle-income voters (with incomes up to $50,000) than had other recent Democratic presidential candidates.

Table 7.2 also shows that the current relationship between *higher* SES and party differs in some interesting ways from that of the New Deal coalition. As a larger proportion of Americans from a wider variety of backgrounds has attended college, voters with a college degree have become somewhat less Republican. In 2008, exit polls showed that a slight majority of college-educated voters supported Obama, as did an even larger majority of those with advanced degrees. Similarly, upper-income people are no longer as distinctively Republican as they used to be—perhaps because this group now contains a larger proportion of professionals, such as teachers and health care specialists, many of whom are concerned with quality-of-life issues such as the environment and women's rights. The identification of many professionals with the Democratic Party is reflected in the support Democratic candidates receive from teachers' unions and trial lawyers.[14] Consistent with this, in 2008, voters with incomes over $100,000 split their votes between Obama and McCain.

The impact of SES should not be overstated. SES has been less important as a basis for party loyalty in the United States than in many other Western democracies,[15] and even at the height of the New Deal, the SES differences between the parties were less clear than the parties' rhetoric would suggest. Some groups locate themselves in the "wrong" party from an SES point of view; for example, white fundamentalist Protestants have voted Republican in recent years even though their average income is closer to that of the average Democrat than to the average Republican.[16] Because SES divisions between the Republicans and Democrats can be fuzzy, the parties do not usually promote blatantly class-based appeals; they try to attract votes from a variety of social groups.

Sectional (Regional) Divisions

Historically, the greatest rival to SES as an explanation for American party differences has been sectionalism. Different sections of the country have often had differing political interests. When a political party has championed these distinct interests, it has some-times united large numbers of voters who may disagree about other issues.

The most enduring sectionalism in American party history was the one-party Democratic control of the South. Well before the Civil War, white southerners shared an interest in slavery and an agricultural system geared to export markets. The searing expe-rience of that war and the Reconstruction that followed made the South into the "Solid South" and delivered it to the Democrats for most of the next century. The 11 states of the former Confederacy cast all their electoral votes for Democratic presidential candi-dates in every election from 1880 through 1924, except for Tennessee's defection in 1920. Al Smith's Catholicism frightened five of these largely Protestant states into the Republican column in 1928, but the New Deal economic programs brought the South back to the Democratic Party from 1932 through 1944.

As we will see later in the chapter, however, the civil rights movement was the opening wedge in the slow process that separated the South from its Democratic loyal-ties. Even now (Table 7.2, section C), southerners are still slightly more Democratic in their basic partisan leanings than nonsoutherners, thanks largely to the overwhelming Democratic partisanship of southern blacks. But this Democratic edge is much less pro-nounced than it had been until the 1960s, and in voting behavior, southern states are now predominantly Republican.

At times, the party system has also reflected the competition between the East, which used to dominate the nation's economy, and the South and West. In the first years of the American republic, the Federalists held on to an ever-narrowing base of eastern financial interests, while the Democratic-Republicans expanded westward with the new settlers. Jackson aimed his party appeals at the men of the frontier, and the protest movements that thrust William Jennings Bryan into the 1896 campaign sprang from the discontent of the western prairies and the South with eastern bankers and eastern capi-talism. The geographic distribution of the 1896 presidential vote, with the Democrats winning all but three states in the South and West, and losing all the northern and Border States east of the Mississippi River, is a striking example of sectional voting.

More recently, the Mountain West has sometimes acted as a unified bloc in national politics on concerns that these states share, such as protecting western coal deposits and ranchers against federal environmental laws. But as these states become more urban and suburban, there has been some movement back toward the Democrats. Although every mountain state had a Republican governor in 2000, five of the eight had elected Democrats by early 2008, and Colorado had experienced a particularly dramatic swing from Republican to Democratic control. The change in the northeastern states has been even more striking, from moderate Republican to Democratic, as we will see later in this chapter.

Age

Democrats typically have more support among young adults than Republicans do, espe-cially in recent years. Although the Democratic advantage in party ID appears in all age groups, the party now has its greatest advantage among those who are 18–24 years old and among "baby boomers" aged 49–60. Those in between, especially those ages 34–46, trend Democratic by a smaller margin. These age-related trends in party ID reflect both the greater enthusiasm for Democratic candidates and policies among younger people and also the special circumstances of the era in which each age cohort first experienced politics. For the current 34–46-year-olds, that was roughly the time of the Ronald Reagan presidency, when Republican identification was on the rise.[17]

Religion and Religiosity

There have always been religious differences between the American party coalitions, just as there are in many other democracies. In the early days of the New Deal, Catholics and Jews were among the most loyal supporters of the Democratic Party, although Catholic support for Democrats has declined in recent years (Table 7.2, section D).

Some of the relationship between religion and party loyalty is due to the SES differences among religious groups. Yet religious conviction and group identification also seem to be involved. Internationalism and concern for social justice, rooted in the religious and ethnic traditions of Judaism, have disposed many Jews toward the Democratic Party.[18] The long-standing ties of Catholics to the Democratic Party partly reflected the party's greater openness to Catholic political advancement. Most Democratic National Committee chairs during the past century have been Catholics, and the only Catholic presidential nominees of a major party have been Democrats.

Northern white Protestants have trended Republican ever since the party began, but the relationship is complex. Especially in elections since 1992, we have seen a division between mainline Protestant denominations and white evangelicals. Although white evangelical Protestants had split evenly between Democratic and Republican partisanship as recently as the late 1980s, they have moved decisively toward the Republican Party since then. They are now a substantial part of the Republican base; in 2008, for instance, this group comprised almost a quarter of the electorate and 73 percent of them told CNN pollsters that they voted for John McCain.[19] Increasing Republican support among white "born-again" Protestants, especially in the South, reflects the party's pro-life stand, the social conservatism of many Republican leaders, and their emphasis on traditional values.[20]

More generally, voters who consider themselves very religious are now substantially more Republican than Democratic. In fact, the greatest religious difference in voting preferences in recent elections, and one of the best predictors of partisanship more generally, is not the difference between Catholics and Protestants but between those who attend church or other houses of worship at least weekly and those who attend only rarely or not at all.

Race

A century ago, the Republican Party, which was founded to abolish slavery, was associated with racial equality in the minds of both black and white Americans. When the New Deal's social welfare programs began to help lift blacks and other disadvantaged groups out of poverty, however, the partisan direction of racial politics turned 180 degrees. It is now the Democratic Party that is viewed as standing for racial equality. As a result, blacks identify as Democrats in overwhelming numbers today, as they have since at least the 1960s, regardless of their SES, region, or other social characteristics.

Look at the stark contrast in Section E of Table 7.2: Democrats outnumber Republicans by 81 percentage points among blacks, but there is no Democratic advantage among whites. The last Democratic presidential candidate to win a majority of the votes of whites was Lyndon Johnson in 1964. Interestingly, this is true even though blacks tend to be much more conservative than other Democrats on issues such as same-sex marriage and abortion.[21] The vital importance of civil rights to black Americans has outweighed the impact of these other issues, however; there is no closer tie between a social group and a party than that between blacks and the Democrats.

Ethnicity

Latinos, who are now more than one in every seven U.S. residents, have surpassed non-Hispanic blacks as the nation's largest minority group. Although Latinos have long exercised voting strength in states such as New Mexico, California, and Texas, they cast only 9 percent of the votes nationwide in the 2008 election. But because they are the fastest-growing segment of the population, both parties have made serious efforts to attract Latino voter support.

Most Latino voters are Democrats, but their diverse ethnic roots produce a more varied voting pattern than that of blacks. The wealthy Cuban émigrés who settled in Miami after Fidel Castro took power in the 1950s tend to be conservative, strongly anti-Communist, and inclined to vote Republican, whereas the larger Mexican American population in California leans Democratic. In 2004, President Bush's proposal to give temporary legal status to undocumented (largely Mexican and Central American) workers met with some success among Latinos, as did the party's advertising in Spanish-language media. But in elections since then, the economic downturn and the hard-line stand taken by many conservative Republicans against illegal immigrants undermined these Republican gains.[22]

Gender

For more than three decades, women have supported Democrats to a greater extent than men have (see Table 7.2, section F). Similar findings can be seen in 2008 exit polls, where 56 percent of women said they voted for Barack Obama for president and 43 percent voted for Republican John McCain—a 13-percent Democratic margin—compared with a 1-percent Democratic edge among men.[23] Although there has been a leftward shift in women's political preferences in many Western democracies,[24] the gender gap in American politics has shown a somewhat different pattern. During the 1980s and 1990s, both men and women became more Republican, but men did so at a faster pace and to a greater degree.[25] Since then, women have returned to the Democratic Party more quickly than men have.

Why should gender be related to partisanship? Men's and women's attitudes differ on some major issues. On average, women express greater support for social programs and less support for defense spending than men do. These differences correspond with the two parties' issue agendas; the Democratic Party emphasizes health care, education, and other social programs, whereas the Republicans put a priority on tax cuts and military strength. People's attitudes toward gender equality and abortion, in particular, have become more closely correlated with their party identification during the past three decades, and when these and other "women's issues" are stressed by candidates, a gender gap is more likely to appear.[26] The national parties also project some lifestyle differences that may affect men's and women's partisanship. Among members of the U.S. House and Senate first elected in 2008, for instance, all but three of the married Republicans list their spouse as sharing their last name, but more than four in ten Democrats had a spouse with a different or a hyphenated last name.[27]

Black women and single women have become particularly distinctive Democratic constituencies. According to CNN's exit poll in 2008, 70 percent of single women (comprising more than one in five voters) supported Obama, compared with only 47 percent of married women.[28] Single women, especially single mothers, are more economically insecure on average than married women are, and thus could be more likely to see government social programs as an ally.

THE CENTRAL ROLE OF ISSUES IN THE GROUP-PARTY LINKAGE

As this discussion of the gender gap suggests, there is a close relationship between the alignment of social groups with parties and the parties' stands on issues. A group's presence in a party coalition indicates that many of the group's members—white evangelical Christians, for instance—have some shared reactions to major issues and candidates, which have drawn them to one party rather than the other. To keep their support, the party is likely to express solidarity with the group's concerns, to speak its language, and to feature some of the group's leaders in its conventions and campaigns.

This relationship between social groups and parties' stands is dynamic; it can change over time, as a party adapts its stands on issues to pick up new sources of support, or as a group senses that another party is becoming more sensitive to its concerns. Consider, for example, the fact that as recently as 1988, there was no relationship between the abortion issue and party ID; attitudes toward abortion cut across party lines, dividing Democrats from Democrats and Republicans from Republicans.[29] By that time, however, pro-choice activists had gained strength in Democratic ranks and had committed the party to policy stands that left many conservative Democrats, including white evangelical Christians and southerners, feeling alienated from their national party.

Some of these conservatives, many of them pro-life on abortion, saw an opportunity to be heard within the Republican Party and were welcomed as a new source of Republican support. As they became a larger proportion of the voters in Republican primaries, they encouraged their new party's candidates to take stronger and clearer pro-life stands. Over time, Republican Party leaders and activists responded to these new Republican enthusiasts by incorporating stands against abortion, same-sex marriage, and embryonic stem cell research into their platform and faith-based initiatives into their rhetoric.

As a result, abortion has become a partisan issue. As Table 7.3 shows (see section A), more than 60 percent of those who feel that abortion should be the woman's own choice now consider themselves Democrats (strong and weak Democrats and Democratic "leaners"). On the right side of the table, you can see in the "Dem. minus

TABLE 7.3 Issue Attitudes and Party Identification, 2008

	Democrats (%)		Independents (%)			Republicans (%)			
	Strong	Weak	Closer to Dem.	Closer to Neither	Closer to Rep.	Weak	Strong	Dem. Minus Rep.	Cases
A. Abortion									
Own choice	28%	14	21	9	11	11	6	35	410
In between	14%	15	15	12	14	17	14	−1	463
Illegal	12%	14	9	19	12	9	26	−12	145
B. Government spending on services									
More	28%	17	22	11	8	8	5	46	473
Same	16%	14	20	13	14	12	13	11	226
Less	6%	7	7	5	19	26	30	−55	263
C. Government role in providing jobs and a good standard of living									
Gov. help	36%	17	19	10	9	4	5	54	312
In between	23%	15	18	16	12	10	6	28	200
Help self	6%	11	16	10	16	20	21	−24	497
D. Government role in improving position of blacks									
Gov. help	39%	17	22	7	5	6	4	63	409
In between	21%	19	19	11	11	9	9	30	438
Help self	11%	11	14	11	15	18	20	−17	1076
E. Government spending on defense									
Decrease	30%	18	22	9	8	10	4	48	327
Same	14%	16	16	12	11	15	16	4	544
Increase	14%	15	10	10	15	12	25	−13	226
F. Ideological self-identification									
Liberal	40%	24	22	5	3	4	1	78	444
Moderate	16%	18	25	17	12	9	4	34	486
Conservative	7%	6	5	5	17	26	34	−59	716

Note: Totals add up to approximately 100 percent reading across (with slight variations due to rounding). Dem. minus Rep. is the party difference calculated by subtracting the percentage of strong, weak, and leaning Republicans from the percentage of strong, weak, and leaning Democrats. Negative numbers indicate a Republican advantage in the group. The number of cases is weighted to account for the oversample of blacks and Latinos in the survey.

Source: 2008 American National Election Study, University of Michigan; data made available by the Inter-University Consortium for Political and Social Research.

Rep." column that among those who favor abortion rights, Democrats outnumber Republicans by more than two to one, and among those who feel abortion should be illegal, there are 12 percent more Republicans than Democrats. This issue shows a clear evolution in the relationship between the parties' issue stands and their coalitional bases; on other issues, such as attitudes toward labor unions, both parties' stands and coalitions have been quite stable for many decades.

Polarization of the Two Parties' Coalitions on Issues

The data in Table 7.3 show that the two parties in the electorate are impressively polarized in their attitudes toward some major issues. These party differences in attitudes closely track the issue preferences of key groups in the parties' coalitions. Democrats, for instance, are much more favorable than are Republicans (sections B and C) to welfare state programs: maintaining government spending on services and a government role in providing jobs for the unemployed. Blacks, lower-income people, those with only a high school education, and those in blue collar or unskilled jobs—all important groups in the Democratic coalition—are especially likely to favor government provision of these services. The recipients of these services and jobs tend to be lower SES people, whose Democratic leanings can be seen in Table 7.2. Note, however, that factors other than an individual's own SES, such as people's perceptions of how the economy is doing as a whole, can have at least as much impact on their views on these issues.[30]

People also differ markedly by party on issues such as civil rights and defense spending (see Table 7.3, sections D and E). On racial policy, since the 1960s, Democrats have been much more likely to favor a government role in helping minorities than Republicans are. Recall from Table 7.2 the strong tendency for blacks, who are much more likely than whites to support government efforts to integrate schools and fair treatment in jobs, to identify as Democrats. And there is a truly striking party difference between those who call themselves liberals and those who identify themselves as conservatives (Table 7.3, section F). As one pollster puts it, "We have two massive, colliding forces . . . One [the Republican coalition] is rural, Christian, religiously conservative, with guns at home. . . . And we have a second America [the Democratic coalition] that is socially tolerant, pro-choice, secular, living in New England and the Pacific coast, and in affluent suburbs."[31] Party divisions increasingly reflect differences that have been termed "the culture wars."[32]

In short, there is a close and reciprocal relationship between the stands a party takes and the groups that form the party's core support. Parties take positions on issues to maintain the support of the groups in their existing coalition. Sometimes party leaders use issue positions to draw members of other social groups to the party, as both parties are now doing to win the support of Latino voters. At times, it is the group that tries to put its concerns on the party's agenda, as we have seen in the case of the abortion issue. As these newer groups become a larger force within the party coalition, the party's leadership will try to firm up their support with additional commitments on their issues. In recent years, this process has led to a growing division on issues between the two parties' coalitions.

THE DEVELOPMENT OF THE SIXTH PARTY SYSTEM

The alignment of social groups with the parties now differs in some significant ways from that of the New Deal coalition. That should not be surprising; the political environment has changed a lot during the past 70 years. Once World War II brought an end to the Depression in the United States, some groups that had benefited from government assistance under Roosevelt moved up into the growing middle class. In return for this economic gain, however, they found themselves paying higher taxes to support those who still needed the assistance; that led many people to reevaluate the costs and benefits of the welfare state in their own lives. At the same time, the issue of race, which had been held in check by Roosevelt's deft maneuvering, was pushed to the top of both parties' agendas by activists hoping to change their parties' stands.

The party system has changed in other important ways since the New Deal as well. Democratic dominance gave way, at least for a time, to close competition between the parties. The party organizations do not expect to anoint candidates now, run their campaigns, or hand out patronage jobs. Rather, the party organizations work primarily to help fund and support campaigns that are run by candidates and their paid consultants. And the relationship between party ID and election results has changed. Until 1952, the elections of the New Deal party system had usually been *maintaining elections*, in which the presidential candidate of the majority party—the party with the most identifiers—normally won. Since 1952, most national elections have been *deviating elections*—those in which short-term forces such as candidate characteristics or issues are powerful enough to cause the defeat of the majority party's candidate. Racial issues have figured prominently in this change.

Major Changes in the Parties' Supporting Coalitions

Liberal northern Democrats in the late 1940s pressed their party to deliver on the long-delayed promise of civil rights for blacks. When Democratic administrations responded and used federal power to end the racial segregation of schools and public accommodations such as restaurants and hotels, some conservative white southerners felt betrayed by their national party. They found an alternative in 1964 when Republican presidential candidate Barry Goldwater opposed the Civil Rights Act. Goldwater argued that no matter how much Republicans supported civil rights, the party's commitment to smaller government and states' rights precluded the federal government from forcing integration on reluctant state governments.

Soon after, when the Voting Rights Act restored southern blacks' right to vote, their overwhelmingly Democratic voting patterns led the national Democratic Party to become even more liberal on race and related issues. Both national parties, then, had markedly changed their positions on this issue. The Democrats moved from an acceptance of segregation in the South to a commitment to use government as the means to secure rights for black Americans. The Republicans reacted against the big-government programs of the New Deal with a stand in favor of states' rights and small government, even at the cost of the party's traditional pro-civil rights stand.[33]

These changes in the parties' positions on race led to a slow reformation of their constituencies.[34] Table 7.4 shows changes between the 1950s and 2008 in the representation of various groups within the Democratic and Republican Parties in the electorate. Look first at the dramatic changes with regard to race. Blacks were only 6 percent of the Democratic Party in the electorate, on average, between 1952 and 1960; at this time, of course, very few southern blacks were permitted to vote. In the 2000–2008 period, on average, blacks constituted 22 percent of all Democrats, and Latinos, Asian Americans, and Native Americans added another 11 percent, for a total of one-third of Democratic

TABLE 7.4 Change in the Parties' Coalitions, 1952–1960 to 2000–2008

	Democratic Voters (%)		Republican Voters (%)	
	1952–1960	2000–2008	1952–1960	2000–2008
Blacks	6	22	3	2
Latinos, Asian Americans, and Native Americans	1	11	0	9
Southern whites	24	16	8	32
Northern whites	69	51	89	58
Upper income	40	35	46	45
Middle income	30	30	26	30
Lower income	31	35	28	25
Protestant	61	56	83	62
Catholic	31	26	14	27
Jewish	6	4	2	1
Other, no religion	2	14	2	11
Married	82	56	79	71
Unmarried	18	44	21	29

Note: Entries are the proportion of all Democratic or Republican Party identifiers, among those who say they voted, who belong to the group named in the first column.

Source: American National Election Studies data for 1952–1960, calculated by Alan Abramowitz and excerpted with kind permission from Abramowitz, Voice of the People (New York: McGraw-Hill, 2004), p. 87, and for 2000–2008 calculated by Nathaniel Birkhead.

voters. The change was especially profound in the South; by 2000, blacks made up a majority (52 percent) of the Democratic voters in the Deep South states of Alabama, Georgia, Louisiana, Mississippi, and South Carolina.[35]

At the same time, southern whites, who were a quarter of the Democratic partisans in the 1950s, dropped to just 16 percent in the 2000s (and this is probably an exaggeration of Democratic strength in the South, because change in people's party ID often lags behind changes in their voting behavior). Surveys show that in 1956, 87 percent of white southerners called themselves Democrats, but in 2000 only 24 percent did so.[36] The Democratic Party's loss was the Republican Party's gain; southern whites had increased from a mere 8 percent in the 1950s to almost a third of the Republican Party in the electorate in the 2000s. Consistent with the change in the national parties' stands, it was the conservatives among these southern whites—and among other groups as well, including males, married people, and Catholics—who were more likely to move to a Republican identification.

This change was part of a more profound shift in the parties' regional bases. In the mid-1950s, as you can see in the upper part of Figure 7.1, almost half of all Democrats in the U.S. House were southerners. By 2009, the drop in Democratic support among white southerners left the party's House contingent much more regionally balanced. Republicans in the House, on the other hand, have moved from one regional base to another. In 1954, the great majority of Republican House members were from the Midwest and Northeast, and a substantial number of northeastern Republicans were liberals and moderates. Now the Northeast is predominantly Democratic—in fact, in the 2008 elections not a single Republican U.S. House member was elected from New England, for the first time ever—and the Republican House contingent is weighted toward southerners.

Democratic House Seats by Region, 1954 and 2009

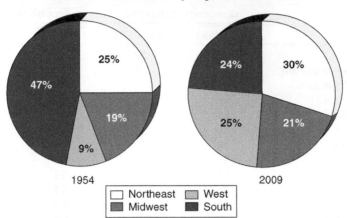

1954   2009

Northeast   West
Midwest   South

Republican House Seats by Region, 1954 and 2009

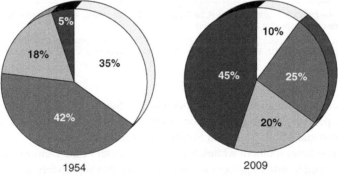

1954   2009

FIGURE 7.1   Democratic and Republican House Seats by Region, 1954 and 2009
Source: CQ Weekly, April 20, 2009.

Another shift has been the interesting income difference between the two parties. As noted above and as Table 7.4 shows, lower-income people are becoming a larger part of the Democratic coalition, whereas middle-income people (but not those with higher incomes) are more prominent among Republicans. And people's income relates differently now to the new issues—those involving religiosity, gender, and sexual identity—that divide the parties. Although SES predicts individuals' positions on economic policies pretty well, that is not the case with people's attitudes toward "values" issues such as stem-cell research.[37]

In sum, the current Democratic Party in the electorate differs from the New Deal coalition in several important ways. Although it continues to include blacks and Latinos, lower-income and less-educated whites, and young people, the Democrats have lost a portion of union members and Catholics and most white southerners. On the other hand, as the box on page 134 shows, the party has gained support among liberals, Northeast and West Coast residents, unmarried people, gays, and those who don't consider themselves religious. Although the Republican coalition is still heavily white, married, and Christian, its Protestant base has shifted from mainline denominations to evangelical churches. Religiously observant whites have become the largest single group of Republican supporters,[38] and the party now has a southern base. Republicans have also gained more support from Catholics, men, rural or exurban people, and those who define themselves as conservatives.

From Democratic Majority to Close Competition

The second major change has been the gradual wearing away of Democratic dominance in party identification. In the 1950s and early 1960s, many more Americans called themselves Democrats than Republicans or independents (see Figure 7.2). The Democratic edge began to erode after 1964, but Republicans were not immediately able to capitalize on the Democrats' losses. In fact, the proportion of Republican identifiers declined from 1964 through the 1970s, Democrats retained control of Congress, and split-ticket voting was fairly common. The proportion of "pure independent" identifiers increased, and there was a steady stream of independent and third-party candidates.[39] These changes in partisanship struck many scholars as resembling a *dealignment*, or a decline in party loyalties.

Yet as we have seen, even as both parties were losing adherents nationally, signs of the coming change were apparent in the South. The movement toward Republican partisanship in southern states began to speed up in the late 1960s. Republican candidates

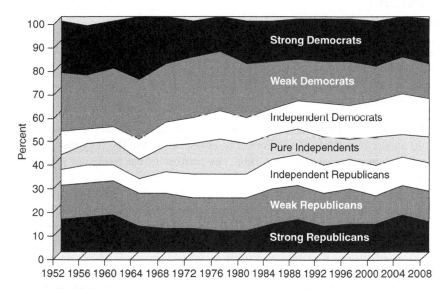

FIGURE 7.2   Change in the Proportions of Democrats, Republicans, and Independents, 1952–2008.

Note: The data for this figure can be found in Table A.2 on page 314. The small percentage of "others" (apoliticals and third-party identifiers) is not included.

Source: American National Election Studies, University of Michigan; data made available by the Inter-University Consortium for Political and Social Research.

THE DEMOCRATIC COALITION IN 2008

Group (% of the Voting Population)	Percent Reporting a Democratic Vote for President
African American (13%)	95
Latino (9%)	67
Jewish (2%)	78
Income under $15,000 (6%)	73
Income under $50,000 (38%)	60
Didn't complete high school (4%)	63
Postgraduate education (17%)	58
Never attend church (16%)	67
Labor union member (12%)	60
Live in an urban area (30%)	63
Unmarried (34%)	65
Unmarried women with kids (6%)	74
Live in Northeast (21%)	59
Gay, lesbian, or bisexual (4%)	70
Age 18–29 (18%)	66
Liberal (22%)	89
Disapprove of U.S. war in Iraq (63%)	90

Source: CNN exit poll, at www.cnn.com/ELECTION/2008/results/polls/#USP00p1 (accessed May 10, 2009).

reaped the fruits. In 1960, there was no Republican candidate on the general election ballot in almost two-thirds of southern U.S. House districts. The only real competition was in the Democratic primary. By 1968, the number of these one-party House races had been cut by half.[40]

The speed of partisan change increased again during the 1980s. Across the nation, for the first time in 50 years, young voters were more likely to call themselves Republicans than Democrats.[41] Two powerful reasons were President Ronald Reagan's popularity and the increased efforts of evangelical Christian groups to promote Republican affiliation. Republicans gained a majority in the U.S. Senate in 1980 that lasted six years, and in 1994, the GOP won control of both houses of Congress for the first time in 40 years. Republicans were now competing effectively with the Democrats in statewide races in the South, and in 1994, there was a Republican majority among the region's Congress members and governors for the first time since Reconstruction. In fact, in recent years, most Republican leaders in the U.S. House and Senate have been southerners. Although this Republican surge weakened after 2005, it clearly left its mark on public policy during the 1990s and early 2000s.

How Can We Characterize These Changes: Realignment, Dealignment, or What?

A number of researchers have argued that these changes can best be called a party realignment—a significant and enduring change in the patterns of group support for the parties, usually (but not always) leading to a new majority party. We have certainly seen the big changes in group support for the parties; the Republican coalition has become more southern, more evangelical, and more conservative, and a Democratic Party that used to draw much of its strength from the white South now depends to a much greater extent on the votes of blacks, liberals, and secularists. These significant shifts have affected the parties' electoral prospects. After the 2004 election, in which President Bush carried almost 85 percent of southern counties, the Democratic Party chair of the sole southern white-majority county in Alabama won by Democrat John Kerry said, "We [Democrats] are out of business in the South."[42]

Even more important, these changes in the parties' coalitions affect their policy stands. A Democratic Party that draws a substantial minority of its followers from among blacks is likely to take different stands from a Democratic Party that depended heavily on conservative white southerners. Southern whites have provided the critical mass for their new party, the Republicans, to adopt more socially conservative positions, not only on civil rights, affirmative action, and racial profiling, but also on health care, abortion, women's rights, aid for inner cities, and support for private schools. Chapter 15 shows these changes in the two parties' platforms. Further, as the policy preferences of blacks, southern whites, and evangelical Christians have become more consistent with their partisanship, each party has become more homogeneous internally, and more distinct from the other party on issues, than had been the case in decades; the Democratic Party's identifiers in 2010 are much more consistently liberal than was the Democratic Party in the electorate in the 1970s, and Republican identifiers are even more homogeneously conservative.

As added support for the realignment perspective, the successes of Republican presidential candidates since 1968, the growth of the GOP in the once-Democratic South, and the Republican takeover of Congress in 1995 are often cited as evidence that the Democrats are no longer the real majority party.[43] The Bush administration tried diligently to create a Republican majority by attracting a larger proportion of Latino, Catholic, and black votes and by working with evangelical preachers to promote voter turnout among conservative Christians.[44] But Democratic congressional and presidential victories have put at least a temporary end to this line of argument. And as Chapter 6 indicated, some analysts suggest that the trend has reversed: that the Democratic majority will continue to expand, because groups that have become the backbone of the Republican Party—in particular, white, married Christians—are declining as a share of the voting population, especially among younger voters.[45]

Problems with the Idea of Realignment

There are both practical and theoretical reasons why other scholars are reluctant to use the *R* word (realignment) to describe these changes. In practical terms, although Republican strength increased until recently, Democrats still hold the edge among party identifiers. And in a theoretical sense, the idea of realignment is difficult to apply with any certainty. How much change has to occur in the parties' coalitions in order to call it a realignment?

As political scientist David Mayhew points out, there are no clear standards for sorting elections into periods of realignment as opposed to nonrealigning periods.[46]

Changes in the partisanship of southern whites and blacks are highly significant. Yet in several ways the parties retain their New Deal character. The Democrats remain the party of the disadvantaged and of minority racial and religious groups, but the minorities have changed; as Catholics have entered the mainstream of economic and political life, they have divided more evenly between the two parties, but the Democrats still represent the majority of lower-income, black, Latino, gay, and nonreligious people. And even if the movement of blacks and white southerners has been dramatic enough to propel the United States into a new party system, when did that system begin? Was it during the 1960s, when southern blacks regained the right to vote and the civil rights movement shook the South? Was it in the 1980s, when southern partisan change accelerated and Ronald Reagan attracted many new voters to the Republicans? Was it in the early 1990s, when Congress finally came under Republican control? Or does it encompass all of these periods in a constantly evolving (so-called "secular") change?

The debate will rage on as to whether the concept of realignment is a valuable tool in understanding change in the party system. Perhaps a more useful approach is to recognize that there are many different kinds of party changes and that we have seen all of them to at least some degree in the past 50 years. The evidence for party organizational change, as presented in Chapters 3 and 4, is convincing. There is little doubt that the Democratic dominance of the New Deal party system gave way to more of a balance in national party strength. And whether we call it a realignment or not, there has been enough change in the two parties' coalitions to produce a palpable shift in campaign and congressional debate. When Democrats call for federally funded embryonic stem cell research and Republicans are opposed, and when Democrats support civil unions for same-sex couples, whereas Republicans agree with the pope on abortion, we know that there is a broader agenda in national politics than simply the economic conflicts of the 1930s and 1940s.

At the beginning of the second decade of the 2000s, then, the American electorate is composed of three groups of roughly comparable size. There is a group of Democrats, including liberals, lower-income people, and minorities, whose size shrunk a bit in recent decades but seems to have recovered. There is a group of Republicans that has expanded and then contracted again, dominated by conservatives, southerners, and churchgoers. And there is a third group that could truly be termed *dealigned*, in that it feels no lasting party loyalties and usually stays out of political activity.[47] Because of the demonstrated ability of both major parties to bounce back from defeat, and because so many Americans consider themselves independent of party, it is also an electorate capable of producing mercurial election results. The trajectory of American politics, then, has the potential for rapid change.

CHAPTER 8

Parties and Voter Turnout

Democrat Barack Obama won most of the votes in New Jersey and Virginia in the 2008 presidential race. A year later, voters in both states elected Republican governors. What caused the party switch? One big reason was voter turnout; many Democrats who were pulled to the polls by Obama in 2008 chose to sit out the 2009 election, and their party's candidates lost. The Democrats and Republicans must not only gain adherents but also bring them to the polls on Election Day and, if possible, discourage those who oppose the party's candidates from turning out to vote.

Parties can do so in three ways. Historically, each party has had to make sure that its likely supporters gained the *right* to vote. The early Democrats, for example, fought to expand voting rights to include renters and other nonproperty owners—groups that would naturally favor Democratic candidates and stances rather than Federalist or Whig ideas. Once its supporters have the right to vote, the party can promote policies that make voting *easier and more accessible* to them (and less accessible to its opponents). Laws governing the ease of voting may seem nonpartisan, but they often have partisan effects in practice. State laws requiring a prospective voter to show a photo ID, for instance, cause controversy because they may increase the burden on some types of people more than on others. (Drivers' licenses are the most common form of photo ID, but people who can't afford a car or who are unable to drive because they are physically disabled—groups that are more likely to support Democratic candidates—will need to exert more effort to get the required photo ID.) Other such laws include requirements that a prospective voter bring proof of citizenship to the polls and decisions by state and local governments to expand the opportunities for casting a ballot, such as early and absentee voting.

Finally, party organizations and their candidates can work actively to bring more of their supporters to the polls in a particular election. This *voter mobilization* has become a key focus in competitive elections. Democrats benefited greatly in 2008 from the rise in blacks' and Latinos' voter turnout relative to 2004 and the slight decline in the voting rate of whites, especially older whites; these turnout shifts were due in part to differences in effectiveness between the two parties' get-out-the-vote (GOTV) efforts. But voter mobilization can be controversial as well. Conservatives accused a community organization called ACORN of using fraudulent practices to mobilize lower-income and minority voters in 2008; ACORN retorted that its activities helped to counteract what it termed "voter suppression" by Republican-related groups.

As we examine these party efforts, we need to consider their impact on American democracy. Voter turnout in the United States is relatively low. Despite the widespread assumption of big turnout increases in 2008, less than 64 percent of eligible voters went to the polls—essentially unchanged from 2004 and well below the turnouts of most other industrialized democracies. Granted, the drop in turnout from the 1970s through the 1990s has ended, at least for the present. But we need to ask why voter turnout in American elections is comparatively low and what responsibility the parties bear for these low turnouts.

ELECTIONS: THE RULES AFFECT THE RESULTS

The rules in politics, as in everything else, are never neutral. Each rule of the electoral process—such as who is eligible to vote or when elections must be held—affects different parties and candidates differently.[1] For example, if polling places close at 6:00 P.M. (as they do in Indiana and Kentucky), so factory and office workers find it hard to get to the polls on time, then the Democratic Party may lose a disproportionate number of votes. If the state makes it easy to vote by mail, then any local party organized enough to distribute mail-in ballots to its supporters will benefit.

Reformers have struggled with the parties to influence the rules governing voting. These battles have generally taken place at the state level, because the Constitution allows the states to decide who is eligible to vote. The national government has acted occasionally, however, most often through constitutional amendments, to keep states from imposing especially offensive restrictions on voting. The story begins with parties' efforts to expand or limit voting rights.

EXPANSION OF THE RIGHT TO VOTE

White male citizens were given the right to vote earlier in the United States than in any other democracy. In the early 1800s, largely due to prompting from supporters of the Democratic-Republicans (who expected to benefit from the change), the states gradually repealed the property, income, and taxpaying qualifications for voting by which they had so severely limited male suffrage.[2] By 1860, no states required property holding, and only four required substantial taxpaying as a condition for voting. About a century later, the Supreme Court, and then the Twenty-fourth Amendment, finally ended even the small poll tax as a requirement for voting.[3]

Women did not win the right to vote in all states until much later. By the mid-1870s, activists had begun to press state governments to let women vote. The Nineteenth Amendment, forbidding states to deny the vote on grounds of gender, was finally ratified in 1920. The most recent change, the constitutional amendment lowering the voting age to 18 for all elections, was ratified by the states in 1971.

The history of black Americans' voting rights is more complex—a story not only of human rights but also of partisanship. Some New England states granted suffrage to blacks before the Civil War. The Fifteenth Amendment, adopted after that war with support from the Republican administration, declared that no state could abridge the right to vote on account of race. (Most blacks supported Republicans, who had championed the emancipation of slaves.) But the federal government soon turned its attention to other matters, and Democratic-run southern states worked effectively to keep blacks from voting, as we will see. By the early 1900s, black turnout in the South had dropped to negligible levels. It remained that way in most southern states until the 1960s, when the Democratic Party, then the majority in Congress, changed its stance on civil rights, and federal authorities began to enforce the Fifteenth Amendment and new voting rights laws on the reluctant states. This change in stance, as Chapter 7 showed, altered the Democratic Party's supporting coalition.

RULES AFFECTING ACCESS TO VOTING RIGHTS

Although the right to vote has been expanded enormously since the early 1800s, states have continued to pass laws governing access to the vote. Many of these regulations were promoted by the Progressive movement in an effort to weaken the political parties in the late 1800s and early 1900s. These restrictions have greatly affected the parties' functioning.

The Secret Ballot

American elections did not always use secret ballots. In the early 1800s, in many areas, voters simply told the election officials which candidates they preferred. Gradually, this "oral vote" was replaced by ballots printed by the parties or candidates. The voter brought the ballot of a particular party to the polling place and put it in the ballot box. The ballots of different parties differed in color and appearance, so observers could tell how an individual had voted. That was how the party "machine" wanted it; if party leaders had done a favor for someone in exchange for a vote, they wanted to be sure they had gotten their money's worth.

To discourage vote buying and to weaken the party machines, Progressives pushed for a new ballot system, which came into widespread use in the 1890s. Called the Australian ballot after the country where it originated, these ballots were printed by the government and marked by the voter in secret. Because the ballot is administered and paid for by the government, this reform involved the government in running elections, which opened the door to government regulation of the parties. It also enabled voters to split their tickets—to vote for the candidates of more than one party on the same ballot.[4]

The Progressives did not succeed in doing away with the *long ballot*, however, in which each state's voters are asked to elect large numbers of state and local officials who would be appointed in other democracies. To cast a meaningful vote on each of 60 or 70 state and local offices, citizens would need to spend a lot of time gathering information, a task most citizens do not find fascinating. That drives down voter turnout. People who do vote may cast ballots for some offices, but not others. This partial voting, called roll-off, is most often seen on minor offices and referenda in which as many as 20 or 30 percent of the voters abstain.[5] The voter fatigue caused by the long ballot leads people to use various shortcuts to make their choices. Party identification is the most common shortcut— an influence the Progressives would clearly have wanted to avoid.

Citizenship

Prior to 1894, at least 12 states permitted noncitizens to vote,[6] although some required the individual to have applied for American citizenship. Since the 1920s, all states have required that voters be U.S. citizens. This is the biggest legal barrier to voting; millions of adults, most of them in California, Florida, Texas, and New York, work and may even pay taxes but cannot vote until they are "naturalized" as citizens, a process that can take years to complete. Given their average income levels and ethnicity, these noncitizen residents would be more likely to vote Democratic than Republican.

Residence

For most of American history, states could require citizens to live in a state and locality for a certain period of time before being allowed to vote there. Southern states had the longest residence requirements (which kept migrant farmworkers from voting). In 1970, Congress limited states' residence requirements to a maximum of 30 days for voting in presidential elections. Since then, almost half of the states have dropped these requirements altogether. Even so, many Americans move frequently, and those who have moved recently are much less likely to vote, in part because they must take the time and initiative to find out where and when they need to register.[7]

Registration

Another major obstacle to voting is the registration requirement—the rule in most states that citizens must register in advance in order to vote in an election. During much of the 1800s, voters needed only to show up on Election Day to cast a ballot, or to be listed on the government's voting roll—the same rules that most European democracies use today. Progressive reformers in the late 1800s urged states to require advance registration in order to limit voter fraud by party bosses. That increased the motivation needed to vote because it doubled the effort involved: one trip to register and a second trip to vote. These registration requirements reduced the high turnout levels of that time.[8]

THE SPECIAL CASE OF VOTING RIGHTS FOR BLACK AMERICANS

Legal barriers to voting were especially effective in denying the vote to southern blacks. The electoral system was manipulated in the South by a variety of laws, capricious election administration, and intimidation and violence when these subtler methods were not effective. The result was that although blacks had been granted the right to vote in the 1860s, they were denied access to the polls in the former Confederacy and some neighboring states for almost a century afterwards.

The Long Struggle for Voting Rights

For years after the end of Reconstruction, southern states and the Supreme Court played a game of constitutional "hide and seek." States would devise a way to disenfranchise blacks, the Court would strike it down as unconstitutional, and the states would find another. One example was the "white primary." Faced with the threat of blacks voting in the Democratic primary, some states declared the party to be a private club open only to whites; therefore, blacks could not vote in the primary. The Republican Party barely existed in the South at this time, so the candidate who won the Democratic primary was assured of winning the general election. It took 21 years of lawsuits and five Supreme Court cases to end this practice.[9]

In addition, most southern states required payment of a poll tax in order to vote—just one or two dollars, but often demanded well before an election, with the stipulation that the taxpayer keep a receipt and present it weeks later at the voting booth. And local election officials in some states used tests to decide who was "literate" enough to vote. These laws were intentionally directed at the poor and uneducated black population.

Southern lawmakers also designed endless delays and other technicalities to prevent blacks from registering to vote (see box on this page). Those who kept trying were often faced with economic reprisal (the loss of a job or a home) and physical violence. It is not surprising, in this relentlessly hostile environment, that only 5 percent of voting-age blacks were registered in the 11 southern states as late as 1940.[10]

Because courts were less able to counter these extra-legal hurdles, reformers turned to Congress and the executive branch. The federal Voting Rights Act of 1965, extended

---

BARRIERS TO BLACK REGISTRATION IN THE SOUTH

In their account of the civil rights movement in the South, Pat Watters and Reese Cleghorn describe how blacks were prevented from registering by simple but effective administrative practices:

Slowdowns were common. Separate tables would be assigned to whites and Negroes [the customary term for African Americans before the mid-1960s]. If a line of Negroes were waiting for the Negro table, a white might go ahead of them, use the empty white table, and leave. In Anniston, Alabama, a report said the white table was larger, and Negroes were not allowed in the room when a white was using it. Another variation was to seat four Negroes at a table, and make three wait until the slowest had finished, while others waited outside in line. These methods were particularly effective when coupled with the one or two day a month registration periods. . . . In one north Florida county, the registrar didn't bother with any of these refinements, and didn't close his office when Negro applicants appeared. He simply sat with his legs stretched out across the doorway. Negroes didn't break through them.

Source: Pat Watters and Reese Cleghorn, *Climbing Jacob's Ladder* (New York: Harcourt Brace Jovanovich, 1967), pp. 122–123.

in 1982 and 2006, authorized the U.S. Justice Department to seek injunctions against anyone who prevented blacks from voting. When the Justice Department could convince a federal court that a "pattern or practice" of discrimination existed in a district, the court could send federal registrars there to register voters. It could also supervise voting procedures in states and counties where less than 50 percent of potential voters had gone to the polls in the most recent presidential election.[11]

This unprecedented federal intervention in state elections, combined with the civil rights movement's efforts to mobilize black voters, enabled the black electorate to grow enormously in the South. By the 1990s, black registration finally reached a level close to that of white southerners (for current figures, see Figure 8.1.) In the process, the conflicts between these new black voters and southern whites ate away at the Democratic Party from within and caused dramatic changes in the two parties' supporting coalitions.

From Voting Rights to Representation

Even after blacks gained voting rights, some states continued trying to dilute the impact of black votes. The federal government responded with a new twist on an old practice. Every ten years, after the U.S. Census, state legislatures must redraw the boundaries of

FIGURE 8.1   Black Voter Registration in the South, 1960 and 2008.
Note: Bars show the number of blacks in the two years who were registered to vote, as a percentage of the voting-age citizen population.
Source: U.S. Census Bureau, at www.census.gov/population/www/socdemo/voting/cps2008.html, Table 4B (accessed July 21, 2009).

congressional and state legislative districts so that these districts remain equal in population size. This ***legislative redistricting***, ordered by the Supreme Court in the 1960s to stop state legislatures from overrepresenting rural areas and underrepresenting bigger cities,[12] has often been used for political gain by resourceful politicians. *Gerrymandering*, or drawing district lines to maximize one's own party's strength and disadvantage the other party, is common and is usually permitted by the courts.[13] For years, in the case of black Americans, it was common for legislators to draw legislative district lines in order to divide black voters among several districts, so as to weaken their voting strength, or to pack black voters into a few districts so that pro-civil rights candidates won these districts by large, wasteful majorities.

After the 1990 census, the first Bush administration pressed southern states to redraw congressional district lines so as to create some districts with a majority of black or Latino voters, called *"majority-minority" districts*. The argument was that these districts would usually elect minority legislators to Congress and thus improve the representation of black Americans. Many of these districts were created by an interesting alliance of black and Latino Democrats with white Republicans, and they did increase the number of congressional seats held by black Americans.

Another effect of these majority–minority districts, however, was to elect more Republicans to Congress from the South—one reason why Republicans supported their creation. Because the districts are fashioned by packing as many (heavily Democratic) black voters into a district as possible, the neighboring districts are left with a higher proportion of whites and Republicans. According to one estimate, "for every overwhelmingly black Democratic district created, there is a good chance of creating two or more districts that are overwhelmingly white and Republican."[14] In turn, Democratic state legislatures try to pack the GOP vote into as few districts as possible, in order to elect more Democratic representatives. A closely divided Supreme Court has rejected the most flagrantly engineered of these majority–minority districts, but has ruled that race can be an element in redrawing district lines, as long as it is not the controlling factor.[15]

Getting Blacks' Votes Counted

Achieving fair representation for black Americans is limited by the fact that between 13 and 17 percent of black males have lost voting rights because they have had felony convictions. Mandatory sentences for drug use appear to target drugs used more often by blacks, and almost all states deny felons the right to vote, at least while they are behind bars. More generally, estimates are that more than 4 million Americans of all races have lost their right to vote because of a felony conviction.[16] Predicting from their SES and race, most of these people would probably vote Democratic. So, although black turnout rates are much higher now than they were in the mid-1900s, more subtle challenges to blacks' voting rights remain.

EFFORTS TO LIBERALIZE VOTING RULES

Concern that registration and the large number of other restrictive rules were holding down voter turnout has led to waves of proposed reforms.[17]

Election Day Registration

North Dakota does not require its citizens to register at all, and nine other states have passed laws to allow citizens to register and vote on the same day, known as *Election Day Registration (EDR)*. These states tend to have higher turnout rates,[18] because citizens can cast a ballot even if they do not get interested enough to take part until the last, most engaging days of the campaign.[19] But in the great majority of states, prospective voters must still take the initiative to find out where and when to register, make the effort to do so, and then register again whenever they move or fail to vote for a number of years. One expert estimated that about 9 million eligible people, many of whom are less educated, lower income, or residentially mobile, tried but were unable to register in time for the 2008 election.[20]

"Motor Voter" Laws

Another effort to ease restrictive registration rules was the so-called *"Motor Voter" law*, passed in 1993, which required the states to let citizens register to vote at driver's license bureaus, by mail, and through agencies that give out federal benefits. Voter registration surged in many areas as a result. Some opponents of "motor voter" feared that it would result in voter fraud or in increased numbers of low-income, Democratic votes on Election Day. Most studies have shown, however, that although stricter registration rules are linked with lower voter turnout, reforms to ease these rules, including "motor voter," do not necessarily increase turnout substantially. Those who register at these alternate sites are less likely to vote than are other registrants.[21]

Early and No-Excuse Absentee Voting

To increase the convenience of voting, two-thirds of the states allowed some form of early voting in person in 2008 or no-excuse absentee voting, in which an individual can request an absentee ballot without having to explain why. In Oregon, all voting is now conducted by mail. As a result, about 30 percent of American voters cast their ballots prior to Election Day—a substantial increase over 2004. Early and no-excuse absentee voting did not seem to expand turnout, however. Rather, it redistributed the votes over a six-week period; voting in some states began as early as late September.

Spreading voting out over a longer period proved to be a boon for local election officials, because it helped identify problems with voting systems (see below), which could then be fixed by Election Day. But it posed challenges for parties and candidates; the traditional plan of building a campaign toward a big finish on Election Day doesn't work very well if large numbers of voters cast their ballots in October. To take advantage of early and no-excuse absentee voting, party organizations must be prepared to explain these new options to their likely supporters and to mobilize early voters. In 2008, many Republican campaigns had difficulty adapting to this rules change. The national party had held very effective GOTV drives on the weekend before several recent elections, but this program did not function as well when so many people voted early. The Obama campaign took account of the change, incorporating a mobilization of early voters into its voter registration activities.

THE VOTER ID CONTROVERSY

These efforts to liberalize the requirements for voter participation have provoked a reaction in several state legislatures, concerned that such reforms as EDR and "motor voter" will promote voter fraud by making it easier for ineligible people to register or for registered voters to cast more than one ballot. To prevent this, some states have recently tightened the rules by requiring people to present certain documents at the polls. That affects people's access to the vote.

Voter ID Laws

Many states have passed or are considering laws requiring voters to show a state or federal government-issued photo ID card at the polls. Proponents, usually Republicans, contend that the laws are needed to limit vote fraud. Democratic opponents argue that vote fraud at the polls is extremely rare and that larger numbers of poor, minority, and disabled people—groups that tend to support Democrats—might lose their chance to vote simply because they are less likely to have driver's licenses and passports. In 2008, the U.S. Supreme Court upheld an Indiana law requiring a government-issued photo ID in order to cast a ballot.[22] Studies show, however, that these rules have often been applied in an arbitrary way; blacks are more likely to have been asked by election officials to show identification than whites are, regardless of the state's voter ID laws.[23]

Proof of Citizenship

Missouri voters in 2008 rejected a proposed state constitutional amendment that would have required all voters to bring documents to the polls (usually, an original birth certificate, naturalization papers, or a passport) proving that they are American citizens. Arizona already requires voters to prove citizenship. Supporters of these laws say they are needed to curb voting by noncitizens. Others claim that, as with voter ID laws, poor and disabled people and minorities have a harder time obtaining the required documents, which require a fee and travel to the relevant government office, and could therefore have their access to the ballot taken away improperly.

State legislatures frequently vote on other bills that would expand or contract the ease with which individuals can vote. These include legislation allowing people to vote at malls and grocery stores, creating more precinct polling places, and sending absentee ballot requests and sample ballots to all registered voters. In general, Democrats have been more likely to favor these changes than Republicans have; it is often assumed (though not necessarily proved) that less-educated and lower-income people, who tend to identify as Democrats, would be more likely to cast a ballot if voting were made less costly in time and effort.

VOTING SYSTEMS: ARE VOTES COUNTED FAIRLY?

Once people have gotten to the polls, most of us assume that their choice of candidates will be registered accurately. At least, we *would* have made that assumption until the aftermath of the 2000 presidential race. Recounts prompted by the closeness of the vote showed that on 1.5 to 2 million ballots (about 2 percent of all those cast), the counting machines found no presidential vote or votes for more than one candidate; these voters' ballots, then, were not counted. Some of these "undervotes" or "overvotes" could have been intentional, but studies showing that these problems occurred much more frequently in some types of voting machines (such as punch-card systems) suggest that the voting system itself may have been the culprit.[24]

In other cases, analysts charged that confusing ballot layout, such as the so-called "butterfly ballot" used in Palm Beach County, Florida, in 2000, led many voters to cast their ballot for a different candidate than they had intended (see Figure 8.2). This was an especially worrisome issue in Florida, which decided the election for President Bush by a margin of only 537 votes. Other problems included malfunctioning voting machines and lines so long that would-be voters gave up and went home.

Why does this happen? Voters cast ballots at almost 700,000 voting machines in 200,000 voting precincts across the nation. The precincts are tended by about 2 million

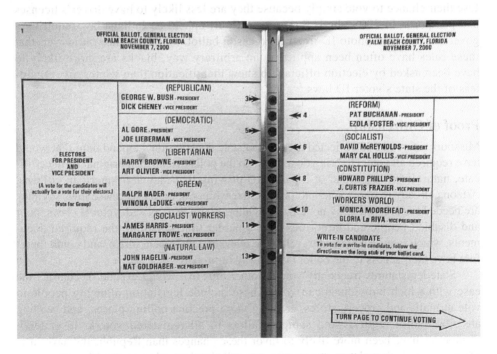

FIGURE 8.2   The Famous Palm Beach, Florida, "Butterfly Ballot."
This ballot format was designed by a Democratic official in Palm Beach County to make it easier for visually challenged older voters to read. As illustrated in this graphic by Daniel Niblock of the South Florida *Sun-Sentinel* (showing the angle at which most voters would have seen the ballot), the problem was that the punch-card holes did not always line up with the candidates' names, so in order to vote for Al Gore, whose name was second on the list of candidates, voters had to punch the *third* hole.
Source: Robert Duyos/South Florida Sun-Sentinel. Reprinted by permission of the *South Florida Sun-Sentinel*. Photograph by Susan Stocker.

poll workers who are typically poorly paid, lightly trained partisan volunteers. Simple human error is as likely to occur in running elections and counting votes as it is in any other large-scale activity. Because elections are decentralized, voters in one state, even in one county, may be treated differently from voters in another.

In particular, counties differ in their ability to pay for the most reliable (and costly) voting systems. The result is that error-prone systems are more likely to be found in poorer and minority-dominated counties, which tend to vote Democratic. The U.S. Commission on Civil Rights reported in 2001 that although it found no evidence of a systematic effort to disenfranchise blacks, they were ten times more likely than whites to have their ballots undercounted or rejected in the 2000 Florida vote because they lived in districts with less reliable voting systems.[25]

In the wake of these revelations, Congress passed the 2002 Help America Vote Act (HAVA) devoting more than $3 billion to help states upgrade their voting systems, set minimum federal standards, and create computerized statewide voter registration rolls. Many counties used the money to buy electronic—touch screen or direct-recording electronic (DRE)—voting machines. In 2006, over 80 percent of all voters used some form of e-voting, more than a third of them for the first time.

That produced new problems. The e-voting systems raised issues familiar to anyone who has used a college computer lab: computer crashes, programming errors, and the possibility of hacking and rigged machines. One Florida newspaper found that voters in counties using touch-screen machines were six times more likely to have their vote go unrecorded as were voters in counties using optical-scan devices, like those often used to grade multiple-choice exams.[26] Another issue was that HAVA granted the right to cast a "provisional" ballot to anyone whose eligibility to vote was challenged by an election official. But Congress set no uniform national standards as to which of these provisional ballots should be counted, which produced concerns about partisan and unequal treatment.

Many counties abandoned these touch-screen machines in time for the 2008 election. Yet problems persisted (see box on page 148). According to one study, 3 million registered voters were prevented from voting in that election due to a variety of administrative failures: their names were accidentally purged from or not recorded on the registration rolls or recorded improperly, or they didn't bring the proper identification to the polls.[27] These are challenging problems to solve; even though accurate and reliable voting systems are vital to a democracy, cash-starved counties and state governments may find it difficult to devote the necessary resources to elections, which take place at most only once or twice a year, when they face daily demands to fund other crucial services, such as law enforcement, garbage collection, road repair, and schools.

THE LOW TURNOUT IN AMERICAN ELECTIONS

These problems with voting systems, as well as efforts by parties to change the rules for casting a vote, take on special importance in light of the relatively low turnout rates in American elections. From the 1970s to 2000, turnout dropped to a degree that generated widespread concern. Only between 51 and 57 percent of voting-age Americans made it to the polls in the presidential elections between 1992 and 2000—low turnouts even by American standards.[28]

DEMOCRACY ON THE CHEAP: IS EVERY VOTE COUNTED?

After almost a decade of concern about voting machines, problems remain:

- In 2008, 22 states (and about a third of all voters) used electronic touch-screen voting machines that provide no paper record of each vote. That means there's no possibility of an independent recount. Screens can freeze, and experts worry that programmers could rig an election. Even machines with paper records, which can be verified by the voter before leaving the machine, can have printer jams.

- Wisconsin used a new statewide database to verify voter registrations in 2008. When names were moved into the database, any voter whose date of birth was not recorded was automatically given the birth date January 1, 1900. According to the database, then, 95,000 of Wisconsin's voters were 108 years old. Six members of the state elections board—all retired judges—ran their registrations through the system; four were incorrectly rejected because of data discrepancies between their registration information and other official records, such as a wrongly listed age or middle initial.

- In at least one precinct in Washington, DC, people waited for hours to vote— not because of the record turnout but because poll workers didn't like the precinct's electronic touch-screen voting machines and had hidden them.

- There has been a big increase in mail-in ballots in recent elections. Anticorruption laws prevent party workers from "helping" voters mark their ballots at the polls, but there is no guarantee that mailed-in ballots will be free from such influence.

As one expert put it, "We'd never tolerate this level of errors with an ATM. The problem is that we continue to do democracy on the cheap."

Sources: Ian Urbina, "High Turnout May Add to Problems at Polling Places," New York Times, November 2, 2008, p. 1; Mary Pat Flaherty, "Thousands Face Mix-Ups in Voter Registrations," Washington Post, October 18, 2008, p. A1; Deborah Hastings, "Pollworkers Can Make Some Strange Decisions," Hoosier Times, February 24, 2008, p. D2.

The political world was different in 2004. Feelings were still raw from the 2000 presidential election; this led to a closely fought 2004 campaign in which a variety of groups mounted feverish GOTV drives. The 2008 presidential election, the first in which a black and a woman candidate were front-runners for a major party nomination, generated at least as much excitement. Many observers expected voter participation to rise dramatically as a result.

There was some good news in both 2004 and 2008 for proponents of high turnouts. In 2004, about 64 percent of eligible voters went to the polls—the highest voting rate in the United States since 1968 (see Figure 8.3).[29] After an all-time-low turnout of 15 percent in the 2006 congressional primaries, the 2008 presidential nomination race produced record-breaking participation in many states' primaries and caucuses. Yet turnout in the 2008 general election was about the same as in 2004.

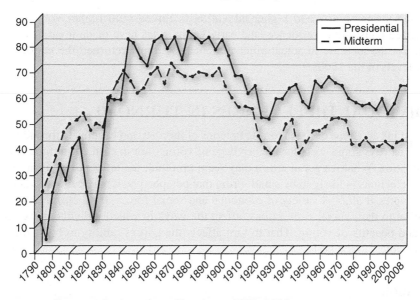

FIGURE 8.3   Turnout in American Elections, 1790–2008.

Note: These are the percentages voting for president and for the office with the highest vote in midterm elections, calculated as described in note 28 to this chapter.

Source: Data are from Walter Dean Burnham, "The Turnout Problem," in A. James Reichley, ed., *Elections American Style* (Washington, DC: Brookings Institution, 1987), pp. 113–114, updated for presidential elections since 1984. Midterm data since 1986 come from Curtis Gans, Director of the Center for the Study of the American Electorate.

Some groups' turnout rates did increase substantially in 2008. Turnout was up by almost five percentage points among blacks (even higher among young blacks) and about three percentage points among Latinos and Asians. Young people's voting rate rose. The turnout increases were selective, however. Among first-time voters, who made up 11 percent of the electorate, 69 percent voted for Obama.[30] And although Democratic turnout went up by 2.6 percentage points, turnout declined by 1.3 percentage points among Republicans and by about one point among whites.

Turnout rates in American elections have been higher at other times, particularly toward the end of the 1800s.[31] In more recent times, presidential turnout reached 65 percent in 1960, and turnout in off-year elections peaked at 49 percent in 1966. But even these percentages are low compared with other countries. In almost no other industrialized democracy does such a small share of the voters take part in choosing the most important government officials. In contrast, voters in nations such as Sweden and Denmark regularly turn out at rates of 80 percent or more, and voter turnout in the 2007 French presidential election reached 85 percent.

WHY DON'T MORE AMERICANS VOTE?

Even taking account of higher turnouts in 2004 and 2008, many observers wonder why voter participation in the United States is not much greater. For several reasons, voting turnout should have risen dramatically since the mid-1900s.[32] Educational levels have increased substantially, and higher education is linked with higher voter turnout. Liberalized registration, residence, and early voting rules have made it easier to cast a ballot. Yet the increase in actual voter turnout has simply returned the nation to the voting levels of the 1960s.

INDIVIDUAL DIFFERENCES IN TURNOUT

We can think about the decision to vote in terms of its costs and benefits to the individual. Each of us pays some costs for the privilege of voting, not in cash but in time, energy, and attention. What we get in return may seem minimal; the influence of a single vote in most elections is likely to be small. From that perspective, it may be remarkable that anyone votes at all.[33] A variety of economic and social forces, from citizens' levels of education to their social connections, affect the ways in which individuals weigh the costs and benefits of voting. That in turn affects the parties' ability to bring different types of voters to the polls.

Education

The biggest difference between voters and nonvoters is their level of education; less-educated Americans, who tend to identify as Democrats, are much less likely to vote[34] (see Figure 8.4, section A). Because of the close relationships between education, income, and job status, poorer people also vote in lower proportions. More education helps people understand the political system and locate the information they need to make political choices. People with more education are more likely to feel that they ought to vote, to gain satisfaction from voting, and to have the experience with meeting deadlines and filling out forms that will be necessary to register and vote.[35]

This relationship between education and voting sounds so obvious that we would expect to see it everywhere. Yet the relationship is weaker in many other democracies, where labor parties and other groups work to bring less-educated and lower-income people to the polls, which compensates for the dampening effect of lower educational levels on voter turnout.[36] And we must still account for the fact that rising educational levels in the United States have not brought even greater voter turnout.

Youth

Although the gap has been shrinking, younger Americans, disproportionately Democratic in their party ID, have long been less likely to go to the polls than are older people (see Figure 8.5). Younger people are no less likely than their elders to take part in other community activities, such as volunteer work.[37] But their political knowledge and interest have lagged behind; their interest in service has not extended to include political service. In a recent survey, the only occupation young people (age 26 and under) rated less attractive than being an elected official was farming.[38]

Analysts thought it would be different in 2004. Surveys showed that young people were paying more attention to the election and were more likely to consider it important than had been the case in 2000. And in fact, turnout among young voters increased; almost 5 million more people under the age of 30 showed up at the polls in 2004. But turnout

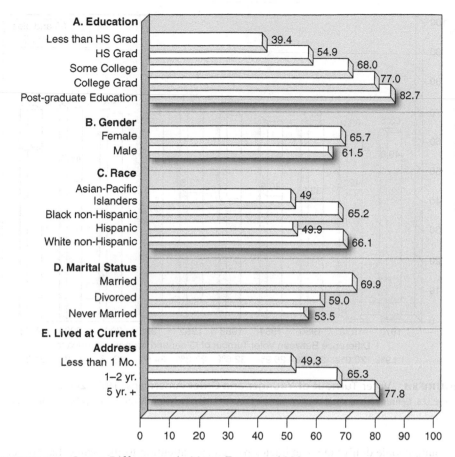

FIGURE 8.4   Group Differences in Voter Turnout, 2008.

Note: Bars show the percentage of each group who reported having voted in the 2008 presidential election, based on the voting-age citizen population.

Source: U.S. Census Bureau data, at www.census.gov/population/www/socdemo/voting/cps2008.html, Tables 6, 10, 11, 15a, and 15b (accessed July 21, 2009).

increased among all other age groups as well, so the proportion of young people going to the polls rose only from 16.4 percent to 18.4 percent of the total.[39] There was a massive increase in the youth vote during the early 2008 primaries, but only about a 2 percent increase in the general election relative to 2004. This increase was notable primarily because the youth vote was much more one-sidedly Democratic in 2008 (a 34 percentage point margin for Barack Obama) than it had been in 2004 (an 8 percentage point margin for Democrat John Kerry).

Why does the lower turnout of young adults matter? There are some interesting differences in attitudes between younger and older generations. Current young adults, on average, are more likely to favor privatizing public services (for instance, letting people invest some of their Social Security taxes in the stock market) than older people are, and also more tolerant of interracial dating and same-sex marriage.[40] When large numbers

FIGURE 8.5 Voter Turnout of Younger and Older Americans, 1972–2008.

Source: U.S. Census Bureau data, at www.census.gov/population/www/socdemo/voting/cps2008.html, Table 5 (accessed July 21, 2009)

of young people don't vote, candidates pay greater attention to the issues that concern those who do vote. Social Security, Medicare, and prescription drugs rank high on the campaign agenda because older people, for whom these issues are important, have higher turnout rates than younger adults do.

Gender and Race

For many decades after getting the right to vote, women voted less often than men, but women's increasing education levels and changes in women's roles have largely eliminated this gender difference (see Figure 8.4, section B). Any remaining racial differences in voting (see Figure 8.4, section C) are due almost entirely to the average differences in education and occupational status between whites and blacks,[41] and these were overcome in 2008 by the great enthusiasm for the Obama candidacy among black voters. Hispanic and Asian Americans have the lowest voter turnout rates.

Social Connectedness

People who have a lot of social ties—those who belong to several organizations and are closely connected with friends and family—are much more likely to vote than others are. Contact with politically knowledgeable people increases that likelihood.[42] These organizations and knowledgeable people probably help to mobilize voters. Voting is also more common among those who are well integrated into the community through home ownership, long-time residence, church attendance, or a job outside the home. Even marriage or the loss of a spouse affects the likelihood that an individual will vote (see Figure 8.4, sections D and E).[43]

Some forms of social connectedness have declined in recent decades. Americans are less inclined to attend religious services now and less likely to be married. These declines may counteract the effects of rising educational levels and liberalized registration rules, by weakening the social networks that stimulate voter participation.

Political Attitudes

Some "civic attitudes" predispose individuals to vote: feelings that government is responsive to citizens (***external political efficacy***) and can be trusted to do what is right (***trust in government***), and a sense of responsibility to take part in elections (***citizen duty***).[44] These civic attitudes have faded in recent decades. Many relatively well informed, well educated young people have become cynical about government and politics. More education and easier access to the vote, then, do not tempt them to become politically involved.[45] And variations in the strength of people's partisanship are also connected with voting; when party ID weakened in the 1970s, turnout declined.[46]

THE IMPACT OF THE CURRENT CAMPAIGN

Declines in civic attitudes and social connectedness help to explain why voter participation has not increased in the United States in tandem with increases in educational levels and liberalized voting rules. Yet turnout does rise in some elections, and party activity has been responsible for some of these increases.

The Excitement of the Election

Voter participation is usually highest in presidential elections and lowest in local races.[47] A main reason is that presidential races are highly publicized and usually exciting. Because of the publicity, people will not have to put much effort into locating information about the candidates, and because of the excitement of the race, they will probably pay more attention to the information they encounter. Both of these conditions reduce the costs of voting and increase its appeal.

Close Competition

Hotly contested races bring voters to the polls; in addition to their excitement, competitive elections give voters more assurance that their vote will matter.[48] The presidential elections of 1992, 2004, and 2008 had the highest turnouts in recent decades. Both 1992 and 2004 were highly competitive. Although the 2008 election was not as close, it was a hard contest for pollsters to predict; throughout the race, analysts wondered whether some voters might be lying to poll takers about their willingness to vote for the first

WHY DIDN'T YOU VOTE?

Here's why people registered to vote said they didn't cast a ballot in 2008:

Too busy	18%
Sick or disabled	15
Not interested	13
Didn't like the candidates	13
Out of town	9
Registration problems (among registered citizens)	6
I forgot	3
Inconvenient polling place	3
Transportation problems	3
Other	18

And here's why others didn't register to vote:

Not interested	39%
Missed the deadline to register	14
Permanent illness or disability	5
Did not know where or how to register	4
Did not meet residency requirement	4
My vote won't make a difference	4
Other	31

Source: U.S. Census Bureau data, at www.census.gov/population/www/socdemo/voting/cps2008.html, Table 12 (accessed July 21, 2009).

black presidential nominee in American history, and thus, whether the outcome would be closer than the polls were forecasting. Turnout rose especially in states that were newly competitive in 2008, such as Virginia, Indiana, and North Carolina, and dropped in some noncompetitive states.[49]

PARTY EFFORTS TO MOBILIZE VOTERS

One of the most important determinants of voter turnout levels is the degree to which the party organizations, as well as campaigns and organized interests, mobilize to get out the vote on Election Day. People go to the polls when somebody encourages them to do so. Person-to-person contact tends to be more effective in increasing turnout than are mail or phone appeals.[50] Personal canvassing is especially useful in mobilizing first-time voters; in 2004, three-fifths of new voters said they came to the polls because "my family or friends encouraged me to vote," compared with only one-fifth of repeat voters.[51]

Face-to-face voter mobilization had become less common in the late 1900s. But during the past decade, a number of groups have developed programs to increase turnout among their supporters. Civil rights groups worked closely with the Democratic Party in the early 2000s to bring more blacks to the polls. Organized labor mounted a major GOTV drive in 2000 and again in 2006, built on union members' contacts with other members and their friends and neighbors. One analyst writes, "Voter mobilization is . . . among the plausible explanations for increasing voter participation levels over the past three presidential elections."[52]

Conventional wisdom says that because nonvoters tend to come from groups usually inclined to vote Democratic, such as lower-income and less-educated people, voter mobilization drives should help Democratic candidates. That is why proposals to make registering and voting easier are often assumed to benefit the Democrats. It explains why organized labor spends so much money and effort on registration and GOTV campaigns. It even explains politicians' belief that rainy weather is Republican weather, in that Republicans will come to the polls anyway.[53]

Conventional wisdom is not always correct, however. As we have seen, close contests, dramatic conflicts, and exciting candidates can bring less involved people to the polls, and these conditions are not always generated by Democratic candidates. In fact, Republican presidential candidates have won most of the large-turnout elections in the past five decades.[54]

Do Party Efforts Diversify the Electorate?

Have these party mobilization drives helped to create an American electorate that more closely reflects the diversity of the American people? Or have they simply increased the representation of those already inclined to vote?

Recall that party organizations hope to mobilize only those voters likely to support their candidates. Yet researchers find that both parties tend to contact higher-income and older people more than they contact less wealthy and younger people, a tendency that has increased in most recent elections.[55] This does not mean that Democrats are misinformed about the voting tendencies of these groups. Rather, it reflects the fact that wealthier and older people are more likely to have stable addresses and phone numbers than are, for instance, highly mobile college students, so party activists can find them more easily. It also stems from the experience of both parties that it is easier to activate those already predisposed to vote than it is to entice previous nonvoters to the polls.

As a result, most voter mobilization drives do relatively little to increase the turnout of groups that have had low voting rates over time. The most recent exception was the 2008 Obama campaign. Its organizers set out to expand the playing field with respect to voter turnout, because many of Obama's most likely supporters were a part of groups with traditionally low turnout. In addition to minority race and ethnic groups, the campaign especially targeted young people who had recently become eligible to vote. Their efforts paid off. One pollster estimated that Obama won the vote of people under age 30 by about 8.3 million votes; Obama's overall margin in the popular vote was about 8 million.[56]

The Obama campaign is trying to maintain these mobilization efforts in the run-up to 2010 and 2012. Obama for America's extensive e-mail list and contact database was turned over to a new organization within the Democratic National Committee called

Organizing for America, which cut its teeth in 2009 on a grassroots campaign to mobilize support for President Obama's proposed budget and policy initiatives.

The Challenge to the Parties

One argument in favor of democracy is the notion that the best decisions are made when the responsibility for decision making is most widely shared. This would seem to be an argument for the widest possible participation in elections (see "Which Would You Choose?" below).[57] Yet we have seen that in current American politics, turnout is lower than in most other democracies; nearly four in ten potential voters do not cast a ballot. Further, the nonvoters are more likely to come from disadvantaged groups: young people, Asian and Latino Americans, those with fewer economic resources and greater need for government help. Groups that have more resources—education, higher incomes, majority status—are those already in the habit of voting.

WHICH WOULD YOU CHOOSE?

WE NEED EVERY VOTE . . .

Democracy is most vibrant when all views are heard. When as many people as possible take part in elections, government is more likely to come up with the creative solutions needed to solve problems.

Politicians pay more attention to the needs of those who vote than to those who don't. So the views and interests of the nonvoters, though real, may go unrepresented.

The most committed voters tend to be older, more educated, and more affluent than other citizens are. These people will get more than their fair share of government benefits and attention from elected officials anxious to get their votes.

It is the alienated and dissatisfied people who stay away from the polls. They can become ripe for extremist appeals. It's better to bring them into the political system where they can voice their concerns in more productive ways.

LET SLEEPING DOGS LIE . . .

Those who are least likely to vote are also the least well informed and the least interested in government. Why should we encourage them to take part in elections? If they don't care enough or know enough to vote, shouldn't we be grateful that they stay home?

If people have the right to vote and choose not to, maybe this means they are satisfied with things as they are. If they really wanted change, they could use their votes to obtain it.

If we relax registration and residence requirements to encourage more people to vote, we're opening the floodgates to vote fraud: people voting more than once or voting under other people's direction.

American democracy has been strong enough to survive impeachments, scandals, and candidates who lose the presidency even though they won the popular vote. If it ain't broke, why fix it?

What responsibility do the parties bear for these low turnouts? Party organizations are among the main sponsors of voter mobilization drives. They have the capacity to recruit large and diverse groups of people into politics. But parties, like individuals and other groups, are self-interested; they want to stimulate turnout only among their likely supporters and to limit turnout by those unlikely to vote for their candidates. And they find it easier to locate and contact people who have already joined the voting population. In practice, then, the parties usually adjust their mobilization strategies to the electorate as it currently exists; they don't often work hard to attract new voting groups, especially the disadvantaged.

The fact that the active electorate in the United States is not as diverse as the nation's population probably reduces the amount of conflict in American politics and the range of political interests to which the parties must respond. Understandably, candidates and elected officials think more about the needs of those who take part in elections than those who don't. For example, studies show that members of Congress direct more federal spending to counties in their district with higher voter turnout than to those with lower turnout.[58] The cost, however, is that in the area of voter participation, the American parties have fallen short of fulfilling their democratic capabilities.

Part Four

PARTIES, NOMINATIONS, AND ELECTIONS

As elections draw near, the distance between the party in government and the other two sectors of the parties—their organizations and their identifiers—shrinks. During campaigns, party activists work to energize party identifiers and bring them to the polls to vote for the party's candidates. The importance of winning elections encourages all three parts of the parties to work together and reconcile their differences—at least until the votes are counted. Elections also link the parties at different levels of government. The process of nominating and electing a presidential candidate binds the state and local parties to the national party, at least for a while, just as a statewide election focuses the energies of local party organizations and leaders within the state.

There is good reason why elections ought to encourage cooperation within the party. When candidates run more capable campaigns, they improve not only their own ability to attract money and other resources but also that of their party organization. When candidates are elected, their party's activists are more likely to see action on their issue agendas. When a party's candidate wins the governorship or the local executive office in some areas, then party leaders may gain access to patronage jobs, which in turn can bring more activists into the party organization. In the effort to win, candidates and party activists have to mobilize as many of the party's identifiers as possible. Because victory holds so many attractions for all three parts of the party, it is a powerful lure for them to work together.

All this cooperation does not come easily. Almost every aspect of the electoral process, and especially the nominating process, can also pit the needs of one part of the party against those of another. Whenever primaries are used to select a party's candidates, there will be times when party voters choose a nominee regarded as a disaster by party leaders. Efforts by the party organization to raise money will compete with candidates' own fund-raising. Candidates choose which issues they will emphasize, which advisers they will hire, and which strategies they will adopt, and these choices will affect the image of the party as a whole, even when the party's leaders and activists do not share these preferences. Once in office, the party's candidates may have reason to ignore or downplay some questions that are "hot button" issues to party activists.

In addition to the competition within each party, the parties also compete on the larger electoral stage with other political organizations. Groups such as single-issue organizations, labor unions, religious lobbies, insurance companies, and other business groups involve themselves in campaigns in order to achieve their political goals. Some of these groups work very aggressively to help candidates get nominated, raise money, influence public opinion, and win elections. Democratic state party leaders, for example, will probably have to compete with environmental groups, women's rights groups, civil rights organizations, pro-choice activists, and unions representing teachers, trial lawyers, and government employees to get the attention of a Democratic candidate for statewide office.

This competition and cooperation is guided by a set of rules, just as the cooperation and competition in a basketball game are. These rules range from laws to standard practices, and, as in basketball, they have a tremendous impact on the results. One of these "rules" is the widespread use of primary elections, which poses a major challenge to party organizations in their effort to control the nomination of candidates. Other influential "rules" include the laws and practices that govern campaign fund-raising.

The first two chapters in this section focus on parties' involvement in nominating candidates. Chapter 9 explores the nomination process in general, and Chapter 10 considers the fascinating and peculiar practices through which the parties select their presidential candidates. In Chapter 11, we turn to the role of parties in general elections, and Chapter 12 discusses money in politics. The constant search for dollars to run campaigns gave rise to extensive reform efforts in the 1970s and the passage of a new campaign finance reform law in 2002. This chapter traces the flow of money into campaigns and considers how it can both expand and contract the influence of parties on their candidates.

CHAPTER 9

How Parties Choose Candidates

In addition to public opinion polls, drive-through restaurants, and other means of democratizing life, Americans invented primary elections. In a primary (more formally known as a *direct primary*), the party electorate chooses which candidates will run for office under the party's label. Then, in a later *general election*, all voters can make the final choice between the two parties' nominees for each office. To American voters neck-deep in primaries during an election season, this may seem like the "normal" way for parties to nominate candidates. But in reality, it isn't. Although the idea of a primary election has spread recently, candidates in most of the rest of the democratic world are still selected by party leaders, activists, or elected officials, not by voters.[1]

These differences in nomination procedures explain a great deal about the contrasts between American party politics and those of other democracies. The shift to primaries forced the American parties to develop a different set of strategies in supporting candidates, contesting elections, and trying to hold elected officials accountable than we would find in nations that do not hold primaries.

The direct primary permeates every level of American politics. The great majority of states use it in all nominations, and the rest use it for most elective offices. It dominates the presidential nominating process (see Chapter 10). Even though it is just the first of two steps in electing public officials, it does the major screening of candidates by reducing the choices to two in most races. The selection of nominees in the primary can affect the party's chance of winning the general election. In areas where one party dominates, the voters' only real choice is made in the primary. What led to the use of this two-step election process? How does it work and how well does it serve the needs of voters, candidates, and parties?

HOW THE NOMINATION PROCESS EVOLVED

For the first 110 years of the American republic, candidates for office were nominated by party caucuses and, later, by party conventions. In both cases, it was the leaders and activists of the party organizations who chose the party's nominees, not the rest of the voting public.

Nominations by Caucus

In the early years, as the parties began to establish local and state organizations, they held local party caucuses to choose candidates for county offices. Caucuses of like-minded partisans in Congress continued to nominate presidential and vice-presidential candidates. Similar caucuses in state legislatures nominated candidates for governor and other statewide offices. These caucuses were generally informal, and there were no procedures for ensuring that all the major figures of the party would take part.[2]

Nominations by Convention

As the push for popular democracy spread, these caucuses came to be seen as an aristocratic elite—"King Caucus"—that ignored public opinion. In 1831, a minor party called the Anti-Masons held a national convention to nominate its presidential candidate, in the hope of getting enough press attention to gain major party status. The Jacksonian Democrats held their own convention in time for the 1832 election. From then on, through the rest of the century, conventions were the main means of nominating presidential candidates. These conventions were composed of delegates chosen by state and local party leaders, often at their own lower-level nominating conventions.

These large and chaotic conventions looked more broadly representative than the caucuses but often were not. Delegates were chosen and the conventions managed by the party leaders. Reformers denounced the convention system as yet another form of boss rule. By the end of the 1800s, the Progressive movement led the drive against conventions. Journalists called "muckrakers" wrote stories about party leaders crushing any outbursts of democracy at national conventions.[3]

Nominations by Direct Primaries

The Progressives proposed a new way to nominate candidates. Instead of giving party leaders the power to choose, they suggested, let the voters select their party's candidates for each office directly. This direct, primary (or first) election reflected the Progressives' core belief: that the best way to cure a democracy's ills was to prescribe larger doses of democracy. Robert M. La Follette, a Progressive leader, argued that in a primary, "The nomination of the party will not be the result of 'compromise' or impulse, or evil design [as he felt it was in a party-run caucus/convention system] . . . but the candidates of the majority, honestly and fairly nominated."[4]

Some southern states had already used primaries at the local level in the years after the Civil War, to legitimize the nominees and settle internal disputes in their one-party Democratic systems. In the first two decades of the twentieth century, all but four other states adopted primaries for at least some of their statewide nominations. This was a time when one party or the other dominated the politics of many states—the most pervasive one-party rule in American history. It might be possible to tolerate the poor choices made by conventions when voters have a real choice in the general election, but when the nominees of the dominant party have no serious competition, those shortcomings were harder to accept. So the Progressives, who fought economic monopoly with antitrust legislation, used the direct primary as their major weapon in battling political monopoly.

Although the primary was designed to democratize the nominating process, many of its supporters hoped that it would go further and cripple the political party itself. They felt that the best way to weaken the parties was to take away the party organization's most important power—the nomination of candidates—and give it instead to party voters. In fact, some states, such as Wisconsin, adopted a definition of the party electorate so broad that it included any voters who chose to vote in the party's primary on Election Day.

Primaries were not the first cause of party weakness in the United States. If party leaders had been strong enough throughout the country when primaries were proposed, then they would have been able to stop the spread of this reform and keep control of the nominations themselves. But primaries did undermine the party organizations' power even further. Elected officials who were nominated by the voters in primaries were unlikely to feel as loyal to the party organization as were officials who owed their nominations to party leaders. Because of the existence of primaries, party leaders in the United States have less control over who will receive the party nomination than in most other democracies. In some states, the reforms required that even the party organization's own leaders be chosen in primaries; the result was that the parties risked losing control over their own internal affairs.

THE CURRENT MIX OF PRIMARIES AND CONVENTIONS

Although conventions are no longer common, they are still used to nominate candidates in a few states and, most notably, in the contest for the presidency. Because states have the legal right to design their own nominating systems, the result is a mixture of primaries and conventions for choosing candidates for state offices.

All 50 states now use primaries to nominate at least some statewide officials, and most states use this method exclusively.[5] In four southern states, the party may choose to hold a convention instead of a primary, but only in Virginia has the convention option been used in recent years, as a means of unifying the party behind a particular candidate. Other states use conventions for some purposes. Iowa requires a convention when no candidate wins at least 35 percent of the primary vote. Three states (Indiana, Michigan, and South Dakota) use primaries for the top statewide offices but choose other nominees in conventions. Seven (Colorado, Connecticut, New Mexico, New York, North Dakota, Rhode Island, and Utah) hold conventions to screen candidates for the primary ballot, though candidates in Connecticut can now bypass the convention by filing a petition signed by 2 percent of party members in the state or district.[6] This variety of choices reminds us that, in spite of the national parties' growing strength, the state and local parties still hold a great deal of independent power.

TYPES OF PRIMARIES

States also differ in the criteria they use to determine who can vote in their primaries. There are three basic forms, although each has many variations.[7] In states with so-called "closed primaries," only voters who have formally declared their affiliation with a party can participate. This makes it easier for party activists and identifiers to keep their party's choice of nominees in their own hands. Voters in states with "open primaries" have more freedom to choose which party's primary they want to vote in. And in a few states, Democratic and Republican candidates for state and local offices have all run on the same primary ballot, so a voter can select some candidates of each party.

Closed Primaries

A slim majority of the states hold *closed primaries*, in which there must be a permanent record of the voter's party affiliation before he or she can vote in that party's primary. In most of these states, voters have to register as a Democrat or a Republican prior to the election.[8] Then they receive the primary ballot of only their own party when they arrive to vote. If they want to vote in the other party's primary, they must formally change their party affiliation on the registration rolls prior to the primary. States with traditionally strong party organizations, such as New York and Pennsylvania, are among those that have been able to keep their primaries closed.

In some other states, whose primaries are often called "semiclosed," voters can change their party registration at the polls, or they can simply declare their party preference at the polling place. They are then given their declared party's ballot and, in a few of these states, are considered to be enrolled in that party. This allows independents and even the other party's identifiers to become "partisans for a day" and vote in a party's primary. From the point of view of the voter, these semiclosed primaries are not very different from an open primary. The difference is important from the party's perspective, however, because in many semiclosed primaries there is a written record of party registration that can then be used by party organizations to target direct mail and other appeals to the people who claim to support them.

Open Primaries

Citizens of most other states can vote in the primary of their choice without having to state publicly which party they favor.[9] In these *open primaries*, voters receive either a consolidated ballot or ballots for every party, and they select the party of their choice in the privacy of the voting booth. They can vote in only one party's primary in a given election. Many of these states have histories of Progressive strength.

Blanket Primaries

The state of Washington adopted the *blanket primary* in 1935. It gives voters even greater freedom. The names of candidates from all parties appear on a single ballot in the primary, just as they do in the general election, so that in contrast to an open primary, a voter can choose a Democrat for one office and a Republican for another. Alaska later adopted the blanket primary as well.

California voters approved an initiative in 1996 to hold a blanket primary. Proponents said it would boost voter participation in the primary, which it did, and encourage the choice of more moderate candidates. Party leaders saw it differently. They claimed that the plan prevented the party's loyal supporters from choosing the candidates who best represented their views. That, they said, violated their First Amendment right to freedom of association and kept the party from offering a clear and consistent message to the voters. In 2000, the U.S. Supreme Court sided with the parties and gave the right to decide who votes in a primary, at least in California, back to the party organization.[10] California then moved to a semiclosed primary. The Alaska Republican Party followed, but Alaska's Democrats and two minor parties have continued using the blanket primary. In 2008, Washington adopted a type of blanket primary called a *"top two" system*, in which the top two vote getters for each office, regardless of party, advance to the general election.

Louisiana has used a version of the "top two," sometimes called a "nonpartisan" primary. As in a "top two" primary, all candidates are listed on the same ballot, no matter what party they belong to. But if one candidate for an office wins more than 50 percent of the votes in the primary, he or she is elected to that office immediately. A runoff between the top two vote getters is held in the general election only if no candidate for the office wins an outright majority in the primary. The state recently switched to a type of closed primary for U.S. House and Senate as well as presidential primaries, but stayed with the nonpartisan primary for state and local races. These shifts occur as state party leaders work to protect their party's interests in the nominating process under changing political conditions.

WHY DOES THE TYPE OF PRIMARY MATTER?

These varieties of primaries represent different answers to a long-standing debate: Is democracy better served by competition between strong and disciplined parties or by a system in which parties have relatively little power? The closed primary reflects the belief that citizens benefit from having clear choices in elections, which can best be provided by unified, strong parties; therefore, it makes sense for a party's candidates to be selected by that party's loyal followers. In contrast, open and blanket primaries are closer to the view that rigid party loyalties can harm a democracy, so candidates should be chosen by all voters, regardless of party.

Most party organizations prefer the closed primary in which voters must register by party before the primary. It pays greater respect to the party's right to select its candidates. Prior party registration also gives the parties a bonus—published lists of their partisans. Further, the closed primary limits the greatest dangers of open and blanket primaries, at least from the perspective of party leaders: crossing over and raiding. Both terms refer to people who vote in the primary of a party that they do not generally support. They differ in the voter's intent. Voters *cross over* in order to take part in a more exciting race or to vote for a more appealing candidate in the other party. *Raiding* is a conscious effort to weaken the other party by voting for its least attractive candidates.

Studies of primary contests in Wisconsin and other states show that crossing over is common in open primaries. Partisans rarely cross over in off-year gubernatorial primaries because that would keep them from having a voice in other state- and local-level party contests. But in a presidential primary, or when only a few offices are on the ballot, both independents and partisans often cross over. In the 2006 Rhode Island Senate race, for example, more Democrats and independents voted in the open Republican primary than Republicans did. These crossover voters often support a different candidate than the party's partisans do. In the Rhode Island race, crossover voting led to a victory for the more moderate Republican candidate, who was closer to the views of the Democrats and independents voting in the Republican contest.

Candidates, then, take the type of primary into account in building their campaign strategies. More moderate candidates for president, and those with a nontraditional appeal or a more independent image, often campaign especially hard in states with open primaries, where they can benefit from the support of crossover voters. They encourage crossovers in these primaries by discussing issues that appeal to the other party's voters.[11] In 2008, Barack Obama beat Hillary Clinton by a larger margin among crossover Republicans and independents than among self-identified Democrats. Thus, he did better in open primaries such as Wisconsin's, where a larger proportion of the votes came from independents and crossovers, than he did in closed primaries (see Figure 9.1). Even in New York, the state Clinton represented in the Senate, Obama was able to hold down her margin of victory because of his support among the small percentage of primary voters who told pollsters that although they were registered Democrats, they actually considered themselves independents.

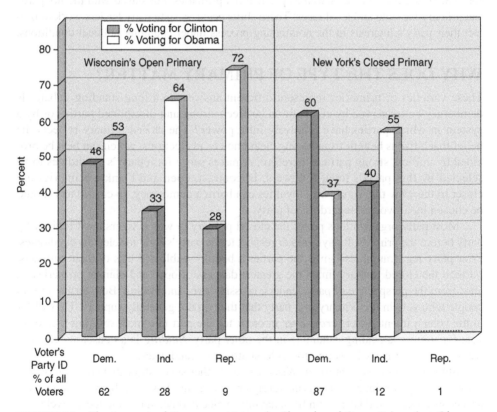

FIGURE 9.1   The Impact of Crossover Voters in Closed and Open Primaries: Obama vs. Clinton, 2008

Note: Bars show the percentage of voters in Wisconsin's open primary and New York's closed primary casting a ballot for Hillary Clinton and Barack Obama, by party identification. The much larger numbers of independent and Republican voters in Wisconsin's open primary gave Obama a big advantage in that state. *Source:* Entrance and exit polls conducted by Edison/Mitofsky for the National Election Pool, at http://projects.washingtonpost.com/2008-presidential-candidates/primaries/exit-polls/topics/party-identification (accessed May 22, 2009).

Organized raiding would be a bigger problem. It is a party leader's nightmare that opponents will make mischief by voting in the party's primary for the least appealing candidate. In fact, some intense voices in both parties encouraged raiding in 2008. Conservative radio personality Rush Limbaugh exhorted conservatives in states with open primaries to vote in the Democratic rather than the Republican primary and to cast their ballot for Clinton, who was then running behind Obama. That, Limbaugh hoped, would drag out the Democrats' nomination battle and weaken them in the general election. Similarly, liberal blogger Markos Moulitsas (founder of the Daily Kos) urged Democrats to request a Republican ballot in Michigan's open primary and vote for Mitt Romney, whose campaign was on its last legs, to force the Republicans into a longer and more expensive struggle. Studies of open primaries have found little evidence of raiding, however. Voters usually cross over to vote their real preferences rather than to weaken the party in whose primary they are participating.[12]

HOW CANDIDATES QUALIFY

States also vary in the ease with which candidates can get their names on the primary ballot and in the support required to win the nomination.

How Do Candidates Get on the Ballot?

In most states, candidates get on the primary ballot by filing a petition. State election laws specify how many signatures the petition has to contain—either a specific number or a percentage of the vote for the office in the past election.[13] States vary a lot in the difficulty of this step. Some have complicated rules requiring lots of signatures, designed to favor party insiders. In some other states, a candidate needs only to appear before the clerk of elections and pay a small fee. A few states even put presidential candidates on the ballot if they are "generally recognized" to be running.

These simple rules have consequences for the parties. The easier it is for candidates to get on the ballot, the more likely it becomes that dissident, or even crackpot, candidates will enter a race and engage the party's preferred candidates in costly primary battles. Sometimes such candidates even win. In states with easy ballot access, citizens can be treated to grudge campaigns, in which people file to oppose the sheriff who arrested them, for instance, or who simply enjoy the thought of wreaking havoc in a primary.

Runoffs: When Too Many Candidates Get on the Ballot

What if the leading candidate in a primary gets less than a majority of the votes? In most states' primaries, a plurality is enough. Almost all the southern and border states, however, hold a runoff between the top two candidates if one candidate does not win at least 50 percent of the vote. During the long period of one-party Democratic rule of the South, Democratic factionalism often produced three, four, or five serious candidates for a single office in a primary. The runoff was used to ensure a majority winner in order to present a unified face to the electorate and to ward off any challenges from blacks and other Republicans.

In recent years, the southern runoff primary has become controversial. Citing instances in which black candidates who received a plurality in the first primary lost to whites in the runoff, recent studies show that runoffs disadvantage minority groups.[14]

WHAT PARTIES DON'T LIKE ABOUT PRIMARIES

The Progressives designed the direct primary to break the party organization's monopoly control of nominations, and, in important respects, it did. In the process, it compromised parties' effectiveness in elections more generally.

Difficulties in Recruiting Candidates

Candidate recruitment has never been an easy job, especially for the minority party. The direct primary makes the challenge even more difficult. If an ambitious candidate can challenge the party favorite in the dominant party's primary, he or she is less likely to consider running for office under the minority party's label. So, some argue, the minority party will find it even harder to recruit good candidates for races that it is not likely to win. Little by little, the majority party becomes the only viable means of exerting political influence and the minority party atrophies.[15]

This argument should not be taken too far. One-party politics declined after primaries became more common. And even in areas dominated by one party, the internal competition promoted by primaries can keep officeholders responsive to their constituents.[16] Nevertheless, the fact that party organizations cannot guarantee the outcome of their own primaries means that they have less to offer the candidates they are trying to recruit.

The Risk of Unattractive Nominees

Normally, only about half as many voters turn out for a primary as for a general election.[17] If this smaller group of primary voters is not representative of those who will vote later, then it may select a weak candidate—one who, because of his or her issue stands or background, may not appeal to the broader turnout in the general election. Imagine the discomfort of Democratic Party leaders in southern California, for instance, when a former official of the Ku Klux Klan captured the Democratic congressional nomination in a multicandidate primary race. In particular, primary voters might be tempted to choose a candidate who is more extreme than the party's supporters as a whole.

Another reason why primary voters might choose a weak candidate is that in a race in which all the candidates are of the same party, voters cannot use their party identification to select candidates, and many voters may not have any other relevant information available. They may choose a candidate because his or her name is familiar or may simply vote for the first name listed on the ballot (see "We Nominated . . . WHO?" on page 169). If the nominations were made by a party convention, it is often argued, convention delegates would know the prospective candidates better, so they would not be prone to these misjudgments.

WE NOMINATED . . . WHO?

When voters choose a party's candidates in a primary election, sometimes the results are puzzling. Voters in the 2002 Missouri primary, for example, selected Allen Hanson as the Republican candidate for state auditor, the office responsible for rooting out waste and abuse in the state budget. Hanson, it turns out, had spent nine months in a Minnesota jail for felony theft and swindling. He defeated Jay Kanzler, the general counsel of highly respected Washington University in St. Louis, who had been endorsed by several Missouri Republican leaders. Kanzler had raised $107,000 for his primary campaign. Hanson raised less than $500 but won about 65 percent of the vote. What was the secret of Hanson's success? Neither candidate was well known to the voters, and Hanson's name was listed first on the ballot. After the primary election, state Republican leaders urged Republican voters not to support this Republican candidate.

A columnist for the *St. Louis Post-Dispatch* warned that this lapse was not the only problem with Missouri elections. Earlier in 2002, one of the state's U.S. senators brought his 13-year-old springer spaniel onto the Senate floor to display the dog's voter registration card as proof that there was vote fraud in St. Louis. The columnist concluded, "They say that people get the kind of government they deserve. This is not a happy thought."

Sources: Quote from Kevin Horrigan, "Missouri Elections: 'Show Me' the Madness," *St. Louis Post-Dispatch*, August 11, 2002, p. B3; and Juliet Eilperin, "Mo. GOP: Felon's Win Is a Fluke," *Washington Post*, August 12, 2002, p. A4.

Divisive Primaries

Primaries can create conflict that may reopen old party wounds or produce new ones. Activists who had campaigned for the losing candidate in a primary may sit out the general election rather than work for their party's nominee. Many Democrats feared that this would happen in 2008 when some supporters of Hillary Clinton, indignant about her loss, refused to back Barack Obama once he won the party's nomination.[18] The charges raised by a candidate's primary opponent are often reused by the opposition in the general election, a source of free campaign help to the other party. If a divisive primary is expensive, it may eat up much of the money the primary winner will need to run an effective campaign in the general election.

A divisive primary could be especially damaging if the losing candidate refuses to take "no" for an answer and runs in the general election anyway, as an independent or minor-party candidate. The sore loser could draw enough support to destroy the chances of his or her primary rival. In 2006, for example, Sen. Joe Lieberman (D-CN) lost a bitter Democratic primary but then filed to run in November under the banner of the newly created Connecticut for Lieberman Party (see page 14). Lieberman was reelected, calling himself an "independent Democrat." In the great majority of states, however, "sore loser" laws and simultaneous filing deadlines prevent primary losers from using this kind of end run to get on the general election ballot.

Despite these concerns, divisive primaries don't always weaken a party. Running in a competitive primary contest might make the winner an even stronger candidate in the general election, as happened in the 2008 Democratic presidential race. And at times, when an incumbent candidate has shown signs of diminishing support due to scandal or change in the district, the national party has encouraged viable challengers. Although that might provoke a divisive primary, it could also increase the chance of a primary winner who can hold the seat for the party in the fall (see box on this page).

The large numbers of safe House seats can increase the incidence of divisive primaries. After the redistricting that followed the 2000 U.S. Census created so many safe congressional seats, several ambitious candidates saw primary elections as their best and least expensive way to win a House seat. That attracted the attention, and the lavish spending, of dozens of national interest groups who wanted to change the ideological orientation of Congress by supporting a challenger who shared their views.

The Democrats are famous for their internal disputes, but we can see just as many divisive primaries in the Republican Party: for instance, when candidates linked to the Christian Right challenge Republicans who are more moderate on social issues.[19] Other groups, including the antitax Club for Growth, have financed primary campaigns as a way to warn other Republicans that they will face a primary opponent if they don't take the strictest possible antitax position.[20] When Sen. Arlen Specter of Pennsylvania

---

A PITCHER BALKS AT HIS PARTY'S EFFORT TO MAKE HIM WALK

Jim Bunning was elected to the Hall of Fame as a major-league pitcher, but he was not as highly honored for his later career in the U.S. Senate. In 2006, *Time* magazine declared him to be one of the five worst senators in the nation. Though he was a Republican in a very Republican state, he eked out a surprisingly narrow reelection victory in 2004. In the run-up to his next race in 2010, Bunning continued to show a penchant for odd remarks and what a colleague called "behavior issues," including a quick temper. Bunning claimed that in his 2004 campaign, his opponent's supporters had sent "little green doctors pounding on my back" to rough him up. He told reporters that his Republican colleague from Kentucky, Senate Minority Leader Mitch McConnell, was a "control freak." Partly as a result, he was not able to raise much campaign money in 2009. The National Republican Senatorial Committee (NRSC) worried that he'd lose reelection—and the party would lose a Republican seat.

Bunning insisted that he would run again. Reporters learned, however, that NRSC officials had met with a possible Republican challenger for the seat. Bunning's Democratic challenger in 2004, Daniel Mongiardo, was also raising money for a rematch, as were other prominent Democrats. An incumbent is usually a good bet for reelection, but Bunning's weaknesses as a candidate led his party to risk a divisive primary in order to have a stronger candidate in the general election. Bunning announced in 2009 that he would retire from the Senate, which reportedly caused jubilation at the NRSC.

Sources: Joseph Gerth, "Bunning: McConnell a 'Control Freak,' *Louisville Courier-Journal*, May 19, 2009, p. 1; Mark Leibovich, "Republicans Look for a Reliever in Kentucky," *New York Times*, March 6, 2009, at www.nytimes.com/2009/03/06/us/06bunning.html (accessed May 22, 2009).

changed his affiliation from Republican to Democratic in 2009, he cited the difficulty of winning a Republican primary against a Club-backed candidate as a major reason.

Problems in Holding Candidates Accountable

When candidates are chosen in primaries rather than by party leaders, the party loses a powerful means of holding its candidates and officeholders accountable for their actions. In England, for example, if an elected official breaks with the party on an important issue, party leaders can usually keep him or her from being renominated. If the party cannot prevent the renomination of a maverick officeholder, then it has no way of enforcing loyalty. That, of course, is just what the Progressives had hoped. Thus, primaries have the following drawbacks:

- Primaries permit the nomination of candidates hostile to the party organization and leadership, opposed to the party's platform, or out of step with the public image that party leaders want to project.
- Primaries create the real possibility that the party's candidates in the general election will be an unbalanced ticket if primary voters select all or most of the candidates from a particular group or region.
- Primaries greatly increase campaign spending. The cost of a contested primary is almost always higher than that of a convention.
- Primaries extend political campaigns, already longer in the United States than in other democracies, to a length that can try many voters' patience.

THE PARTY ORGANIZATION FIGHTS BACK

Parties are clearly aware of the threats posed by primary elections, but they are just as aware that a direct attempt to abolish primaries would fail. So party organizations have developed a range of strategies for trying to limit the damage primaries can cause. The success of these strategies varies; some local parties have been able to dominate primaries effectively, but others have neither the strength nor the will to try.

Persuading Candidates to Run (or Not to Run)

The surest way to control a primary is to make sure that the candidate the party favors has no opponent. Some party organizations try to mediate among prospective candidates or coax an attractive but unwilling candidate to run. If they have a strong organization, they may be able to convince less desirable candidates to stay out of the race, perhaps by threatening to block a candidate's access to campaign money. Even if they have little to offer or withhold, many party leaders have the opportunity to try to influence prospective candidates' decisions; researchers have found that almost 70 percent of nonincumbent state legislative candidates discussed their plans to run with local party leaders before announcing their candidacy.[21]

Endorsing Candidates

Some of the stronger state parties, such as those in Massachusetts and Minnesota, go beyond this informal influence and offer some form of preprimary endorsement to the candidates they prefer. Recall that in several states, at least one of the parties holds a convention to formally endorse candidates for state office. Usually, a candidate who gets a certain percentage of the convention's vote automatically gets his or her name on the primary ballot, though candidates who are not endorsed by the party can still be listed on the ballot in several of these states by filing a petition. Endorsements are sometimes accompanied by campaign money and organizational help. In some other states, including Illinois, Ohio, and Michigan, party leaders may meet informally to endorse some candidates.

Do these endorsements influence voters? The record is mixed. Formal endorsements can often discourage other candidates from challenging the party's choice in the primary and can keep some interest groups from flooding a race with outside money in support of a nonendorsed candidate. Besides, the process of winning a formal endorsement usually involves the candidate in so many face-to-face meetings with party activists that the resulting visibility, and the resources that the endorsing party can provide, can give the endorsed candidate some vote-getting benefits.[22]

On the other hand, since 1980, when there has been competition in the primary, the endorsed candidate has won only about half the time—a big drop compared with the success rate of endorsed candidates in the 1960s and 1970s.[23] Some states have passed laws preventing parties from endorsing candidates in advance of the primary. When the parties are restricted to offering informal endorsements before the primary, their effectiveness is even more limited. These informal endorsements are not listed on the ballot. As a result, only the most politically attentive voters are likely to know that the party is supporting a particular candidate, and they are the ones least in need of the guidance provided by a party endorsement.[24]

Providing Tangible Support

If the party is not able to prevent a challenge to its preferred candidates, then it must fall back on more conventional approaches. It may urge party activists to help the favored candidates circulate their nominating petitions or offer party money and expertise to these candidates. It may publish ads announcing the party's endorsements or print reminder cards that voters can take right into the polling booth. On the day of the primary, the party organization may help to get party voters to the polls.

Although state and local parties vary in their efforts to influence primaries, recruiting candidates is probably the most frequent form of activity. Trying to clear the field for a favored candidate is less common. In most parts of the country, parties are only one of a number of groups encouraging men and women to run for office. Local business, professional, and labor groups; civic associations; ethnic, racial, and religious organizations; and other interest groups and officeholders may also be working to recruit candidates. The party organizations that seem best able to control candidate recruitment are generally those that endorse and support candidates in the primary itself.

CANDIDATES AND VOTERS IN THE PRIMARIES

Two facts help make the primaries more manageable for the parties: often only one candidate runs for each office in a primary and the majority of voters do not vote in them. The party may be responsible for one or both of these situations. There may be no competition in a primary, for example, because of the party's skill in persuading and dissuading potential candidates. The result is that nomination politics can be more easily controlled by aggressive party organizations.

Many Candidates Run Without Competition

All over the United States, large numbers of primary candidates win nominations without a contest. Probably the most important determinant of the competitiveness of a primary is the party's prospects for victory in the general election; candidates rarely fight for the right to face almost certain defeat. Primaries also tend to be less competitive when an incumbent is running (unless the incumbent is already thought to be vulnerable), when parties have made preprimary endorsements, and when the state's rules make it harder to get on the ballot.[25]

The power of incumbency to discourage competition is one of the many ironies of the primary. In an election in which voters cannot rely on the party label to guide their choices, name recognition and media coverage are important influences. Incumbents, of course, are more likely to have these resources than are challengers. To dislodge an incumbent, a challenger will often need large amounts of campaign money, but few challengers can raise large campaign budgets. By weakening party control of nominations through the direct primary, then, Progressive reformers may have unintentionally made it harder to defeat incumbents.

. . . And Voters Are in Short Supply

If competition is scarce in primaries, so are voters. Turnout tends to be especially low in the minority party's primary, in primaries held separately from the state's presidential primary, and in elections in which independents and the other party's identifiers are not allowed to vote.[26] In addition to the lack of competition in many primary contests, the fact that no one is elected in a primary probably depresses turnout; a race for the nomination lacks the drama inherent in a general election that is followed by victorious candidates taking office.

Southern primaries in earlier years were the one great exception to the rule that few people vote in primaries. Because winning the Democratic nomination in a one-party area was tantamount to winning the office itself, competition and turnout in Democratic primaries were relatively high. When the Republican Party became more competitive in the South, however, the Democratic primaries lost their special standing. The result is that participation has declined in southern primaries. Republican primaries are attracting many more voters now because their candidates' prospects in the general election have greatly improved, but the GOP increase has not been large enough to offset the drop in Democratic turnout.[27]

The primary electorate is distinctive in several ways. Many primary voters are strong party identifiers and activists, which makes them more responsive to party endorsements of certain candidates. As would be expected, people who vote in primaries have higher levels of education and political interest than nonvoters do. Until recent years, they were often found to hold more extreme ideological positions than those of other party voters and to be more intense in their ideological commitments,[28] though this bias can be moderated by the use of open primaries.[29] Because primaries usually attract such a small sample of the eligible voters, they can be more easily dominated by well-financed organized interests, such as antitax or antiwar groups, than can general elections.

Primary voters often make unexpected choices. Because primary campaigns tend to get little media coverage, the candidates are often not well known. Thus, the voter's choice in a primary is not as well structured or predictable as that in a general election. Many voting decisions are made right in the polling booth. It is small wonder that parties are rarely confident about primary results and pollsters find it hard to predict them accurately.

THE IMPACT OF THE DIRECT PRIMARY

Americans have had a century of experience with the direct primary. On balance, how has it affected us? Has the primary democratized nominations by taking them out of the hands of party leaders and giving them to voters? Has it weakened the party organizations overall? In short, have the Progressives' hopes been realized?

Has it Made Elections More Democratic?

Many more people vote in primaries than take part in conventions or caucuses; in that sense, the process has been made more democratic. But the democratic promise of primaries is cut short by the number of unopposed candidates and the low levels of voter turnout. If voters are to have meaningful alternatives, then there must be more than one candidate for an office. If the results are to be meaningful, then people must go to the polls.

By its very nature, however, the primary tends to discourage participation. Would-be candidates are put off by the cost of an additional race, the difficulty of getting on the primary ballot, and the need to differentiate themselves from other candidates of their party. The lack of party cues reduces the quantity and quality of voter participation. If widespread competition for office and extensive public participation in the nominating process were goals of the primary's architects, then they would be seriously disappointed.

The direct primary has not fully replaced party leaders in making nominations. Caucuses and conventions are still used, most visibly in presidential nominations, although they are more open than they used to be. And as we have seen, parties can influence the competition in primaries. If only 25 percent of registered voters go to the polls, then 13 percent will be enough to nominate a candidate. Parties count on the fact that a large part of that group will be party loyalists who care about the party leaders' recommendations. Thus, strong party organizations—those able to muster the needed voters, money, activists, and organization—can still have a big influence on the results.

Even so, trying to influence primary elections is very costly and time-consuming, even for strong parties. The large number of elected offices in the United States, from senator to surveyor, forces party organizations to be selective in trying to affect primaries. Parties sometimes stand aside because picking a favorite in the primary might heat up old resentments or produce new ones. Of course, the greatest fear of party leaders is that if they support one candidate in a primary and the other candidate wins, they could lose all influence over the winning officeholder.

In some ways, then, the primary has been a democratizing force. In competitive districts, especially when no incumbent is running, voters have the opportunity for choice envisioned by the reformers. In all districts, the primaries place real limits on the power of party leaders. Parties, even strong ones, can no longer award a nomination to anyone they choose. Research in some other nations shows that in comparison with systems where party leaders select the candidates, primaries can help the weaker party choose a candidate with greater voter appeal.[30] And the primary gives dissenters a chance to take their case to the party's voters, so it offers them a potential veto over the party leaders' preferences.

How Badly has it Harmed the Parties?

On the other hand, is it possible to say that the direct primary has strengthened democracy in the United States if it weakens the political parties? From the risk of divisive primary races to the added campaign funding and voter mobilization that they require, primaries strain party resources and create headaches for party leaders and activists. Even though some state party organizations have been able to maintain some control over their primaries by making preprimary endorsements or holding conventions to nominate some candidates, the bottom line is this: When a party organization cannot choose who will carry the party label into the general election, the party has been deprived of one of its key resources.

The direct primary has redistributed power within the parties. The Progressives' goal was to shift the power to nominate candidates from the party organization to the party in the electorate, but a funny thing happened along the way. Because candidates (especially incumbents) can win the party's nomination even when they defy the party organization, the idea of party "discipline" loses credibility. Just as the direct primary undercuts the ability of the party organization to recruit candidates who share its goals and accept its discipline, it prevents the organization from disciplining partisans who already are in office. The primary, then, empowers the party's candidates and the party in government at the expense of the party organization. This sets the United States apart from many other democracies, in which the party organization has real power over the party in government.

Primaries also contribute to the decentralization of power in the American parties. As long as the candidates can appeal successfully to a majority of local primary voters, they are free from the control of state or national party leaders. In all these ways, the direct primary has gone beyond changing the nominating process; it has helped to reshape the American parties.

Is the Primary Worth the Cost?

How to nominate party candidates has been a controversial question since political parties first appeared in the United States. It raises the fundamental question of what a political party is. Are parties only alliances of officeholders—the party in government? That seemed to be the prevailing definition in the early years when public officials nominated their prospective colleagues in party caucuses. Should the definition be expanded to include the party's activists and leaders? The change from a caucus to a convention system of nominations, in which the party organization played its greatest role, reflects this change in the definition of party.

Should we extend the idea of party well beyond the limits accepted by most other democracies and include the party's supporters in the electorate? If so, which supporters should be included—only those willing to register formally as party loyalists or anyone who wants to vote for a party candidate in a primary election? The answer has evolved over the years toward the most inclusive definition of party. Even though the Supreme Court insists that the parties' freedom of association is vital, the "party," especially in states with an open or blanket primary and, in practice, in semiclosed primary states, has become so permeable that its boundaries are hard to define.

The methods we use to nominate candidates have a far-reaching impact. The Jacksonians promoted the convention system in order to gain control of the party from congressional party leaders. Progressives used their preference for the direct primary as a weapon with which to wrest control of the party and, ultimately, the government from the party organization. Because of the importance of nominations in the political process, those who control the nominations have great influence on the political agenda and, in turn, over who gets what in the political system. The stakes in this debate, as a result, are extremely high.

CHAPTER 10

Choosing
the Presidential
Nominees

The 2008 Democratic nomination race between Hillary Clinton and Barack Obama was one of the closest, most hard-fought, and most expensive that Americans had seen in recent decades. Clinton, a New York senator (and former first lady), and Obama, who represented Illinois in the U.S. Senate, battled one another for more than a year and a half and spent two-thirds of a *billion* dollars in the process. Aiming to become the first female major-party nominee for president, Clinton ran the kind of campaign that would have been expected of a front-runner. Obama, who would be the first black major-party nominee, ran an insurgent effort powered by organizational skill and a close reading of the party's complex nomination rules. As we explore how presidential candidates are nominated, a look at the contrast between these two campaigns will help us understand how the process has changed over time.

Formally, each of the two major parties nominates its candidate for president at the party's national convention, held every four years. In reality, the convention delegates simply ratify the choices that have been made months before the convention, by voters in their states' delegate-selection events (see box on page 178). Most states use primary elections, the benefits and drawbacks of which were explored in the last chapter, for that purpose.

THE MOVE TO PRESIDENTIAL PRIMARIES

It took decades for primaries to become established in the presidential nominating process. Florida passed the first presidential primary law in 1901, and many other states quickly followed. The use of primaries soon faded, however. Advocates may have lost faith in the effectiveness of primaries; opponents probably worked hard to get rid of them and restore party leaders' control over nominations. By 1936, only 14 states were still holding primaries to choose their delegates to the national conventions that select the parties' presidential candidates. That number had hardly changed by 1968.[1]

HOW A PRESIDENTIAL CANDIDATE IS CHOSEN

Step 1: *Assessing Their Chances.* Many people who think they might have public support—governors, senators, House members, people well known in another field—consider running for president. They take private polls to see how much backing they would have and how they are viewed by the public. To assess their chances of getting the resources they'd need, they contact fund-raisers and potential donors and try to get well-respected consultants to commit to their candidacy. They visit states with early primaries and caucuses to gain support from local officials.

Timing: Typically, several years before the presidential election.

Step 2: *Entering the Race.* Those who feel they have a good chance—and some who don't—set up exploratory committees to raise money for advertising and to fund their increasingly frequent trips to Iowa, New Hampshire, and other states with early delegate-selection events. Then they formally declare their candidacy and work to get on every state ballot.

Timing: Typically, at least two years before the presidential election.

Step 3: *Primaries and Caucuses.* Voters cast a ballot in their states for the candidate they want their party to nominate for president. Most states hold primary elections for this purpose; the rest use participatory caucuses and state conventions. Delegates are chosen to represent each state and to vote in the party's national convention for the candidates selected by the state's voters.

Timing: Between early January and early June of each presidential election year.

Step 4: *National Nominating Conventions.* The delegates vote in their party's convention to ratify the choice of presidential candidate made by the voters in the nominating season (Step 3) and the candidate's choice of a vice-presidential nominee and to adopt a party platform.

Timing: By tradition, the party that does not currently hold the presidency holds its convention first, normally in August; the other party's convention is held soon after.

Step 5: *General Election.* The two major parties' candidates run against one another.

Timing: From the conventions until the first Tuesday after the first Monday in November.

In most states, then, state and local party leaders regained the power to choose delegates to the national conventions. The selection was usually done in a series of party-controlled meetings, called caucuses, beginning at the local level and culminating in statewide party conventions. Even in many states that held primaries, voters could take part in only a "beauty contest" to express their preferences about presidential candidates; the delegates who went to the national convention and actually chose the candidates were selected elsewhere. A fascinating story began to unfold in 1968, however, in which the national Democratic Party took control of the delegate-selection process away from the state parties and gave new life to the movement toward presidential primaries.

Turbulence in the Democratic Party

The 1968 Democratic convention was a riotous event. Struggling with the painful issues of civil rights and American involvement in the Vietnam War, the convention nominated the party leaders' choice, Vice President Hubert Humphrey, as the Democratic presidential candidate, even though he hadn't run in a single state primary. Antiwar activists within the party protested that Humphrey's nomination did not fairly reflect the views of most Democrats. To try to make peace with their critics, the national party leaders agreed that the next convention's delegates would be selected in a more open and democratic manner.

A party commission chaired by liberal senator George McGovern of South Dakota (and later by Representative Donald Fraser of Minnesota, and known as the *McGovern–Fraser Commission*) recommended, and the Democratic National Committee (DNC) and the next Democratic convention approved, major changes to increase the influence of insurgent Democrats in the 1972 nominating process. One of the striking elements of this story is the remarkable ease with which state Democratic Party leaders accepted rule changes that greatly reduced their power over the awarding of the party's greatest prize, the presidential nomination.[2]

In trying to comply with the complicated new rules recommended by McGovern–Fraser, many states stopped using caucus–convention systems and reinstituted primaries.[3] The remaining caucuses were guided by strict party requirements that delegates be selected in open and well-publicized meetings. Techniques formerly used by state party organizations to control the caucuses were outlawed. In the process, not only were the delegate-selection procedures radically changed, but also the principle was established that the national party, not the states or the state parties, makes the rules for nominating presidential candidates.

Once the reform genie was let out of the bottle, it was hard to contain. The Democrats tinkered with their presidential nomination process prior to almost every election for the next 20 years. First, they used national party leverage to make the process more open and more representative of women, blacks, and young people. Then, the Democrats "fine-tuned" the rules by requiring proportional representation (PR), so that voter support for candidates was more faithfully represented in delegate counts. Starting in 1980, in order to bring party leaders (and their "peer review" of candidates) back into the process, many elected and party officials were guaranteed a vote at the convention as uncommitted "superdelegates" (to be discussed later).

The result has been a stunning transformation of the process by which the Democrats select their presidential nominees. Many state legislatures responded to the new Democratic requirements by changing state election laws to require primary elections in both parties. Thus, the Republicans became the unwilling beneficiaries of the Democratic reforms. Republicans have preserved their tradition of giving state parties wide latitude in developing their own rules, however, which has kept the national party out of much of the rules debate.

Presidential Primaries and Caucuses Today

Each state decides whether to choose its delegates to the parties' national conventions in a primary election or a series of caucuses. Although primaries are more common, states can change their method of selection from one presidential election to the next (see Figure 10.1).

A state holding a primary selects a date on which its eligible voters can go to a polling place (or cast an absentee ballot) and choose a candidate to become their party's presidential nominee. The popular vote for each candidate determines how many of the state's delegates will go to the party's national convention supporting that candidate. The list of delegates who will represent each candidate is usually approved by the candidate or his or her agent. This all but guarantees that the popular vote for candidates will be faithfully translated into delegates committed to the respective candidates at the national convention, even though no laws require delegates to support the popular vote winner in their state.[4]

Other states use a longer delegate-selection process that begins with precinct caucuses. In these meetings, party identifiers are invited to gather in local schools or other public areas, often for an hour or more, to debate which candidates for president will best represent their party and the issues they believe in. Then they choose delegates to communicate their presidential preference to caucuses at higher levels, typically at the county, congressional district, and then the state level. The state's final delegate slate for the national convention is determined at the higher-level conventions. The first-in-the-nation

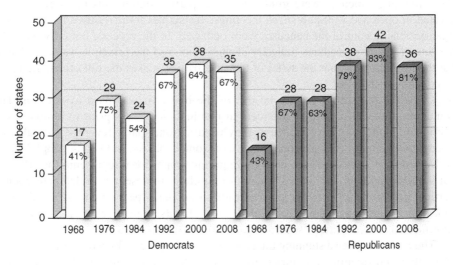

FIGURE 10.1   Change in the Number of Presidential Primaries, 1968–2008.

Note: The number above each bar is the number of states that held primaries to select delegates (not purely advisory primaries) in that year; inside the bar is the percentage of convention delegates elected in those primaries. All 50 states plus Washington, DC, are included, but not the territories (American Samoa, Guam, Puerto Rico, Virgin Islands) or Democrats Abroad. Delegate percentages include Democratic superdelegates. The two parties' national committees decided in 2007 to take away delegate votes from states that held primaries prior to February 5, 2008, without national party permission.

Sources: For 1968–1992, Michael G. Hagen and William G. Mayer, "The Modern Politics of Presidential Selection," in William G. Mayer, ed., *In Pursuit of the White House 2000* (New York: Chatham House, 2000), pp. 11 and 43–44. Figures for 2000 were kindly provided by Mayer and were calculated by the author for 2008 from data provided by the National Association of Secretaries of State.

Iowa caucuses, for example, began with precinct meetings in January 2008, but Iowa's national convention delegates were not chosen until the district and state conventions in April and June.

The selection of delegates in the caucus states attracted little media coverage until 1976, when a little-known Democratic governor, Jimmy Carter, made himself a serious presidential candidate by campaigning intensively in Iowa and winning an unexpectedly large number of delegates. After that time, the Iowa caucuses joined the New Hampshire primary as the first and most significant delegate-selection events. From 1980 till 2004, an estimated half to three-quarters of the media coverage of the nomination race focused on these two states' events.[5] To dilute their impact in 2008, the DNC allowed Nevada and South Carolina, states with large minority populations, to move up their delegate-selection events as well.

Candidates campaign differently in a caucus state than they do in a primary. Because the turnout at caucuses is much smaller and consists mainly of party activists, winning caucuses requires early and extensive organizing to appeal to these likely caucus-goers. (In contrast, media ads are better suited to reach the larger turnout of voters in a primary.) As we will see, a major reason for Obama's success in winning the Democratic presidential nomination was that his campaign understood this to a greater extent than the Clinton campaign did, so he deployed extensive field organizations and won big victories in several caucus states early in the nominating season.[6]

THE RACE TO WIN DELEGATE VOTES

Every presidential nomination in both parties since 1956 has been won on the convention's first ballot, and since 1968, that first-ballot nominee has always been the winner of the most delegates in the primaries and caucuses. How does a candidate get to that coveted spot?

The "Invisible Primary"

Almost all serious presidential candidates begin several years before the election to take polls, raise money, identify active supporters in the states with early contests, and compete for the services of respected consultants. The competition heats up during the year before the first primaries and caucuses. Journalists are competing at this time as well; they each want to be the first to predict who will win the nomination. The indicators they use are the candidates' standing in polls and their fund-raising success. This process of early fund-raising and jockeying for media attention and public support has become so important to the eventual result that it has come to be called the *invisible primary* or the "money primary."[7]

Prospective candidates who fall behind in the money chase are likely to be winnowed out of the race even before most Americans have had the chance to assess their capabilities. In 2007, for instance, several candidates, including former Tennessee senator Fred Thompson, lost the invisible primary because of their lackluster fund-raising and media reviews. Those who raise more than expected, in contrast, can greatly improve their chances. Obama's surprisingly strong fund-raising during the first three months of 2007, when he attracted more donors than Clinton did and pulled in almost as much money ($25 million to her $26 million), vaulted him out of the pack to become Clinton's main rival for the Democratic nomination.

Candidates' Strategic Choices

Those regarded as serious candidates near the end of the "invisible primary" must decide how much effort and money to put into each of the early primary and caucus states and which of their issue positions and personal qualities to emphasize. The most important factor in making these decisions is the candidate's standing in the race. Someone who enters the election year as a front-runner, for example, normally has to demonstrate overwhelming support in the early delegate-selection events. Otherwise, his or her supporters' and contributors' confidence may be so badly shaken that the candidate's hopes for the nomination fade. In 2008, for instance, Hillary Clinton based her strategy for winning the Democratic nomination on creating a sense of inevitability about her candidacy. That strategy was undermined big time by her loss in the Iowa caucuses.

A number of other formal and informal "rules" structure the nominating process and affect campaigns' strategic choices. One is that a candidate who expects to do especially well among independents will need to concentrate resources in states with open primaries, in which independents and other partisans can vote (see Chapter 9). In fact, in 2007, supporters of John McCain urged California Republican leaders to open the party primary to independents, which would have helped McCain, after the state decided to move its primary to an earlier date.

The Democrats' rules of the game differ from those of the Republicans. Recall that the Democrats' nomination reforms require the use of PR, so that a candidate with significant support will not be shut out in any state. Since 1988, candidates who win at least 15 percent of the vote in primaries and caucuses get approximately the same share of the delegates as they received of the popular vote. For instance, when 36 percent of voters in the 2008 New Hampshire Democratic primary chose Barack Obama, approximately the same percentage of New Hampshire's delegation was directed to vote for Obama in the Democratic National Convention to be the party's nominee.

The Republicans, in contrast, use some form of a winner-take-all system in most states: The candidate who gets the most votes in a state primary or caucus wins all or most of the state's delegates. This winner-take-all rule makes a big difference in the results.[8] For example, John McCain won 33 percent of the vote in the 2008 Missouri Republican primary, and former Arkansas governor Mike Huckabee and former Massachusetts governor Mitt Romney were close behind with 32 and 29 percent, respectively. Although the three candidates were separated by fewer than 22,000 votes, all 58 of the state's convention delegates were assigned to the narrow winner, McCain; Huckabee and Romney got none. In contrast, when Obama lost a primary narrowly to Clinton, under the Democrats' PR rules, he got almost as many delegates as she did. As one reporter put it, "the Republican who kills the buffalo gets all the meat; the Democrat has to crouch around the campfire and share it with his brethren and sistren."[9] The Republicans' winner-take-all rules allowed McCain to build a big lead in delegates fairly quickly and to clinch his party's nomination much earlier than Obama did.[10]

Win Early or Die

The strongest imperative is the need to win early. Victories early in the nominating process create momentum. They attract more media coverage for the candidate and, in turn, more name recognition among voters. The candidate looks more and more unstoppable, so it is easier to raise money, which makes later victories more likely. The other candidates fall further and further behind.

In recent elections, the nomination process has become highly *"front-loaded"* (see box on page 184). Many states have moved their primaries forward in the election calendar to benefit from the attention attracted by these early contests, as well as the campaign spending that comes with it. This can affect the issues discussed in the race; Iowa's first-in-the-nation status means that ethanol use, favored by Iowa's corn farmers, gets more attention from presidential candidates than it would receive otherwise. In 2008, front-loading nearly pushed the first delegate-selection events into the "invisible primary"; Iowa and New Hampshire moved their caucuses and primary to the first week in January, and several big states, including California, Illinois, and New York, advanced the dates of their primaries. More than 40 percent of the delegates to both parties' conventions were selected on February 5, termed "Super Tuesday."

Comparing the Clinton and Obama Strategies

Taking account of these rules, presidential candidates have chosen many different types of approaches to the nomination race. Consider the contrast between the Clinton and Obama campaigns in 2008. At first, the race was seen by many as the story of an old pro, backed by her party's most experienced advisers, who would quickly demolish an inexperienced young upstart. Except that the old pros fought among themselves rather than doing their homework, and the young upstart had advisers who studied the rules, formed a tightly disciplined team, and understood cutting-edge technologies.

Clinton ran a relatively traditional race as the "establishment" candidate for the nomination.[11] Her strategy, as we have seen, was based on the assumption that if she started early and established the belief that she was the presumptive nominee, then the contest would be over within a month of the Iowa caucuses. She hoped to win the big states of Ohio, Pennsylvania, California, and New York, and she expected that her experience, contacts, and support from women's and labor groups would smooth her way in other states.

Obama's organization didn't gear up in earnest until January of 2007—very late for a modern nomination race. Obama and his advisers knew that he couldn't challenge Clinton's great strengths—her almost-universal name recognition and her (and her husband's, former President Bill Clinton) extensive relationships with state Democratic officials and activists. Obama's staff had to design a different route to the nomination. Under the Democratic Party's PR rules, a candidate could gain a big lead in delegates only by winning landslide victories. That wasn't very likely to happen in most of the big, Democratic-leaning states, where both Obama and Clinton had substantial support.

So Obama's staff put enormous effort into states where Democratic candidates didn't usually campaign, and thus where Clinton's advantages were barely perceptible. These dominantly Republican states, including Idaho, Utah, Alaska, and Kansas, tend to be

FRONT-LOADING THE NOMINATION PROCESS

In the first presidential election after the Democratic nomination reforms, the New Hampshire primary—the lead-off event of the 1972 nominating season—was held during the first week in March. By that week in 2008, the Republican race for the nomination was already over. The first presidential selection event in 2008 was the Iowa caucuses, held less than two weeks after Christmas 2007. Holiday decorations vied for space with presidential campaign yard signs and posters.

It is old news by now that the nomination race has become "front-loaded." States have increasingly pushed their delegate-selection events closer to the beginning of the election year, when they would get more media coverage, bring in more money from campaign advertising, and, they thought, give the state's voters more of a chance to influence the choice of their parties' nominees. By tradition, the first events are the Iowa caucuses and the New Hampshire primary. Because the prime positioning of these states—neither one very typical of either party's national constituency—had often been criticized, the DNC agreed to let Nevada and South Carolina add their delegate-selection events to the early days of the 2008 primary season, and thus increase the voice of Latinos and African Americans in the nominating process. That opened the floodgates, and soon, Michigan and Florida also decided to hold their events before the DNC-authorized "window" opened on February 5. The DNC warned both states that they would lose all their convention delegates if they went ahead; both did, anyway.

But the joke turned out to be on the states that rushed ahead. Although the winner-take-all Republican events produced a nominee in less than two months, Hillary Clinton staged a comeback in New Hampshire after losing the Iowa caucuses, and from that point on, neither Democratic candidate was able to open up a commanding lead in delegate votes. The proportional representation required by DNC rules, just as the party's reformers had hoped, gave the second-ranking candidate chance after chance to remain a contender. Obama did not wrap up the nomination until early June. So in fact, in the Democratic race, the states at the rear of the calendar, particularly Ohio, Pennsylvania, Indiana, and North Carolina, had enormous influence on the outcome.

Front-loading has several important effects on the nominating process. It forces presidential candidates to raise money very early. It gives an extra boost to the candidates who were front-runners during the "invisible primary." When there are only a few days between the earliest primaries and the rest, the cost of a strategic mistake in these early events could be very high. This "rush to judgment," as two political scientists call it, makes the nominating system "less deliberative, less rational, less flexible and more chaotic."

Sources: Andrew E. Busch and William G. Mayer, "The Front-Loading Problem," in William G. Mayer, ed., *The Making of the Presidential Candidates 2004* (Lanham, MD: Rowman & Littlefield, 2004), pp. 1–43 (quotation at p. 15); and Mark J. Wattier, "Presidential Primaries and Frontloading," prepared for Ray C. Bliss Institute of Applied Politics, "State of the Party: 2004 & Beyond," University of Akron, October 5–7, 2005.

more rural, often western, and with growing concentrations of higher-income profession-als in their cities. In 2008, many of these states held caucuses, where the kind of organiza-tional effort and volunteer enthusiasm closely associated with the Obama campaign can pay dividends in voter turnout. Because caucuses attract much smaller turnouts than primaries do, "mobilizing a few thousand people in a caucus state can have as much impact as getting several hundred thousand voters to the polls in a primary state."[12] Obama's staffers recruited large numbers of activists—college students and other young people, blacks, affluent professionals—in these states, most of which scheduled their caucuses early in the nomination season.

In Idaho, for instance, the Democratic Party chair said of the Obama campaign, "It was the most impressive political organization I've seen in my thirty-one years here."[13] The organization used ground-war strategies (see Chapter 11) to increase turnout among Obama supporters, and it succeeded very well. Clinton's campaign, following the traditional plan of focusing on states with the most delegates, made no organized effort at all in the state. Obama beat Clinton in Idaho by 62 percentage points and won the great majority of its delegates.

With similar efforts, he won a series of landslides, and big delegate leads, in other caucus states. But Obama's narrower win in Iowa was even more important. Not only was Iowa's the first delegate-selection event of 2008, but it was also largely white. By winning Iowa, Obama showed that he could do well in a state with only a tiny black population and few major cities.

In the more traditional Democratic states, with their larger trove of delegates, the Obama campaign's aim was to hold down the size of Clinton's victories. Under the PR rules, a narrow loss would give Obama almost as many delegates as Clinton in these states. Obama's energetic organization again targeted blacks in big cities, students in college towns, and affluent suburban voters, whereas the Clinton cam-paign focused on older voters, women, Latinos, and blue-collar whites. The Obama efforts were effective; slim Clinton victories in the later primary states did not bring her enough delegates to surmount the small lead that Obama had built with his land-slide wins in the early caucuses.

Because Obama's delegate lead was narrow, however, the nomination fight didn't end until early June, when the last of the states held their primaries. Democratic activists feared that the drawn-out nomination race would weaken Obama's chances against McCain in the fall. Instead, the lengthy nomination contest proved to be a bless-ing in disguise. The Democrats were forced to organize in almost every state and thus to "field-test" local and state organizers. Large numbers of new voters registered as Democrats. The close race brought out big Democratic turnouts, which gave the Democrats expanded voter lists to use in the general election campaign. And although some Clinton supporters refused to accept Obama as their nominee when the battle ended, and some even worked actively for Republican John McCain in the fall, the Democrats' worst fear—that the party would be split during and after the national con-vention—did not materialize.

Obama's execution was not perfect; in the second half of the nominating season, his prospects suffered from the kinds of verbal slips, embarrassing associations, and simple fatigue that bedevil most candidates. But his superior game plan—his ability to stimulate enthusiasm among volunteers, his staff's extensive organizational work, their detailed knowledge of the Democratic Party's nomination rules, and their ability to use the rules to their advantage—made the difference. Interestingly, although Obama's campaign was widely regarded as innovative, in fact it simply applied new technology to a time-honored approach to winning elections: contacting voters individually and bringing them to the polls.

What Is the Party's Role?

The party organizations' interests in the nominating process are not necessarily the same as those of the presidential candidates. State and local parties want a nominee who will bring voters to the polls to support the party's candidates for state and local offices; a weak presidential candidate may hurt their chances. Party leaders also generally prefer early agreement on a presidential candidate. A hotly contested race carries the risk of increasing conflict within local and state parties, which might weaken them in the general election.

Historically, state parties protected their interests by selecting delegates uncommitted to any candidate and then casting the state's delegate votes as a bloc for a particular nominee. The ability to swing a bloc of delegates to a candidate could increase the state party's influence at the convention. But the current nominating system prevents the state parties from sending an uncommitted delegation. In most primary states, it is the candidates who set up their delegate slates, so the delegates' first loyalty is to the candidate. In caucus states, delegates committed to a candidate simply have greater appeal to caucus participants than do uncommitted delegates.

Party leaders, then, have a harder time protecting the party's interests in a nominating process that is dominated by the candidates and their supporters. The Democrats tried to enhance the party's role in 1984 by setting aside delegate seats at the national convention for elected and party officials. These *superdelegates*—all Democratic governors and members of Congress, current and former presidents and vice presidents, and all members of the DNC—were meant to be a large, uncommitted bloc now totaling almost 20 percent of all delegates, with the party's interests in mind. But because the nomination race concluded so quickly in most election years, superdelegates did not play an independent role in the nominating process.[14]

The closeness of the delegate count during the 2008 nominating season raised concerns that the superdelegates' votes might actually decide the race. Some observers hinted darkly that this could raise suspicions about "boss rule." The suspicions were probably unfounded. All the superdelegates are either elected officials, who have a natural interest in maintaining constituent support, or party leaders, whose aim is to choose the candidate to head their ticket who is most attractive to voters. In fact, although Clinton seemed to have greater superdelegate support early in the nominating season, this changed as Obama's slim lead in the elected delegates grew. In several cases, superdelegates switched their presidential preference (as superdelegates are allowed to do) to reflect the primary or caucus vote of their own constituents. In practice, then, superdelegates did not act as an independent voice for the party's interests. The presidential candidates in 2008, as in past nominations, owed their selection largely to their own core supporters, rather than to the party organization. This limits the party organization's ability to influence the president once he or she has been elected.

VOTERS' CHOICES IN PRESIDENTIAL NOMINATIONS

The move to primaries has greatly increased citizen participation in the process of nominating a president. What determines the level of voter participation and guides the voters' choices in these contests?

Who Votes?

Turnout varies a great deal from state to state and across different years in any one state. The Iowa caucuses and the New Hampshire primary usually bring out a lot of voters because of the high media attention to those early contests. More generally, turnout tends to be higher in states with a better-educated citizenry and a tradition of two-party competition—the same states where there is higher turnout in the general election. The nature of the contest matters, too. Voters are most likely to participate in early races that are closely fought, in which the candidates spend more money and the excitement is high, all of which increase interest in the election.[15]

Are Primary Voters Typical?

However, turnout is lower in primary than in general elections, especially after the parties' nominations have been largely wrapped up. Are the people who turn out to vote in presidential primaries, and who therefore choose the nominees for the rest of the public, typical of other citizens? Critics of the reforms have charged that they are not and, thus, that candidates are now being selected by an unrepresentative group of citizens.

We can explore this question in several ways. When we compare presidential primary voters with nonvoters, we find that those who vote in primaries are, in fact, better educated, wealthier, and older, but then, so are general election voters. A more appropriate comparison is with party identifiers because primaries are the means by which the party electorate chooses its nominees. Using this comparison, just as is the case with primary voters more generally, voters in presidential primaries tend to be slightly older, better educated, more affluent, better integrated into their communities, and less likely to be black or Hispanic, but the differences are not substantial.[16] Concerns remain, however, as we have seen in Chapter 9, that primary voters may hold more extreme views than does the party electorate more generally.

Do Voters Make Informed Choices?

Another criticism of the primaries is that voters do not make very well-informed decisions. Compared with voters in the general election, primary voters seem to pay less attention to the campaign and to have less knowledge about the candidates. Especially in the early contests, voters are influenced by candidate momentum, as bandwagons form for candidates who have won unexpectedly or by a large margin. Candidates' personal characteristics influence voters in the primaries,[17] but issues often have only a minor impact. The result, so the argument goes, is a series of contests decided mainly on the basis of short-run, superficial considerations.[18]

Many analysts think that this is too strong an indictment, however. They feel that voters respond with some rationality to the challenge of having to choose among several candidates in a short campaign without the powerful guidance provided by party labels.[19] Although it may seem unproductive to support a candidate simply because he or she has momentum, primary voters often find only minor issue differences among their party's candidates and just want to pick the candidate with the best chance of winning the presidency. Momentum seems to matter especially when voters are being asked to sort through a pack of candidates about whom they know little[20] and when there is no well-known front-runner.[21] Even then, the candidates who move to the head of the pack are usually subjected to more searching evaluations, which give voters more reasons to support or oppose them. In short, even though primary voters often have less information about the candidates than do general election voters, the basis for their decisions may not differ very much from those in general elections.[22]

Do Primaries Produce Good Candidates?

Both the current primary-dominated system and the earlier caucus–convention system have attractive and unattractive qualities. Talented candidates have been nominated by both and so have less distinguished candidates. The earlier nominating system tended to favor mainstream politicians, those who were more acceptable to the party's leaders, including some candidates who had earned their nomination through party loyalty rather than through their personal appeal or their skills at governing. Primaries are more likely to give an advantage to candidates whose names are well known to the public and those who have the support of issue activists and people with intensely held views.[23]

Compared with the earlier, party-dominated nominating process, the current system gives presidential candidates a better chance to demonstrate their public support, raise more campaign money, and test their stamina and ability to cope with pressure. On the other hand, candidates' performance in the primaries may not be a good indicator of their likely competence in the White House. The front-loading of the current system also increases the risk that party voters will choose a nominee too hastily and later experience buyer's remorse.

ON TO THE NATIONAL CONVENTIONS

Once the states have chosen their delegates in primaries and caucuses, the Democratic and Republican delegates assemble as national parties in conventions. These mass meetings bring together the party organization and activists and the party in government, but the main purpose of the convention—to select the party's presidential nominee—has already been accomplished in those primaries and caucuses. Aside from formally approving the candidates who have won the most delegates, what is left for the convention to do?

Roots of the Conventions

The national party convention is an old and respected institution, but it began, at least in part, as a power grab. In 1832, the nomination of Andrew Jackson as the Democratic-Republican candidate for president was a foregone conclusion, but state political leaders wanted to keep Henry Clay, the favorite of the congressional caucus, from being nominated as vice president; they preferred Martin Van Buren. So these leaders pushed for a national convention to make the nominations. In doing so, they wrested control of the presidential selection process from congressional leaders. By the time the Republican Party emerged in 1854, the convention had become the accepted means through which major parties chose their candidates for president and vice president. Ever since 1856, the two major parties have held national conventions every four years.

What Conventions Do

Months before the convention, its major committees begin their work (see box on this page). What these committees decide can be overruled by the convention itself, which acts as the ultimate arbiter of its own structure and procedures. The convention warms up with a keynote address by a party "star," showcases as many of its popular older leaders and attractive new faces as possible, and reaches a dramatic peak in the nomination of the presidential and vice-presidential candidates. This general format has remained basically the same for decades.

Approving the Platform   In addition to nominating candidates, the convention's main job is to approve the party's *platform*—its statement of party positions on a wide range of issues. The platform committee often begins public hearings long before the convention opens; Republicans invited public comments on the Internet in 2008, and Democrats held 1,600 "listening sessions" to hear individuals' views. The finished platform is then presented to the convention for its approval.

Party platforms don't always get much respect. Even party leaders sometimes ignore them; in 1988, Democratic presidential candidate Michael Dukakis referred

---

KEY COMMITTEES OF THE NATIONAL PARTY CONVENTIONS

The national conventions have four important committees:

Credentials deals with the qualifications of delegates and alternates. In earlier years, fierce battles sometimes took place over the seating of delegations—for example, in the 1964 Democratic convention, when the all-white Mississippi delegation was challenged as being unrepresentative of all Mississippi Democrats. The state procedures are regularized now, so this committee is no longer as crucial.

Permanent Organization selects the convention's officials, including the chair, secretary, and sergeant at arms.

Rules sets the rules of the convention, including the length and number of nomination speeches. The committee may also debate the procedures to be followed at future conventions.

Platform (or *Resolutions*) drafts the party's platform for action by the convention. Because internal party battles focus increasingly on issues, this committee takes on special importance.

to only about half the pledges in his party's platform, ignoring those designed to appeal to supporters of rival candidates.[24] Because they are approved in nominating conventions whose main purpose is to choose a presidential candidate, platforms usually reflect the candidate's views, or the bargains that the candidate has been willing to make to win support or preserve party harmony.[25] So a platform usually lists the policy preferences of various groups in the party's (and the candidate's) supporting coalition. Platforms are also campaign documents, intended to help the party's candidates win their races.

Yet platforms are much more than just a laundry list of promises. They often define the major differences between the parties, as the leading scholar of party platforms shows.[26] As a result, they can provoke spirited debates because many delegates care deeply about this statement of the party's beliefs on such issues as abortion, taxes, pollution, and American involvement in the world (see Chapter 15).

Formalizing the Presidential Nomination   Many years ago, when a party's nominee was actually chosen at the national convention, several rounds of balloting were usually needed to agree on a nominee. When the first ballot did not produce a majority, intense bargaining would follow. The leading candidates would try to hold their own supporters while negotiating for the votes of state delegations that had come committed to minor candidates. In recent years, however, one candidate has won a majority of delegate votes well before the convention starts, so only a single round of balloting has been necessary.

Approving the Vice-Presidential Nominee   The day after the presidential nominee is chosen, delegates vote again to select the vice-presidential candidate. This, too, is ceremonial; presidential nominees choose their own running mates and conventions ratify their choice.[27] In years past, the vice-presidential nominee was selected by the (usually exhausted) presidential candidate at the time of the convention. Now, presidential nominees announce their "veep" choice before the convention begins, often as a means to gain more voter support.

Launching the General Election Campaign   The final business of the convention is to present the party's presidential candidate to the American public. The candidates hope that the glowing portrayal presented by the convention will produce a boost in public support, known as a "convention bounce."

Many other events take place at the conventions as well. Lobbyists host lavish dinners and receptions to curry favor with elected officials. Even though they get federal funding, conventions are funded largely by big donors with an interest in federal policies—corporations (especially for the Republicans), unions (for the Democrats), and wealthy individuals.

WHO ARE THE DELEGATES?

Convention delegates help to shape the public's image of the two parties. Who are these delegates?

Apportioning Delegates Among the States

The national parties determine how many delegates each state can send to the convention. The two parties make these choices differently. The Republicans allocate delegates more equally among the states; the Democrats weigh more heavily the size of the state's population and its record of support for Democratic candidates.

These formulas affect the voting strength of various groups within the party coalitions, as they do in the two national committees (see Chapter 4). The GOP's decision to represent the small states more equally with the large states has advantaged its conservative wing. In contrast, by giving relatively more weight to the larger states with stronger Democratic voting traditions, the Democrats have favored the more liberal interests in their party, and in particular, urban areas with large minority populations.

How Representative are the Delegates?

The delegates to the Democratic and Republican conventions have never been a cross section of American citizens or even of their party's voters. White males, the well educated, and the affluent have traditionally been overrepresented in conventions. Reflecting their different coalitional bases, since the 1930s, Democratic delegations have had more labor union members and black Americans, and Republican conventions have drawn more Protestants and business entrepreneurs.

Demographics   Since the nomination reforms, the delegates of both parties have become more representative of other citizens in some ways and less representative in others. The Democrats used affirmative action plans after 1968 to increase the presence of women, blacks, and, for a brief time, young people. At the 2008 Democratic convention, more than a third of the delegates were people of color (compared with only 6 percent of Republican delegates), and since 1980, the DNC has required that half of the delegates be women. The percentage of female delegates at Republican conventions has increased during this period as well, without party mandates. The DNC has urged state parties to recruit more low- and moderate-income delegates, but their lesser political involvement and the high price of attending a convention stand in the way. So conventions remain meetings of the wealthy and well educated (see Table 10.1). In 2008, for instance, 34 percent of Republican delegates and 22 percent of Democrats said they were millionaires, the largest proportion in over a dozen years, and most had postgraduate education.[28]

Political Experience   We might assume that delegates would be recidivists, making return appearances at convention after convention. But that was not the case even before the reforms; even then, most delegates at each convention were first timers. With the move to primaries, the percentage of newcomers jumped to about 80 percent before declining to 57 percent in 2008. The decline became more marked when the Democrats granted convention seats to politically experienced superdelegates. Even if many delegates are new to conventions, however, the great majority are long-time party activists. In 2008, most of a random sample of delegates reported that they had been active in their party for at least 20 years, and a majority said they currently hold party office.

TABLE 10.1 How Representative Were the 2008 Democratic and Republican Convention Delegates?

	Dem. Delegates (%)	Dem. Voters (%)	All Voters (%)	Rep. Voters (%)	Rep. Delegates (%)
Gender					
Female	49	58	54	56	32
Race					
Black	23	23	12	2	2
White	65	72	83	93	93
Latino	11	9	8	10	5
Education					
HS graduate or less	5	42	37	32	4
Some college	12	28	30	29	15
College grad	26	17	21	28	31
Postgraduate	55	13	12	11	50
Total family income					
Under $50,000	10	43	39	31	5
Over $75,000	70	26	31	39	66
Religion					
Protestant	43	52	55	61	57
Evangelical or born-again*	14	23	27	39	33
Catholic	26	23	24	25	30
Jewish	9	5	3	1	3
Other or none	18	19	17	12	8

*Asked in a separate question, so percentages for "religion" do not add up to 100 percent.

Source: Data on convention delegates are from New York Times/CBS News polls taken during July 16–August 17, 2008, of Democratic National Convention delegates (n=970) and July 23–August 26 for Republican delegates (n=854). "Voters" are all registered voters in nationwide polls (n=1014) taken by the same polling organization during August 15–20, 2008.

Issues Convention delegates are more extreme in their views and more aware of issues than most other voters are. In 2008, Democratic delegates were slightly more likely to call themselves very liberal (19 percent) than were Democratic voters (15 percent) and about twice as likely to consider themselves liberal or very liberal as was the average voter. Forty percent of Republican delegates called themselves very conservative, compared with 30 percent of GOP voters and only 15 percent of all voters. Delegates' views, then, are very polarized by party.

The distance between delegates and their party's voters varies from issue to issue. As Table 10.2 shows, although Democratic delegates in 2008 were more liberal than most voters on several key issues, they came closest to the views of Democratic voters

TABLE 10.2 Views on Issues: Comparing Delegates and Voters in 2008

	Dem. Delegates (%)	Dem. Voters (%)	All Voters (%)	Rep. Voters (%)	Rep. Delegates (%)
Providing health care coverage for all Americans is more important than holding down taxes	94	90	67	40	7
Abortion should be permitted in all cases	58	33	26	13	5
Illegal immigration is a very serious problem for the country now	15	36	49	64	58
Many of the tax cuts Congress passed in 2001 should be made permanent	7	34	47	62	91
United States did the right thing in taking military action against Iraq	2	14	37	70	80
Environmental protection should be a higher priority for government than finding new energy sources	25	30	21	9	3
Gay couples should be allowed to legally marry	55	49	34	11	6
Gun control laws should be more strict	62	70	52	32	8

Note: Figures are the percentage of each group who agreed with the statement.

Source: Data on convention delegates are from New York Times/CBS News polls taken during July 16–August 17, 2008, of Democratic National Convention delegates (n=970) and July 23–August 26 for Republican delegates (n=854). "Voters" are all registered voters in nationwide polls (n=1014) taken by the same polling organization during August 15–20, 2008.

(and all voters) in favoring health care coverage for all Americans, environmental protection, and gun control. Republican delegates most closely resembled other Republicans, as well as the average voter, in their views on the importance of illegal immigration, but scored well to the right on other questions. Democratic and Republican delegates differed most from one another on health care coverage and the Bush tax cuts. So although supporters of the McGovern–Fraser reforms had hoped that the new system would better represent the views of most party identifiers than the old party-leader-dominated system did, the reforms have not made much difference in that regard.[29] The real effect of the reforms has been to link the selection of delegates more closely to candidate preferences. As a result, when an issue-oriented candidate does well in the primaries and caucuses, more issue-oriented activists become convention delegates. That may not make the conventions more representative of the party in the electorate, but it may offer clearer choices to voters.

Amateurs or Professionals?   The reforms were also expected to result in delegates with a different approach to politics. Using the terms described in Chapter 5, some convention delegates can be described as amateurs, others as professionals. Amateurs are more attracted by issues, more insistent on internal party democracy, and less willing to compromise. Professionals, in contrast, are more likely to have a long-term commitment to the party and to be more willing to compromise on issues in order to win the general election.

There is some evidence that the Democratic Party's reforms had, as intended, reduced the presence of party professionals between the 1968 and the 1972 conventions.[30] As we have seen, however, the party later moved to reverse this trend by adding superdelegates. Research shows that both before and after the reforms, delegates have remained strongly committed to the parties and their goals.[31] It may be that for both professionals and amateurs, involvement in this very public party pageant strengthens delegates' commitment to the party's aims.

Who Controls the Delegates?   It would not matter how representative delegates are if they act as pawns of powerful party leaders. In fact, for most of the history of party conventions, that is exactly how the state delegations behaved. State party leaders and big-city mayors had a commanding presence, especially at Democratic conventions.

Now, however, strong party leaders no longer control the convention by dominating their state delegations. When the Democrats eliminated their long-standing unit rule in 1968, through which a majority of a state delegation could throw all the delegation's votes to one candidate, they removed a powerful instrument of leadership control. Perhaps the most powerful force preventing state party leaders from controlling the conventions is the fact that the delegates in both parties now come to the conventions already committed to a candidate. That makes them unavailable for "delivery" by party leaders. If anyone controls the modern conventions, then, it is the party's prospective nominee for president, not leaders of the state parties.

HOW MEDIA COVER CONVENTIONS

In addition to all these changes in the convention's delegates and power centers, media coverage of conventions has changed significantly. On one hand, conventions have been reshaped and rescheduled to meet the media's needs.[32] On the other hand, ironically, media attention to the conventions has declined sharply in recent years.

Beginning with the first televised national party conventions in 1948, TV journalists and politicians found ways to serve one another's interests. In the early days of television before the convenience of videotape, networks were desperate for content with which to fill broadcast time, so they covered the party conventions live, from beginning to end. The convention became a major story for TV news, like the Olympics, through which it could demonstrate its skill and provide a public service. Reporters swarmed through the convention halls, covering the strategic moves of major candidates, the actions of powerful party leaders, and the reactions of individual delegates.

For party leaders, television coverage offered a priceless opportunity to reach voters and to launch the presidential campaign with maximum impact. So they reshaped the convention into a performance intended as much for the national television audience as for the delegates. Party officials gave key speaking roles to telegenic candidates, speeded up the proceedings, and moved the most dramatic convention business into prime-time hours. More and more, the aim of the convention shifted from the conduct of party business to the wooing of voters.

These two sets of goals, however—the networks' interest in a good story and the parties' interest in attracting supporters—increasingly began to conflict. Once the nomination reforms took effect, and the choice of the parties' presidential candidates was settled before the convention started, conventions lost most of their suspense. To hold viewers, media people searched the conventions for new sources of excitement, such as potential conflicts. But party leaders had no interest in making their disputes public; that would interfere with the positive message they were trying to convey. As the conventions' audience appeal continued to decline, the major networks reduced their coverage markedly. Although convention junkies still can turn to cable TV to watch the entire convention, coverage on ABC, CBS, and NBC decreased from about 60 hours per convention in 1952 to a grand total of 4 hours in 2008.

Media coverage, of course, is not always a boon for the parties. Television's capacity to dramatize and personalize can make a convention come to life for its audience, as it did in covering the struggles in the Democratic convention hall and streets of Chicago in 1968, which led to the nomination reforms. However, the sight of bloody demonstrators and angry delegates did not help the Democratic Party attract voter support for its candidates that year. Television cameras can encourage some participants to use the convention as a podium to advance their own causes even if they risk undermining the party's interests. For better or worse, the televised conventions of 2008 had become a shadow of their former selves, in which a shrinking audience watched snippets of roll-call votes, shots of people wearing funny hats, and lots of talk among media commentators.

DO CONVENTIONS STILL HAVE A PURPOSE?

Since the nomination reforms, then, conventions have greatly changed. They are no longer the occasions when the major parties actually select their presidential nominees. That happens in the primaries and caucuses; the conventions simply ratify the results. The national conventions have lost much of their deliberative character and independence.

In another way, however, the conventions have become more significant. Because candidates must mobilize groups of activists and voters in order to win primaries and caucuses and because many of these groups are concerned with particular policies, the nomination reforms have made issues all the more important in convention politics. Many delegates arrive at the convention committed not only to a candidate but also to a cause. The pressures exerted by Christian conservatives at recent Republican conventions to preserve the party's stated opposition to same-sex marriage and abortion are a good illustration.

In spite of all these changes—or perhaps because of them—the national conventions are living symbols of the national parties. They provide an occasion for rediscovering common interests and for celebrating the party's heroes. They motivate state and local party candidates, energize party workers, and launch presidential campaigns. They give new party candidates a few moments in the media spotlight. They may not compete with *American Idol* for ratings, but they do remind party activists and identifiers why the party matters to them.

SHOULD WE REFORM THE REFORMS?

The increasing use of primaries in the presidential nominating system was part of a time-honored pattern in American politics: efforts by reformers to break up concentrations of party power. As we have seen, however, the reforms have had many unintended effects as well. Primaries can create internal divisions in party organizations that may not heal in time for the general election. The low turnouts in many primaries and caucuses may increase the influence of well-organized groups on the ideological extremes: the right wing of the Republican Party and the left wing of the Democrats. The results of a few early contests in states not very representative of the nation have a disproportionate effect on the national outcome.[33] In most years, by the time most voters know enough about the prospective nominees to make an informed choice, the nominees have already been chosen. And candidates must invest such an enormous amount of time, energy, and money in the nomination process that the ultimate winner can arrive at the party convention personally and financially exhausted.

But there is no going back to the old system. As the reformers charged, it was controlled by state and local party leaders who were often out of touch with the electorate. It kept many party voters and even party activists out of the crucial first step in picking a president. It violated the desire for a more open, democratic politics, and it did not help presidential candidates learn how to prepare for the most powerful leadership job in the world.[34]

What Could be Done?

Could the reforms' drawbacks be fixed by more reforms?[35] Both parties feel some pressure to do just that. Among Democratic delegates in 2008, only 21 percent claimed to be "very satisfied" with the party's nominating system as a whole.

One possible reform would be to create regional nominating events, in which the states in a given region would all schedule their primaries on the same day. That might bring more coherence to the welter of state contests by limiting the number of dates on which they could be held and reducing the enormous strain on the candidates. For a time in the late 1980s and 1990s, most southern states chose to hold their primaries early in March on a single day, referred to as Super Tuesday. Their aim was to draw greater attention to southern concerns and to encourage the nomination of moderate candidates acceptable to the South. But Super Tuesday has now become a national event, featuring primaries and caucuses in states from every region.

Regional primaries, however, have drawbacks. Which region would go first? Even if the order were rotated from one election to the next, the first region to vote, with its peculiarities and specific concerns, would disproportionately influence the nominations. Regional primaries could still produce all the complaints listed above, from internal party divisions to low turnouts.

The RNC has discussed moving almost all Republican state primaries to three successive Tuesdays late in the nomination season, though Iowa, New Hampshire, Nevada, and South Carolina would retain their early dates. Another option is to hold a national primary in which all the states' primaries and caucuses take place on the same day. In 2008, almost half of the states chose to hold their delegate-selection events on February 5. But a mega-primary has mega-drawbacks; it advantages the candidates with the most money and the highest name recognition, those capable of campaigning in dozens of states at the same time, and reduces the roles of both the party organizations and the states in the process. As is so often the case in politics, there is no "right" answer here— just a series of options, each of which favors some kinds of candidates and interests and disadvantages others.

CHAPTER 11

The General Election

If Abraham Lincoln had run for president in 2008, his campaign manager would have said, "Cancel the torchlight parades and the wall posters, Abe. You need a Twitter feed. You need bloggers. You need Webmasters, database managers, direct mail experts, bundlers, pollsters, and media consultants. And don't forget lawyers; lots of lawyers." Campaigning, always evolving, has been changing at warp speed in recent years.

Until the early to mid-1900s, most campaigns were *party-centered*; party leaders planned and managed candidates' campaigns with the party's interests in mind, just as they do today in most other democracies. It was the state and local party organizations that provided most of the money and volunteers used by candidates. Then a series of changes undermined the ability of parties to control campaigns. Reformers pushed for the adoption of primary elections. Because it can be risky for a party to take sides in a primary, candidates had to create their own campaign organizations to compete for the party's nomination, which they tended to keep and augment after winning the primary. State and local parties were weakened by other reforms, ranging from civil service laws to referenda, and their flow of volunteers lessened (see Chapter 3). New and effective technologies were emerging that could be purchased by wealthy candidates and interest groups just as easily as by parties. Some public relations experts began to specialize in campaign advertising; these professional political consultants were willing to handle the tasks—for a fee, of course—that the parties would have handled for free (or at least for no monetary payment) in earlier times.

These changes freed candidates from having to depend on their parties for volunteers, money, and advice. Campaigns became more *candidate-centered*, focusing on the needs and aims of the candidates rather than the parties. But just as they always have during their long lives, the parties are adjusting to these changes. This chapter will look at the many technologies, information sources, and means of persuasion that candidates now have available for their use and that contribute to the candidate-centered nature of most campaigns. We will also explore the conditions in which party organizations have been able to reclaim an important role in at least some campaigns.

CAMPAIGN STRATEGY

The key factors in designing a general election strategy[1] differ in several respects from those important in a primary. Especially in states with closed primaries (see Chapter 9), campaigning in a primary election tends to focus mainly on the party electorate, whereas the general election audience is much larger, more diverse, and can observe the candidates for a longer time. The general election campaign is also more powerfully affected by whether the candidate's party is in the majority or the minority in that district (see box on this page).

PARTY CAMPAIGN STRATEGIES IN 2012

As the manager of a general election campaign, one of your first critical decisions will be whether to focus on mobilizing your base—your core supporters—or whether you need to appeal to independents and supporters of the other party. If you are running the campaign of the majority party's candidate, you'll win if you can turn out enough of your majority, so you'll probably try to rally your base by appealing to the party's core values. If your party is in the minority, then (as you would in an open primary) you need to promote aspects of your candidate's record or personality that attract independents or to raise issues that cross party lines.

In 2000, the two parties' presidential candidates followed that script. George W. Bush came into the campaign with his party's identifiers in the minority. He stressed that he was a "compassionate conservative" in order to appeal to independents and Democrats. Bush also emphasized bipartisanship and an end to "partisan bickering," just as a minority-party candidate would logically do. As would be expected from a majority-party candidate, Democrat Al Gore emphasized the traditional Democratic core issues of Social Security and Medicare.

When Bush ran for reelection in 2004, he chose a different approach. Although he continued to appeal to independents and weak Democrats by stressing his leadership in the war on terror, Bush's campaign put major effort into energizing its base. Believing that millions of conservative Christians had sat out the 2000 election, presidential adviser Karl Rove used issues such as same-sex marriage and abortion to mobilize those core Bush supporters. Democrat John Kerry's campaign, in contrast, behaved like a minority party by stressing Kerry's record as a Vietnam War hero. Similarly, in 2006, the Republican leadership focused on its conservative and religious base voters, while the Democrats appealed to the moderate center.

Why did the two parties' campaigns switch strategies? In 2004, the Republicans took the unusual approach of appealing to the party's base, even though it was not clearly in the majority, because the party's sophisticated campaign apparatus had become better able to locate and turn out its core supporters. Republican strategists also used specific issues to appeal to voters who would not otherwise be available to Republican candidates: for instance, peeling off some usually Democratic Latinos by appealing to their religious opposition to same-sex marriage. The polarization of the electorate influenced the strategists as well; if the center is shrinking, a centrist appeal makes less sense. The Republican strategy worked in 2004.

But when Bush's approval ratings declined by 2006, the Republican base proved harder to mobilize. The economic recession in 2008 put the Republicans' "base strategy" further in doubt, because the base was getting smaller. For the majority Democrats in that election, the choice was easy: hold the base but use Barack Obama's charismatic appeal to increase turnout and attract moderate suburbanites and independents.

If you were managing a presidential campaign in 2012, which approach would you take? You would need to assess how well Obama's economic stimulus is working, which will help determine whether the Democratic wave that began in 2005 is continuing or has peaked. If you are a Republican strategist, you would have to decide whether to rely on the traditional approach of a minority party and broaden your appeal well beyond your conservative Christian base—and, if you do, whether you'll infuriate the base and weaken yourself further. If your strategy works, you'll be hailed as a genius and your party's candidates for president in 2016 will seek your counsel. If it doesn't, expect frequent mentions on Jon Stewart's "The Daily Show."

In both primary and general election campaigns, however, one of the best ways to win is to already hold the office you seek.[2] Incumbents normally have greater name recognition and more success in attracting (usually favorable) media coverage than do most of their potential opponents. The constituent service provided by their government-paid staff members and their paid travel to and from the district give them a substantial edge over their challengers, unless they throw it away due to scandal. Their access to power makes it easier for incumbents to raise as much campaign money as they think they need, and their experience helps them use it effectively. And incumbents are usually part of the majority party in the district, which helps them win. Because of these advantages, in both types of elections, incumbents often don't need to do more than stress their experience, their trustworthiness, and the benefits they bring to the district, including the "earmarks" in the federal budget that help the district's economy.

Challengers face a much harsher campaign environment. Especially if they have not won any other political office before, challengers do not start with an experienced organization, proven fund-raising skills, or the other incumbent advantages.[3] In the days when party organizations ran campaigns, this might not have been a problem. Now it is. One obvious answer might be to purchase an experienced campaign organization by hiring political consultants, but most challengers do not have the money. Thus, the predictable cycle begins: The challenger lacks an existing organization and enough money to attract the interest of well-known consultants and buy media time, so he or she cannot reach many voters, and without these vital resources, a challenger will not raise enough money to be able to afford either one.

In this resource-poor environment, policy issues such as abortion, health care, and taxes are more important tools for challengers than they are for incumbents.[4] Researchers find that challengers usually do better when they campaign on issues "owned" by their party, such as health care and Social Security for Democrats and national defense and taxes for Republicans.[5] (Even better, of course, is an incumbent opponent who thoughtfully becomes embroiled in a financial or sex scandal within a few months of the election.)

Candidates for open seats (those where no incumbent is running) are more likely to run competitive races. Those who choose to run for the most visible offices—the presidency, governorships, the U.S. Senate—typically start with considerable name recognition, which increases because of the attention given to an open seat race. They can attract enough funds to pay for extensive media campaigns. Their major challenge will be to spend their money effectively and to define themselves to the voters before their opponents get the chance to define them. John McCain's media consultants were trying to define their opponent in the summer of 2008 when they put up an ad calling Barack Obama "the biggest celebrity in the world" and comparing him to Paris Hilton and Britney Spears, to suggest that he was a presumptuous empty suit rather than an experienced president-to-be. (Hilton responded with an ad referring to McCain as "the wrinkly, white-haired guy," another attempt at defining an opponent.)

HOW CAMPAIGNING HAS CHANGED

Incumbents, challengers, and open seat candidates now have campaign tools available to them that would have been the envy of candidates decades ago. Campaigns have found effective ways to apply advances in polling, media use, and computer technology. They have done so with the help of a burgeoning industry of professional campaign consultants.

Professional Consultants

Political consultants deliver a variety of campaign services.[6] Some are general consultants, similar to the general contractors who oversee the construction of a home; others concentrate on the details of mailing lists, Web-page design, or sampling public opinion. Some are experts in the development of media messages and others in how to raise money. Some provide organizational skills; they can organize rallies, coffee parties, and phone banks.

Professional consultants typically work for several different campaigns at a time. Although they work independently of the party organizations, they almost always work with clients from only one party—some consultants restrict themselves even further to one wing, or ideological grouping, within the party—and they normally maintain a cooperative relationship with that party's leaders. In fact, national party committees often play a matchmaking role in bringing together consultants and candidates.

American consultants have also exported their campaign expertise to the rest of the democratic world. Pollster Stan Greenberg, for instance, worked for former President Bill Clinton in 1996. Then he was hired by campaigns for prime minister in England in 1997, Germany in 1998, and Israel in 1999 before signing on to Al Gore's presidential campaign in 2000. In 2005, he advised Britain's Labour Party in the national election, along with another former Clinton pollster, Mark Penn, who later worked on Hillary Clinton's presidential campaign in 2008.

Sources of Information

Computers   Experienced candidates develop a picture of their constituency in their minds. After years of contact with constituents, they know what kinds of people support them and how they believe they can trigger that support again. In past years, this "theory" of the campaign would have guided the candidate's strategy, even if the beliefs were inaccurate or the constituency had changed.

Computer technology now provides a much more sophisticated check on the candidate's beliefs. By entering canvassers' information into databases, party organizations can aim specific appeals at people likely to be sympathetic to those appeals. Fund-raisers can merge mailing lists from groups and publications whose members may be predisposed to favor their candidate and then produce targeted mailings within hours. Using computerized records, "oppo" researchers can locate statements made by the opponent on any conceivable issue.

Polls   No campaign technology has been employed more fully than the public opinion poll.[7] Candidates poll before deciding whether to run for an office in order to assess voters' views and to probe for weaknesses in the opposition. When the campaign begins, polls are used to determine what issues are uppermost in voters' minds and how the candidate's first steps are affecting his or her "negatives" and "positives." Poll data can help the campaign decide whether its ads should emphasize party loyalties or ties with other party candidates. *Tracking polls* can follow the reactions of small samples of voters each day to measure immediate responses to a campaign event or a new ad.

METHODS OF PERSUASION: THE AIR WAR

Because of the large size of most state and federal election districts, candidates (and national parties as well) make extensive use of the mass media, especially television, radio, and the Internet.

Television

Television consumes most of the money of a typical campaign. In the early and inexpensive days of TV, candidates bought large chunks of time to air entire speeches to a nation- or statewide audience. Now, because of television's increased cost and voters' shorter attention spans, campaign messages are compressed into 30-second spot ads that can be run frequently.[8] In several close House races in 2008, for example, virtually every minute of advertising time in the weeks before Election Day was filled with campaign ads. Placement of these spot ads is a major concern of media specialists. Toward the end of the 2008 presidential race, both the McCain and Obama organizations tried to reach out to "security moms" concerned about national defense by running ads on *Oprah*, *The View*, *Live with Regis and Kelly*, and *Rachael Ray*. The value of broadcast advertising in campaigns has been reduced, however, by technology—from the "mute" button to TiVo—that viewers can use to screen out campaign commercials.

Cable TV is a cost-effective alternative to the traditional networks and works well in local campaigns, whose constituencies are too small to warrant buying time in major media markets. Most cable stations, such as TLC and CBN (Christian Broadcasting

Network), have more specialized "niche" audiences than do the bigger networks. This permits campaigns to target their messages (called *narrowcasting*).

Campaigns also try to get as much *free media* (campaigners prefer to call it *earned media*) coverage as possible on TV news and in newspapers. When newscasts and print reporters cover a candidate, the information may seem more credible and "objective" than if it is conveyed through the campaign's own ads. Campaign coverage, however, is normally brief. A study of seven major Midwestern cities during the 2006 campaign found that viewers were exposed to less than two minutes of election news during a typical 30-minute local newscast, most of it about campaign strategy and polls, compared with four and a half minutes of paid political ads.[9] And large numbers of Americans have little or no interest in news, and now have enough other media choices to be able to avoid it altogether—a big change from the 1960s and 1970s, when most Americans watched the same three network newscasts. The political information these news-avoiders receive, then, comes entirely from entertainment programming and campaign ads.[10]

To get free media coverage, campaigns need to provide material that meets the media's definition of "news."[11] If "news" is that which is dramatic, controversial, and immediate, then a candidate is not likely to earn media coverage with yet another reading of a standard stump speech. Dave Barry offers this illustration: "Let's consider two headlines. FIRST HEADLINE: 'Federal Reserve Board Ponders Reversal of Postponement of Deferral of Policy Reconsideration.' SECOND HEADLINE: 'Federal Reserve Board Caught in Motel with Underage Sheep.' Be honest, now. Which of these two stories would you read?"[12] Candidates who depend on free media need to stage campaign events that use the tamer, political equivalent of the underage sheep: dramatic confrontations, visually exciting settings, or meetings with well-known or telegenic people.

The Internet

First used by candidates in 1996, Web sites are now a part of every major campaign and many local races as well. Campaigns can reach their supporters directly on the Internet, thus bypassing the needs and biases of the broadcast media. Many Web sites ask visitors to register, which allows the campaign to contact them later via e-mail. By loading spots or longer ads online—on the free video-sharing site YouTube, for instance—campaigners can get their messages nationally distributed without paying for costly TV time. During the 2008 primary season alone, more than 1,000 videos on Barack Obama were posted on YouTube and viewed more than 53 million times.[13]

Not all voters have ready access to the Internet, but its use has expanded rapidly. In a 2009 poll, 55 percent of the entire adult population, and three-quarters of all Internet users, reported having gone online during the 2008 election to get campaign news or information—more than double the online news audience in 2000. People under the age of 30 are most likely to be Internet users, not surprisingly, but older adults who use the Internet are almost as likely to watch political videos and share election news online as younger people are.[14]

New uses of the Internet develop with each election. In the 2008 presidential race, the buzzword was *viral marketing*, in which campaigns can spread a message exponentially by sending it into social networks such as e-mail, texting, Facebook, and blogs, and urging each recipient to forward it to his or her already existing network of contacts. Hillary Clinton was the target of the first viral attack of the 2008 campaign when an Obama supporter posted a video on YouTube portraying Clinton as Orwell's Big Brother, droning on until a young woman hurls a sledgehammer at a giant video screen showing Clinton's image. Within two weeks, the video had received a million hits; it spread like a virus after viewers sent its Web address to their e-mail contacts and linked it to blogs, and others heard about it in newspapers and on TV. All these uses vastly increase a campaign's reach at little or no cost.

Ads on Internet sites are another effective way to reach potential supporters. Obama spent ten times as much as Clinton for pop-up ads on the Internet sites of major newspapers, Google searches, and also on blogs operated by the "netroots," liberal activists who were particularly friendly to the Obama campaign. These pop-ups were intended not just to raise money but also to recruit volunteers to knock on doors and register voters for the candidate. Although most people do not visit political blogs, journalists do, which increases the blogs' impact.

Social Networking Sites ("Socnets")   Many candidates maintain profiles on Facebook and other social networking sites. The Obama campaign created its own socnet, called MyBarackObama, or MyBO, on which supporters could contact one another. Eventually, MyBO hosted 2 million profiles.

E-mail   E-mail has the great advantage that it is cheaper than regular mail; fundraising appeals using direct (regular) mail cost about 40 cents for each dollar raised, compared with about one penny per dollar raised on the Internet.[15] Online fund-raising, first used effectively by John McCain in 2000 and Howard Dean in 2004, played a vital role in elevating Obama and Republican Mitt Romney to the status of serious presidential candidates in 2008.

Several groups and campaigns amassed huge e-mail lists in the 2008 campaign. The King Kong of these lists was the Obama campaign's, with more than 13 million e-mail addresses. Online contributions accounted for an estimated two-thirds of the candidate's record-breaking $750 million in contributions. The campaign sent more than 7,000 discrete messages to its e-mail list, for a total of over a billion e-mails. Many of the messages were targeted specifically to certain groups—for instance, people who had donated small sums to the campaign. Hillary Clinton's smaller list, a still-impressive 2.5 million e-mail addresses, brought in additional funds after the election to retire the candidate's substantial debt when it was rented to a variety of other candidates and groups. The Republican National Committee (RNC) and the liberal organization MoveOn.org also maintain extensive e-mail lists.

THE GROUND WAR: "UNDER THE RADAR"

The broadcast media are an efficient way to reach large numbers of citizens. Their greatest strength, however, the breadth of their reach, is also one of their greatest weaknesses. (The other is their high cost.) If you were running for office, you would want to target different messages to different kinds of people so that you could speak to each individual about the issue that most concerns him or her.

Increasingly, candidates are turning to more carefully targeted appeals. These are known collectively as the *ground war*: nonbroadcast activities such as house-to-house canvassing and computer-targeted mailings and phone calls that permit communication with selected groups of people. These ground-war techniques were used with great sophistication by Republican campaigns in 2004. The 2008 Obama campaign organization surpassed even that standard for personal as well as online contact (see box on this page).

Direct Contact by Mail, Text, and Twitter

Direct Mail   By merging mailing lists of people who are of special interest to a campaign, consultants can direct personalized letters to millions of people who might be inclined to respond to a particular appeal. A candidate who wants to appeal

---

WHAT MADE THE OBAMA CAMPAIGN SO EFFECTIVE?

The Obama campaign's strategy was unusual for a presidential race, according to Campaign Manager David Plouffe. Most presidential campaigns have spent 70–75 percent of their funds on broadcast media advertising. The Obama campaign's media expenditure was less than 50 percent. Instead, the campaign's first priority was the ground war—the block-by-block, phone-by-phone effort to contact as many individuals as possible. Obama had won the nomination, his managers felt, because he had a much more extensive and effective field organization than Hillary Clinton did. In the general election, "we knew that we had to get really good turnout," Plouffe said, "and we thought that a human being talking to a human being . . . is the most effective in communication." When the Obama organization found that it had raised more than enough money during the fall campaign, it did buy a lot of broadcast time in September and October, "but we could've won without that," according to Plouffe. The McCain campaign, in contrast, put relatively little effort into the ground war.

Plouffe credited the lengthy Democratic nomination race against a "formidable" and aggressive Clinton candidacy with toughening up the young Obama organization for the general election race against Republican John McCain. The long march of primaries and caucuses "made us a stronger general election candidate. A lot of our dirty laundry was aired, and we had practice in testing a campaign . . . we went into the general election in very much fighting shape." McCain's campaign, Plouffe said, "careened from message to message, strategy to strategy. We had one message, one strategy."

And, of course, the economic meltdown and Obama's calm response to it, the unpopularity of President Bush, and the excitement generated by the first African American major-party nominee for president didn't hurt either.

Sources: Lloyd Grove, "World According to . . . David Plouffe," at www.portfolio.com/views/columns/the-world-according-to/2008/12/11/David-Plouffe-Interview (accessed June 4, 2009); Anne E. Kornblut, "Measured Response to Financial Crisis Sealed the Election," *Washington Post*, November 5, 2008, p. A1.

to pro-gun voters, for example, could send computer-generated letters to people on mailing lists of the National Rifle Association, donors to other pro-gun candidates, and subscribers to hunting magazines. Because these messages are designed to be read by sympathetic individuals in the privacy of their homes, direct mail appeals can be highly emotional and inflammatory, appeals that would not work well in the "cool" medium of television.

Text Messaging   In addition to Obama's mammoth e-mail list, his campaign collected a million cell phone numbers from people who had agreed to receive text messages from the campaign. Supporters typically got 5–20 texts a month, targeted to the individual's location and interests. In battleground states on Election Day, every voter who had signed up for Obama texts got at least three such messages reminding him or her to vote and to bring others to the polls too.

Twitter   The 2008 election was the first in which Twitter, a free social networking site, received campaign use. Campaigners can send "tweets," messages of up to 140 characters, to update supporters. Tweets can be used effectively to respond quickly to an opponent's attacks —or to distribute those attacks more widely.

Canvassing and Phone Banks

In the days of machine politics, party organizations sent their patronage workers and other volunteers to the homes of people who might vote for party candidates, to give them information about the party ticket. Although candidates' staffs now can tweet, call, and e-mail just as easily as party leaders can, canvassing does not lend itself as readily to candidate-centered campaigns. It takes a lot of volunteers to go door-to-door, and for most of American history, party organizations were more likely than individual candidates to have the requisite numbers of canvassers.

Canvassing efforts became less common in the mid-1900s, when party organizations had more difficulty finding volunteers. But in recent years, the parties have developed more sophisticated forms of canvassing to turn out their base voters and other targeted groups. Voter contacting by the parties has increased dramatically.

Microtargeting   Door-to-door canvassing is especially efficient when a party's target voters all live in the same area. Republican strategists learned in the early 2000s, however, that Republican voters are not as concentrated geographically as Democrats tend to be. Thus, they reasoned, they would have to identify these sympathizers individually instead, using commercial databases. Party staffers collected data on people's viewing habits, magazine subscriptions, purchasing preferences, and voting patterns. They learned that people who watch Fox News, country or religious stations, or the Golf Channel, drive BMWs rather than Chevys, go to exercise clubs after work, drink bourbon or Coors beer, and watch college football are inclined to support Republicans. They also confirmed that a lot of conservatives don't trust the mainstream media.

Using these demographic data and public opinion research, the Bush–Cheney campaign and the RNC, in coordination with Republican state and local parties, worked to cherry-pick likely Republican voters in the 2004 election. This is known as *"microtargeting"* or "niche marketing." In particular, they identified 7 million Republicans and 10 million conservative-leaning independents who had not voted regularly in the past. Then they classified these targets into a series of types and determined which issues were the most likely to anger voters in each type. One voter type could be approached with a mailing or a phone call about same-sex marriage; another might receive an appeal about terrorism. All these data were entered into the national Republican database called *Voter Vault*.

The success of the Republican effort prompted the Democrats to catch up. In 2008 exit polls, 26 percent of respondents said they were contacted personally by the Obama campaign, compared with just 18 percent reporting contact by McCain.[16] The A.F.L.–C.I.O., the giant labor federation, contributed extensively to the Democrats' canvassing efforts in 2006 and 2008.

These contacts can be made even more efficiently, though probably not as persuasively, by phone. In 2008, many campaigns brought supporters to a central location (a *phone "bank"*) with telephones—often a business, union, or party or campaign headquarters, or even an empty building where volunteers could use their cell phones—to dial lists of numbers identified by the campaign's microtargeting. Even cheaper are *robocalls*, in which volunteers or computers can direct automated phone calls to large numbers of people on a campaign's target list. Robocalls are often used to send a negative message or to do *"push polling"* —attack messages disguised as public opinion polls. In high-profile races, households often receive several of these calls a night as the election approaches.

Negative Campaigning

It has become a staple of political consulting that, when a candidate is falling behind in the polls, one of the quickest ways to recover is to "go negative." Attacking an opponent is not new; politicians since the earliest days of the republic have been the focus of vicious attacks. Concern about negative campaigns has increased recently, however, because they can be spread so much faster and farther by new technologies.

Harsh negative ads sometimes attract news coverage, which carries their message to even more people. Information about the savage ads of the "Swift Boat Veterans for Truth" in the 2004 campaign, making the unsubstantiated claim that John Kerry had not deserved the medals he was awarded in the Vietnam War, reached between half and three-quarters of respondents in national surveys even though the ads were broadcast in only seven small media markets, such as Green Bay and Wausau, Wisconsin. Interest groups and party organizations are more likely than the candidates themselves to use negative themes in their ads and direct mail.[17]

Does negative campaigning work? Some researchers find that negative campaigns drive down turnout because they increase voter cynicism. Others suggest that negative ads are particularly memorable and emotionally engaging, which actually increase voter information and turnout.[18] There is some evidence that the timing of negative ads matters; before an individual chooses a candidate, negative ads can be informative and useful, but after the individual has made his or her choice, attack ads are more likely to depress turnout, especially among people who are not strong partisans.[19] No matter what their real impact was, however, the Swift Boat ads were widely assumed to have seriously hurt Kerry's campaign in 2004, so presidential candidates in 2008 drew the lesson that they needed to respond immediately and strongly to negative ads, rather than to ignore them.

These campaign tools have been used in a variety of ways in recent elections:

The 2004 Campaign

Attention focused heavily in 2004 on a few highly competitive campaigns. Because the two parties were so evenly matched in the U.S. House and Senate, and because the overwhelming majority of House incumbents were expected to coast to easy wins, the parties and many interest groups ignored most congressional races and focused their resources on two or three dozen competitive seats as well as the presidential race. In the presidential contest, the air wars were limited to between 12 and 20 "battleground" states at any given time. Voters in eight of the ten biggest media markets—New York, Los Angeles, Chicago, Washington, San Francisco, Boston, Dallas, and Houston—saw no sustained advertising for either presidential candidate because their states were regarded as locked up for one candidate. The residents of the targeted states and districts were hit by a virtual hurricane of campaign advertising.

Although most campaigns continued to be candidate-centered in 2004, there were signs of more party-centered activity in these very competitive races. In particular, the national Republican Party geared up for an unprecedented ground-war campaign. To counteract the expected canvassing drives by labor unions and the Democrats, the national Republicans had been conducting a series of experiments on how best to reach voters. They had field-tested a program in 2002 in which the GOP flooded precincts in competitive states with Republican volunteers and paid staffers, especially during the last 72 hours of the campaign. This *"72-hour project"* was expensive, costing $200 million, but observers felt that it increased Republican turnout by about 3 percent in 2002 over that of the last midterm election, and Republicans won most of the close contests, maintained control of the House, and narrowly regained control of the Senate.[20] Thus the Republicans expanded the model in 2004. A full year before the election, the RNC and the Bush campaign were already training thousands of volunteers to recruit canvassers for a massive "72-hour project." Because the president was unopposed for the Republican nomination, the full force of his huge campaign budget could be focused on the general election.

The Kerry campaign and the national Democrats put effort into the ground war as well. But much of Kerry's canvassing and almost 40 percent of his TV advertising was done by independent groups, who raised money in order to help the Democratic ticket compete under the constraints of the 2002 campaign finance reforms (see Chapter 12). By law, these independent groups were not allowed to consult with the Kerry campaign in planning or conducting their activities, nor could they ask people directly to vote for Kerry, so their messages and efforts were not always closely integrated with those of the campaign.

In the end, the Bush volunteers had an easier sell. A large majority of Bush voters were enthusiastic about their candidate, whereas a lot of Kerry voters were motivated mainly by their dislike of Bush. The Kerry campaign won about 8 million more votes than Democrat Al Gore in 2000, while Bush increased his by about 11 million. As one analyst wrote, "Kerry did well. Bush did better."[21] Bush eked out a narrow victory, and his party kept control of the House and slightly increased its Senate majority.

Democrats Regain the Advantage in 2006

Republican candidates anticipated a much tougher race in 2006. The climate of public opinion had changed. Bush's approval rating was dropping markedly, in part because of growing public discontent with the war in Iraq. As anti-Republican feeling grew, more and more previously "safe" Republican incumbents started looking over their shoulders. The number of competitive House races, estimated to be about 35–45 at the beginning of the 2006 campaign, jumped to more than twice that number.

The national Republican Party continued to trust its tested ground-war techniques. In view of the changed political climate, however, Republican strategists decided to start the microtargeting and canvassing campaign sooner and to expand it to include a larger portion of independents. To counteract the anti-Bush tide, the national party planned to spend more than 90 percent of its funds on negative ads attacking the Democrats.

Democratic candidates sought to attract voter support by linking their Republican opponents to Bush. As the campaign progressed, Democrats gained other targets, including several Republican Congressmen who were linked to a corrupt lobbyist, and Rep. Mark Foley (D-FL), who resigned after having sent sexually explicit e-mails and IMs to underage House pages. Anti-immigration speeches by some Republican conservatives undercut the party's recent efforts to appeal to Latino votes.

On Election Day, Democrats rode a wave just as the Republicans had in 1994. With a net gain of 31 seats in the House and 6 in the Senate, Democrats took control of both houses of Congress for the first time in 12 years. The Democratic trend, which was especially strong in the Northeast, was built on substantial support from moderates and independents as well as Democratic identifiers.

The Old and the New in 2008

Democratic strength continued to build in 2008 as Bush's popularity hit new lows. The Obama campaign chose a strategy that would have looked very familiar to leaders of the powerful urban party organizations of the late 1800s: use extensive networks of personal contact to engage voters and get them to the polls. The main difference was that, just as effective party politics has always adapted to new technologies, Obama's organization successfully used the Internet, text messaging, cell phones, and other high-tech tools to contact voters. By 2008, as Chapter 4 showed, the DNC and several other Democratic-leaning groups had matched and perhaps even surpassed the Republicans' microtargeting skills. Using the DNC's upgraded Vote Builder databank as well as data from the privately owned Catalist, the Obama campaign designed an extensive ground game.

It was not always clear that Obama would win the presidential race convincingly, however. In many ways, Republican John McCain was the Obama campaign's worst nightmare. As a self-proclaimed "maverick" and reformer, McCain was able to draw distinctions between himself and President Bush. McCain was a war hero, a longtime political presence in comparison with Obama's relative inexperience in national politics, and a personality attractive to independents. McCain's campaign sought to overcome Democratic trends by portraying Obama as an elitist who did not "share our values," similar to Bush's successful characterizations of Kerry in 2004 and Al Gore in 2000. Obama fought to keep the focus on the Bush administration's failures. Although the polls showed Obama with a slight lead during the summer of 2008, McCain pulled ahead after the Republican convention. But the financial disaster of mid-September, and McCain's unsteady response to it, broke McCain's new momentum and foreshadowed Obama's victory in November.

Perhaps the most notable accomplishment of Obama's campaign, building on its massive fund-raising and effective use of new technologies, was its ability to expand the playing field. Democratic presidential campaigns in the recent past had targeted a group of reliably Democratic East and West Coast states and then aimed to pick up just enough "battleground" states (typically, Ohio, Pennsylvania, and Florida) to reach an Electoral College majority. Obama's staffers tried to create more alternative ways to win. They put particular effort into some previously Republican states, such as Colorado and Virginia, whose demographic profile was becoming more favorable to Democratic candidates.

In the end, the Obama efforts paid off. Several states, including Virginia and Indiana, gave their electoral votes to a Democratic presidential candidate for the first time in 44 years. Obama won not only every state that Kerry had carried in 2004 but also nine former Bush states, plus one electoral vote from Nebraska. Minorities (especially blacks), women, city dwellers, upscale suburbanites, and liberals formed the core of Obama's victory. Republicans held their own in Appalachia and other areas with large white, evangelical populations and even improved their performance in the Deep South, among whites. As always, however, the results were interpreted in different ways, depending in part on the agenda of the observer (see box on this page).

WHY DID THE DEMOCRATS WIN IN 2008?

Many Democrats argued that voters wanted change; the public was done with President Bush and welcomed the chance to support hope, dynamism, and better economic times.

Many conservative Republicans believed that voters prefer conservative government but they no longer saw the Republican Party as conservative. Republicans in Congress had supported big-spending projects and strayed from the party's core values in other ways.

Many moderate Republicans contended that because Republican leaders had put so much emphasis on hot-button social issues such as opposition to stem cell research, moderate suburban voters saw the party as extremist. Republicans need to be more of a "big tent," including those with differing views on abortion and related issues.

It is common for different groups to interpret (or "spin") the meaning of an election differently, to support their own preferred views. Journalists, who are the targets of the spin, often become cynical about it. Jon Margolis, former national political reporter for the *Chicago Tribune*, claims that he switched to the sports beat because he said he'd never seen a sports story that read, "The Chicago Cubs defeated the St. Louis Cardinals today by a score of 2–1. The Cardinals denied it."

Sources: Tom Davis, "The Way Back," *The Ripon Forum* 43 (2009), at www.riponsociety. org/forum109a.htm (accessed June 4, 2009); Margolis quoted in Ronald D. Elving, "Campaign Data Can Be Calculated Nonsense," *CQ Weekly*, August 19, 1995, p. 2602.

Political activists then turned their attention to the crucial midterm contests of 2010. Governors and state legislators chosen in that election are responsible for redrawing legislative districts—those for Congress and state legislatures—after the 2010 census is completed. This legislative redistricting will make a big difference in the parties' prospects for 2012, when the ground and air wars can be expected to heat up again.

DO CAMPAIGNS MAKE A DIFFERENCE?

Because campaigns attract so much media attention, money, and effort, many people naturally assume that campaign events are responsible for the election's outcome. Yet careful statistical analysis shows that election results can normally be predicted fairly well from conditions that existed before the campaign began, such as the incumbent's previous poll ratings, economic conditions, and the distribution of party loyalties in the district. That doesn't leave much room for campaigns to determine the outcome. Instead, it seems to suggest that campaigns simply remind voters of these longer lasting conditions and, in this way, help them move toward a largely preordained outcome.[22]

Does this mean that the relative strengths and weaknesses of candidates' strategies are not important? Researchers have used a variety of methods to measure campaign impact, and, not surprisingly, they have reached a variety of conclusions.

The Argument that Campaigns Matter

A look at John McCain's journey—from a nearly broke and discredited presidential candidacy in July 2007 to victory in the Republican nomination race a year later—would suggest that at least in some cases, some aspects of a campaign must have an impact. McCain's resurgence stemmed in part from events outside his control, including a declining death rate in the war in Iraq, but also in part from his campaign's efforts, such as its successful use of town-hall meetings with voters in the pivotal New Hampshire primary.

What has been found to make a difference? A long line of evidence, supported by both parties' experience in recent elections, suggests that canvassing has a small but meaningful effect on both turnout and voters' choices.[23] Canvassing probably makes more of a difference in local elections than in presidential races because there are fewer alternative sources of information in local contests. Researchers find that door-to-door canvassing is more effective in activating voters than phone contact is; conversational phone calls are more effective than those in which the caller reads a prepared script, and both door-to-door and phone contact are more effective than mailings,[24] though the quality of the contact can matter at least as much as the medium.[25] Researchers find that where a party is active, its vote share can increase by at least a few percentage points, which could be the critical margin in a close race.[26]

Television news and advertising—and the money that pays for the ads—can also influence voters' decisions, especially when they provide new information about a candidate.[27] Even with the big increase in voter contacts by the party organizations, many more people see the campaign on TV. Campaign debates and other events have been found to influence voters' decisions under some circumstances.[28] Newer media make a difference too. All these sources of campaign information, taken together, seem to improve citizens' knowledge and increase voter turnout.[29]

Various elements of campaigns, including media ads and coverage, affect some voters differently from others, depending on the voter's party identification and level of interest in politics. For instance, those with limited political interest may pick up only a little information about campaigns, but the few bits of information that break through—often, perceptions of a candidate's likeability—could have a substantial impact on their attitudes.[30] As a rule, campaign communications are most effective in bringing weak partisans back into the fold when they have had doubts about their party's candidate.[31] More generally, the information that campaigns provide can affect the importance voters attach to various aspects of the race, such as a candidate's views on the economy or his or her age or ethnicity.[32] Media attention also "primes" viewers to look for some qualities in candidates rather than others.[33] This kind of media impact is indirect and hard to measure, but its effects could be profound.

The Argument That They Don't

There are several reasons why campaigning may have only a limited effect, however. First, television news, ads, and ground-war activities offer viewers a wide range of conflicting messages about candidates—positive, negative, and neutral information and opinions, all mixed together. The inconsistency of these messages makes it harder for a campaign to have a single, consistent impact on viewers' minds.[34]

We know that voters pay selective attention to media and other campaign communications. They tend to surround themselves with friends, information, and even personal experiences that support their beliefs and loyalties.[35] The politically aware may pick and choose among the differing messages and ignore those that conflict with their own opinions. Most campaign communications, then, probably have the effect of activating and reinforcing the voter's existing political inclinations, as they always have.[36] That can explain why so much campaign effort is directed at getting people out to vote—to act on whatever opinions they already hold—rather than at trying to change their voting decision.

Some Tentative Answers

There is much left to learn about the effects of campaigns. In the information-rich environment of current campaigns and among the large numbers of independents, the potential for campaigns to shape voters' perceptions may be greater than it has ever been. There are times when dramatic events during a campaign may actually decide the outcome and when even well-established candidate images can be revised (see box on page 215). The impact of campaigns, however, will continue to be limited by the same forces that have always constrained it: voters' tendency to pay attention to the messages with which they already agree and their ability to tune out most political messages altogether.

CANDIDATE-CENTERED OR PARTY-CENTERED CAMPAIGNS?

The campaign techniques that we have explored in this chapter have affected the balance of power in campaigns between parties and candidates. Broadcast media, which need a large audience, tend to focus on individual personalities rather than institutions such as parties. Tools such as direct mail, Internet ads, and TV advertising are available to any candidate who can pay for them; they let candidates communicate with voters without the party's help. The technologies that have developed since the mid-1900s, in short, have helped candidates run their campaigns independently of the party organizations. If the American parties had been as strong organizationally as those in many other nations when these technologies developed, then they might have been able to monopolize the use of TV and other media for campaign purposes. But in fact, as we have seen, the American parties have always struggled to maintain their power in a political culture hostile to their functioning.

Many of the nation's electoral rules also make it easier for campaigns to be candidate-centered. The American electoral process has few institutions, such as parliamentary-cabinet government or proportional representation, which would encourage voters to see elections as contests between parties for control of government. Instead, rules ranging from campaign finance regulations to the separate scheduling of national and state elections encourage candidates to run as individuals, not as members of a party ticket, and make it hard for parties to coordinate the campaigns of several candidates. Progressive reforms strengthened this tendency. The direct primary, as we have seen, allows candidates to run without the party organization's approval.

As a consequence, it is the candidates and their advisers, not the parties, who make the strategic decisions in most campaigns. Candidates have their own headquarters and staffers rather than using the party's facilities. Candidates maintain their own relationships with voters rather than relying on the party organization as an intermediary. Party organizations, rather than running campaigns, often work instead to enhance the appeal of individual candidates, and they compete with consultants, interest groups, and others for the chance to do so.

Party Influence in Competitive Campaigns

The parties, however, are fighting back. The large sums of money that have flowed into the national parties in the past three decades have helped them to assist individual campaigns with money and other services.[37] As Chapter 4 noted, soft money enabled party organizations to pour millions of dollars into campaign ads in a few battleground states until 2004. Since then, massive party fund-raising and voter contact drives have increased the party presence in more races.

The national parties' visibility has increased especially in the most highly competitive Senate and House elections. That is where party organizations have used independent spending to make the biggest financial impact, in some cases spending even more than the candidates themselves do. But because independent spending does not allow the parties to coordinate their efforts with their candidates, much less to run their campaigns, party-funded ads have sometimes stressed different themes from those the campaign preferred to emphasize and, frequently, more negative messages than the campaign's own advertising.[38] Because voters rarely pay attention to the source of any particular message, candidates have gotten blamed for negativity and claims that they have not made. In most races, however, the party's role is not nearly as noticeable.

The Continuing Struggle Between Candidates and Party Organizations

An expanded party role in campaigns makes economic sense. Party organizations can distribute appeals for a number of candidates at the same time and register voters to help the entire ticket. Parties can buy media advertising and consultants' services for use by several candidates at cost-effective prices. Party organizations can coordinate Election Day activities for all the party's candidates, provide poll-watchers to guard against voting irregularities, send cars to get people to the polls, and check voter lists to mobilize nonvoters late in the day.

This efficiency is bought at the cost of limiting each candidate's independence, however. Party organizations and candidates do not always have the same goals. The party, aiming to maximize the number of races it wins, puts its scarce resources into the most competitive campaigns and spends as little as possible on the races it considers hopeless. Each candidate, in contrast, is committed above all to his or her own victory and to gaining the resources needed to achieve it, no matter how unlikely that victory may be. The party, in its drive to win every competitive race, is likely to do whatever it takes, whether through negative or positive campaigning. The candidate, in contrast, has to face the voters; a constant barrage of attack ads may make a candidate less appealing.

The result is a continuing struggle between party organizations and candidates—the party in government—for control of campaigns. In most elections, the candidates are winning the fight. Although the parties have more to offer candidates than they did just a few years ago, party organizations still contribute only a fairly small percentage of candidates' overall spending in all but a few races. In contrast, European parties often provide more than half the funding used by most candidates.

Candidate-centered campaigning has an important effect on governing. When they control their own campaigns, winning candidates can develop personal relationships with their constituents, unconstrained by party ties. Candidates are free to form close alliances with interest groups, which enhance the ability of these groups to influence public policy. In short, candidate-centered campaigning strengthens the power of the party in government relative to that of the party organization. It also poses an important question: If strong party organizations can help to hold elected officials accountable for their actions, then how much accountability do voters get from a candidate-centered politics?

THE REINVENTION OF HILLARY CLINTON

While she was First Lady, Hillary Clinton's public image was not a pollster's dream. Although she was beloved by many liberals, a lot of conservatives disliked her intensely. Scores of Republicans saw her as a strident feminist, a dyed-in-the-wool liberal, and the author of a national health care proposal that gave much of the business community fits. Tabloids called her cold, calculating, and overly ambitious.

Her public role changed in 2000 when, even before leaving the White House, Clinton won a close contest for New York's open Senate seat. On her return to Washington, Senator Clinton's actions surprised a lot of Hillary haters. She asked for a seat on the Armed Services Committee. She came out in favor of the death penalty and collaborated with several conservative Republican senators, including some who had fought hard to impeach and convict her husband.

Then she announced that she was running for president in 2008. As she had done for many years, Clinton spoke publicly about prayer and faith and encouraged those on both sides of such divisive issues as abortion to find common ground. She stressed her Midwestern roots and her advocacy for children's causes rather than her high-powered legal career.

Clinton was a formidable candidate in the Democratic primaries. She received almost 18 million primary votes and came very close to winning the nomination. Her campaign stumbled, oddly, in its understanding of the party's nomination rules—an unexpected lapse for a candidate steeped in party politics. Although her loss to Barack Obama was a crushing blow, Clinton moved quickly to champion an Obama victory in the general election. Soon after Election Day, President Obama named her his Secretary of State, responsible for overseeing the administration's diplomatic efforts all over the globe, including the women's rights initiatives she had championed.

It isn't easy for someone with a polarizing image and a long political history to change her public image. But as a writer for *New York Magazine* put it, "No two people are more adept at writing their own story than the Clintons."

Sources: Anne E. Kornblut and Perry Bacon, Jr., "Clinton Makeover Accents her Midwestern Roots," *Washington Post*, June 3, 2007, p. A1; Chris Cillizza, "Hillary Clinton Re-Imagined," at voices.washingtonpost.com/thefix/2009/01/hillary_clinton_re-imagined.html?hpid=topnews (accessed June 4, 2009).

CHAPTER 12

Financing
the Campaigns

In 2008, members of the U.S. Senate running for reelection spent an average of $7.8 million each on their campaigns.[1] If you had to raise that much money, you would need to collect about $25,000—what some people pay for a year in college—*every week* of your six-year term. If you went a week without asking for money, then you'd need to raise $50,000 the following week. That is, of course, in addition to the time you'd need to spend learning about legislation, working with other senators, voting on bills, and communicating with constituents.

Why does it cost so much money to win an office whose salary is $174,000 a year? The escalation in campaign spending has many causes. As candidates have come to depend on paid professionals, television, and computers, money has become key to mobilizing the resources needed for a viable campaign. So candidates, especially for statewide and national office, are not likely to be taken seriously unless they start with a big campaign budget or a proven talent for fund-raising.

Until the campaign finance reforms of the 1970s, much of the money used in campaigns was collected and spent in secret. Candidates were not required to disclose how they raised funds, and contributors were often unwilling to make their names public. The few laws governing campaign contributions were full of loopholes.

As a result of the 1970s reforms, we now have a flood of data about campaign spending and contributions. The regulation is mind-boggling in its complexity. It is constantly under assault by candidates and contributors looking for loopholes through which they can pursue their aims. Despite all this change, the basic questions remain the same. How much money is spent to elect candidates to office, and who spends it? Who contributes the money? What is the party's role in funding campaigns? How much influence does money have on politics, and to what extent have campaign finance reforms been able to control its influence?

HOW MUCH MONEY IS SPENT ON CAMPAIGNS?

Campaigns for all levels of office in the United States cost well over $5 *billion* collectively in 2008—an enormous increase over the amounts spent on campaigns in earlier decades. Inflation has reduced the purchasing power of the dollar during this period, so the real, inflation-adjusted increase is not nearly as dramatic. But the growth in real spending since 1996, which has coincided with the increasing polarization of the major parties, is impressive by any standard.

Presidential Campaigns

The 2008 presidential race was, hands down, the most expensive political campaign in American history (see Figure 12.1). It began as a wide-open contest: the first presidential election in almost 80 years in which no sitting president or vice-president was running for reelection. Democrats sensed the chance of a big victory due in large part to President Bush's unpopularity. But perhaps the biggest reason for the unprecedented spending was the uncommon fund-raising skill of some of the candidates, Barack Obama in particular.

Obama's fund-raising talent became apparent during the invisible primary in 2007. By the end of December, he had already raised more than $100 million. He collected almost as much during the first two months of 2008 alone, a large proportion of it from small donors on the Internet. Obama's organization used a novel approach in Internet fund-raising. Rather than just repeatedly asking supporters for money, as most other candidates have, his staff worked to build relationships with likely donors, informed

FIGURE 12.1   Total Spending by Candidates, Parties, and Groups in Presidential Elections, 1960–2008.

Note: Estimates are for two-year cycles ending in the presidential election years. Inflation-adjusted figures are computed by deflating the actual expenditures using the Consumer Price Index (with 1960 as the base year). *Sources:* John C. Green, ed., *Financing the 1996 Election* (Armonk, NY: M. E. Sharpe, 1999), p. 19; FEC data for 2000–2008, at www.fec.gov. Consumer Price Index deflator is based on Table 702 in the U.S. Census Bureau, *The 2009 Statistical Abstract*, www.census.gov/compendia/statab/tables/09s0702.pdf (accessed June 28, 2009).

them about new developments, and encouraged them to volunteer as canvassers and at campaign events. This approach, combined with Obama's singular appeal, enticed more than 3 million people to contribute to his campaign.

Obama raised over $750 million in 2007–2008, more than all Democratic and Republican presidential candidates combined had collected in the 2004 election cycle. He and his Republican opponent, John McCain, pulled in and spent a total of almost $1.1 billion in the 2008 primaries and the general election campaign (see Table 12.1). But perhaps the most striking feature is that Obama, the Democrat, greatly outraised and outspent his Republican rival. Until Democrat John Kerry came close to matching George W. Bush's overall fund-raising in 2004, the Republican advantage in raising money had been one of the certainties of presidential campaigning.

As sections II and III in Table 12.1 show, other groups also spent a great deal on the presidential race, though not as much as the candidates themselves. Taxpayers pick up part of the tab for the two parties' national conventions; contributions from corporations and other interests cover the bulk of the cost. And the candidate nominated by each major party can choose to receive public funds for the general election. The catch is that he or she is then limited to spending no more than the public funds provided (except money the candidate can raise to pay lawyers and accountants to deal with federal campaign finance laws, called "compliance costs").

Only McCain accepted the public funding; thus, he could spend no more than the $84.1 million he received from the government for his general election campaign. Obama, riding the wave of his fund-raising success in the primaries, guessed that he could raise much more than $84 million between his nomination and Election Day, so it would make sense for him to turn down the federal funds and avoid the spending limit that accompanied them. He guessed right; in September alone, the Obama fund-raising machine took in a record-shattering $150 million—almost twice what he would have received in total federal funding, and quadruple the biggest sum any candidate had raised in one month in any previous presidential race.

In addition to public funding, party organizations spent millions in the presidential campaign. The parties can put money into presidential races in four different ways. They can use *coordinated spending*: money spent by party organizations *in coordination with* a candidate's campaign to purchase services such as media advertising or polling for the campaign. Parties, as well as individuals and other political groups, can also spend as much as they choose independently, to expressly support or oppose a candidate, as long as they do so *without consulting with their candidate*. This is known as *independent spending*. Almost all the party independent spending in the 2008 presidential race came from the Republican Party. When McCain fell far behind Obama in the money chase, and then agreed to accept public funds for his general election campaign, he was vastly outspent by Obama and needed his party's help to remain competitive.

Parties are also allowed to split the cost with a candidate's campaign on *"hybrid" ads*, which mention both the presidential candidate and other party candidates, and to *mobilize voters through grassroots efforts*. Party spending has become increasingly important, though the parties' role in American campaigns pales in comparison with most other democracies, where the party organizations, not the candidates, do most of the campaign spending.

TABLE 12.1 What It Cost to Nominate and Elect a President, 2008

I. Prenomination Receipts and Spending	Amount (in millions of dollars)	
	Raised	Spent
Republicans	**472.4**	**450.2**
McCain	219.6	202.1
Romney	105.2	105.1
Huckabee	16.1	16.0
All others	131.5	127.0
Democrats	**752.4**	**539.4**
Obama	424.2	224.8
Clinton	223.9	215.8
All others	104.3	98.8
II. Conventions		
Public funding for party conventions		33.6
Private funding:		
Republican		62.4
Democratic		61.9
III. General Election		
Candidate Funds		
Public funding for major-party candidates (McCain only)		84.1
General election receipts and spending (Obama only)	321.5	504.5
Third-party receipts and spending (Nader)	4.0	3.8
Compliance costs		46.4
Party Funds (nomination and general)		
Parties' coordinated expenditures		25.3
Parties' independent expenditures		54.6
Parties' contributions to "hybrid" ads financed jointly with candidates		106.0**
Group Funds (nomination and general)		
PAC and individual independent spending		114.2
Spending by 527 groups		202.1*
Spending by 501(c) groups		195.9*
Internal communication costs		18.1
Electioneering communications by groups		27.8

*Although most of this spending went into the presidential race, an unspecified portion was spent on House and Senate campaigns. The figures represent groups that raised $200,000 or more by the end of November 2008.

** Estimates from party officials; no official figures are available at this writing, nor are there data for parties' voter-mobilization (field operation) efforts.

Sources: Based on FEC data as of September 12, 2009. Data on 527 and 501(c) groups from the Campaign Finance Institute. I am grateful to Christian Hilland, Anthony Corrado, and Michael Malbin for their help.

A variety of other groups and individuals also pay for advertising and voter mobilization. "Internal communication costs" in Table 12.1 are the funds spent by labor unions and corporations to urge their members to vote for a particular candidate. Unions, corporations, and membership associations also spent millions on "nonpartisan" voter mobilization, to register voters and get them to the polls on Election Day. (Spending by PACs and 527 groups will be discussed later.)

Congressional Campaigns

In contrast with the presidential election, spending in congressional races declined from that of the previous election: from $1.4 billion in 2006 to about $1.3 billion in 2008 (see Figures 12.2 and 12.3). The feverish fund-raising by the presidential candidates probably dried up some of the usual sources of contributions to House and Senate campaigns. In addition, because only one-third of all Senate seats are up for election in any given year, the mix of states in that group has a big impact on the amount of money spent. In 2006, Senate seats in both New York and Pennsylvania were at stake, and each of those races cost about $46 million in candidate spending, slightly more than each candidate for the French presidency was allowed to spend nationwide in the final round of the 2007 French national election. In the 2008 cycle, fewer large states had Senate contests, so the totals dipped. The biggest sums were spent in the highly competitive contests in Minnesota (where the two candidates combined to spend $40 million), Kentucky ($32 million), and Georgia ($23 million).

Incumbents greatly outraise and outspend their challengers in every election year, and their financial advantage continued in the early 2000s. In 2008, the average

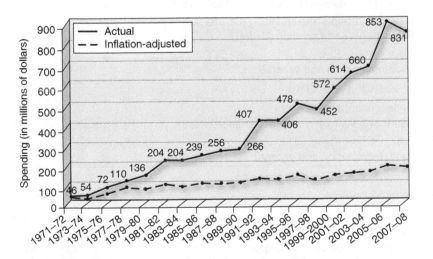

FIGURE 12.2 Total Spending by Candidates in House Campaigns, 1971–1972 to 2007–2008.

Note: Inflation-adjusted figures are computed by deflating the actual expenditures by changes in the price level as measured by the Consumer Price Index (yearly averages) using 1972 as the base year.

Source: FEC press releases for each election year. CPI deflator is the same as that listed for Figure 12.1.

FIGURE 12.3 Total Spending by Candidates in Senate Campaigns, 1971–1972 to 2007–2008.

Note: Inflation-adjusted figures are computed as in Figure 12.1.

Source: FEC press releases for each election year. CPI deflator is the same as that listed for Figure 12.1.

House incumbent raised about $1.4 million for his or her campaign, compared with about $489,000 for the average major-party challenger.[2] In Senate races, incumbents collected an average of $7.8 million compared with about $3.4 million for challengers. Out of each dollar raised in a House race between an incumbent and a challenger, then, the average major-party challenger accounted for only about 26 cents, and in a Senate race, a little more than 30 cents. This challenger disadvantage in Senate races was even greater than usual. Candidates for open seats—those where no incumbent is running—were able to raise more than challengers did but not nearly as much as incumbents: an average of $1.5 million in House races and $5.8 million in Senate campaigns.

Although Republican candidates and organizations have usually held a fund-raising edge over Democrats in congressional campaigns, the size of that advantage depends on which party controls Congress. When the Republican Party won majorities in both houses in 1994, their status as the majority party gave the Republicans an increasing financial advantage going into the next two congressional elections. The Republican edge waxed and waned in the early 2000s, depending in part on which states were electing senators in a given year. But in 2006, the pro-Democratic tide of public opinion permitted Democratic candidates to match or beat the Republicans' fund-raising, and the Democrats took advantage of their majority status in Congress to maintain their fundraising edge in 2008. Although Republican Senate incumbents raised a bit more than their Democratic colleagues, Democratic Senate challengers pulled in four times more money than Republican challengers did, and most types of Democratic House candidates outraised the Republicans.

State and Local Campaigns

Much less is known about spending practices in the thousands of campaigns for state and local offices, mainly because there is no central reporting agency comparable to the national Federal Election Commission (FEC). The range in these races is enormous. Many local candidates win after spending a few hundred dollars. On the other end of the scale are some top-dollar mayoral races. In 2009, Michael Bloomberg spent more than $100 million of his own money to win a third term as mayor of New York—about $91 for each voter in that election.

Campaigns for governor in large states often cost as much as, or more than, races for the U.S. Senate. California typically sets the records. The major candidates in the 2003 election to recall California governor Gray Davis managed to spend a total of $83 million in only 77 days. Winning a state legislative race in a large state is an increasingly expensive proposition as well. In 2007, for example, some legislative campaigns in New Jersey cost more than $1 million each, largely because their "local" media originate in the expensive markets of New York and Philadelphia.[3] Even state Supreme Court elections have become big-spending contests, replete with attack ads. In a 2007 state Supreme Court race in Pennsylvania, eight candidates raised a total of almost $9.5 million, more than double the amount raised two years earlier, and most of it came from business interests and trial lawyers who have a big stake in the judges' rulings.[4]

These figures must be kept in perspective. As substantial as the spending has been, the total cost of all American campaigns still doesn't match the amounts some large corporations spend each year to advertise fast food and cigarettes (see box on this page). Although fast food is a big part of many people's lives, our futures are affected more profoundly by the choices made in state and federal elections. So, to the extent that campaigns give us the chance to learn about the strengths and weaknesses of the people

---

CAMPAIGN SPENDING: TOO MUCH OR TOO LITTLE?

What will $5 billion buy in the United States?

- Less than half of the cigarette advertising and promotion run in 2005
- Five times the advertising budget of McDonald's for 2008
- 18 percent of the amount spent in American gambling casinos in 2008
- One Nimitz-class aircraft carrier (not counting operating costs)
- All the political campaigns run at all levels of government by and for all candidates in 2008

Sources: American Medical Association, at www.ama-assn.org/amednews/2008/09/15/hlsb0915.htm (on cigarette advertising); *Ad Age*, at adage.com/article?article_id=131600 (on McDonald's); Amanda Finnegan, "Report: Last Year Was Second Most Profitable for Industry," *Las Vegas Sun*, May 18, 2009 (on gambling); and http://en.wikipedia.org/wiki/Aircraft_carrier (on aircraft carriers; all accessed June 14, 2009).

who would govern us, the amounts spent on campaign advertising could be considered a real bargain.[5] There are important questions to be asked, however, about the motivations of contributors and the fund-raising disparities among candidates.

WHAT IS THE IMPACT OF CAMPAIGN SPENDING?

Money does not buy victory, but it certainly doesn't hurt. In the general election for president, both sides usually have enough money to reach voters with their messages, so the candidate with the largest war chest does not gain an overwhelming advantage. Money matters more in the early months of the nomination race for president, especially in buying the early visibility that is so vital to an underdog. In later primaries and caucuses, when the candidates are better known, a monetary edge does not necessarily lead to a win. For instance, in the 2008 nominating season, Obama lost the popular vote to his main rival, Hillary Clinton, in several large state primaries that were held after Super Tuesday even though he had outspent Clinton in these states by a factor of three or four to one.

In congressional elections, where we have even more evidence on the impact of campaign spending, most researchers find that money does make a real difference. The more challengers can spend when they run against incumbents, the better their chances are of victory. The same is not always true for incumbents. Gary Jacobson found that the more incumbents spend, the worse they do in the race.[6] It is not that incumbent spending turns voters off, but rather that incumbents tend to spend a lot when they face serious competition. A big budget for an incumbent, then, typically means that he or she has (or worries about) an unusually strong challenger.

Other researchers disagree and report that when incumbents spend more, they do get a return in terms of votes. The dispute turns on thorny questions about the proper way to estimate the impact of spending, but there is general agreement on three points. First, House incumbents rarely face a serious challenge for reelection. Second, challengers need a lot of money to have a chance of beating an incumbent. Third, when they do have a strong opponent, incumbents may not be able to survive the challenge by pouring more money into their reelection effort.[7] For political scientists, measuring the effects of campaign spending is a challenging task. For candidates, the answer is simple: more is better.

WHERE DOES THE MONEY COME FROM?

Candidates raise their campaign funds from five main sources: individuals, political action committees (PACs), political parties (including the party in government), the candidates' own resources, and public (taxpayers') funds. There are no other sources from which candidates can raise large amounts of money. Campaign finance reform, then, cannot do much more than require a different mix among these five or try to eliminate one or more of these sources altogether.

Individual Contributors

Most of the money contributed directly to candidates comes from individuals, not parties or PACs (see Table 12.2), and the number of small donors is growing. In the 2008 elections, individuals accounted for 55 percent of the contributions to House

TABLE 12.2 Sources of Campaign Funds for Presidential and Congressional Candidates (in millions of dollars)

	Presidential, 2007–2008					
	Democrats		Republicans		Total	
	Nomination	General	Nomination	General	Nomination	General
Individuals	$699.7	$320.0	$389.9	$0	$1089.6	$320.0
Candidates	13.2	0	45.7	0	58.9	0
PAC and party direct	2.7	1.0	2.4	0	5.1	1.0
Party coordinated*	0	6.4	0	18.9	0	25.3
Party independent*	0	1.1	0	53.5	0	54.6
Public funds	17.5	0	2.6	84.1	21.0	84.1
Legal, accounting	0.2	0	1.2	46.4	1.4	46.4
Other	5.6	0.5	6.2	0	11.8	0.6
Total	$738.9	$321.5	$448.0	$130.5	$1,187.8	$452.1

	Congressional, 2007–2008						
	Democrats		Republicans		Total		Grand Total
	House	Senate	House	Senate	House	Senate	
Individuals	$260.6	$137.1	$204.1	$113.6	$466.2	$250.9	$712.2
Candidate contributions	8.7	1.5	8.1	1.6	17.4	3.2	20.5
Candidate loans	18.2	1.0	20.7	7.6	39.5	8.6	48.2
PACs	182.1	33.4	113.2	44.6	295.3	78.0	373.3
Party	0.7	0.5	1.4	0.4	2.1	0.9	3.0
Party coordinated*	4.6	6.4	6.0	6.1	10.6	12.4	23.0
Party independent*	81.0	71.0	31.7	38.6	112.7	109.6	222.3
Other receipts	21.5	34.9	22.7	16.4	44.3	51.4	95.6
Total	$491.8	$208.4	$370.2	$184.2	$864.8	$393.0	$1,258

*Party coordinated and party independent expenditures are spent on behalf of the candidate rather than given to the campaign, so they are not included in the totals at the bottom of the table. Figures for Democrats and Republicans do not always add up to the sums in the "total" columns because the latter also include funds for minor party candidates. "Other receipts" include interest, dividends, and vendor and individual refunds.

Sources: FEC data: for the presidential nomination race, as of September 11, 2009; for party funding, as of May 28, 2009, and for general-election congressional races as of December 29, 2009.

candidates and 66 percent of the money given to Senate candidates—a substantial increase over 2000. Data on state elections are harder to obtain, but individual givers probably provide the majority of funds here as well.[8]

The nature of the individual contributor has changed, however. Before the 1970s campaign finance reforms, congressional and presidential candidates were allowed to take unlimited sums of money from individuals. For example, insurance magnate W. Clement Stone and multimillionaire Richard Mellon Scaife donated a total of $3 million to President Nixon's reelection campaign in 1972. Well-supported fears that these "fat cats" were getting something in return for their money—preferential treatment ranging from tax breaks to ambassadorships—led Congress to pass the *Federal Election Campaign Act*

(FECA) amendments of 1974, which limited an individual's donation to any federal candidate to $1,000, as we will see.

For the next two decades, these limits seemed to work. Because of the reforms, congressional campaigns were financed not by a handful of big givers but by a large number of people making small (under $1,000) donations. That was also true of the nomination phase of presidential campaigns. Even so, this expanded group of small donors remained a very small percentage of the population, and they were likely to be older, wealthier, more conservative, and Republican than the average American voter and more likely to be male than female.[9] But they resembled the typical American much more closely than the Stones and the Scaifes did.

The $1,000 limit meant that campaigns had to learn new ways to separate prospective donors from their money. When "fat cats" were the preferred funding source, they were wooed by star-studded dinners and personal visits and phone calls with the candidate. The small contributors are usually solicited by mail and e-mail. Online fund-raising has surged since 2004, mainly benefiting Democrats. In 2008, two-thirds of Obama's campaign treasury came via the Internet, in relatively small amounts (the Obama staff estimated that the average online donation was $80), and often from repeat donors.[10]

Political Action Committees

PACs are political groups, other than party organizations, whose purpose is to raise and spend money to influence elections. Most PACs have been created by corporations, labor unions, or trade associations. Corporations and unions are not allowed to give money directly to federal campaigns, so in order to contribute, they must set up a PAC. The corporation, trade association, or union then becomes the PAC's "parent" group and can support the PAC as it begins its work of raising money. Other PACs have no sponsoring organizations; these so-called *nonconnected PACs* are usually ideological groups of the right or the left. This category also includes *leadership PACs*—those set up by incumbents to distribute money to other incumbents or challengers in their party. Members of Congress contribute to other candidates to gain their support in elections for party leadership positions in Congress or because their Hill committee has insisted that they "share the wealth." PACs can give money directly to candidates and party organizations and can also spend it on independent expenditures or issue ads (see pages 232–235).

The number of PACs grew markedly in the 1970s and 1980s; there were about 4,600 by early 2009. In particular, corporate and nonconnected PACs have proliferated; corporate PACs increased from 15 percent of the 1974 total to 35 percent by 2009, and nonconnected PACs grew from 0 to 35 percent. Corporate committees are the biggest PAC givers overall; together with trade association PACs (most of which are business related), they provided almost two-thirds of the PAC contributions to federal candidates in 2008. Labor union PACs gave less than a quarter as much. But because labor unions give almost all their PAC money to Democrats, they help to compensate for the usual Republican edge in business contributions (see Table 12.3).

One main reason for the growth of PACs was the campaign finance reforms of the post-Watergate years, which permitted PACs to donate up to $5,000 per candidate, whereas individuals could give only a maximum of $1,000. The reforms also explicitly permitted corporations doing business with government to have PACs. Federal court

TABLE 12.3 The Top Ten List of the Biggest PACs (in Contributions to Federal Candidates, 2007–2008)

Rank	PACs	Contributions to Federal Candidates		
		Total (in millions of dollars)	Percentage to Democrats	Percentage to Republicans
1	National Association of Realtors	4.0	58	42
2	Electrical Workers*	3.3	98	2
3	AT&T Inc.	3.1	47	52
4	National Auto Dealers Association	2.9	34	66
5	National Beer Wholesalers	2.9	53	47
6	American Bankers Association	2.8	42	58
7	International Association of Fire Fighters*	2.7	77	23
8	American Association for Justice (Trial Lawyers)	2.7	95	4
9	Operating Engineers Union*	2.7	87	13
10	Laborers Union*	2.5	92	8

*Labor union PACs. Totals do not always add up to 100 percent due to rounding error.

Source: FEC data from the Committee for Responsive Politics, at www.opensecrets.org/pacs/toppacs.php?cycle=2008&Type=C (accessed March 18, 2009).

decisions and the FEC confirmed the legality of PACs and the right of sponsoring organizations to pay their overhead expenses (as long as the PAC's political funds are collected and kept in a fund separate from the sponsoring organization's regular assets and revenues). Once their legality was clarified and their fund-raising advantages became obvious, their numbers exploded.

Although PACs spent a total of $1.2 billion in the 2008 elections, they are not generally a major source of funds for presidential candidates. In the 2008 campaign, PACs gave a total of just $4.4 million to candidates seeking their party's presidential nomination. PACs put the bulk of their money into congressional races; they gave a total of $373.3 million to House and Senate candidates in 2008 (Table 12.2). Because House candidates are less well-funded overall than Senate candidates, PAC money accounts for a higher proportion of House campaign budgets. Overall, PACs typically provide about a quarter of the revenue for congressional campaigns. In addition to their direct contributions, PACs put $98.8 million into independent expenditures for and against presidential candidates and $36.4 million for and against congressional candidates in 2008.

Candidates and parties work hard to get PAC money. Both parties' Hill committees connect their candidates with PACs likely to be sympathetic to their causes. Campaigners also seek PAC help directly, assisted by directories that list PACs by their issue positions, the size of their resources, and their previous contributions. Incumbent Congress members invite PACs or the lobbyists of their parent organizations to fund-raising parties in Washington. In fact, since the late 1990s, a number of members of Congress have hired PAC directors and lobbyists to be treasurers of their campaign committees or leadership PACs and engaged them as active fund-raisers for the member's campaign. This certainly raises the PAC's profile for the incumbent. PACs take the initiative as well. Unlike most individual donors, they are in the business of making political contributions, and they don't necessarily wait to be asked.[11]

What do PACs buy with their donations to congressional campaigns? Most PAC money is intended to gain access for the giver: the assurance that the legislator's door will be open when the group hopes to plead its case on legislation. The result is that most PAC contributions go to incumbents—in 2008, more than $10 for every $1 that was donated to a challenger. There is little advantage, after all, in getting access to a likely loser. PAC money, like individual donations, therefore flows to the party with the most incumbents. So even though corporate PACs generally prefer to give to Republican candidates, they gave most of their House donations to the majority Democrats in 2008.

It seems likely that PAC contributions help them get access to lawmakers. What elected officials will slam the door on representatives of interests that donated money to their campaigns? It is harder to determine, however, how intently they listen and whether the PAC's concerns will influence their legislative behavior. There is not much evidence that PAC contributions affect the recipients' roll-call votes,[12] although legislators who receive PAC money do seem to be more active on congressional committees on behalf of issues that concern their PAC donors.[13]

There are many reasons why PAC money rarely "buys" votes. Because most PACs give much less than the $5,000 maximum per candidate, many PACs could be considered small donors. PACs give most of their money to incumbents, who normally have an easy time raising other campaign funds. PACs generally support legislators who have shown that they already favor the PAC's interests. That limits the opportunity for PAC money to change legislators' votes. PAC influence is also limited because they have so much competition—from party leaders, constituents, and other PACs—for the ear and the vote of a legislator. Their influence tends to be greatest when they represent powerful interests in the legislator's district, when they are not in conflict with his or her party's position, and when the benefit they seek is of little concern to anyone else (such as a small change in the tax laws that gives a big break to a particular corporation).

Parties

At the time of the 1970s reforms, the party organizations didn't have enough money to be big players in congressional or presidential races. Now that the parties are raising much more money from individuals, elected officials, PACs, and other interests, their role in campaigns—especially in the few highly competitive races—is more substantial. The two parties raised a whopping $1 billion in the 2000 election cycle and almost matched that amount in 2002, despite having no presidential candidates on the ballot. Even after Congress prevented party committees from collecting unlimited "soft money" (see pages 232–233), party fund-raising increased to $1.2 billion in 2004 and $1.6 billion in 2008.

In congressional races, parties are allowed to make small contributions (up to $5,000) directly to candidates' campaigns. In 2008, for example, national party committees gave a total of $3 million directly to House and Senate candidates. More substantial are the two parties' coordinated spending—the funds they spend on behalf of their candidates and in coordination with the candidate's campaign, typically for services such as television and radio ads and polling. Coordinated spending is useful to the party because party committees have more control over how the money is spent than they do in making direct contributions to candidates.

Federal law limits the parties' coordinated expenditures in each race. As of 2009, each party was permitted to spend $43,700 per House race, except in states with only one House district, where the limit was $87,300. The state party can spend the same amount or authorize another party committee to do so. In Senate campaigns, the limit varies with the size of the state's voting-age population: from $87,300 in Delaware to $2.4 million in California.[14] Nationwide, the two parties put $23 million in coordinated spending into House and Senate races in 2008. Altogether, then, each party could put more than $100,000 in direct and coordinated spending into a House race and much more into a Senate race. But in most races, the parties' direct and coordinated expenditures still amount to only a small fraction of congressional candidates' total spending.

Since 2004, however, the national parties have greatly expanded their role in a smaller number of targeted congressional campaigns by using TV ads funded with independent spending. In 2006 and again in 2008, the two parties put a remarkable $222 million into independent expenditures in House and Senate races. Most of the party money spent independently on House elections in 2008 was used for negative ads, as was almost all of the independent spending in Senate races ($108 million out of the total of $110 million). The parties spent more than $15 million independently on the close Senate contests in Minnesota (where the race was not decided in favor of Democrat Al Franken until the summer of 2009) and Oregon. In fact, in the Oregon campaign and in some highly contested House races, party independent spending matched the total amount spent by the candidates themselves.

As Chapter 4 showed, members of the party in government have become important campaign contributors in recent congressional elections. Party leaders and other members of the House and Senate are now expected to make major contributions to their congressional campaign committees from their personal campaign accounts and leadership PACs and by raising money for the party and its endangered candidates. These contributions indicate the value that incumbents place on their congressional parties in the effort to reach their policy and political goals.

But the greater party role in campaigns depends on party fund-raising success, which may be slowing. After the economic downturn of late 2008, in which both small and big donors were hit by the falling stock market and industry losses, party committees saw their fund-raising fall sharply to a greater extent than after previous elections. As the party out of power, the Republicans' national committees felt the decline acutely, but the Democratic committees were hard hit as well.

The Candidates Themselves

Candidates, as they always have, continue to spend their personal wealth in trying to win political office. In 2008, about 7 percent of House candidates' campaign funds came from their own pockets in the form of contributions and loans. Senate candidates gave and loaned themselves less than 4 percent of their total campaign funds (Table 12.2). Self-funders often lose, but a candidate's willingness to contribute his or her own funds can reassure voters of the candidate's commitment. After Hillary Clinton's lead in the 2008 Democratic nomination race began to slip away, she loaned her campaign an initial $5 million, which helped her compete seriously in the large number of Super Tuesday primaries and caucuses. Not all candidates have the means to make these large loans, however; in 2008, the only presidential candidates who made substantial contributions to their own campaigns were Clinton and Republican Mitt Romney, a multimillionaire businessman.

Public Funding

Congress voted in the early 1970s to let taxpayers designate a dollar (now $3) of their tax payments to match small contributions to candidates for their party's presidential nomination and, as noted above, to foot most of the bill for the major-party presidential nominees in the general election. The intent was to reduce corruption by limiting the role of private funds. In 2008, the federal government paid out $105.1 million in public matching funds in the nomination and general election campaigns—much less than in 2000 or 2004. None of the major candidates accepted matching funds for the nomination race, largely because these funds come with strict spending limits in each state and for the nomination race as a whole. And when Obama announced his intention to decline federal funding in the general election and faced little public backlash, though he was the first general election candidate to do so in the 35 years of the FECA reforms, the fate of the current public funding system was sealed. Congress has chosen not to extend public funding to its own races.

Money in State and Local Campaigns

State campaigns generally follow a pattern similar to those at the national level. Individual donors are the most important source of candidates' campaign funds, followed by PAC contributions, and then, at greater distance, by party and candidates' personal funds. There are exceptions, of course. In an increasing number of states, parties' legislative leaders and caucuses are donating to state legislative candidates. Individual donors are even more important in local campaigns because parties and PACs play a lesser (although expanding) role at this level.

REFORM OF THE CAMPAIGN FINANCE RULES

For years, American campaign finance laws were a flimsy structure of halfhearted and not very well-integrated federal and state statutes. Reformers tried periodically to strengthen legal controls over the raising and spending of campaign money. A new episode of reform was under way in the early 1970s when the Watergate scandals broke. The revulsion caused by these fund-raising scandals produced the most extensive federal law on the subject in U.S. history: the *Federal Election Campaign Act (FECA)* amendments. The Supreme Court invalidated some of these reforms in 1976. Congress then revised the law and did so again in the late 1970s. The resulting legislation put limits on federal campaign contributions and spending and set up a system of public funding for presidential campaigns.

Contribution Limits

In the hope of ending big contributions from "fat cats," FECA limited the amounts of money an individual, a PAC, and a party organization could give directly to a candidate in each election (primary or general) in a given year. These limits apply only to federal campaigns—those for the president and Congress. The money contributed under these regulations is called *hard* (or *federal*) *money*—funds raised and spent in accordance with the FECA's rules. A new reform in 2002 raised the limits for the first time in almost 30 years (see Table 12.4).

Public Disclosure

Another main aim of the reformers was to make the sources of campaign money public. They felt that voters could make a more informed choice if they were armed with information as to who had contributed to the various candidates. So FECA required that congressional and presidential candidates publicly disclose their spending and the names, addresses, and occupations of all contributors of $200 or more. All donations to a federal candidate must go through and be accounted for by a single campaign committee; before the reforms, candidates could avoid full public disclosure by using a complex array of committees. Each candidate must file monthly or quarterly reports on his or her finances during the campaign through December 31 after the election.

Earlier legislation had tried and failed to achieve this goal. The new law improved the quality of reporting by creating the FEC to collect the data and make them available. The FEC's power is limited by inadequate funding, but even so, its public files, available on the Internet (www.fec.gov), have provided a wealth of campaign finance information for journalists and scholars.

TABLE 12.4 Limits on Campaign Contributions Under Federal Law, 2010

	Limits on Contributions		
	Individual ($)	Political Action Committee ($)	State or National Party Committee ($)
To candidate or candidate committee per election	2,400	5,000*	5,000+
To all candidates combined, per two-year cycle	45,600	No limit	No limit
To a national party committee per year (An individual's total contribution to all PACs and party committees per two-year election cycle is limited to $69,900, with no more than $45,600 of this amount to go to PACs and state and local parties.)	30,400	15,000	—
To a state or local party committee per year	10,000	5,000	No limit
Total per two-year election cycle	115,500	No limit	No limit

*If the PAC qualifies as a "multicandidate committee" under federal law by making contributions to five or more federal candidates, the limit is $5,000. Otherwise, the committee is treated as an individual with a limit of $2,000.

+ The limit is $5,000 for contributions to presidential and House candidates. National and Senate (campaign) party committees can contribute a joint total of $42,600 to each U.S. Senate candidate per election.

Note: These are the limits on so-called "hard-money" contributions for the 2010 elections. Individual limits are indexed for inflation; PAC limits (and individual limits to PACs and state parties) are not.

Source: Federal Election Commission, at www.fec.gov/pages/brochures/contriblimitschart.htm (accessed July 18, 2009).

Public Funding of Presidential Campaigns

As another means of removing "interested money" from elections, Congress passed laws in 1971 and 1976 to provide public (tax) funding for presidential candidates. To get the money, a candidate for a party's presidential nomination must first raise $5,000 in contributions of $250 or less in each of 20 states, as a way of demonstrating broad public support. After that, public funds match every individual contribution up to $250. (This was intended to encourage candidates to focus on small contributions.) And as noted earlier in this chapter, each major party's candidate can choose to take public money to pay for his or her general election campaign. In addition, the two major parties each received $16.8 million in public funds to help pay for their 2008 national conventions.

The public funding treats minor-party candidates differently. They receive only a fraction of that total and then only after the election if they have received at least 5 percent of the vote. Once they have reached that milestone, they qualify to receive their payment before the next presidential election. Because of the need to pay cash for many campaign expenses, this provision of FECA adds to the difficulty of financing even a modest third-party campaign. Ross Perot, the Reform Party candidate in 1996, is the only minor-party candidate ever to qualify for public funding.

Spending Limits

Candidates for president who accept this public funding in the race for their party's nomination must also accept spending limits in each of the 50 states and in the nomination race as a whole. Candidates who accepted these matching funds in 2008 were allowed to spend no more than about $50 million in the nomination race. These spending limits have not kept up with the fast-rising cost of presidential campaigns. As a result, although the availability of public money has helped lesser-known candidates stay in the race and thus provide voters more choices, no viable presidential candidate is likely to accept public funding in 2012 unless Congress votes to raise the amounts of matching funds and raise the spending limits dramatically.[15]

Congress tried to limit spending in House and Senate campaigns as well. The Supreme Court ruled in *Buckley v. Valeo*,[16] however, that restrictions on a candidate's spending infringed on the candidate's right to free speech; those restrictions could be justified only in the case of a candidate who accepts public funding. Congress could apply spending limits to its own campaigns, then, only as part of a plan for subsidizing them with public money. That would mean subsidizing their challengers' campaigns as well. For congressional incumbents, who are normally quite capable of outspending their challengers, this was not an appealing idea.

THE LOOPHOLES THAT ATE THE REFORMS

This set of reforms was far-reaching. Yet, not long after the legislation was passed, those affected by it began to find and exploit loopholes in its provisions. The FECA amendments of 1979 and action by the FEC and the Supreme Court steadily chipped away at the framework of the FECA reforms.

Independent Spending

If an interest group or individual runs an ad to support a candidate and works with the campaign in doing so, then the law treats that ad as a campaign contribution. But as long as the individual or group does not coordinate its advertising with a candidate's campaign, it is regarded by the Supreme Court as *independent spending,* and the group is permitted to spend unlimited amounts of money on it. The Court majority's reasoning in *Buckley v. Valeo* was that free speech is fundamental to democracy, and since "free" speech normally costs money to disseminate through radio, television, and other media, Congress cannot limit the amount that groups or individuals can spend on campaign ads that are run independent of a candidate's campaign. In 1996, the Supreme Court said that political parties could spend independently on campaigns as well, and the Court applied this ruling in 2003 to publicly financed presidential campaigns.[17] Since then, party money has moved heavily into independent spending; in recent congressional races, as we have seen, the parties have put much more money into independent spending than into coordinated spending. In 2008, Democrats in close races got a big boost from their party's substantial advantage in independent expenditures. Similarly, PAC independent spending rose sharply in 2008; labor unions and trade associations were the biggest independent spenders.

The advantage of independent spending, for a party, is that the communication can call expressly for the election or defeat of a candidate, and there are no limits on how much the party can spend. The disadvantage of this spending is that, by law, it cannot be coordinated with the candidate's campaign. So the parties had to segregate the staffers involved with independent spending from those who worked with the candidates. Their only legal way to alert a candidate to the party's efforts was to hope for media coverage describing the extent and content of the party's planned advertising.

Independent spending poses many challenges for a democracy. For one, it can encourage irresponsible campaign attacks. Most independent spending is used to fund attack ads designed to raise the negatives of the candidate's opponent. That was true of 80 percent of the parties' independent spending in 2008, as well as millions of dollars of independent spending by other groups such as the Service Employees International Union (against McCain) and Vets for Freedom (against Obama). If a *candidate* launches an outrageous attack, voters can protest by voting for his or her opponent. However, if a party, interest group, or individual runs an outrageous ad as an independent spender, who can be held responsible? The independent spender can't be punished at the polls; he or she isn't running for anything. And because independent spenders, by definition, are not supposed to be coordinating their efforts with a candidate, is it fair to punish the candidate for the offensive ad? Therefore, independent spenders are free to say whatever they wish, and the candidate they favor can't be held accountable.

Soft Money

As a means of strengthening state and local party organizations, Congress amended FECA in 1979 to exempt from federal regulation any money raised and spent by state and local parties for party-building and voter-mobilization activities. This and other funding that the FEC permitted parties to raise outside the FECA limits, as long as it was used for nonfederal (in other words, state or local) party activity, came to be called *soft money*.

The law was interpreted to allow unlimited contributions not only to be donated to state and local parties but also to pass through national party committees on their way to the state parties. So, although FECA permitted individuals to give no more than $1,000 each to a federal candidate per election, citizens—and corporations and unions as well—could also give unlimited amounts of money to party organizations as soft money. These funds could not be spent directly on federal campaigns, but they could pay for any nonfederal portion of a campaign effort, and they had a tendency to migrate wherever they were needed.

In effect, then, soft money became a way for individuals and PACs to launder large campaign contributions through a party organization. The parties pushed hard to get the money. In a letter made famous by a Supreme Court case, for example, then-Republican National Chair Jim Nicholson sent a draft of the party's health care legislation to the drug company Bristol-Myers Squibb and asked for any suggested changes—and a $250,000 contribution to the RNC.[18] Fat cats, in short, had reentered the building. It was not the law's stated intention for soft money to become an end run around the limits on hard money, but the difficulty of monitoring the uses of these funds made it so. In most states, soft money could be raised not only from individuals and PACs but also from corporations' profits and labor union dues—funds that could not be donated directly to federal candidates under FECA.[19]

Tremendous sums flowed through the soft-money conduit from the early 1990s until 2002, when it was banned at the federal level. In the 2002 election cycle, the national parties' last-ditch drive to beat the deadline for soft money resulted in an impressive intake of $496.1 million. Soft money had become so attractive a source of funding, especially for the Democrats, who did not have as many hard-money donors, that in 2002 it comprised more than half of the Democratic Party's receipts and more than one-third of the Republicans' (see Figure 12.4).[20]

Issue Advocacy Ads

Soft money has been used to pay some of the party organization's overhead expenses and for registration and get-out-the-vote (GOTV) drives. Most soft money, however, has been used to fund *issue advocacy ads* (*issue ads* for short). These are political ads that do not include the terms "elect," "vote for," "support," or "oppose." As long as an ad does not use these "magic words" or ones like it, the courts define it as "issue advocacy" instead of election advertising (or *express advocacy*). Therefore, it falls under the First Amendment's right to freedom of expression and cannot be regulated by FECA. The Democratic National Committee was the first to exploit this loophole to support President Clinton's reelection in 1996.[21]

Here are examples of ads that met the definition of "issue advocacy" in the 2008 campaign, funded in these cases by interest groups:

> "Call Mike Huckabee. Ask why he supported all those taxes." (funded by the conservative Club for Growth, a 527 group opposing Huckabee in the Iowa caucuses)[22]
>
> ". . . . Was Obama afraid that the public would learn about his extreme position . . . ? Will Obama now apologize for calling us liars when we were the ones telling the truth?"[23] (funded by the National Right to Life Committee)

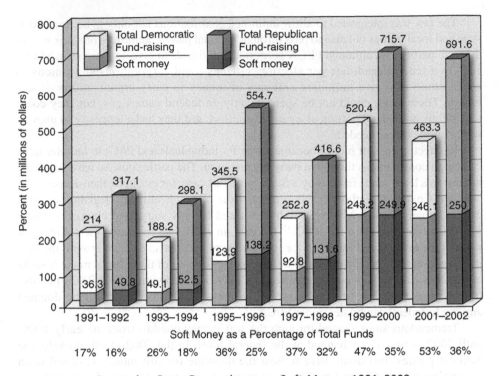

FIGURE 12.4 Increasing Party Dependence on Soft Money, 1991–2002.
Note: Bars represent total party fund-raising and the portion of it received in the form of soft money for each election cycle.
Source: FEC data, issued by press release on March 20, 2003.

These certainly sound like campaign ads. But because they don't use the "magic words," they are considered to be issue advocacy and thus could be funded with unlimited amounts of soft money. Issue advocacy gives these groups, as well as corporations, unions, and big individual donors, a perfectly legal way around the spending limits imposed by FECA (see Figure 12.5). Why does this make sense? The Supreme Court has ruled that the right of individuals and groups to express their ideas freely carries more weight than concerns about campaign corruption. The result is that in some recent campaigns the volume of issue ads funded by interest groups threatened to drown out the voices of the candidates.

From the candidate's perspective, that can be a mixed blessing. As is the case with independent spenders, the issue ads run by outside groups may convey different messages than the campaign would prefer. The ads are usually negative and often make extreme claims, which can outrage some voters. Some candidates' poll numbers have declined after being "helped" by a group running issue ads.[24] These ads frequently try to hold down voter turnout for the opposing candidate by raising doubts about the oppo- nent, rather than to encourage turnout for the candidate they favor. And many of the groups that run issue ads have generic-sounding names in order to disguise their source of funding; the United Seniors Association, for instance, would appear to be a group of senior citizens but was actually funded mainly by big pharmaceutical companies.[25]

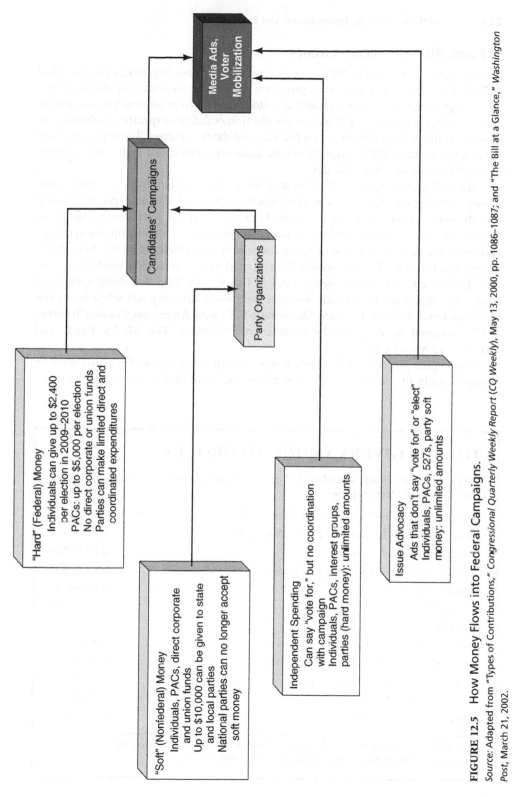

FIGURE 12.5   How Money Flows into Federal Campaigns.

Source: Adapted from "Types of Contributions," *Congressional Quarterly Weekly Report (CQ Weekly),* May 13, 2000, pp. 1086–1087; and "The Bill at a Glance," *Washington Post,* March 21, 2002.

"Hard" (Federal) Money
Individuals can give up to $2,400 per election in 2009–2010
PACs: up to $5,000 per election
No direct corporate or union funds
Parties can make limited direct and coordinated expenditures

"Soft" (Nonfederal) Money
Individuals, PACs, direct corporate and union funds
Up to $10,000 can be given to state and local parties
National parties can no longer accept soft money

Independent Spending
Can say "vote for," but no coordination with campaign
Individuals, PACs, interest groups, parties (hard money): unlimited amounts

Issue Advocacy
Ads that don't say "vote for" or "elect"
Individuals, PACs, 527s, party soft money: unlimited amounts

Media Ads, Voter Mobilization

Candidates' Campaigns

Party Organizations

527 and 501(c) Advocacy Groups

A major development in the 2004 campaign was the increase in political groups called "527s." This odd name refers to the provision of the U.S. tax code that allows certain tax-exempt groups to raise and spend unlimited sums on issue advocacy in campaigns as long as they do not expressly call for the election or defeat of specific candidates and do not coordinate their activities with federal candidates or parties. These groups could register voters, run GOTV drives, broadcast issue ads, send direct mail, and distribute voter guides, among other activities.

When Congress voted in 2002 to stop the national parties from accepting soft-money contributions, Democrats worried that their party, which had depended heavily on soft money, would be greatly outspent. In particular, if the 2004 Democratic presidential nominee accepted matching funds in the primaries, and thus hit the spending ceiling in the early spring, the campaign would be overwhelmed by the huge hard-money treasury of the Bush campaign. So with seed money from a few wealthy individuals, Democratic activists created several 527 groups in 2003 that could spend soft money to support the Democratic nominee with issue advocacy ads when his or her funds ran low. The biggest of these Democratic 527s were Americans Coming Together (ACT), created to do ground-war voter mobilization, The Media Fund, and MoveOn.org Voter Fund.

The engine powering their creation was a small group of wealthy partisans with strong (mainly liberal) ideological commitments. More than a quarter of the funds

THE TOP GIVERS AMONG 527 GROUPS

These were the biggest-spending 527 groups (and their partisan leanings) during the 2007–2008 election cycle:

American Federation of State, County, Municipal Employees (Democratic)	$30.7 million
Service Employees International Union (Democratic)	$27.8 million
America Votes (Democratic)	$24.5 million
American Solutions for Winning the Future (Republican)	$23.0 million
EMILY's List (Democratic)	$12.9 million
The Fund for America (Democratic)	$12.1 million
Patriot Majority Fund (Democratic)	$8.1 million
Change to Win Political Education (Democratic)	$7.8 million
College Republican National Committee (Republican)	$7.5 million
The Presidential Coalition (Republican)	$6.0 million
Club for Growth (Republican)	$5.9 million
RightChange.com (Republican)	$5.6 million

Source: 527 Disclosure Reports filed with the Internal Revenue Service; data as of February 8, 2009, provided by the Campaign Finance Institute.

raised by all 527 groups combined in 2004 came from only 15 individuals, who together gave a total of $125 million. The two biggest donors, financier George Soros and insurance magnate Peter Lewis, each contributed $23 million to Democratic-leaning 527s.

At first, Republicans found it difficult to build their own network of 527s. Publicity about corporate scandals made business leaders uneasy about contributing to these controversial groups. The RNC instead asked the FEC to stop 527s from giving to campaigns. When the FEC declined, Republican groups, such as the Swift Boat Veterans for Truth and Progress for America geared up quickly during the summer of 2004, raised tens of millions of dollars, and began putting up ads, though they were still outspent four to one by Democratic 527s. All federal 527s combined raked in a total of $433 million in 2004, which replaced part but not all of the soft money the national parties had received in 2002.[26] Spending by 527s declined to about $200 million in 2008, but it was just as concentrated as in earlier years, with the bulk of the money provided by labor unions and contributors of at least $500,000 each.

These groups were clearly partisan; their ads were designed to promote specific candidates, just as PACs' and parties' issue ads have been. They could use individual donations to broadcast issue ads right up to Election Day, some of which were among the most vicious attack ads of the campaigns. And although they were not permitted to coordinate their activities with candidates' campaigns, there is little doubt that they have done so. In 2004, the coordination was much more effective on the Republican side; Democratic 527s didn't always follow the Kerry campaign's lead in their advertising. As a result, to keep its message from being distorted by outside groups, the Obama campaign discouraged donors from giving to 527s in the 2008 campaign.

Congress voted in 2000 to require 527s to disclose their contributors and expenses. Later, the FEC added further regulations on their fund-raising, treating 527s funding federal candidates more like PACs. As a result, several organizations, including the U.S. Chamber of Commerce, moved their political activity from 527s into another category of types of groups organized as nonprofits. These groups, collectively called 501(c)s, offer donors additional benefits. As long as federal campaign activity is not their "major purpose," 501(c)s do not need to disclose the names of their donors. Contributions to some of these groups are tax-exempt (so donors can write off the contributions on their taxes), and they can spend unlimited soft money on voter registration and guides, mailings, phone banks, canvassing, and ads that "educate" voters on issues, and other campaign activities. With money raised mainly from wealthy individuals and businesses, 501(c)s spent approximately $200 million in the 2008 election (including $36 million by the Chamber), largely in support of Republican candidates and conservative causes.[27]

Clearly, then, each time Congress has moved to close a loophole in campaign finance, candidates, interest groups, and other big donors have been able to find alternative channels for putting substantial sums into political campaigns. Each of these channels is useful for certain kinds of fund-raising and spending. So an organization might choose to set up several different types of groups: a 501(c) to do voter education with money that the givers do not want to be disclosed, a 527 for issue advocacy and ground-war activities, also with soft money, and a PAC to provide direct financial contributions to candidates in limited amounts.

WHAT DID THE 1970s REFORMS ACCOMPLISH?

With loopholes this large, there was reason to wonder if the federal regulation actually regulated anything. Public funding and money raised under the limits of FECA had been swamped by massive quantities of issue advertising, paid for largely by unregulated soft money. What did the reforms accomplish?

Intended and Unintended Effects

At first, the FECA reforms seemed to achieve *most* of their goals. They slowed the growth of campaign spending in presidential races, at least in spending by the candidates' own campaigns, for about three decades. Prior to the reforms, presidential campaign expenditures had tripled between 1960 and 1972. Real spending increased more slowly from 1972 to 2000, and spending actually declined in three of these eight elections. In the early days of the reforms, the contribution limits made small donations more valuable than ever to candidates, which broadened the base of campaign funding. The reforms also opened much of the campaign finance process to public scrutiny.

Like all reforms, however, the campaign finance laws of the 1970s had some worrisome, unintended effects. One of the largest was the imbalance between hard-money contributions to candidates, which are limited, and the unlimited spending that soft money, issue advocacy ads, and independent expenditures made possible. The cap of $1,000 on hard-money contributions held until 2002, although inflation had greatly eroded its value during that time. These relatively low ceilings on individual contributions made soft money and independent spending all the more attractive to parties and interest groups. Both these forms of spending raise real questions of accountability and bring back the types of money—big money from individuals and corporate and union treasuries—that the sponsors of FECA had hoped to clean out of federal campaigns.

In the long run, then, the reformers' efforts failed to meet one of their major goals: reducing the influence of "interested money." Currently, probably no more than 1 percent of Americans give money to any federal candidate,[28] and only about one-fourth of 1 percent give $200 or more.[29] The other givers are groups—corporations, labor unions, and other organized interests—that want something specific from lawmakers. Whether they get what they want is not always clear, but we can assume that they wouldn't be spending so much if they thought they were getting nothing in return.

Effects on the Parties

For the first two decades after FECA was passed, the prevailing view was that the reforms had harmed the party organizations. By limiting parties' direct contributions to presidential and congressional candidates, FECA treated the parties as no more privileged in the campaign process than were PACs or other groups. In addition, the public funding of presidential campaigns went to the candidates themselves, not to the parties, as it does in most other democracies. That creates more distance between the party organization and the presidential campaign.

Since 1996, however, the loopholes in the reforms, including independent spending, soft money, and issue advocacy, gave the national parties the means to raise and spend much more money than ever before. Large amounts of party money went into TV and radio advertising and beefed-up voter-mobilization programs. State and local parties, energized by money received from the national parties and by their own fund-raising success, became more involved in campaigns. Some put major effort into the labor-intensive grassroots work that was the staple of party organizations in an earlier era. Soft money allowed the parties to play more of a role in the most competitive races than had been the case in more than half a century. Party organizations invested some of their new riches in long-term state and local party-building.[30] However, very few of the party-funded issue ads even mentioned the party labels, so they probably did not help to strengthen the parties' ties with voters.[31]

ANOTHER TRY: THE BIPARTISAN CAMPAIGN REFORM ACT (BCRA)

The unintended effects of the 1970s reforms—and some of the intended effects as well—created pressures for new reforms. They also led to cynicism about the chance for genuine change. When respondents were asked in a Fox News poll whether they were more likely to see Elvis or to see real campaign finance reform, Elvis won 48 percent to 31 percent.[32]

Nevertheless, in 2002, thanks to the dogged determination of Senators John McCain and Russ Feingold and another set of fund-raising scandals, Congress passed the *Bipartisan Campaign Reform Act* (known as *BCRA*, pronounced BICK-ra).[33] In order to cut off the soft-money "end run" around federal contribution limits, BCRA banned soft-money contributions to national parties. State and local parties can still accept soft money from individuals, corporations, and labor unions in amounts up to $10,000 per donor per year. They can spend this money in combination with hard money to run generic voter registration and turnout drives, and they can still collect unlimited soft-money donations for use in state elections. Beyond that, state parties can now spend only hard money on federal election activities.

BCRA also limited the use of issue ads. It applied the term *electioneering communications* to issue ads that mention a federal candidate, even if they don't use the "magic words" of express advocacy (such as "vote for," "elect," and "defeat"). These "electioneering" ads could not be aired within 60 days of a general election or 30 days of a primary unless they were funded entirely by federally regulated hard money or by soft money contributed only by individuals. Ads funded by corporations or unions could not be run during this "window," though they could still be aired at other times. The restriction applied only to broadcast media ads directed at targeted audiences, however, so advocacy groups could continue to use soft money for direct mail, phone banks, and voter registration during this time, and many groups did move their soft money into these activities.[34] And the Supreme Court loosened even this restriction on broadcast ads in 2007, permitting many of these ads to be run at any time.

In addition, BCRA increased the individual contribution limit to $2,000 for federal campaigns, raised the overall limit on individual contributions to candidates, parties, and other political committees combined, and provided that these limits would rise with inflation. An even higher limit was set for candidates whose opponents were self-funded, and who could therefore spend unlimited amounts of their own money to run (the "millionaires' amendment"; the Court struck down this provision in 2008 on the ground that it limited candidates' free speech).

Although most congressional Democrats voted for the bill, Democratic leaders worried that their party's fund-raising would be seriously undercut once BCRA took effect. For decades, Republicans had been more successful than Democrats in raising hard money; many more of the individuals able to contribute $2,000 to a campaign are Republicans. Between 1996 and 2002, Democrats had been able to narrow the fund-raising gap somewhat by raising soft money from big donors such as labor unions and some wealthy individuals. Eliminating this soft money, they thought, would increase the Republican advantage. In fact, the RNC, with its extensive hard-money donor base, had three times as much cash on hand at the beginning of 2004 as did the DNC.

Big and Small Contributions in 2004 and 2008

The ink on the legislation was barely dry, however, when new loopholes had been opened. As we have seen, unlimited amounts of soft money could still be donated to groups such as 527s and 501(c)s, which can then spend the money on campaigns. BCRA also exempted the host committees for the parties' national conventions from the ban on soft money. As a result, wealthy individuals, corporations, and labor unions were still able to contribute unlimited amounts to the national parties to help pay for the conventions. Donors gave a total of $124 million to the parties' host committees in 2008.

And raising the limit on individual donations from $1,000 to $2,000 encouraged greater use of an older practice called **bundling**. Although individual contributions to a campaign are limited, an individual or interest group can solicit large numbers of these individual donors, combine ("bundle") their contributions, deliver them to a campaign, and take credit for a much more substantial donation without breaking the letter of the law. Groups such as the pro-choice EMILY's List and the antitax Club for Growth have given bundled donations totaling hundreds of thousands of dollars to a single candidate. Because these are hard-money donations, they can be used for almost any purpose in campaigns. Although bundling is a clear effort to dodge the contribution limits, it has not been ruled illegal.

The 2004 Bush reelection campaign took bundling to new heights, and presidential candidates in 2008 built on this foundation. McCain backers who collected at least $250,000 in donations were rewarded with the title "Innovators," and those who raised more than $100,000 were called "Trailblazers." When the campaign ran short of funds, it exhorted the Innovators to bundle another $250,000 and become known as "Super-Innovators." By mid-August of 2008, McCain had received $75 million from 534 bundlers, and Obama had pulled in $63 million from 561 bundlers,[35] over 100 of whom raised at least half a million dollars each. Most of the bundlers have been corporate CEOs and lawyers, lobbyists, and developers who, like other big donors, have interests in the policies being made by the federal government.[36] Some restrictions were placed on bundling after the 2008 election: lobbyists who raise more than $15,000 for a candidate on two or more occasions must disclose their contributions.

On the other end of the financial scale, raising the individual contribution limit probably helped to jump-start the campaigns of some lesser-known candidates as well. The first task of any candidate is to gain recognition as a contender; that requires a lot of money. So in 2008, almost every presidential candidate began the invisible primary by raising a majority of his or her funds from donors of $1,000 or more. Raising the individual limit to $2,000 thus permitted relative unknowns such as Mike Huckabee and Sam Brownback to find enough money to pay for the advertising that brought media attention and name recognition. For most candidates, it was only after having passed this threshold of recognition that they could prospect for small contributions.

The Obama campaign was heralded for receiving a larger proportion of its funds from small donors—those whose contributions added up to $200 or less—than did any of his Democratic rivals and most of the Republican candidates. Yet his campaign got an even greater share of its funding from donations aggregating to $1,000 or more; Obama simply outraised his rivals in every category. So both the front-runners and the also-ran candidates gained advantages from the higher limit on individual contributions.

The Parties Survived BCRA

Just as federal candidates learned to cope with the changes wrought by BCRA, the national parties also found alternative ways of raising funds. The national party organizations were able to replace most of the big soft-money contributions that had become so important to their efforts prior to BCRA. Starting in 2006, more than a third of the money raised by the national party committees came in small contributions, three times as much as the money coming from contributors of $20,000 or more. Much of this substantial growth in small donations has come via Internet fund-raising. A great benefit of the Internet is that contributions can be received immediately, with the click of a mouse, rather than weeks later as in the case of direct mail.[37]

State and local party organizations have not fared as well under BCRA as their national counterparts. After the ban on soft-money transfers from the national party organizations, state and local parties' fund-raising declined somewhat, especially in the case of Democratic parties. As a result, many state parties reduced their broadcast activity, direct mail, and phone banking (see Chapter 4). In particular, state parties' broadcast ads for federal candidates, on which these parties spent $236 million in 2000, nearly disappeared after BCRA. Many state parties helped to make up for these losses by increasing their own fund-raising efforts. But most found it challenging to comply with the complicated provisions of the new law.[38]

In short, BCRA has not had the impact that its promoters envisioned. It did force the parties to change the ways they raised and spent money. The parties adapted by increasing their hard-money fund-raising and by developing more intensive programs to reach small donors. More recently, donors have been able to give much larger sums to joint fund-raising committees (called "victory committees") that benefit the candidates and their national and state parties. But many of the aims of the reform process—to limit interested money and to slow the growth of campaign spending—are almost as far out of reach now as they were before the FECA became law.[39] The amount of private money flowing into campaigns is greater than ever. The Supreme Court has steadily carved away many of BCRA's provisions and appears ready to keep carving.

State Regulation and Financing

Candidates for state office are governed by the 50 different sets of state regulations. The Watergate scandals triggered a reform movement in many states during the 1970s, focusing mainly on requiring public disclosure. The movement has broadened since then. When the federal government pushed a number of conflict-filled issues (abortion policy, for example) back to the states, interest group and PAC activity at the state level increased as a result, and so did efforts to regulate it. As of 2009, 36 states limited campaign contributions by individuals—a right upheld by the Supreme Court in 2000. Almost as many either prohibited or limited PAC donations and regulated labor union contributions, and all but six regulated corporate contributions.[40] More than half of the states restrict party contributions to campaigns. Some states have even limited self-funding by the candidates themselves—a step that the Supreme Court would not let Congress take in federal elections.

A growing number of states have ventured into public funding for state elections. Several states (such as Arizona, Maine, Minnesota, New Jersey, Vermont, and Wisconsin) and even some cities (such as Portland, Oregon, and New York City) now provide optional public funding for at least some types of candidates, though it typically covers only part of the campaign's costs.[41] In most states, as at the federal level, the agencies designed to enforce these rules are small and poorly funded, and public support for these programs, as seen by taxpayers' willingness to direct their tax money to these funds, has declined sharply.

MONEY IN AMERICAN POLITICS

Both before and after these reforms, money has played a bigger role in American elections than in those of most other democracies. The sheer size of many constituencies in the United States leads candidates to buy expensive mass media time. The large number of elected officials combined with frequent primary and general elections has produced a year-round election industry. Fund-raising occupies a great deal of the candidates' time even after they are elected, which takes public officials' time away from a thoughtful consideration of the public's needs (see box on page 243) and may give big contributors undue influence on public policy. And because many contributors have strong, even extreme views on issues, the polarization of the two parties in government is increased.

Campaign finance in Britain works very differently. British election campaigns run for only about 30 days, and candidates and parties cannot buy TV and radio time for ads during this period. Instead, British parties get free time on the government-run BBC network; each major party can air only five TV ads of five minutes in length, each shown only once. British campaigns are organized around their national party leaders, but there is considerable integration between the local parliamentary candidate and the leader rather than the largely separate campaigns of American congressional and presidential candidates. Campaign spending is pocket change by American standards; each party is permitted to spend no more than about $33 million a year. On the other hand, interested Britons have the opportunity to watch daily, and often contentious, news conferences by the parties' leaders.

The American system of campaign finance has its consequences. The fact that candidates dominate the fund-raising in American campaigns gives them greater independence from their party organizations once they take office. The parties are working hard to increase their role in the raising and spending of campaign money. Their ingenuity was sorely tested by FECA and then by BCRA, but both parties have shown a lot of resilience in adapting to these reforms. Their need to adapt will continue; in the area of political money, reform is always a work in progress.

... AND YOU THOUGHT *YOUR* FRESHMAN YEAR COST A LOT!

They called him Landslide Joe after Joe Courtney, a Democrat, won the closest U.S. House race in the nation in 2006; he beat Republican incumbent Rob Simmons by 83 votes. But his victory celebration didn't last long. Simmons and other possible Republican opponents, he knew, were already raising money to unseat him in 2008. Estimating that he would need $2–3 million to win in 2008, the Democratic Congressional Campaign Committee (DCCC) urged Courtney to raise between $200,000 and $300,000 by March 31, 2007, as his first step toward reelection. Doing so would increase his chance of getting future help from the DCCC. Under House rules, Courtney can't make campaign fund-raising calls from his House office, so he walked to the DCCC offices regularly to use one of the 38 phones available for Democratic Congress members raising money. On one morning, when Courtney arrived accompanied by a reporter, all 38 phones were in use and some incumbents were waiting in line.

Courtney exceeded his first fund-raising goal on March 31. But there was another fund-raising goal to meet during the next three months. By the time of the 2008 election, he had fulfilled the DCCC's aims; the $2.4 million he raised had deterred experienced Republican candidates from opposing him. He greatly outspent his inexperienced and underfunded Republican challenger, and he won reelection comfortably, with 65 percent of the vote.

But then, the money chase started again. Courtney raised another $150,000 during the first three months of 2009, and soon after, a Republican challenger declared his intent to oppose Courtney in 2010. Having achieved his dream of winning a seat in Congress, Courtney would like to work on health care reform, especially on extending insurance coverage to all children and improving care for mental illness. If he doesn't raise the money necessary to get reelected, however, he won't get the chance. House and Senate members typically spend at least a third of their time raising money for their next election. "It just never stops," Courtney says. "Never."

Sources: Michael Leahy, "House Rules," *Washington Post*, June 10, 2007, p. W12; fund-raising data from the FEC.

Part Five

THE PARTY
IN GOVERNMENT

Taking action on climate change was a major goal of the new Obama administration. So in June 2009, the House Democratic leadership called for a vote on a bill to set up a cap-and-trade system for greenhouse gases. It was a highly controversial step; conservatives termed the bill a "climate tax" and pressed hard for its defeat. President Barack Obama and his staff worked the phones intensively to encourage House Democrats to pass it. The bill did pass the House—but 44 Democrats, including James Marshall of Georgia and Chet Edwards of Texas, voted no.

Obama, the House Democratic leadership, and the 44 who voted down the climate change bill are all members of the Democratic *party in government.* As you recall from Chapter 1, the party in government includes *any elected or appointed public officials* who see themselves as belonging to that party. They are vitally important to the party as a whole because it is the members of the party in government who pass and enforce laws. They, rather than the party organization or the party electorate, are the people who can legislate the party's proposals on college student loans, pornography, gun control, and abortion.

So if Obama and the Energy 44 are part of the same party in government, why did they disagree on this bill? The Democratic Party in government, like its Republican counterpart, is a diverse group. In addition to the party in Congress, consisting of everyone elected to the House or the Senate as a Democrat, and the Democratic president, the Democratic Party in government includes Democrats who work for federal, state, and local administrative agencies; Democratic governors and state legislators; Democrats who serve in local elective and appointive offices; and even judges (and Supreme Court justices) who see themselves as Democrats.

The design of the American political system works against a unified party in government. Because members of Congress such as Marshall and Edwards are elected separately from the president, they do not need to act as a single Democratic or Republican "team." They deal with different constituencies and pressures, so they may have different ideas from one another as to what their party in government should be doing. Congressional candidates are not chosen to run by their party organization; rather, they become the party's candidates by winning voter support in primary elections. Thus, the separation of powers, combined with federalism and the use of direct primaries, are formidable obstacles to the development of a united party working at all levels of government to achieve a single, coherent set of policy goals. In fact, in cases such as the climate change bill, the House Democratic leadership encouraged some Democratic representatives, elected from Republican-leaning districts, to vote no on the bill in order to please their constituents and win reelection.

For decades, reformers have dreamed of an alternative. One of the most discussed is the idea of *party government*, also called *responsible parties*. Its proponents suggest that American democracy would be improved if the parties were to offer clearer and fuller statements of their proposed policies, nominate candidates pledged to support those policies, and then see to it that their winning candidates enact those programs.[1] The parties would then let voters choose not only between candidates but, more importantly, between alternative sets of policies and be assured that the winning set would be put into effect. That would greatly strengthen the parties' role in American politics. Local, state, and national parties would work together as the main link between citizens and the uses of government power. Voters, the argument goes, would be better able to hold their government accountable.

Several European parties do behave more like responsible parties. In Britain, for example, the parliamentary system encourages the kind of legislative party unity that the advocates of responsible parties have in mind. The House of Commons selects the government's chief executive, the prime minister, from its own ranks; he or she must keep a legislative majority in order to stay in office. To do so, the parliamentary party is also likely to consult with the local party organizations that nominate candidates. This creates a powerful incentive for responsible parties. The party in government then tries to carry out a program that was adopted with the help of party leaders, activists, and members at party conferences.

Could this work in the United States? Probably not. The design of the American system is not likely to change. Because of the separation of powers, Democrats can hold a majority in Congress while a Republican sits in the White House, or one party can dominate the House while the other controls the Senate. In fact, in the past half-century, divided control of government has been the norm at the national level and in most states. That makes it difficult for a party to implement all its preferred policies; instead, legislation is likely to involve compromise. Even at times when one party controls both Congress and the presidency, the legislative party might not always be in perfect agreement with its White House colleague, as an exasperated President Obama realized. The party organization can't guarantee that all the party's candidates, selected in primary elections in differing constituencies across the nation, will run on the party's platform. And the party electorate is still connected only loosely to the party organization.

However, the Democrats and the Republicans have been acting more like responsible parties in recent years. Congress and state legislatures now divide more along party lines than they have in decades. Partisanship has a major influence on the staffing of top executive offices and the appointment of judges. As more citizens are being attracted to party work because of particular issues that concern them, the pressure builds for greater party responsibility.

As a result, government policies change depending on the makeup of the party in government. After Republicans won majorities in both the House and Senate in 1994, for instance, an Associated Press analysis showed that federal spending levels changed to reflect the priorities of the newly dominant Republicans. Cuts in public housing grants, food stamps, and child-care programs took money away from poor rural and urban areas, while increases in business loans and farm subsidies gave more federal spending to suburbs and farm areas. These are real, tangible indicators of a shift in priorities associated with the change in congressional party control, even though the presidency remained in Democratic hands.[2] Major policy shifts occurred again when the Democrats won Congress in 2006, and especially when a Democrat was elected to the White House in 2008. It would be too strong to call the result an American twin of British party government, but we are probably safe in describing it as a distant cousin.

Why have these changes occurred? What does this party polarization mean for American politics? The chapters in Part Five address these questions of party influence in government. Chapters 13 and 14 examine the roles of the parties in the organization and operation of the legislature, the executive branch, and the courts. Chapter 15 looks at the degree to which party government can be said to exist in American politics.

CHAPTER 13

Parties in Congress and State Legislatures

Joseph Cao was the first Republican elected to the U.S. House from New Orleans in many years. A few weeks after arriving in Congress in 2009, he told reporters that he was leaning toward supporting President Obama's massive economic stimulus package, which could help many of his constituents who were still suffering from the economic devastation of Hurricane Katrina. The Republican Party leadership in the chamber expressed strong opposition to the Democratic stimulus package. "The party's chief deputy whip," a blogger reported, "stood near Cao during the entire vote." That clarified the situation for Cao, who voted against Obama's stimulus.[1]

The pressure on Joseph Cao is one of many examples of increasing party power in Congress. Both houses of Congress and almost all state legislatures are organized by party. Party leaders in these legislative bodies have more influence over their workings today than was the case during most of the 1900s. Each of the four congressional parties—the House Democrats, House Republicans, Senate Democrats, and Senate Republicans—is more unified internally, and legislative voting is more intensely partisan now, than it has been for decades. Congressional Republicans differ sharply on important issues from their Democratic colleagues.

The parties' more central role in Congress has not come easily. To be effective, they must fight an uphill battle against the system's design. One of the most basic rules of American politics, the separation of powers, undermines efforts at party unity. In a political system without a separation of powers—a parliamentary regime, such as that of Great Britain—the party that wins (or can put together a coalition of parties to win) a majority of seats in the legislature becomes the governing party; its leader becomes the prime minister, who in practice heads the executive as well as the legislative branch. If a majority of legislators vote that they have "no confidence" in the governing party's policies, then either the governing cabinet must be reshuffled or the legislature must be dissolved and its members sent home to campaign for their jobs again. So there is a strong incentive for the legislative party to remain united.

American legislators do not face these pressures. They can reject the proposals of a president, a governor, or a leader of their own legislative party without bringing down the government and having to face a new election. Their constituents probably will not punish them for doing so. Yet in Congress and many state legislatures in recent years, several forces are encouraging members of each legislative party to hang together.

To some analysts, these increasing levels of party unity don't reflect the power of *party* in legislative life. Rather, they suggest, legislators rely on their own preferences on issues when they vote, and to an increasing extent, conservative legislators have sorted themselves into the Republican Party and liberals into the Democratic Party.[2] However, there is ample evidence that party leadership, organizational reforms, and changes in the parties outside of Congress have expanded the roles of the legislative parties and the power of their leaders.[3]

HOW THE PARTIES ARE ORGANIZED IN CONGRESS

Soon after the founding of the American government, members of Congress created political parties to serve their needs. These legislative parties coordinate ideas about public policy, set priorities, divide up the workload in moving legislation, try to get the party's bills passed, hold their leaders accountable, protect the party's reputation, and help party candidates get elected and reelected.[4] The congressional parties are independent of the national, state, and local party organizations but have ties to these organizations.

The members of each legislative party come together in meetings (called *caucuses* by the House Democrats and *conferences* by the Senate Democrats and both Republican parties) to select their party's leaders (see box on page 251). They also structure the chamber itself by nominating candidates for its presiding officer (the Speaker of the House of Representatives or president pro tempore of the Senate) and approving procedures for appointing party members to congressional committees.

The majority party dominates the organization of both houses. In the House, the majority party's elected leader, the Speaker, has extensive power over the chamber's operations. The majority party leadership controls the action in committees and on the floor and chooses the chairs of all the committees. Most of each committee's members come from the majority party, by a margin that is often larger than the majority's margin in the chamber. The Democrats held the House majority from the early 1950s until 1995 and regained it in 2007. In the Senate, the majority leader manages floor action, to the degree that floor action can be managed in that highly individualistic institution. Democrats won a Senate majority in 2007, but Republicans were in the majority from 1981 to 1987 and for most of the period from 1995 to 2007.

Changes in the Power of House Party Leaders

Congressional party leaders, especially those in the House, were very powerful a century ago, weaker for most of the 1900s, and are now in a position of strength again. These changes reflect differences in the degree to which a party's members in Congress are willing to accept strong leadership. Because party leaders in Congress are chosen by the votes of all members of their legislative party, their power is, in effect, delegated to them by their party caucus (or conference) and they serve subject to its approval.[5]

PARTY LEADERSHIP POSITIONS IN THE HOUSE AND SENATE

Each party creates its own leadership structure in each house of Congress; the individual leaders are elected by the entire party membership of the chamber. At the top of the hierarchy is the party leader (called the *majority* or *minority leader*, depending on whether the party controls the chamber). In the House of Representatives, the *Speaker* ranks above the majority leader as the true leader of the majority party. These party leaders have assistants called *whips, and senior, deputy or assistant whips*, who tell members the party's position on bills, try to convince them to vote the way the party leadership wants, and keep a head count of each bill's supporters and opponents.

Each congressional party also has several specialized leadership positions. There is a *conference* or (among House Democrats) *caucus chair* to head the meeting of all party members. Other chairs are selected for the *Steering Committee*, which assigns party members to committees; the *Policy Committee*, which identifies the party's position on proposed legislation and sets issue priorities; the *Campaign Committee*, which provides campaign support to the party's congressional candidates; and any other committees the legislative party may create. Variations do occur; House Democrats, for example, have a single Steering and Policy Committee.

The Revolt Against "Czar" Cannon   Years ago, power in the House of Representatives was highly centralized in the hands of the Speaker. In the first decade of the 1900s, powerful Speaker Joe Cannon chaired the Rules Committee, the "traffic cop" through which he could control the flow of legislation to the floor. He appointed all standing committees and their chairs, putting his chief supporters in key positions, and generally had the resources and sanctions needed to enforce party discipline.[6] In 1910, however, dissidents within his own party combined with the minority Democrats to revolt against "Czar" Cannon. For decades after that, Speakers were not able to muster the kind of power that Cannon commanded. Instead, they had to operate in a much more decentralized House in which party discipline could be maintained only through skillful bargaining and strong personal loyalties. Successful Speakers during this era, such as Sam Rayburn and Tip O'Neill, were skilled negotiators rather than commanders.[7]

Growing Party Coordination   In the late 1960s, House Republicans enhanced party coordination by giving rank-and-file party legislators more opportunity to influence policy through the party conference. During the 1970s, under the prodding of the reform-minded Democratic Study Group and the wave of liberals elected in the wake of the Watergate scandals, Democrats took more serious steps toward the same goal by strengthening both the party caucus and, then, the party leadership.

Until that time, chairs of the standing committees that dealt with proposed legislation were selected using the *seniority rule*: the longest-serving member of the majority party on a committee automatically became its chair. Because of this rule, members of the majority party could win a chairmanship simply by being reelected to Congress many times, even if they did not support their party leadership's position on issues—

in fact, even if they voted with the *other* party more often than with their own. That gave long-serving party members a base of power in Congress independent of the party leaders. Committee chairs could, and often did, use that power in an autocratic manner.

To enhance its own power and to give rank-and-file Democrats more rights on their committees, the Democratic caucus weakened the seniority rule in the mid-1970s. The caucus gave itself the right to challenge committee chairs by secret ballot. Soon after, the caucus did replace a few committee chairs with less senior Democrats.[8] By reducing the autonomy of the committee chairs, this reform expanded the power of their main competitors, the party leaders. That fundamentally changed the structure of authority within the Democratic-run House and the behavior of committee chairs and those who wanted to become chairs.

The power to assign members to committees was vested in the new Steering and Policy Committee chaired by the Speaker. The Speaker was also allowed to choose, with the caucus's approval, the chair and other Democratic members of the Rules Committee, whose independence had formerly been a thorn in the side of the party leadership. Thus, the Speaker gained more power over the careers of other party legislators and over the fate of the bills that they wanted to pass. The whip system, a set of deputies responsible for informing their party colleagues about the party's stands and for finding out how many members are supporting those stands, was enlarged and made more responsive to party leaders.[9]

The Gingrich Revolution

The Republican minority had had no input into the Democratic procedural reforms of the 1970s and 1980s. But in 1994, Republicans won a majority of House seats for the first time in 40 years, after a campaign centered on a set of conservative policy pledges known as the "Contract with America." The election of a number of new conservative members made the House Republicans even more cohesive. Most of these newcomers had gotten campaign help from Rep. Newt Gingrich, then the second-ranking Republican leader in the House, and credited him with engineering their party's unexpected takeover. They elected Gingrich Speaker and gave him unprecedented authority to push the Republican agenda.

One of the most important tools given to the leadership by the House Republican conference was the power to set aside the seniority rule. The leadership could now pick all the committee chairs on the basis of their commitment to bringing the party's desired bills to the floor, and each committee chair was limited to a six-year term. Why did the committee chairs agree to such a sharp reduction in their power? Republicans had only a slender majority in the House, and they faced a Democrat, Bill Clinton, in the White House. Perhaps GOP members were willing to accept strong party discipline to have a better chance of achieving the goals of the Contract.[10] Or perhaps the change reflected the chairs' personal loyalty to Gingrich, or even fear for their political careers if they resisted. It was a giant step in the expansion of party power in the House, and Gingrich became the strongest Speaker since Cannon.[11]

The result, at least initially, was a level of party discipline with which "Czar" Cannon probably would have felt comfortable. When the ten sections of the Contract with America came to a vote in the House, out of a possible 2,300 Republican voting decisions (ten provisions times 230 Republican House members), there were a grand total of only

111 "no" votes; 95 percent of Republican votes supported the party leadership's position. To a greater extent than in almost a century, the party discipline was directed toward achieving the congressional party's policy goals.

... And the Change to Democratic Control

Later in 1995, Gingrich's aura of invincibility started to crumble. When a standoff on the national budget between President Clinton and House Republicans led to a shutdown of the government, Gingrich and his colleagues got the blame. The Speaker was dogged by charges of ethics violations and declining popularity ratings. House Republicans were frustrated by his uneven leadership style. An aborted effort to oust him from the Speakership in 1997 had quiet help from some other Republican leaders. Then, when the GOP lost a net of five House seats in the 1998 election, many House Republicans demanded new leadership, and Gingrich resigned.

His successor, Dennis Hastert, did not begin by demanding unshakable party discipline, and his party colleagues, in 1999, were not as inclined to give it. Committee chairs were allowed to take the lead on most legislation. But the Republican leadership maintained control over the chairs' selection. After the first term-limited chairs had to step down in 2001, those who hoped to take their places were in the unusual position of having to submit to interviews by top party leaders as well as to the judgment of the party's backbenchers before the appointments were made.

After the Republicans gained seats in the 2002 elections, the party leaders' power again rose to a new level. The new Majority Leader, Tom DeLay, was nicknamed "The Hammer" for his iron-fisted use of power. DeLay called on business lobbyists to help pressure Republican House members to support the party's positions. The term limit on the Speaker was eliminated, seniority rules were undercut even more in order to move loyal leadership allies into powerful subcommittee chairs, and party leaders cracked down on Republicans who refused to follow the party's lead.[12] Democrats complained that they were being shut out of conference committees and prevented from offering amendments on bills. The Republican leadership was remarkably effective in pushing legislation through the House.

DeLay was forced to step down in 2005 after being indicted for campaign finance violations. A drop in President Bush's public approval ratings made it more difficult for DeLay's successor, John Boehner, to deliver Republican votes. Moderate Republicans joined with Democrats to shoot down the leadership's bills on health care, tax cuts, environment, and other issues. Legislative party cohesion and party leaders' power, then, depends not only on broad policy agreement but also on the party's standing in the wider political environment and the skills of the party leaders.

When the Democrats regained control of the House in 2007, they preserved many of these Republican reforms. To be able to deliver on their campaign promises and keep their majority, the Democratic Party leadership shut out the minority Republicans in the legislative process with as much enthusiasm as the Republicans under Gingrich and DeLay had shut out the Democrats. The incoming Speaker, Nancy Pelosi, imposed more party discipline on committee chairs than had been customary under previous Democratic Speakers. Although Pelosi tended to appoint as chairs the most senior committee members, and the term limits for chairs were abolished in 2009, the chairs were now expected to vote with the party leadership and to raise a great deal of money for the campaigns of party candidates. The rules changes have made members' advancement in the House and their ability to pass legislation dependent on their loyalty to the party and its leadership. Because members are much better able to achieve their individual goals when their party holds a House majority, they have good reason to work hard on their party's behalf.[13]

What Caused This Stronger Party Leadership?

One main reason why individual party members in the House have been more willing to accept strong party leadership since the 1970s is that the members of each party have become more ideologically cohesive—more inclined to agree with their party colleagues on issues.[14] As Chapter 7 shows, white southern voters were leaving the Democratic Party in increasing numbers at this time, so fewer conservative southern Democrats were being elected to Congress. Democratic House members, then, were more uniformly liberal than had been the case in many years. The sharp gulf that had separated southern Democrats from northern Democrats during the mid-1900s had become an easily bridged creek. Because of the committee reforms, the remaining conservative southerners were losing their strongholds of committee power. Congressional Republicans were becoming more ideologically unified as well and were energized by the conservative policy leadership coming from President Ronald Reagan in the 1980s.

When a party is ideologically cohesive, it is easier for the party caucus to agree on a unified position on legislation. The members of each of these united parties can better trust that their leaders will share and promote their policy concerns and protect their reelection interests. In addition, the two congressional parties were more at odds with one another on issues during this period than they had been for some time. So the legislators of each party became more willing to grant power to their legislative party leaders, including the power to pressure straggling legislators to fall in line, in order to pass the party's legislation.[15]

This account of the reasons for stronger party leadership is called *conditional party government*, or *CPG*. It stresses that as the two parties' supporting coalitions in the electorate become more polarized, the party members representing them in Congress become more polarized as well—in short, the members of each legislative party will become more similar to one another in their preferences on issues and more different from the members of the other party—and thus, party members in Congress will grant their party leaders more power to pursue those shared policy goals.[16] The theory of CPG is not yet as precise as it needs to be, but it has been widely accepted as an explanation of these changes.[17]

Note that some party leaders have been more willing than others to make use of these new sources of power. Speaker Jim Wright, during his brief tenure as party leader in the late 1980s, took advantage of congressional reforms to become one of the most assertive Democratic leaders in decades. His successor, Thomas Foley, was not as inclined to aggressive partisanship and returned to a more collegial style. More recent Speakers and party leaders have used and expanded these party leadership powers with relish.

Parties in the "Individualist" Senate

Clearly, the job of a House party leader is challenging, but the work of the Senate's party leaders is more like herding cats. By the mid-1970s, Barbara Sinclair explains,[18] the U.S. Senate had moved from an institution governed by elaborate "rules" of reciprocity, specialization, and apprenticeship, in which powerful committees dominated the legislative work, to a much more individualistic body with a more collegial distribution of power. Increasingly, and with avid media attention, members of the Senate established themselves as national spokespersons on various policy questions. Once they had become political "stars," these senators expected to participate more fully in the Senate's work, on their way, many hoped, to greater glory and higher office.

This change combined with institutional features of the Senate to produce the threat of stalemate. A leading institutional feature is the unique Senate rule of the filibuster—the right of extended debate, used to talk a bill or a nomination to death if the votes are not available to defeat it in any other way. It takes 60 votes to stop a filibuster, a number that is very difficult to achieve. As a result, even the threat of a filibuster is enough to stop legislation in its tracks, so members of the minority (and, on occasion, disgruntled members of the majority party) have been able to wrest control of the legislative agenda away from the majority by making more frequent use of such threats in recent years.

By this time, changes in southern politics had led to greater party polarization in the Senate, just as they had in the House. Issues reaching both houses of Congress were often contentious. Add to this a more partisan Senate and a set of rules that permitted any member to tie up the work of the institution for an indefinite period, and the result is a desperate need for a legislative traffic cop. Increasingly, it has been the party leadership in the Senate that has tried to direct the traffic. Individual senators have come to depend on their party leaders to promote the legislative party's interests, both inside and outside the Senate chamber. So even though the Senate majority leader still defers to committee chairs to a greater extent than his House counterpart (the Speaker) does, Senate party leaders have slowly expanded their power. Term limits were placed on committee chairs in 1995, and in 2005 the majority leader got the right to name half the membership of the most valued Senate committees, without needing to follow seniority.

The Senate's rules make it harder for the majority to govern than is the case in the House; they do not allow as much centralization of power in the party leadership.[19] So the Senate's majority and minority party leaders consult extensively with their party colleagues, rather than command them, to build the unanimous consent agreements that allow bills to be brought to a vote without risking a filibuster by an unhappy senator. But even in the Senate's more individualistic environment, party leaders now play a more important role.[20]

Parties in the State Legislatures

As in Congress, the legislative parties organize the legislatures in almost every state.[21] They structure everything from the legislative leadership to its committees. The power of the legislative parties varies, however, depending in part on the legislature's rules and on the personal skills and resources of the party leaders. In a few state legislatures, daily caucuses and strong party leadership make for a party every bit as potent as the Republicans in the 1995–2007 U.S. House. In others, especially the traditionally one-party states, party organization is weaker than it was in Congress before the reforms of the 1970s.

Most state legislative party leaders have a lot of power over the day-to-day workings of the legislature. They do not usually have to defer to powerful committee chairs. The party leaders can appoint the members and chairs of these committees, often without having to consider the members' seniority, so they can choose chairs and members on the basis of their support for the party leader personally or for their views on issues that the committee will consider. Party leaders also exercise their influence through the party caucus. In many states with strong two-party systems, party leaders call meetings to give members information about upcoming bills, learn whether their membership is united or divided on an issue, and encourage legislators to support the party's position. Leaders in a few of these states even try, occasionally, to get the caucus to hold a "binding" vote that calls on all members to support the party's position on an important issue. Where the state parties are not as strong, it is more common for the party caucus simply to offer information or allow leaders to hear members' opinions but not to try to build consensus.[22]

In sum, although the parties' legislative organizations look similar across the states—their party leadership positions are fairly uniform—they differ in their behavior. Party leaders' power can vary even between the two houses of the same state legislature, as do the influence and effectiveness of the party caucus.[23]

METHODS OF PARTY INFLUENCE

How do legislative parties and their leaders exercise their power? What resources can they use to influence their members' behavior?

Carrots and Sticks

Congressional party leaders have a variety of tools available to affect the behavior of their party colleagues. They tend to rely more on incentives than on punishments because the most effective punishments are limited in their use and occasionally have been known to backfire. The most powerful punishment would be to remove a maverick legislator from his or her seat in the House or Senate. Except in rare cases, however, such as that of Ohio Democrat James Traficant, who was in jail when the House expelled him in 2002, party leaders do not have that power. Only the legislator's constituents can do that, and they are not likely to serve as agents of the congressional party leadership. Thus, representatives and senators can normally vote against their party's leadership, or against major bills proposed by their party's president, without fear of losing their jobs.

Even the in-your-face disloyalty of supporting the other party's presidential candidate in an election has not been punished consistently in Congress. In 1965, the House Democratic caucus stripped committee seniority from two southern Democrats who had supported the Republican presidential candidate, Barry Goldwater, the year before. In 2008, however, Senator Joe Lieberman was allowed to keep his position as chair of the Senate Homeland Security and Governmental Affairs Committee by his Democratic colleagues even after running for reelection as an independent, speaking at the Republican convention in support of its presidential candidate, John McCain, and campaigning extensively with him. Democratic senators feared that punishing Lieberman would cause him to defect to the Republican side, which could endanger the Democrats' Senate majority.

Perhaps the most famous example of the weakness of party penalties is the story of Phil Gramm, elected as a Democratic representative from Texas in 1978. The House Democratic leadership gave Gramm, a conservative, a seat on the prestigious House Budget Committee in return for his promise to cooperate with party leaders. But in 1983, members of the Democratic caucus were outraged to learn that Gramm had leaked the details of secret Democratic Party meetings on the Reagan budget to Republican House members. The caucus took away Gramm's seat on the Budget Committee.

Gramm did not accept his fate quietly. He resigned from the House and then ran—as a Republican—in the special election held to replace him. His constituents reelected him to the House and later to the Senate as a Republican. In fact, he was soon back on the House Budget Committee, courtesy of the Republican leadership! As long as legislative party leaders cannot keep a party maverick from being renominated and reelected and in districts where voters are not impressed by a legislator's party loyalty, party influence will be limited. So this step is taken only rarely.

In short, House and Senate party leaders have only a few punishments at their command when trying to unify their parties and using these punishments might do more harm than good. There is always the risk that punishing a legislator will cause him or her to defect or lose his or her seat to the other party or will give the party leadership a bad public image. So party leaders tend to rely more on the incentives they have at their command to achieve party loyalty. They can offer or withhold desirable committee assignments to cultivate party support. They can give speeches and raise money for a member's reelection effort. The parties' congressional campaign committees, with their campaign funds and services, have been a major factor in promoting party cohesion on legislation.[24]

Party leaders can also help in passing a member's bills and promoting federal projects in the member's district. They can give members useful information about the status of a bill on the legislative schedule. Some researchers find that junior members of Congress are more likely to vote with their party than are more senior members, perhaps because the newer legislators have greater need for the information or other resources that party leaders can provide.[25] And leaders can use their personal relationships with party colleagues to cajole them through careful listening or more hard-edged persuasion. On a House vote on school vouchers, for example, a reporter described House Republican leaders surrounding a Kentucky Republican who had opposed the leadership on this bill the week before. A senior Democrat, "Representative David R. Obey (D-WI) took to the microphone. 'Is anyone from the office of the attending physician present?' he deadpanned. 'I understand someone's arm is being broken.' " The Republican did decide to vote for the bill.[26]

Agenda Control

According to *cart el theory*,[27] another vital source of party leaders' power is their ability to control the legislative agenda. When party leaders can control which bills will come up for a vote, they can derail legislation that could divide their party's members or damage the party's image, and they can forward bills that help the party keep its majority. In recent decades, both parties, when they held a House majority, have adopted rules that concentrate these powers of agenda control in the party leadership. Bills are now debated under restrictive rules, set by a leadership-controlled Rules Committee, which prevent involvement by the minority and often by majority party members as well. Legislation is increasingly combined into "omnibus" bills so broad in scope that individual members have to rely on the party leadership to understand their content. Conference committees, which previously included representatives of both parties to iron out differences between the House and Senate versions of a bill, are now held only rarely and often exclude the minority party. Party leaders negotiate the content of legislation at points in the process that they would not have controlled several decades ago.[28]

PARTY INFLUENCE ON LEGISLATIVE VOTING

When is this party influence most effective? In voting on a bill, a member of Congress could be swayed by any of several forces: not only party, but also his or her beliefs about the proper size of government or about the issue at hand, or pressures from the president, campaign contributors, or constituents. Yet researchers have found that the parties in Congress play an important role in members' voting patterns, whether through the direct impact of party leaders' persuasion, the majority party's agenda control, or because of the ability of a member's partisanship to structure issues and create loyalties within his or her own mind.

How Unified Is Each Legislative Party?

Several measures can be used to determine how often members vote with their party. The first, the *party vote*, is the proportion of roll calls on which most Democrats vote one way on a bill and most Republicans vote the other way. The second, *party unity scores* (or *party support*), is the degree to which legislators vote with their party's majority on these party votes.

Party Votes   A very demanding test of party voting would be the percentage of all legislative roll calls in which at least 90 percent of one party's members vote yes and 90 percent or more of the other party vote no. By such a strict test, party discipline appears regularly in the British House of Commons and the German Bundestag, but not as often in American legislatures. Under Czar Cannon, about a third of all roll calls in the House met this standard of party discipline. From 1921 through 1948, that dropped to only 17 percent,[29] and it declined steadily to about 2 to 8 percent in the 1950s and 1960s. During approximately the same period in the British House of Commons, this striking party division occurred on almost every roll call.

Since the late 1990s, however, there has been a notable increase in "90 percent votes" in Congress. In 2009, for example, both houses were almost perfectly divided by party on a number of major issues (see Figure 13.1, case 1), including President Obama's massive economic stimulus spending program, climate change, and taxes. The most striking evidence of party voting could be seen in 2003, when House

Case 1: Should President Obama's economic stimulus program become law?

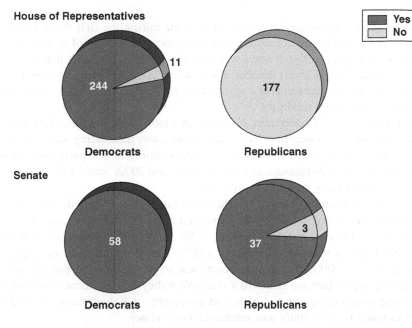

House of Representatives

| | Yes |
| | No |

244 — 11

Democrats

177

Republicans

Senate

58

Democrats

37 — 3

Republicans

Case 2: Should the State Children's Health Insurance Program (SCHIP) be reauthorized and expanded, paid for partly by an increase in the cigarette tax?

House of Representatives

249 — 2

Democrats

40
137

Republicans

Senate

57

Democrats

32 — 9

Republicans

FIGURE 13.1 Congressional Party Unity and Disunity, 2009.

Note: The figure shows the numbers of Democrats and Republicans in the Senate and House casting "yes" and "no" votes on the bills named. Senators Bernard Sanders (I-VT) and Joe Lieberman (I-CT) are counted as Democrats because they caucus with the Democrats.

Source: CQ Weekly, February 2, 2009, pp. 264 and 268 (Obama stimulus bill, House; and SCHIP, Senate); January 19, 2009, p. 144 (SCHIP, House), and February 16, 2009, p. 368 (Obama stimulus bill, Senate).

Republicans voted *unanimously* 44 percent of the time during the first three months of the year, as did their Democratic counterparts on almost one-fourth of all roll calls. The number of unanimous roll-call votes was higher in all of 2003 than it had been in more than 40 years.[30] These levels dropped a little after 2003 but rose again beginning with President Bush's second term. In a system of separated powers, this is a remarkable demonstration of party solidarity.[31]

The 90 percent standard is too strict, however, for a look at the American legislative experience over time. So researchers have focused on a less demanding measure: the *party vote*, or the percentage of roll calls in which the *majority* of one party opposed a majority of the other. By this measure as well, the 1990s and 2000s produced the highest levels of congressional party voting in many years.

Let's start where senators think we should—with the Senate. During the late 1960s and early 1970s, a majority of Democrats opposed a majority of Republicans in only about one-third of all Senate roll-call votes. By 1995, the figure was up to 69 percent, the highest recorded in the Senate since the 1950s. That dropped to an average of 54 percent in the early 2000s; because the Senate was so closely divided, party leaders avoided bringing highly partisan issues to a vote unless they felt confident of winning. But when these issues *did* come to a vote and a majority of Republicans opposed a majority of Democrats, party unity was substantial (see below).

Party voting has been even more prevalent in the House at times. In the late 1800s, congressional party voting was common (although still far below that of the British Parliament). This was a time when the parties were competitive in most congressional districts, party leaders wielded considerable legislative authority, and Congress was a much less professionalized institution. After 1900, following a decline in the party-based link among candidates for different offices and the development of a more professionalized Congress,[32] party voting decreased markedly. The start of the New Deal party system in the 1930s increased the frequency of party votes for a time, before it fell again to twentieth-century lows (of 27 percent) in 1970 and 1972.

Beginning in the mid-1980s, party voting in the House has reached levels not seen since the New Deal; a 50-year high of 73 percent was recorded in the rancorous 1995 session (see Figure 13.2). As with the Senate, these levels were not sustained after 1995; the figure generally remained in the 40 to 55 percent range through 2008.

States vary in their levels of party voting, both across the states and within a given state from one political generation to the next. We are most likely to see party voting in states where the two parties are closely balanced in strength in the legislature, so both parties feel they have a chance to get their bills passed. It is also more common where the two parties represent distinctive groups of voters—for example, in urban, industrialized states where Democratic strength is concentrated among union members and blacks in the big cities, and Republican state legislators tend to represent suburban and rural districts that are largely white and conservative. As is the case in Congress, state legislative parties are more likely to accept strong party leadership when the parties are highly polarized. Party voting in southern states such as Texas and Florida, then, has increased since the 1990s.[33]

Party Support   To what extent do legislators support their party on party votes? From the late 1930s into the 1960s, conservative southern Democrats often crossed the aisle to

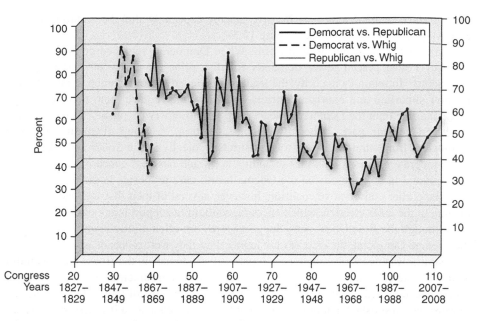

FIGURE 13.2   Party Voting in the House of Representatives, 1835–2008.

Note: Entries are the percentage of roll-call votes on which a majority of one party opposed a majority of the other party. Because party voting tends to decrease in the even-numbered years, as an election approaches, the data are averaged across the two sessions of each Congress.

Sources: For 24th through 36th Congresses, Thomas B. Alexander, *Sectional Stress and Party Strength* (Nashville, TN: Vanderbilt University Press, 1967). For 37th through 93rd Congresses, Jerome B. Chubb and Santa A. Traugott, "Partisan Cleavage and Cohesion in the House of Representatives, 1861–1974," *Journal of Interdisciplinary History* 7 (1977), 382–383. More recent data are from *CQ Weekly*, reported in December or early January issues.

vote with Republicans in the House and Senate, and their defections were tolerated by the decentralized party leadership of that time. This cross-party alliance, known as the ***conservative coalition***, came together to oppose civil rights bills and Democratic labor and education proposals, and lowered party support scores, especially among the Democrats.

The reshaping of the Democratic Party's supporting coalition in the South seriously undercut the conservative coalition in the 1960s and 1970s. As the conditional party government theory suggests, when the Voting Rights Act brought southern blacks into the electorate, some conservative southern Democrats in Congress became Republicans and others were defeated by more moderate and liberal Democrats. Thus Democrats in Congress became more unified in their policy views. Now, congressional Democrats tend to represent different types of districts from their Republican colleagues, face different pressures from party activists and organized interests, are recruited from different professions, and hold different personal views on major issues. Party organizational reforms, discussed earlier in the chapter, made it easier for the Democratic leaders to unite their party.[34] The new Republicans elected from the South contributed to the growing conservatism of congressional Republicans in the 1970s and early 1980s, and since that time, nonsouthern Republicans have become more conservative as well.[35]

This produced a marked increase in party support, especially after the Republicans won control of Congress in 1995 (see Figure 13.3).

The increase has not been uniform. When Democrats regained control in 2007, Speaker Pelosi placed fewer demands for discipline on newly elected moderate Democrats. To retain its majority, the leadership needed these freshmen to be reelected in their suburban and exurban districts, which would require them to vote a more moderate line than the Democratic leadership would otherwise push.[36] Many of these freshmen became part of the "Blue Dog Coalition," a group of about 50 House Democrats from rural and small-town districts, typically in the South and West, who take moderate positions on issues including taxes and business concerns. Their voices were pivotal in negotiations on the Obama health care proposals in 2009. In contrast with the earlier conservative coalition, however, several of their districts had voted for Obama in the 2008 election, which encouraged them to support many of his initiatives. So, although the Blue Dogs' party support scores are often a little lower than those of the average Democrat, these scores are higher than they were a decade ago.

Similarly, a declining number of Republican moderates in the House and a handful in the Senate continue to break with their party on environmental, fiscal, and social issues because their constituencies differ from those of most of their GOP colleagues. For instance, a substantial minority of Republicans figured that voting against an expansion of federally funded children's health insurance in 2009 (See Figure 13.1, case 2),

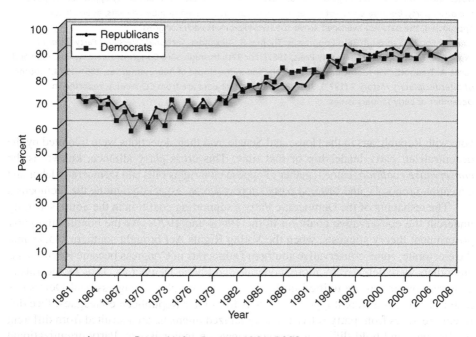

FIGURE 13.3   Average Party Unity Scores, 1961–2008.

Note: Entries are the average percentages of members voting in agreement with a majority of their party on party votes—those in which a majority of one party voted against a majority of the other party. Figures for the House and Senate are averaged.

Source: CQ Weekly, December 15, 2008, p. 3332.

as their party leadership asked, would harm their prospects of reelection. As long as the American parties cannot protect legislators from constituency pressures, and as long as what it means to be a Republican in New York differs from what it means to be a Republican in Alaska, party cohesion will suffer.

These are the exceptions, however. In 2008, House Republicans voted with their party's position 87 percent of the time, as did a full 92 percent of Democrats, and the comparable figures for the Senate were 83 percent for Republicans and 87 percent for Democrats. In the first six weeks of the new Congress in 2009, House and Senate Democrats voted with their party more than 96 percent of the time, and House Republicans were almost as cohesive at 94 percent. When the Americans for Democratic Action (ADA), a liberal group, examined how often legislators voted with the ADA's position on 20 key votes, the average score for Democratic House members in 2008 was 89 percent and that of Republicans was 22 percent.[37] These sharp differences give most voters a clear choice when electing House members and senators.

Greater Polarization of the Congressional Parties

In short, both the House and the Senate are more polarized now than they have been since the late 1870s (see Figure 13.4). Although the major cause of this polarization has been the change in southern party coalitions, anticipated and encouraged by party leaders, the

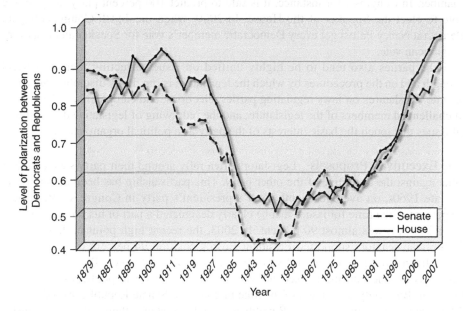

FIGURE 13.4   Party Polarization in Congress, 1879–2008.

Note: Entries are the difference in mean DW-NOMINATE scores between the Democratic and Republican Parties in each house for each Congress. These scores estimate the position of each legislator on a liberal–conservative dimension by using the scaling of roll-call votes; higher values (closer to 1.0) mean greater difference between the parties.

Source: Keith T. Poole, http://pooleandrosenthal.com/Polarized_America.htm#POLITICALPOLARIZATION (accessed June 27, 2009).

declining competitiveness of House elections may have had an impact as well. If a House district has been drawn to favor the incumbent's party, then the most likely source of a successful challenge is an ambitious candidate in the incumbent's party, running against him or her in a primary election. In a primary, a Republican incumbent is most likely to be challenged from the right; for Democratic incumbents, challenges tend to come from the left. That encourages House members to move toward the extreme of their party rather than toward the center; one study finds that a credible primary challenge moves a typical candidate for Congress fully 10 points along a 100-point conservative-to-liberal scale.[38] Thus, safer House seats, at least in the current political climate, may well discourage moderation or compromise across party lines.

When Are the Parties Most Unified?

Students of Congress and state legislatures find that three types of issues are most likely to prompt high levels of party voting and party support: those touching the interests of the legislative party as a group, those involving support of or opposition to an executive program, and those that clearly divide the party's voters.

Issues That Touch the Interests of the Legislative Parties   produce the greatest party unity. Among the best examples are the basic votes to organize the legislative chamber. In Congress, for instance, it is safe to predict 100 percent party unity on the vote to elect the Speaker of the House. In 2009, when the 111th Congress began, Democrat Nancy Pelosi got every Democratic member's vote for Speaker and lost every Republican vote.

The parties also tend to be highly unified on issues affecting their numerical strength and on the procedures by which the legislature is run. Party discipline runs high in state legislatures on laws regulating parties, elections, and campaigning; the seating of challenged members of the legislature; and the redrawing of legislative district lines, all issues that touch the basic interests of the party as a political organization.

The Executive's Proposals   Legislators often rally around their party's executive or unite against the executive of the other party. This partisanship has been mounting. In the late 1960s, on average, members of a president's party in Congress voted about 60 percent of the time for issues that he clearly designated a part of his program; by the early 2000s, it was almost 90 percent. In 2003, the recent high point in these scores, Republican senators supported President Bush's position 94 percent of the time and Republican House members did so on 89 percent of these votes. Bush's support in Congress declined during his second term in office—House Republicans voted with President Bush only 64 percent of the time in 2008 and Senate Republicans did so only 70 percent of the time—as many Republicans tried to distance themselves from Bush's unpopularity in preparation for the 2008 elections.[39] But President Obama's proposals quickly repolarized the parties.

Conversely, the opposition party's support for a president's program has decreased steadily,[40] at least until the terrorist attacks of 2001 briefly interrupted the downward trend. Since the 1980s, the opposition supported the president's proposals only about one-third of the time, on average. The Clinton presidency is an excellent example of this party polarization with regard to the executive. In the early years of Clinton's first term, Democrats' support for their president was higher than it had been since the mid-1960s, and Republicans' support was relatively low. The president became an even more powerful partisan trigger in 1998, when Clinton was impeached by the House for lying about his sexual relationship with a White House intern. Sparked by strongly antagonistic congressional party leaders on both sides of the aisle, the House vote to impeach and the Senate vote to acquit Clinton were close to being party-line votes. An expert observer wrote, "On what everyone claimed was a conscience vote, 98 percent of Republican consciences dictated a vote to impeach the president, while 98 percent of Democratic consciences dictated the opposite."[41] In 2000, Clinton's last year as president, there was a difference of almost 50 percentage points between Republicans' and Democrats' support of the president's position.

When the president's party in Congress marches in lockstep with the president's proposals, then it is important to ask whether Congress continues to play an independent role in the business of governing. The other party's united opposition can be a potential check on the executive, of course. But especially in the House, where even a slim majority can exercise a great deal of control, there have been periods of time when a highly partisan leadership has ceded congressional power to the executive branch.

Policies Central to the Party System   Legislative parties are also more unified on issues that fundamentally divide the parties in the electorate—the "label-defining" issues.[42] At the time of the Civil War, the questions of slavery and Reconstruction generated the greatest cohesion within each party and the clearest divisions between the two parties. These issues were displaced by conflicts between farm and industrial interests in the 1890s. Now the parties are most internally cohesive on the role of government in the economy and in people's personal lives, including taxes and the regulation of business. In many state legislatures, for instance, an attempt to change the rules governing the hiring of teenagers by local businesses will pit one unified party against another, as will environmental issues, the rights of women and minority groups, and aid to agriculture. In Congress, a similar set of issues—social welfare, environmental, and tax policy—has produced the most cohesive partisan voting.[43]

COMPARING PARTY POWER IN CONGRESS AND STATE LEGISLATURES

In sum, based on what we know about the role of parties in the U.S. House and Senate and the state legislatures, we can draw some conclusions about the conditions most likely to produce strong legislative parties.

Party Polarization and Cohesion   When a party's legislators represent similar constituencies (for instance, when Republicans throughout the state or nation all get significant support from Christian conservatives and very little support from blacks), they are more likely to hold similar views, and party cohesion increases. This greater party cohesion, combined with greater distance between the two parties in the nature of their constituencies and their views on issues, encourages legislators to accept strong party leadership in order to translate those views into policy. Legislative party strength has long flourished in northeastern states such as Connecticut and New Jersey, where the two parties have quite different bases of support.[44] Increasing party polarization at the national level has been associated with an increase in party strength in Congress as well, especially in the House, whose rules, as we have seen, permit greater control by the leadership.

Greater Interparty Competition   There is an interesting relationship between the competitiveness of the two parties and the degree of party voting. At the level of the individual legislator, those from marginal districts, where the two parties have relatively equal shares of the electorate, are less likely to vote with their legislative party than are those from safer districts. Two characteristics of marginal districts encourage a legislator to be highly sensitive to the constituency. First, both parties in marginal districts often have strong organizations and appealing candidates, so the opposition is a credible threat. Second, in many marginal districts, the groups that support Democrats or Republicans differ from those more typically associated with the party. When party voters in a district hold different views from the national or state party on a big issue, a representative will usually need to bend to constituency wishes in order to get reelected, even if that means opposing his or her legislative party's position.

As we have seen, party leaders may not insist on the member's party loyalty in such situations; they would rather have a legislator who will at least vote for the party's candidate for Speaker than a totally loyal legislator who is defeated for reelection because his or her constituents do not want what the national party is selling. Where constituency and party point in different directions, most legislators remember that their constituents, not their party leadership, gave them their job.

At the level of the legislature as a whole, however, close party competition can increase party voting. When the two parties in a legislature are relatively evenly balanced numerically, "the majority party must stick together to get legislation passed, and the minority party has some realistic chance of winning if it can remain cohesive."[45] Close party competition gives both parties an incentive to remain unified. So do situations in which a governor has been elected from the minority party, which sees the opportunity to pass the governor's program if it stays together.

When a party wins a comfortable majority, under some circumstances it can become flabby and vulnerable to internal squabbles. That was true of many legislative parties in the South during the period of one-party Democratic rule. It is true today in state legislatures in which one party has a lopsided majority, such as the Republicans in the Idaho and Kansas state legislatures.[46] And in the absence of strong leadership, it can even be true when a legislature is evenly divided (see box on page 267).

No Competing Centers of Power   A legislature's standing committees may serve as sources of power rivaling those of the party leaders, as was the case in Congress when seniority was the only criterion for becoming a committee chair. When committee chairs are chosen on the basis of criteria other than party loyalty, then chairs owe less to their party leadership. Seniority is not used as often now in either Congress or state legislatures as a basis for appointing members to powerful positions. Other centers of power in some states—powerful business groups, labor unions, ideological groups, or other big contributors—are often closely allied with one party's leaders.

PARTISANSHIP, GRIDLOCK, AND THE NEW YORK STATE SENATE

After decades in the minority, Democrats won a slim majority in the New York State Senate in 2008. They held it for a scant five months. In early June, 2009, two Democratic state senators switched parties. They were encouraged to make the jump by a billionaire business executive; he had contributed heavily to Democratic campaigns but felt betrayed when the party discussed raising taxes on the wealthy.

The party switchers were not acting out of principle. Democratic legislative leaders had previously bought the support of one, who represented the Bronx (though he apparently didn't live there), with promises of pork-barrel spending. When he asked for state funding of two corporations he had set up, however, the Democratic leaders balked. The other, elected as a Democrat from Queens, was indicted in 2009 for a rather poorly timed criminal act: while waiting to be sworn in to the Senate, he assaulted his female companion with broken glass.

The switch gave the Republicans a one-seat majority. They installed the Bronx Democrat-turned-Republican as the new president pro tempore of the Senate. But the Republican majority was only a week old when the Queens Democrat-turned-Republican turned Democratic again. That left the two parties dead even in Senate strength.

Senate Democrats locked the door of the chamber to keep the Republicans out but didn't have enough senators to constitute the quorum necessary for passing legislation. One day, a Republican senator was spotted walking through the back of the chamber in search of coffee. The Democrats promptly declared that a quorum was present and began voting on bills. New York's governor pleaded with the senators to sort out their disagreements: Taking an unusual approach, he asked for their sympathy for the poor lobbyists who couldn't get their work done under these difficult conditions. Senators managed to withstand that appeal but were more fully convinced by the state comptroller's decision to begin withholding their pay. Finally, the Bronx Democrat-turned-Republican was persuaded to rejoin the Democrats—in return for becoming their majority leader.

The chaos was due in part to the leadership vacuum among Senate Democrats. Latino Democrats, including the two party switchers in this case, objected to the dominance of blacks in the state Senate's leadership, and the legislative party fragmented. The Senate's Republicans, however, had responded to the close party division with a great deal of cohesion. In short, the size of a party's contingent in the legislature interacts with several other factors to determine how unified the party will be.

Sources: Danny Hakim and Jeremy W. Peters, "Door Is Locked, and Senate Is In Gridlock," *New York Times*, June 11, 2009, at www.nytimes.com/2009/06/11/nyregion/11albany.html (accessed June 29, 2009); Nicholas Confessore, "State Senate Coup Exposes Albany's Lack of Order," *New York Times*, June 14, 2009, at www.nytimes.com/2009/06/14/nyregion/ 14democracy.html?_r=1&hp (accessed June 14, 2009).

Other Needed Resources   Where the party organizations have more to offer a legislator, he or she will be more inclined to follow the organization's lead in legislative voting. In Congress and many state legislatures, party leaders can use their power over the legislative agenda to help a member get a desired bill passed. Pork-barrel projects in the member's home district can be moved up or down on the agenda by legislative party leaders to help to maintain the loyalty of their party colleagues, as happens in Congress and in at least some parliamentary democracies.[47] In some states, these material rewards, which also include patronage and other forms of governmental preference, are more abundant than in the national government.

The party organizations outside the legislature can also influence legislative voting if they control important resources. State parties' legislative campaign committees help fund legislative candidates in most states, and legislative party leaders' personal PACs help in some.[48] Given the shortage of campaign funds at this level, many candidates look beyond the legislative campaign committees to the state parties themselves for campaign money and services. The state parties are better prepared to respond now than they have been in the past. Many states place no ceilings on party contributions to campaigns, so parties can make substantial investments, if they wish. Another important resource is influence on the nominating process. The leaders of many state parties have become more active in recruiting legislative candidates, and some may be able to convince local activists to oppose the renomination of candidates disloyal to the party (although that ability can always be undermined by primary elections).

Lesser Legislative Professionalism   Congress has evolved into a highly professional legislative body. Each member controls a sizable and well-paid personal staff and a considerable budget, which are used to meet the member's legislative and reelection needs. Serving in Congress is a full-time job with good pay and benefits. Although state legislatures have become more professional as well, very few provide ordinary members with levels of support that even approach those in the Congress. Staff and budget resources are usually minimal. Most state legislators are lucky to have as much as a private office and a personal secretary. Many state legislatures meet for only part of the year and pay so little that most members must hold other jobs and live only temporarily in the capital. With such limited personal resources, legislators in most states welcome additional help in performing the tasks of legislative life. Party leaders can often provide such help. When a state legislator depends on the party leadership for needed resources, he or she is more likely to listen when a leader calls for party discipline.

Styles of Individual Leaders   Legislative party leaders in the states, like those in the U.S. House and Senate, vary in their willingness to take up the tools of strong leadership. Their leadership styles interact with the situation of their party—whether it is a powerful majority, a competitive party, or a weakened minority—to determine how effectively they function in uniting their party members and getting their bills passed.

THE POWER OF LEGISLATIVE PARTIES

The story that this chapter tells is complex. On the one hand, parties are at the very center of the legislative process. Some even view them as "legislative leviathans" that dominate the business of Congress in order to benefit their individual members.[49] Party affiliation does more to explain the legislative behavior of state legislators and Congress members than does any other single factor in their environment. There has been an increase in party voting and polarization in recent years in both the U.S. House and Senate.

Yet even now, most American legislative parties are not as unified as those of most other democracies. This is another instance in which the fragmenting institutions of American government have left their mark; because of the separation of powers, there is no institutional need for a party to remain internally cohesive, as there is in parliamentary systems.[50] Although the legislative parties in Congress and the states have been strengthened, the primary relationship in American legislatures is between representatives and their constituents rather than between legislators and their party leaders or party organizations (see "Which Would You Choose?").

Under certain conditions, such as when the party's legislative constituencies are more alike in their preferences and more different from those of the other party, the legislative parties will be more unified and party voting will be common. That has been strikingly true in the U.S. Congress and many state legislatures in recent years. Increasing party polarization brought the views of legislative leaders and party voters into closer alignment, and members of Congress are not as likely to face a difficult choice between party and constituency. In the institutional world of American legislatures, however, party leaders can never take their power for granted.

WHICH WOULD YOU CHOOSE?

SHOULD YOUR REPRESENTATIVE LISTEN MORE CLOSELY TO THE PARTY OR TO THE CONSTITUENTS?

To the constituents: This sounds like a no-brainer. If we elect members of Congress, they ought to represent the interests of their constituents, right? We have a single-member district system with candidate-centered campaigns; that encourages us to focus on the qualities of individual candidates rather than on the party's platform or plans. We vote for a candidate, and he or she goes to Washington and is then supposed to do whatever we ask. Why should the legislator listen to the party leadership?

To their party: This constituent-centered approach sounds good, but it isn't realistic. How are members of Congress supposed to know what each of their 700,000 constituents wants? Isn't it better for the two major parties to offer competing answers on issues, press their legislative party members to pass these policies, and then let voters decide whether they like the results? That asks less of us as voters and probably corresponds more closely to the (minimal) time that we are willing to spend on politics. Besides, by taking a longer view, the parties can look beyond local concerns to a broader national interest.

To both: As we have seen, when the various constituencies that a party's legislators represent become more similar in views and more different from those of the other party, then most legislators don't have to choose between constituents and party. At these times, members can vote with their party colleagues and also speak for the interests and voters who, in their view, sent them to the legislature. So party and constituency are not necessarily in conflict.

CHAPTER 14

The Party in the Executive and the Courts

When environmental groups file a lawsuit, they hope it will be assigned to a Democratic judge, or at least a judge appointed by a Democratic president or governor. Business groups hope for a Republican judge. Why would they care? Because they hope that a judge who shares their partisanship will give them a more favorable ruling.

Most other Americans see it differently. They prefer to see courts—including the Supreme Court—as nonpartisan, just as we hope for nonpartisan behavior from police officers and the people who inspect restaurant kitchens. Yet, as we see in this chapter, American judges and executives (presidents, governors, and the bureaucrats or administrators who work in government agencies) have been in the thick of party politics since the nation began. Many presidents and governors behave like party leaders, and although the writers of the Constitution designed an independent federal court system with lifetime appointments, hoping to protect it from partisan controversy, it has never been possible to design judges who are free of party identification. Heated partisan battles over the nomination of Supreme Court judges show clearly that judicial appointments are matters of great partisan concern.

In many ways, partisanship has penetrated more deeply into the executive and judicial branches in the United States than in other Western democracies. As Chapter 2 showed, the push for popular democracy led to the election of public officials who would be appointed to their jobs in most other nations, such as state school superintendents and local judges. When administrators and judges are elected, the door is open to party influence in their elections. Even when these officials are appointed, party affiliation is often a criterion for their appointment.

If partisanship affects their selection, does it also influence the ways in which administrators and judges use their powers? If you sue your landlord to get your security deposit back, will you get a different ruling from a Democratic judge than you would from a Republican? If so, does this reflect party organizations' efforts to influence the behavior of executives and judges? Or is it simply that most people feel closer to one party than the

270

other, and people who consider themselves Democrats tend to share similar attitudes toward political issues, whether they are presidents, voters, or judges, and the same is true of those who identify as Republicans?

PRESIDENTS AND GOVERNORS AS PARTY LEADERS

Presidents don't normally serve as formal party leaders, although they do choose the leadership and shape the functioning of their party's national committee. Yet the successes and failures of presidents, and governors as well, can affect the public image of their parties. As the most visible members of the party in government, presidents often come to personify their party at the national level, just as many governors do within their states. As a congressional aide put it, "The president becomes the face of your party,"[1] as Ronald Reagan was for Republicans during the 1980s and Barack Obama is now for many Democrats.

In recent years, several presidents have become extensively involved in party activities by helping to recruit and campaign with party candidates and raise money for the party. These efforts have strengthened the bond between presidents and the party colleagues in Congress for whom they campaign. Especially in the current polarized atmosphere in Washington and in many state capitals and when the party division in the legislature is close, executives have good reason to nurture their ties with their party's legislators in order to get the votes needed to pass their policies.

The President as Campaigner-in-Chief

Recent presidents have invested a lot of energy in their party's campaign activities. One especially welcome form of help involves raising money; presidents are normally a big draw on the fund-raising circuit. George W. Bush was an unparalleled fund-raiser for Republican congressional and statewide candidates. Even in 2008, when his public approval ratings were rock-bottom, Bush continued to raise millions in private events for Republican candidates.

Presidents can do a great deal more for their party organizations. The state or national party organization often finds itself in the difficult position of trying to convince an attractive but reluctant prospect to run for a governorship, or urging an eager would-be challenger not to oppose a party favorite in a primary. Presidents can be very persuasive recruiters or "decruiters." When the president of the United States calls to encourage the prospect to run, or not to run, that makes the party's job easier.

In 2009, for instance, the governor of New York appointed Democratic U.S. Representative Kirsten Gillibrand to the U.S. Senate seat left vacant when Hillary Clinton became Secretary of State. Gillibrand's appointment worried Democratic leaders; her poll ratings were not high, and they feared that her vulnerability and her moderate stands on issues would tempt other Democrats to enter the 2010 party primary against her. That would produce a costly intra-party struggle, which could drain funds from the general election race. So President Obama joined other Democratic Party leaders in clearing the primary field for Gillibrand. Her strongest potential Democratic challenger reported, "I spoke with President Obama today. He asked me that I not run for the U.S. Senate this year." The challenger complied.[2]

White House leverage doesn't always work, however. In 2006, then-White House Deputy Chief of Staff Karl Rove tried to dissuade Katherine Harris from running for the U.S. Senate from Florida. Harris had made so many political blunders that three campaign managers had quit her campaign, one of whom had programmed his cell phone to play the theme song from "The Exorcist" when Harris called. But the independently wealthy candidate persevered, won the primary, and then, as Rove feared, lost the general election.[3]

The President as the "Top of the Ticket"

Even when the president doesn't actively campaign for other candidates, presidents' actions and records in office, and those of governors as well, can affect the electoral fates of other candidates of their party.

Coattail Effects   The most direct link between presidential success and party victories is traditionally explained by the metaphor of *coattails*. Presidents ran "at the top of the ticket," the explanation goes, and the rest of the party ticket came into office clinging to their sturdy coattails. (Nineteenth-century dress coats did have tails.) This coattail effect was very common in the 1800s when the parties printed their own ballots, so a voter had to cast a ballot for an entire party ticket.

Coattail effects declined from the end of World War II through the 1980s.[4] Members of Congress became extremely good at cultivating their constituency by attending closely to its interests and providing services to individual constituents; this helped to insulate them from outside electoral forces, including presidential popularity.[5] Incumbents gained impressive advantages over their challengers in fund-raising and other campaign resources, especially in House races.

The relationship between presidential and congressional election results has reemerged somewhat since the early 1990s, as the parties have become more polarized,[6] though the size of the effect varies from one presidential candidate to the next.[7] Coattail effects can reach into nonfederal races as well.[8] Thus, many states moved their state legislative and governor elections to years when the presidency was not on the ballot, to insulate state elections from presidential politics.

In a broader sense, a chief executive's appeal can affect the environment in which the parties function. In the great majority of congressional districts, Barack Obama got a smaller percentage of the vote than did the Democratic House candidate in 2008, just as was the case with Ronald Reagan and Republican House candidates in 1980. Even so, many House members credited him with creating an atmosphere that helped other party candidates succeed by boosting the numbers of registered Democrats, energizing young and minority voters, and bringing positive media attention. That encouraged House Democrats to see themselves as part of Obama's "team" and to support his legislative program, at least for the first few months of his presidency.

Coattails Even without the Coat   Presidential leadership may influence election results even when the president is not on the ballot. During the period leading up to a midterm election, voters' approval of the president's job performance usually relates closely to their support for candidates of the president's party.[9] A 2006 poll found that

20 percent of the sample intended their midterm vote as a means to express support for President Bush, and 37 percent said it would be to show their opposition to the president.[10]

Most often, presidents' public approval has dropped by the midpoint of their terms, and the president's party has almost always suffered a decline in its share of House seats in the next midterm election.[11] The president's declining popularity may drag down congressional candidates of his or her party or discourage attractive party candidates from running.[12] Those who disapprove of the president's performance seem to vote in larger numbers in midterm elections than those who approve, and their disapproval can lead them to vote for the other party's candidates.[13] Or it may be that, just as a popular presidential candidate can boost the chances of other party candidates in the presidential year, the president's absence from the ticket may deprive them of this advantage at midterm.

The 1998 and 2002 elections broke this pattern of midterm losses by the president's party. In both cases, voters' approval of the president was either holding steady or increasing. Although President Bush had begun his first term with fairly low approval ratings, his popularity soared to almost 90 percent after the September 11 terrorist attacks and remained consistently above 60 percent as the 2002 election approached. Observers reported that his 90 percent approval among Republicans, in particular, made a difference in close campaigns.[14] But the traditional pattern returned in 2006, when Bush's popularity sank and the Republicans lost both houses of Congress.

In sum, presidents' popularity and success can influence the likelihood that other candidates of their party will win their races. This happens especially if the candidates' advertising emphasizes their connection with the president and if the president campaigns actively for them. What, then, do presidents do with this potential source of influence over their legislative party colleagues?

PARTY LEADERSHIP AND LEGISLATIVE RELATIONS

Presidents and other chief executives draw on all the capital they can generate in order to get their programs passed by Congress and state legislatures. They remind legislators of the coattails and the favors they may have provided. They use whatever public approval they may have as well as their ability to attract media coverage. They appeal to their shared party ties with members of their party in the House and Senate. Members of the president's party know that if they make him or her look bad, they might also make themselves and their party look bad. That can encourage them to rally around the president on important votes, even if they would prefer to vote differently.

To deploy these resources most effectively, chief executives have legislative liaisons: staff people who work with party leaders and other members of Congress or state legislatures to get bills passed. Obama, for instance, picked as his Chief of Staff a former House Democratic leader, Rahm Emanuel, with close contacts on Capitol Hill.

Legislative Support for Executives

Popular support is a valuable resource for the chief executive in getting Congress to go along with his or her programs. President Bush's rise in public popularity after September 11 helped him to gain considerable success on the Hill, and his low public

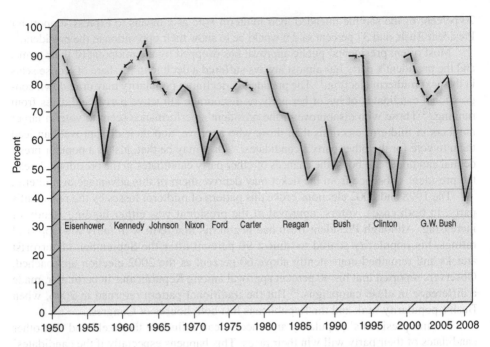

FIGURE 14.1 Presidential Success in the U.S. Congress, 1953–2008.

Note: The entry for each year is the percentage of time members of both the House and the Senate voted in support of the announced position of the president. Years in which the president's party controlled both houses of Congress are indicated by an "x" and connected by dotted lines. Years in which the opposition party controlled at least one house of Congress are indicated by a "." and connected by solid lines.

Source: CQ Weekly, December 31, 1994, p. 3654, and, for 1995–2008, annual December or January *CQ Weekly* issues.

approval dragged down his success rate in 2007 and 2008 (see Figure 14.1). Presidents also do better when their party controls both houses of Congress; these periods of time, as indicated by the dotted lines in the figure, are typically the president's greatest opportunities for success on legislation.

Unified party control of Congress does not *guarantee* success, however. Some legislators of the president's party who represent competitive or "swing" districts may endanger their reelection prospects if they vote in lockstep with the president. And the institutional rivalries designed into a separation of powers system insure that the president's party in Congress will not surrender all its powers to the co-partisan in the White House. As powerful House Democrat David Obey said in 2009, "I'm certainly willing to work with a Democratic president. But I work with him, not for him."[15]

Divided Control of Government   Presidents generally get much less support, of course, when Congress is in the hands of the opposing party. Unhappily for modern presidents, divided government has been the rule, not the exception, in the past five decades. During the same period, almost all of the states have also experienced divided party control of the legislature and the governorship.

In times of divided government, it can be risky for presidents and governors to rely heavily on partisan appeals. Because of the close party division in many legislatures and the unreliability of some legislators of their own party, executives must also curry favor with some legislators in the opposing party. That requires them to walk a fine line, using partisan appeals to legislators of their own party and nonpartisan, or bipartisan, appeals to those in the opposition. There are times when especially effective presidential leadership can get even a Congress controlled by the other party to go along with what he wants. However, American presidents have never been able to gain as much support in Congress as prime ministers naturally enjoy in parliamentary systems.

Governors, in contrast, can often exercise greater party organizational power over the legislators of their party. In the many state legislatures that do not use seniority rules, governors can take an active part in selecting committee chairs and party floor leaders. The average governor has greater control over party rewards and incentives than a president does. On the other hand, governors are not as visible as presidents are, so their coattails and prestige are normally less influential than those of presidents.

PARTY INFLUENCE IN EXECUTIVE AGENCIES

The president is the tip of an iceberg. Below the surface, huge and powerful, lies the rest of the executive branch. The administrators or bureaucrats who work in cabinet-level departments such as Defense and State and in other agencies such as the Environmental Protection Agency (EPA) are charged by the Constitution with carrying out the laws Congress passes. In spite of a burst of deregulation in the 1980s and 1990s, these executive agencies still regulate vast areas of the economy—food safety, prescription drugs, and pollution, for example—under congressional mandates that require a lot of interpretation. The bureaucrats who implement these laws, then, shape policy by applying it. It is they who determine, for example, whether morning-after contraception will be available over the counter rather than by prescription only.

How might party influence affect the people who work in these executive agencies? One possibility is that the president, the partisan who heads the executive branch, might be able to hold all these administrators responsible for putting the party's aims into practice. That, however, turns out to be more difficult than it sounds.

Limits on Presidential Influence: Bureaucrats Have Constituents Too

Perhaps the biggest problem presidents and governors face in enforcing party discipline on their subordinates is the same problem faced by legislative party leaders: constituency pressure. Just as individual legislators try to meet the needs of their constituents, administrators deal with demands from a variety of groups. Top-level administrators know that their best political protection is the support of their client groups. The EPA, for instance, works very closely with the industries it regulates as well as with a variety of professional and citizen groups. If its rulings in applying the Clean Air Act enrage electric power companies or if they outrage big environmental groups, the EPA will be in the political hot seat. Party loyalties do not compete very well with the power of these constituencies; in the executive as well as the legislature, the party has less to give and less to take away than the constituency does.[16]

Many other factors limit an executive's ability to unify an administration and hold it accountable for achieving a party's policy goals. Several of these limits were put in place by Progressive reforms aimed at crippling party power:

- Legislatures can protect top-level bureaucrats from presidential influence by giving them terms of office longer than the president's term, by limiting the president's power to remove them, or by requiring that they be chosen through a merit system rather than by political appointment.

- Legislatures can prevent party control of an administrative agency by requiring that its leadership include members of both parties. The Federal Election Commission board, for example, is traditionally composed of three Democrats and three Republicans—and at least *four* board members must agree to investigate any suspected campaign finance abuse. (This, of course, guarantees gridlock as much as it assures bipartisanship.)

- Top administrators in many states are elected. So voters may choose, say, a Republican for governor and a Democrat for state treasurer to work together in an uneasy alliance.

- Most American executives are term-limited; presidents can run for only two terms, and most governors can serve only one or two consecutive terms. As the end of their term approaches, their authority over other officeholders lessens.

Party Experience Among Bureaucrats

Another way in which party can influence bureaucrats and administrators is that the people appointed to head cabinet departments, such as Health and Human Services, Agriculture, and Labor, have often had a long history of party activity. Most of President Obama's cabinet members are long-time Democratic loyalists. Presidents no longer use these positions as rewards for loyal *party* service; instead, they look for loyalty to the president's *own* aims. Nevertheless, most presidential appointees have been active partisans whose values and political careers have been shaped to a significant degree by their party.

Just below this top level, officeholders are less likely to have party experience. These officials are most often chosen for their administrative skills and only secondarily for their political credentials. The party organization's role in their selection may be minimal. Yet they usually share the president's party affiliation, and the party link can result in a common outlook.

Modern presidents can make only about 3,000 political appointments, however— fewer appointive positions than some governors have—to try to gain control of an executive branch employing several million civilian employees. Many of these appointees are newcomers with little time to "learn the ropes" and little hope of gaining the necessary support of career bureaucrats.[17]

Changing Political Outlooks in the Federal Bureaucracy

In spite of these limits on party control, the federal bureaucracy (and many state bureaucracies) does respond to partisan forces over the long run. As the federal government expanded in the 1930s, President Roosevelt drew people into the career bureaucracy who were committed to his programs. They then became a bulwark against later efforts to weaken these programs, especially as these dedicated New Dealers came to be promoted to more and more senior positions in their agencies.

This pro-Democratic slant could still be seen in the federal bureaucracy decades later. By 1970, Joel Aberbach and Bert Rockman found that nearly a majority of these career bureaucrats said they normally voted Democratic and only 17 percent usually voted Republican. In federal social service agencies, even the administrators who were not Democrats said that they favored liberal policies. So Republican President Richard Nixon, in office at that time, faced a federal bureaucracy that had little sympathy for his conservative agenda. His administration spent a lot of time trying to control the bureaucracy by appointing Nixon loyalists to top bureaucratic positions.[18]

By 1992, however, the bureaucratic environment had changed. In the intervening two decades, Republicans had held the White House for all but four years. When Aberbach and Rockman returned to interview career administrators in comparable positions to those they interviewed in 1970, they now found slight Republican pluralities, although the career executives were still much more Democratic and liberal than the Reagan and Bush political appointees. As older civil servants retired, a new generation, less committed to New Deal and Great Society programs, had been recruited into senior executive positions. Changes in civil service laws further allowed positions formerly reserved for career employees to be filled by political appointees who could be carefully screened by the White House. The bureaucracy was no longer as hostile to Republican initiatives.[19] The Reagan, Clinton, and George W. Bush administrations made serious efforts to put their own stamp on the federal bureaucracy's administration of the laws, sometimes resulting in complaints of political interference in federal agencies' activities.[20]

In short, there is evidence of party influence in the executive branch. But most presidents and governors use their party leadership role to promote their own programs and reelection, not their party's programs. To the extent that the executive's goals are similar to those of his or her party, of course, the party's program benefits. For most American executives, however, the goals and interests of their party organization are secondary to their own policy goals and political careers.

TRACES OF PARTY IN THE COURTS

Courts and judges are affected by party politics as well. Most American judges—even most justices of the U.S. Supreme Court—are political men and women who took office after careers that involved them in some aspect of partisan politics (see box on page 278). The appointment and election of judges has become increasingly partisan and contentious. Because of the nature of the judiciary, however, party influence can be subtle.

Judicial Voting along Party Lines

Hints of party influence appear when we examine the voting in American appellate courts. Judges appointed by Democratic presidents tend to be more liberal than those appointed by Republican presidents on issues such as civil liberties, labor issues, and regulation.[21] In a study of state and federal courts, in comparison with Republican judges, Democratic judges were found to decide more often in favor of the defendant in criminal cases, for the government in tax cases, for the regulatory agency in cases involving the regulation of business, and for the claimants in workers' compensation, and unemployment compensation cases.[22] An environmental research group found that federal judges appointed by Democratic presidents were much more likely to rule in favor of environmentalists than Republican-appointed judges were.[23] These are the kinds of differences that we would expect to find when comparing the views of Democrats and Republicans outside the courtroom.

Similarly, in recent redistricting cases, U.S. District Court judges have tended to uphold plans enacted by their party more than those enacted by the opposing party,[24] and court rulings on states' voter identification laws (see Chapter 8) closely reflect whether the court's majority was nominated by Democratic or Republican officials.[25]

THE PARTISAN BACKGROUNDS OF U.S. SUPREME COURT JUSTICES

Justices Appointed by Republican Presidents

John Roberts (chief justice; appointed by G. W. Bush) served as an aide to the attorney general and the White House counsel in the Republican Reagan administration and was the principal deputy solicitor general in the Republican G. H. W. Bush administration.

John Paul Stevens (Ford) is a registered Republican, though he was never active in Republican Party politics.

Antonin Scalia (Reagan) was named general counsel for the Office of Telecommunications Policy in the Republican Nixon administration and then assistant attorney general under Republican Gerald Ford.

Anthony Kennedy (Reagan) was a Republican activist and campaign donor in California and then became a legal adviser to Reagan as governor.

Clarence Thomas (G. H. W. Bush) served on the staff of Missouri's Republican attorney general and as assistant secretary for Civil Rights and director of the Equal Employment Opportunity Commission in the Republican Reagan administration. Thomas's wife was a senior aide to former House Republican Majority Leader Dick Armey.

Samuel A. Alito, Jr. (G. W. Bush) was assistant to the solicitor general and deputy assistant to the attorney general in the Republican Reagan administration.

Justices Appointed by a Democratic President

Ruth Bader Ginsburg (Clinton) had no formal party positions or appointments prior to her nomination to the Court.

Stephen G. Breyer (Clinton) was a special assistant to the assistant attorney general under Democratic President Lyndon Johnson, assistant special prosecutor in the Watergate investigation, and special counsel and then chief counsel to the Democratic-led Senate Judiciary Committee.

Sonia Sotomayor (Obama) served as a New York County Assistant District Attorney, appointed by a Democratic governor. She was recommended for a federal judgeship by a Democratic senator and nominated by both a Republican (G. H. W. Bush) and a Democratic (Clinton) president.

It is not easy to distinguish the impact of judges' partisanship from other influences, including their career considerations, their law school training, and their desire to protect their professional reputations. Judges show much less party cohesion than legislators do. Yet under some circumstances, Democratic judges rule differently from their Republican colleagues.

What Causes Partisan Behavior on the Courts?

Very little of this apparent partisanship is due to active efforts by Democratic and Republican Party leaders to influence court decisions. In most communities now, openly partisan activity by a judge or pressure by a party leader to decide a case in a certain way would be seen as violating the norms of the judicial system.

A much better explanation for the impact of party on judges' behavior is simply that laws do not interpret themselves. Legislatures write laws using general language, and these general laws must be applied to specific cases with varying features. The judges who apply these laws, like the bureaucrats who administer them, have views on political issues and on how much interpretation is necessary or permissible in applying the law to particular situations.

Among those views are party identifications. Just as the two parties reflect different sets of values, so do their identifiers, including those who become judges. Two judges might vote together on the regulation of business because of values they share about the proper role of government. Those values may have led them to identify with the same party years earlier or were developed out of experience in that party. In other words, it is not usually the external pressure from a party leader but rather the party *in* the judge that can lead judges with similar partisan backgrounds to make similar decisions (see "A Day in the Life," on page 280).

Those who appoint judges to their positions are well aware of the importance of judges' value systems. They know that judges have discretion in deciding some cases and that the choices they make may reflect, at least in part, the judge's own experiences and beliefs. This became a major issue in the confirmation hearings for Obama Supreme Court nominee Sonia Sotomayor, who had argued that her life experience as a Latina could add to the Court's breadth of understanding. So the selection of judges, especially for higher courts that receive the most challenging cases, has traditionally taken into account the values and attitudes of the possible nominees.[26]

Party and Judicial Appointments

Parties can affect the selection of judges in several ways. In many states, party leaders may advise on the nominations of prospective judges. That gives them a means to advance party goals by encouraging the appointment or election of judges who believe in the party's values. It also permits them to further the careers of lawyers who have served the party loyally. Even when party organizations don't have that opportunity, the nomination of judges by a governor or a president permits the influence of the party in government on judicial appointments.[27]

Federal Judges   Presidents nominate candidates for federal judgeships; the Senate must confirm or reject them. Because prospective judges' party and ideology are

A WOMAN'S PLACE IS IN THE COURTHOUSE

Accompanying their parents to a trial, two young girls glanced through the windows of the courtroom next door. "Ooh, look at that!" said one, gazing up at the bench. "She's a judge and she's a girl! I didn't know girls could be judges!"

Circuit Court Judge Mary Ellen Diekhoff, the "girl" on the bench, felt the same way when she was growing up. The daughter of a single mother who worked as a secretary in a steel mill, Diekhoff had never met a lawyer. But "in seventh grade, a very brave teacher decided to take us to the Statehouse in Indianapolis and told us that this is where the laws were made. And I realized that I *loved* the Statehouse." When she got home, she announced to her astonished mother, "I'm going to be a lawyer."

Years later, after law school and a private practice, she became a prosecutor. For 17 years, she got a thorough grounding in the highs and the lows of the justice system by preparing and trying criminal cases. Then, when the only two local women judges retired, she was approached by several people who suggested that she run. Circuit Court judges in Indiana are chosen in partisan elections. She filed as a Democratic candidate and won the third highest vote total in the county.

"I don't think of myself as a partisan when doing my job," she says. "But we are all the product of our life experiences. If you have a civil case where a credit card company is suing a credit card holder, for instance, I could imagine moments where different judges might see the principles in the case differently. It's not honest to say that as a judge, you don't have opinions. A good judge has to say that he or she does have opinions, acknowledge them, and then look through them to apply the law, even in cases where you have to sign some orders that you don't like personally."

Would she prefer not to run in a partisan election? "I can see both sides. It would be better if a judge could run without a party label. It's good that a judge can't say in a campaign, 'I'm in favor of the death penalty,' but if you run for office under a party's flag, people make assumptions about your stands on issues that may not be true. On the other hand, if you're appointed for a lifetime term, that's not always a good idea either. As a judge, you get a lot of respect. As a prosecutor, lots of people would argue with me. But when you become a judge, you walk into the courtroom and everybody stands up. Nobody criticizes you—at least not to your face. If you became a judge fairly young, I could imagine that over time you'd begin to believe that you were invincible. That's dangerous in a democratic society.

"Historically, though, I think that Supreme Court justices and other judges have been able to get past their appointments by partisan officials and think like judges, even if they disappoint the president who appointed them. And that's important; it's the judiciary that will guard the Constitution, and I'm proud to be a part of it."

important indicators of their attitudes and, thus, can affect their decisions in some kinds of cases, every American president for the past century has made at least 80 percent of his judicial appointments from within his own party; the average is higher than 90 percent.

The Reagan and first Bush administrations took special care to screen candidates for their dedication to conservative principles.[28] As a result, their appointees were even more ideologically distinctive (as well as more likely to have been active in party politics) than average among recent presidents. The Clinton administration was less concerned with ideological screening. Clinton also appointed a somewhat lower percentage of federal judges from his own party than most of his predecessors did and was less inclined to choose judges with records of party activity.[29]

George W. Bush's judicial selections returned to the pattern of Reagan and Bush's father. As a result, appellate courts are often the sites of bitter ideological battles between Bush-appointed conservative judges and liberal judges appointed by Democratic presidents. It has become routine for Democratic-appointed and Republican-appointed appeals court judges to attack one another's decisions in their own rulings with terms such as "unconscionable," "absurd," and "alarming."[30]

Senate action on the president's nominations to federal judgeships has become increasingly partisan as well during the last two decades. Early shots were fired in the 1980s and early 1990s, when Senate Democrats and their allies waged major battles over the confirmation of two conservative nominees to the Supreme Court: Robert Bork and Clarence Thomas. (In fact, the former case gave rise to a new verb. When an intense, partisan campaign has been mustered against a nominee, he or she is said to have been "Borked.") By the end of the Clinton administration, the level of partisan animosity over judicial appointments was so high that Republican Senate leaders were refusing to schedule debate on some of the president's nominees.

Both parties have continued this tradition of bare-knuckles partisanship into the 2000s.[31] The atmosphere surrounding judicial appointments has become more and more acrimonious as the parties use these nominations to fire up their core support in the public (see box on page 282).

State Court Judges   State court judges, in contrast, are often elected rather than appointed—a practice used almost nowhere else in the world. Candidates for at least some types of judgeships must run in partisan elections in about a third of the states. Some states use a nonpartisan ballot for judges' races, though party organizations may still endorse their own candidates publicly. In these elections, candidates for judge routinely accept campaign contributions, often from lawyers and groups who will be bringing cases to their courts for a ruling. These contests are attracting increasing contributions and spending.

Even when judges are appointed to their posts, partisanship can still play a role. A number of states have moved toward a "merit appointment" system in which nominating commissions screen prospective judges or recommend a short list to the governor or another official. In these cases, the appointee usually has to run in a retention election within 4–12 years of his or her appointment. Reformers hoped that these long terms and the high probability that the appointee would be reelected (thanks to incumbency) would free judges from party pressures, or even pressures from the governor or president. But partisanship is so often already internalized in the judge's values and preferences that a long-term judgeship merely allows them to flourish.[32]

NOMINATION WARS

Partisan battles over presidents' judicial nominations had been intense for two decades by the time of President Obama's first opportunity to nominate a Supreme Court justice. The president's nominee, Federal Appeals Court Judge Sonia Sotomayor, seemed to be a politically appealing choice. Sotomayor, who had pulled herself out of poverty and graduated from Yale Law School, would be the first Latina ever to serve on the high court. Sotomayor had been previously appointed to federal judgeships by both Republican President George H. W. Bush and Democrat Bill Clinton.

But in the current political climate, nomination battles, stoked by ideological interest groups on the left and right, have become a standard part of the confirmation process. For these groups, a Supreme Court nomination offered the chance to raise campaign funds and whip up supporters. All sides planned their strategies to influence Senate confirmation well before Obama announced his choice.

The Obama administration named a team of presidential and vice-presidential aides to coordinate the effort promoting Sotomayor's nomination. Members of the team coached the nominee through mock Senate confirmation sessions. They worked with liberal interest groups, who asked their supporters to lobby their senators on her behalf, write to newspapers, and, of course, contribute to Democratic groups.

Several Republican senators worried publicly that attacking Sotomayor would hurt the party's image among Latinos. But conservative, pro-family, and Christian evangelical groups were not deterred. They charged that she would be a liberal activist judge and publicized her earlier comment that it is appropriate for judges to consider their personal experiences in their decisions and that under some circumstances, a Latina judge might reach a "better conclusion" on the bench than a white male judge.

Millions of dollars were spent on TV, radio, and Internet ads as well as efforts to shape media coverage of the nomination. All sides exaggerated the nominee's stands to achieve their own political goals. In the end, even a successful nominee must live with the aftermath of the controversy throughout his or her service on the bench.

Sources: Adam Nagourney, "Republicans Weigh Risks of a Supreme Court Battle," at thecaucus.blogs.nytimes.com/2009/05/26/ (accessed July 6, 2009), and Kevin Bohn, "Prepping Sotomayor for hearings," at www.cnn.com/2009/POLITICS/05/28/prepping. sotomayor/index.html (accessed May 28, 2009).

Many European countries have different selection procedures. Someone prepares to be a judge through study, apprenticeship, and then by scoring well on a special exam. In the United States, in contrast, there is no special training process for judges—no exam to take, no advanced degree in "judgeship." Any lawyer can be a judge if he or she can win election or appointment to the job. But although the specialized training process required for judgeships in many European nations limits the impact of party organizations and partisan elections, those who become judges will still have political preferences, many of which will have been shaped by their partisanship.

THE PARTY WITHIN THE EXECUTIVE AND THE JUDGE

When we talk about party influence on executives and judges, then, the best explanation for this influence is that executives and judges are people who hold political beliefs, and those beliefs are often related to the individual's party affiliation. Democrats tend to hold different beliefs about government and the economy than Republicans do, and Democratic judges and bureaucrats, similarly, hold different views from Republican judges and bureaucrats. These party differences are reinforced by partisan elements in the process by which presidents and governors, top executive officials, and most judges are chosen. And the fact that judges and administrators have to interpret laws when applying them allows these differences to be expressed. However, we rarely see much evidence of direct influence by the party organization on bureaucrats and courts. The parties don't have the means to enforce party discipline in the executive or judicial branches.

Reformers have tried to wring partisan considerations out of the selection process; one example is the use of the merit system to appoint officials. There is good reason to try. When citizens suspect that partisan forces are affecting courts and administrative agencies—for instance, when judges campaigning for reelection get big campaign contributions from lawyers and groups whose lawsuits they will later decide, public confidence in courts and administrative agencies can be undermined. But there is no way to eliminate individuals' beliefs and values, including their partisanship, from their selection as administrators or judges or from their behavior in administrative agencies and in court.

CHAPTER 15

The Semi-Responsible Parties

It's ironic. Since the early years of the United States, large numbers of Americans have mistrusted political parties and tried to limit party power. Yet most Americans are partisans, in that they identify themselves as Democrats or Republicans. Why do so many of us feel attached to something we mistrust? Because parties, even when they misbehave, can be extremely useful. They are among the most effective means we have of controlling the awesome powers of government. Unless government's power is controlled—held accountable to the wishes of citizens, to at least some extent—then democracy is at risk.

In part because of public mistrust, the American parties have less power over the functioning of government than do parties in many European countries. In the United States, even when a party has won a majority in government, it still can't guarantee that its promises to the nation—the pledges that it has made in its platform—will be carried out. Unified Republican control of Congress and the White House in the early 2000s, for example, brought the tax cuts promised by the Republican platform but not the limits on the growth of government spending. President Barack Obama has faced resistance from his Democratic co-partisans in Congress as well as from their Republican colleagues on top-priority issues such as health care.

If the parties are not strong enough to hold American elected officials fully accountable, then how can citizens protect their interests?[1] Some argue that the answer is to create a system of truly "responsible parties."[2] The governing party in this system would translate a coherent political philosophy into government action and would then be held responsible for the results.

Others see a more limited problem with party politics. For decades, the American parties have been criticized for being too much alike in their platforms, too centrist, and not clear and specific enough on big issues. Bloggers and other commentators have charged that both parties are under the control of moneyed special interests. The result, they argue, is that government serves the well-financed minorities—corporations, labor unions, single-issue groups—rather than the people.

These two sets of critics—the scholars who favor responsible parties and the ideologically oriented activists—have different perspectives, but at heart they make the same point. They both want the parties to offer clearer and more detailed stands on issues and for the winning party to put its promises to work in public policy. To some extent, their complaints have been answered. The parties' stands on important issues now differ sharply from one another. The Democratic Party is more uniformly liberal now, after many southern conservatives switched into the Republican Party, and the Republicans have followed a more consistently conservative path. In fact, for many Americans, the gulf between the parties has become too wide; in recent surveys, almost half of Americans describe the Democrats as "too liberal" and the Republican Party as "too conservative."[3] Have they become more like "responsible" parties, and does that improve their ability to serve the needs of a democracy?

THE CASE FOR RESPONSIBLE PARTY GOVERNMENT

The idea of *responsible parties*, also called *party government*, offers a vision of a democracy very different from the traditional American commitment to limited government and the equally traditional American hostility to powerful political parties. Champions of party government believe that we need a strong and decisive government to solve social and economic problems. Our political institutions, they feel, may have been well suited to the limited governing of the early years of American history but do not serve us well today, when we need more vigorous government action against challenges ranging from climate change to terrorism.

However, the public must be able to keep this strong government under control. Individuals rarely have the time, information, or desire to play an active political role or even to find out what their elected representatives are doing. Candidate-centered elections can reduce public control as well; it is much harder for voters to monitor hundreds of different candidates than to judge the performance of one governing party.

How Would Party Government (Responsible Parties) Work?

To solve these problems, party government advocates say, we must restructure the political parties and let them hold elected officials accountable.[4] The parties would take the lead in organizing and energizing the government and would, in the process, reinvigorate the other institutions of popular democracy. Party government would work like this:

- Each party would draw up a clear, detailed statement of the principles and programs it favors. It would pledge to carry out those programs if the party wins.
- The parties would nominate candidates loyal to the party program and willing to enact it into public policy if elected.
- Each party would run a campaign that clarifies the policy differences between the two parties, so voters would grasp these differences and vote on that basis.
- Once elected, the party would hold its officeholders responsible for carrying out the party program. Voters could then determine whether they approved of the results and decide whether to keep or defeat the governing party at the next election.

In this system of responsible parties, then, the party's main focus would be on the policies it has pledged to put into effect. Winning elections would not be an end in itself. Nominations and elections would become no more—and no less—than a means to achieve certain public policy goals. *For this to happen, all the elected branches of government would have to be controlled by the same party at a particular time.* The party would bind the divided institutions of government into a working whole, as happens in parliamentary democracies.

What qualifies the party to play this crucial role? In the words of a prominent party scholar, it is because "the parties have claims on the loyalties of the American people superior to the claims of any other forms of political organization. . . . The parties are the special form of political organization adapted to the mobilization of majorities."[5] So parties would hold a privileged position in politics compared with interest groups, their major rivals as intermediaries between citizens and government.[6]

Those who argue for party government do not always agree on the purposes they feel a strong federal government should serve. Many conservatives, once suspicious of a powerful central government, grew to like it better when conservative Presidents Reagan and Bush used their power to urge Congress to eliminate liberal programs. Similarly, liberals who were frustrated by the separation of powers developed greater enthusiasm for the principle when Congress proved capable of checking some of Reagan's and Bush's initiatives. It is easier to like party government, apparently, when your party is in charge. In any case, party government advocates feel that a government pulled together by strong parties would give the public a bigger voice.

THE CASE AGAINST PARTY GOVERNMENT

The proponents of party government are persuasive, but most American political scientists remain unconvinced. Their concerns about party government take two forms. One is the argument that party government would not produce desirable results. The other is that it simply would not work in the American context.[7]

It Would Increase Conflict

First, these skeptics fear that the nature of party government—its dedication to providing clear alternatives on major issues—would stimulate more intense and conflict-filled politics. Legislators, they say, would be bound to a fixed party position and would no longer be free to represent their own constituents and to negotiate mutually acceptable solutions. That would weaken the deliberative character of American legislatures.

Critics of party government also fear that a system that makes parties the main avenue of political representation could undercut the rich variety of interest groups that now exist. Without these other means of representing groups and views, the two major parties might be seriously overloaded. Minor parties would pop up, further fragmenting American politics. In short, critics fear that legislatures would be dominated by rigid, dogmatic political parties unable to resolve problems.

It Wouldn't Work in American Politics

The second major argument against responsible parties is that the idea conflicts with the American government's design. The principles of separation of powers and federalism were intended to prevent tyranny by dividing constitutional authority among the various levels and branches of government. The separation of powers, for example, allows voters to give control of the executive branch to one party and the legislative branch to the other. Elections for Congress take place on a different schedule from presidential elections, so congressional candidates can try to insulate themselves from presidential coattails. Federalism permits different parties to dominate in different states. Any change in these basic principles would require major revision of the Constitution.

American voters have made enthusiastic use of the separation of powers in recent years. Until 1950, the president's party controlled both houses of Congress most of the time. Since then, *divided government* has prevailed: A president or governor faces at least one house of the legislature controlled by the other party (see Table 15.1). That has been true of 22 of the 30 years since 1980. Voters have produced divided party control in most state governments as well since the early 1980s.[8]

Divided government makes responsible party government impossible. When both Democratic-controlled and Republican-controlled parts of the government have their fingerprints on every major piece of legislation, voters find it difficult to figure out which party is responsible for bad policies. Without that ability, voters can't throw out the guilty party and replace it with the opposition.

To party government advocates, divided government helps to explain why the federal government has failed to respond effectively on a number of major concerns from health care to campaign finance. The critics disagree. They contend that unified

TABLE 15.1 Party Control of the Federal Government, 1951–2010

Party Control	Number of Years
Unified	*24*
Democrats control the presidency and both houses of Congress 1951–1952 (Truman), 1961–1968 (Kennedy, Johnson), 1977–1980 (Carter), 1993–1994 (Clinton), 2009–2010 (Obama)	18
Republicans control the presidency and both houses of Congress 1953–1954 (Eisenhower), 2003–2006 (G. W. Bush)	6
Divided	*36*
Democratic president, Republican House and Senate 1995–2000 (Clinton)	6
Republican president, Democratic House and Senate 1955–1960 (Eisenhower), 1969–1976 (Nixon, Ford), 1987–1992 (Reagan, G. H. W. Bush), 2007–2008 (G. W. Bush)	22
President's party controls one house of Congress 1981–1986 (Reagan), 2001–2002 (G. W. Bush)[*]	8

*The Senate was Republican-controlled for the first five months of 2001 until Senator James Jeffords left the Republican Party and the Democrats gained majority control.

Source: Updated from Harold W. Stanley and Richard G. Niemi, *Vital Statistics on American Politics 1999–2000* (Washington, DC: CQ Press, 2000), pp. 34–38.

Note: The names of the presidents during these years are in parentheses.

party government doesn't necessarily produce more significant legislative action, that the federal government has a lot of practice in coping with shared party power,[9] and even that American voters prefer it that way.[10]

The Gingrich Experiment: A Temporarily Responsible Party

Americans did get at least a whiff of party responsibility starting in the mid-1990s. In a move spearheaded by House Republican minority leader Newt Gingrich, the great majority of Republicans running for House seats in 1994 signed a statement they called a "Contract with America." In it, they pledged that if the voters would give the Republicans a House majority, they would guarantee a vote on each of ten pieces of legislation, all embodying conservative principles, within the first one hundred days of the next Congress. The statement concluded, in words that would gladden the hearts of party government advocates: "If we break this contract, throw us out. We mean it."

The Republicans did win a majority of House seats in 1994. They delivered on their promise; once in office, the new Republican leadership used its iron control of the House agenda to vote on each of the bills before the self-imposed deadline. The House Republicans were more unified on these bills than they had been in decades. That, however, is when party government stalled. The Senate Republican majority had not committed itself to the Contract with America and did not feel bound to consider these bills promptly or to pass them. The House Republicans' efforts were further stymied by divided government; a Democratic president had the power to veto any legislation that made it through both houses.

What can we learn from this experiment? As we have seen, the separation of powers is a mighty roadblock in the path of party government. Even the commitment of a legislative party to a set of clear and consistent principles is not enough to produce responsible party government, as long as the president and the other house of Congress are not willing to go along. There is reason to doubt, as well, that most voters appreciated the experiment; although Republicans kept their House majority in the next elections in 1996, so did the Senate Republicans who had not signed the Contract with America, and the Democratic president was reelected as well.

Even when the same party controls the White House and both houses of Congress, as the Democrats have since 2009, there are other obstacles to achieving party government. Because the parties' candidates are chosen by voters in primary elections, parties cannot insist that their candidates remain loyal to the party's program; even candidates who break with their party on important issues can still run, and win, as long as their constituents keep voting for them. Critics of the responsible parties model have also argued that:

- American voters are not issue oriented enough to be willing to see politics only through ideological lenses.
- The diversity of interests in American society is too great to be contained within just two party platforms.
- Each party is too decentralized to be able to take a single, national position on an issue and then enforce it on all their officeholders.
- Americans distrust parties too much, as seen by their frequent efforts to reduce party influence, to accept greater party power.

The idea of a responsible governing party, in other words, seems to its critics to ask too much of the voters, the parties, and the institutions of American government.

PARTY COHESION AND IDEOLOGY

Although genuine party government is unlikely in the United States, it is still possible to nudge the parties in the direction of greater accountability. Some observers suggest that this is happening now, in the only way that would be consistent with the American system of separated powers: that the party in government, party voters, and the party organization are more likely now than in recent decades to agree voluntarily on a clear party program. But there are limits to the parties' cohesiveness on issues.

Are the American Parties Ideological?

An *ideological party* is one with clear and consistent principles on a wide range of questions, from the purpose of government to the essence of human nature. Examples include the old-style Communist parties and the Muslim fundamentalist parties that have arisen in Middle Eastern nations. The principles of an ideological party offer answers to questions such as these: What should the power relationships in the society look like? How should the society be governed and what values should the government try to achieve? What are the appropriate means to achieve these values?

Throughout their long histories, however, the American parties have tended to be more pragmatic than ideological, focusing on concrete problems rather than on the purity of their principles. Ever since their founding, each party has been a blend of its own original tradition (the egalitarian tradition of the Democrats and the Republican tradition of order and industrial capitalism) with those of other groups that associated with it because of personal ties, geographic nearness, or simple expectations of political gain.[11]

Why have the major American parties been relatively free of ideology? Most important, there are only two of them to divide up a tremendous array of interests in American politics. In a system with several parties, a party can cater to one ideological niche in the voting public and still hope to survive. In a diverse two-party system, with many different interests and people to represent, such specialized appeals can be made only by minor parties—or by a major party intent on self-destruction.

Do They At Least Offer Clear Choices?

Even though the two parties are not as ideological as are many European parties, they have come to differ clearly in their stands on specific policies, which can increase voters' ability to hold them responsible. We can see these differences in the platforms they adopt every four years at their national conventions (see box on pages 290–291), in their candidates' speeches, and in the policies they pursue when they win. It would have been hard during the 2008 presidential campaign, for example, to mistake the stands taken by the major Democratic candidates on health care, poverty, and other social programs from those expressed by the Republican candidates. "Republicans mostly believe that the role of government is to foster greater individual economic achievement, even if it leads to more economic inequality," one perceptive analyst writes. "The Democratic philosophy is that the government should provide a safety net, even if it leads to economic inefficiency."[12] These differences, most notably the Democratic commitment to federal social programs and the Republican desire to limit them, have been central principles of the two parties since the New Deal.

PARTY DIFFERENCES ON MAJOR ISSUES: THE 2008 PARTY PLATFORMS

Abortion

Democrats: "The Democratic Party strongly and unequivocally supports *Roe v. Wade* and a woman's right to choose a safe and legal abortion, regardless of ability to pay, and we oppose any and all efforts to weaken or undermine that right."

Republicans: "We . . . affirm that the unborn child has a fundamental individual right to life which cannot be infringed."

Affirmative Action

Democrats: "We support affirmative action, including in federal contracting in higher education . . . "

Republicans: "Precisely because we oppose discrimination, we reject preferences, quotas, and set-asides, whether in education or in corporate boardrooms."

Education

Democrats: "The Democratic Party firmly believes that graduation from a quality public school and the opportunity to succeed in college must be the birthright of every child—not the privilege of the few."

Republicans: "We support choice in education for all families . . . whether through charter schools, vouchers or tax credits for attending faith-based or other nonpublic schools, or the option of home schooling. . . . We will energetically assert the right of students to engage in voluntary prayer in schools and to have equal access to school facilities for religious purposes."

Environment

Democrats: "We will reinvigorate the Environmental Protection Agency. . . . We will restore the 'polluter pays' principle to fund the cleanup of the most polluted sites, so that those who cause environmental problems pay to fix them."

Republicans: "In caring for the land and water, private ownership has been the best guarantee of conscientious stewardship, while the world's worst instances of environmental degradation have occurred under governmental control."

Global Warming

Democrats: "We need a global response to climate change that includes binding and enforceable commitments to reducing emissions, especially for those that pollute the most: the United States, China, India, the European Union, and Russia."

Republicans: "Republicans support technology-driven, market-based solutions that will decrease emissions. . . . Republicans caution against the doomsday climate change scenarios peddled by the aficionados of centralized command-and-control government."

PARTY DIFFERENCES ON MAJOR ISSUES: THE 2008 PARTY PLATFORMS *(continued)*

Gun Control

Democrats: "We believe that the right to own firearms is subject to reasonable regulation."

Republicans: "We uphold the right of individual Americans to own firearms."

Health Care

Democrats: "The government should insure that health insurance is affordable and provides meaningful coverage."

Republicans: "Republicans support the private practice of medicine and oppose socialized medicine in the form of a government-run universal health care system."

Iraq

Democrats: "We will be as careful getting out of Iraq as we were careless in getting in. We can safely remove our combat brigades at the pace of one to two per month and expect to complete redeployment within sixteen months."

Republicans: "To those who have sacrificed so much, we owe the commitment that American forces will leave that country in victory and with honor. That outcome is too critical to our own national security to be jeopardized by artificial or politically inspired timetables that neither reflect conditions on the ground nor respect the essential advice of our military commanders."

Labor Unions

Democrats: "We will strengthen the ability of workers to organize unions. . . . We will continue to vigorously oppose 'Right-to-Work Laws' . . ."

Republicans: "We affirm both the right of individuals to voluntarily participate in labor organizations and bargain collectively and the right of states to enact 'Right to Work' laws."

Same-Sex Marriage

Democrats: "We support the full inclusion of all families, including same-sex couples, in the life of our nation, and support equal responsibility, benefits, and protections. . . . We oppose the Defense of Marriage Act."

Republicans: "A Republican Congress enacted the Defense of Marriage Act, affirming the right of states not to recognize same-sex 'marriages' licensed in other states."

Taxes

Democrats: "We will shut down the corporate loopholes and tax havens and use the money so that we can provide an immediate middle-class tax cut that will offer relief to workers and their families."

Republicans: "We support a major reduction in the corporate tax rate so that American companies stay competitive with their foreign counterparts and American jobs can remain in this country."

Note: You can find the full text of the platforms at www.democrats.org/a/party/platform. html (for the Democrats) and www.gop.com/2008Platform/ for the Republicans)

Each major party has become more unified in its stands during the past few decades as well as more different from the other party. A major contributor was the issue of civil rights. As questions of racial justice emerged as an important focus of national policy in the 1960s and 1970s, white southerners deserted the Democratic Party in increasing numbers and took with them their more conservative views on many other issues. (This story is told more fully in Chapter 7.) This lowered the biggest barrier to unity within the Democratic Party on several issues.[13]

The Ronald Reagan presidency during the 1980s further polarized the parties. Reagan, who was strongly identified with the religious, neoconservative wing of the Republican Party, demonstrated the appeal of a simple vision based on one major idea: less government. His assault on the role of government as it had developed since the New Deal gave a more ideological tone to American politics than had been seen in decades. Since then, more issue-oriented leaders have been selected in both parties,[14] and political ideas, or purposive incentives, have become more prominent in bringing people into party activism. And as Chapter 13 showed, both congressional parties vote more cohesively now than they have in decades. State parties tend to divide along issue lines as well, with Democratic parties more liberal, especially when there is real party competition in the state.[15]

As a result, a change in party control can now make a noticeable difference in public policy. When Democrats won a majority from Republicans in both the House and Senate in 2006, the congressional agenda changed quickly. A bill to raise the minimum wage moved to the head of the legislative line under Democratic control, and both houses began investigations of the Bush administration's actions in Iraq and other policy areas that had long been deferred under Republican rule.

But Internal Divisions Remain

These clear differences on major issues, however, do not add up to the kinds of all-encompassing political philosophies that are found in genuinely ideological parties. Consider, for instance, the interesting relationship between each party's stand on economic policy and its position on issues such as abortion and pornography. Democrats have long stood for an activist federal government in promoting individuals' social welfare but very limited government power over individuals' decisions on abortion. Republicans generally want to loosen the federal government's grip on the economy and environmental regulation but argue for government activism in banning abortion. Nimble advocates could probably construct a rationale as to why these sets of positions are actually consistent. But in reality, these stands coexist within each party's platform because the major parties, as they always have, adjust their policy positions to attract groups of potential supporters—in this case, when Republicans found common cause with conservative Christians and Democrats reached out to pro-choice women—even at the cost of internal consistency.

In addition, because the major American parties are pragmatic and vote-seeking above all, neither party has stayed entirely true to the principles it has articulated. The Republican platform, for example, has long been committed to smaller government. Yet after gaining control of Congress in 1994 and the presidency in 2000, the Republican Party in Congress promoted a number of big-government programs, from a huge ($400–$700 billion) expansion of Medicare entitlements to a major boost in pork barrel spending. Their aim was to keep attracting the votes of constituents who value tangible economic benefits more than abstract principles. A conservative group tracking the 30 Republicans first elected to the House in the Republican sweep of 1994 who were still serving in the House in 2004 found that in their first term, most had sponsored bills that would have had a net effect of cutting federal spending, whereas in 2003–2004, all but two sponsored legislation that would have had a net effect of increasing spending.[16]

Finally, as cohesive as the congressional parties have become, they both deal with some internal dissent.[17] As Chapter 13 noted, the shrinking group of Republican moderates continues to conflict with the much larger Republican Study Committee, which supports conservative principles. The two groups worked to find common ground in 2009 at the request of the party's leadership but still clash on issues such as abortion. The Democrats have at least as long a history of internal conflict on issues.[18] Conflicts occur in state parties as well, such as in Idaho, where rural, mainly Mormon Democrats split from urban liberals on abortion, and Democrats from the logging and mining areas vote differently from urban Democrats on environmental issues.[19]

What about party voters? Is it true, as some ideologues charge, that most Americans are committed to ideological principles and want the Democrats and Republicans to provide more clearly defined ideological choices? Or are party voters bored with, or even alienated by, the programmatic concerns of many party activists?

IDEOLOGY AND THE AMERICAN VOTER

Media reports of election results frequently use the terms "liberal" and "conservative" to describe voters' choices. The question is more complicated for political scientists, who have long debated the nature and structure of citizens' political attitudes.

How Ideological Is the American Public?

An ideological voter, like an ideological party, would not just hold clear attitudes toward some individual issues but would also connect those attitudes into a coherent structure. Careful study of American political attitudes since the 1950s, however, raises serious doubt that most voters can be described as "ideological" or even as very consistent in their thinking about politics.

Analysts have found that many individuals with conservative attitudes on, say, taxes may express moderate or liberal attitudes on other issues, such as gay rights or the environment.[20] We do not necessarily hold a set of fixed stands, such as an unqualified "yes" on all forms of affirmative action and a firm "no" on taxes. Rather, we might feel that affirmative action can help those who need it *and* that it can give an unfair advantage. We can be pulled toward one of these views under some conditions and toward another view under other conditions. Thus, most people react to issues with a degree of ambivalence[21]—a sharp contrast with a more ideological thinker.

This ambivalence permits many of us to hold sets of beliefs that might drive an ideologue to drink. For instance, large numbers of survey respondents say that they want a smaller government with lower taxes *and* a government that provides more services in areas such as antiterrorism, health care, and education. That is understandable; most people would like to pay less but get more. But it is not a likely foundation for consistent thinking.[22]

Even in elections when voters are offered clearly contrasting choices, many voters tend to focus on more pragmatic considerations instead. Reagan campaigned for president in 1980 as a principled conservative, yet many voters supported him in spite of his conservative policy positions, rather than because of them. In fact, in both 1980 and 1984 most voters preferred the policy stands of Reagan's opponent, though Reagan won both elections handily.[23] Voters' judgments turned more on their *retrospective evaluations* of presidential performance—their feelings as to whether the most recent presidency had turned out well—than on Reagan's ideological stance. Because many voters tend to be results oriented, parties and candidates try to stitch together winning coalitions by appealing to a range of qualities—candidates' personal characteristics, group interests, single issues, and feelings about the party in power—rather than by stressing ideological differences.

It is important to note, however, that a growing number of people have been attracted to ideological appeals in recent years. The proportion of people in the American National Election Studies calling themselves conservative or extremely conservative, and liberal or extremely liberal, rose from 19 percent in 1972 to a high of 43 percent in 2008. These voters, who tend to be more interested and engaged in politics, have sorted themselves out more accurately by party in recent years; an increasing proportion of Democrats now call themselves liberals and a substantially greater proportion of Republicans consider themselves conservatives (see Figure 15.1).[24] In 2008, CNN's exit

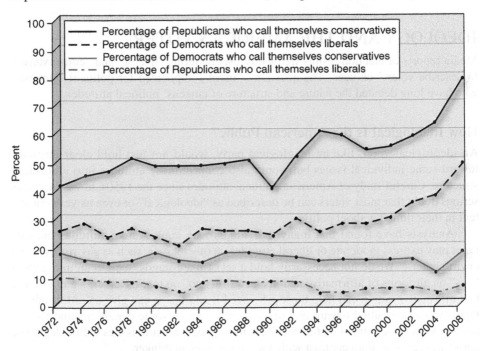

FIGURE 15.1   Increasing Polarization of Democrats and Republicans, 1972–2008

Note: Lines are the percentages of Democrats and Republicans (including strong and weak partisans and "leaners") who classify themselves as liberal (1–3 on a 1–7 liberal to conservative scale) or conservative (5–7) in each year listed.

Source: 2008 American National Election Study, University of Michigan; data made available by the Inter-University Consortium for Political and Social Research.

poll showed that voters who described themselves as liberal or conservative were very likely to pick the "correct" candidate (89 percent of liberals selecting Democrat Barack Obama, 78 percent of conservatives choosing Republican John McCain). Differences between the two parties' activists are even greater.[25]

Changes in the parties' behavior may account for a lot of this "ideological sorting." For several reasons, as we've seen in earlier chapters, party leaders and platforms are more polarized now, and both parties have been increasingly concerned with mobilizing their base in campaigns.[26] Americans are more likely to see a difference between the two parties on big issues (see Figure 15.2) and to divide by party in their attitudes toward candidates and issues.[27] They are more likely to view their own party's ideology as very similar to their own and the other party's ideology as quite different (see Figure 15.3). That may improve many voters' ability to approximate the demands of the responsible parties model.[28]

Even so, a lot of Americans have managed to sit out this polarization so far. Paul Allen Beck refers to "two electorates—one partisan and about evenly divided, the other estranged from party politics."[29] Is the polarized portion of the electorate big enough to sustain a movement toward more responsible parties?

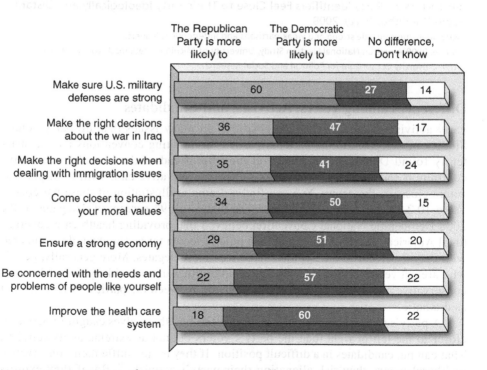

FIGURE 15.2   Percent of Voters Seeing Party Differences on Issues, 2008–2009.

Note: Rows do not always add up to 100 percent because of rounding error.

Source: New York Times/CBS polls conducted April 25–29, July 7–14, and October 10–13, 2008, and March 12–16, April 1–5, and June 12–16, 2009; responses to each question are averaged across surveys. Data at www.nytimes.com/http://www.nytimes.com/ref/us/polls_index.html (accessed July 12, 2009).

FIGURE 15.3   Party Identifiers Feel Close to Their Party Ideologically and Distant from the Other Party, 2008

Note: Identifiers include strong and weak partisans and independent leaners.

Source: 2008 American National Election Study, University of Michigan; data made available by the Inter-University Consortium for Political and Social Research.

Differences among Voters, Activists, and Candidates

Party activists take more extreme positions on many issues than do party voters. Studies of delegates to the national parties' nominating conventions have consistently found Democratic activists on the liberal end of the liberal-conservative continuum and Republican activists on the conservative end, with both parties' voters closer to the center. You can find a dramatic illustration of these patterns in Table 10.2, on page 193. The table shows that a full 94 percent of delegates to the 2008 Democratic National Convention believed that providing health care coverage to all Americans is more important than holding down taxes, for example, compared with only 7 percent of the Republican convention delegates. More generally, people who are actively involved in campaigns and politics are more likely to be liberal or conservative rather than moderate. The division between the parties' voters was not as dramatic.

A party's candidates and officeholders often find themselves caught in between: closer to the left or right than the party's voters but not as extreme as its activists. That can put candidates in a difficult position. If they try to muffle their conservative or liberal views, they risk alienating their party's activists.[30] But if they express those views candidly, more moderate voters may choose not to support them in the next election.[31] It is no wonder that many candidates prefer to remain ambiguous when asked about issues in their campaigns, at least when they speak to general audiences.

These differences between more ideological activists and more flexible candidates can aggravate the tensions among the party organization, the party in government, and the party's voters. Ideologues in both parties complain about the moderation of at least some parts of the party in government. Liberal Democrats objected to what they saw as President Obama's "sellout" on climate change and health care, and many social and fiscal conservatives questioned President Bush's commitment to their causes.

The dilemma of ideology, then, is not whether the American parties can become genuinely ideological parties. That is not likely. The problem is whether the increasing ideological commitment of their activists and of many of their officeholders can be sustained without alienating their more pragmatic supporters. The parties already face a deep well of public suspicion. Much of the public feels alienated from the parties' attachment to organized interests, their affinity for negative campaigns, and their failure to keep their promises.[32] Many Americans, whose tolerance for politics is low, find these sharpened party differences to be a turnoff.[33] As one writer put it, moderates may become more convinced that "politics no longer speaks to them, that it has become a dialogue of the deaf, a rant of uncompromising extremes."[34]

WHEN IS PARTY GOVERNMENT MOST LIKELY?

Responsible parties are hard to achieve. Even the British Parliament, so often cited as a model of party government, has not always had the cohesion and the binding party discipline that a "pure" responsible party government would require.[35] Under what conditions have the American parties come closest to the ideal of responsible parties?

When There Is Strong Presidential Leadership

At times, a strong president—Ronald Reagan and George W. Bush in his first term are good examples—has been able to push Congress to enact important parts of the platform on which he ran for office. That is especially likely, of course, when the president's party controls both houses of Congress. Strong party-oriented presidents can also draw voters' attention to party differences. But the result is likely to be "presidential government" rather than party government; voters are likely to respond to the president's performance rather than that of the party as a whole.

In Times of Crisis

At critical times in American history, the parties have divided in ways that were, if not truly ideological, at least determinedly policy oriented. In the 1936 presidential election, for example, the Democrats and the Republicans offered dramatically different solutions to a nation devastated by the Great Depression. The hardships of that economic collapse probably focused voter attention to an unusual degree on the possible remedies that government could provide. Combined with a campaign centered on the pros and cons of the Roosevelt program for social and economic change, this may well have produced something close to a mandate in the election for both the president and Congress. When strong presidential leadership is combined with crisis conditions, then a degree of responsible party government might be achieved, at least for the duration of the crisis.

When the Parties' Supporting Coalitions Realign

At some times when the parties' supporting coalitions of social groups have undergone real change—often called "realignments"—American politics seems to have most closely approached the requirements for party government. At these times, which often result in the creation of a new party system, the parties have tended to divide more clearly on a single, riveting set of issues, and party leaders, activists, and voters have reached high levels of agreement with one another and major differences with the other party (see Chapter 7).

New party systems typically produce a unified federal government, with the same party controlling both houses of Congress, the presidency, and a judiciary that, through the president's appointment power, comes to reflect the new majority. On only five occasions in American history has one party enjoyed control of Congress and the presidency continuously for more than a decade, and each time, this control was first established during a realignment. Party cohesion in Congress is especially high at the beginning of a new party system. So it is not surprising that major bursts of comprehensive policy change have followed the realignments of the parties' coalitions after the Civil War and during the 1930s,[36] though there have been periods of major policy innovation during periods of divided party control or shorter periods of unified party control as well.

Even at these times, the American version of party government has been a pale imitation of its European counterparts. The realignment of the 1930s, for example, produced a majority Democratic Party by linking a liberal northern wing, attracted to the party because it represented the hopes of disadvantaged groups and championed the developing welfare state, and a conservative southern wing that often opposed both of these goals. The president at the time, Franklin D. Roosevelt, had a congressional majority large enough to achieve many of his policy goals, but he faced opposition within his own party throughout his long career in the White House. In short, even when they have been most unified around a single political agenda, the American parties have still typically contained differing interests and goals.

PARTY GOVERNMENT AND POPULAR CONTROL

To many analysts, the idea of party government, or responsible parties, has continuing appeal. When parties stand for clear principles and voters are offered clear choices in elections, it is easier for citizens to hold government responsible for the policies it produces. That may make for a stronger and more vibrant democracy.

The major American parties are not ideological parties like many in other nations. But the congressional parties and, to some extent, the parties in the electorate have become more cohesive in the past two decades than they have been in a very long time. At the federal level and in many states, there is a marked difference between the parties on basic principles of public policy.

Yet, if the parties are to become more accountable, more like responsible parties in a system of party government, clear differences on issues and greater organizational strength are not enough. There must be some set of basic principles that can connect different issues into a single logical structure for each party, some means by which voters and leaders are able to distill the large number of policy issues into one major dimension or a few so that voters can easily understand and predict the party's stands.

That much structure and coherence will be harder and perhaps impossible to achieve. Too many powerful forces stand in the way. Even if party organizations gain immense new resources, they still won't be able to choose their own candidates; prospective officeholders will still have to attract voter support in primary elections. So candidates will still need to run their own campaigns and raise most of their own campaign money. Primaries give candidates greater independence from their parties than the increase in party resources can counteract. And no amount of party money can buy an exception to the rules of federalism and the separation of powers.

It is not likely, then, that the American parties and voters can meet the demands of the responsible parties model. The party organizations have not grown into the central role that the reformers so valued—that of drawing up a party program and enforcing it on candidates and officeholders. Many would find that to be cause for celebration. Others would remind us that, in a system of government as fragmented as that of the United States, semi-responsible parties make it even harder to accomplish one of the basic tasks of a democracy: holding public officials accountable for their actions.

CHAPTER 16

The Place of Parties in American Politics

T hree decades ago, the American parties appeared to be in decline. Because their troubles seemed to reflect long-term changes in American society, it was easy to assume that the decline was permanent. By the time their decay had become the central theme of books and articles about the parties, however, there were clear signs of resurgence. The parties have grown into different types of organizations than they once were, but in this changed form, they continue to be a fundamental part of the American political landscape.

To conclude this look at the American parties, this chapter will sum up these changes in relation to a simple but important truth: Political parties are powerfully shaped not only by the people who lead and participate in them but also by the environment in which they act. They are profoundly affected by election and campaign finance rules, interest groups, citizens, legislatures, and courts, just as they influence these forces. It is vital to look at the relationships between parties and their environment to understand the changes in party power and functions over time.

PARTIES AND THEIR ENVIRONMENT

Political parties affect their environment in a variety of ways. They recruit individuals into active roles in politics and government. They promote public policies in response to citizens' beliefs, demands, and fears. Through their communications and performance, parties affect public attitudes about the Democrats and the Republicans and about politics more generally. Party organizations and the parties in government structure their own environment even more directly as well: They make the rules governing how the parties' candidates will be nominated and financed and who will have the opportunity to choose them.

In turn, their environment helps to shape the parties' nature, activities, and effectiveness. Three types of environmental factors have been especially important in influencing the American parties as well as those in other Western democracies: the nature of the

TABLE 16.1 How Their Environment Influences the American Parties

Types of Influences	Examples
1. Nature of the electorate	Expansion of the right to vote, citizens' political interest and knowledge, social characteristics of the electorate (age, race, income)
2. Political institutions and rules	
(a) Institutions	Federalism, separation of powers, nature of the presidency, single-member districts
(b) Electoral processes	Direct primary, nonpartisan elections
(c) Laws and regulations	Laws governing campaign finance, structure of party organization, patronage
3. Social forces	
(a) National events and conditions	State of the economy, war
(b) Other political intermediaries	Types of other organized interests, media, independent consultants
(c) Political culture	Attitudes toward parties and politics

electorate, the nation's basic governmental institutions and rules, and the forces that affect the broader society (Table 16.1).[1]

The Nature of the Electorate

The nature and concerns of the voting population are vital influences on a party system. The societal "fault lines" that divide the electorate into opposing groups—race is one of the clearest and most persistent examples in American politics—help to define the parties' issue agendas. So do the social characteristics that make some groups more likely to vote than others.

The right to vote has expanded enormously in the United States. From an extremely limited suffrage—the small proportion of white male adults who owned property—it now includes the great majority of citizens over the age of 18. Political information has expanded as well. Mass media and computers have made information about politics much more accessible, and more citizens have the advantage of higher education, which helps them find and understand the information. Voters have gained unprecedented opportunities to take part in political decisions through primary elections, referenda, recall elections, and Internet access to public officials. Yet people's interest in politics and their feelings of political effectiveness and trust have not increased. So at the same time that these opportunities for participation expanded, voter turnout dropped and, although it has rebounded, remains lower than in most other industrialized democracies.

Turnout did not decline to the same degree among all groups in the population, however. There has been a steeper decline among lower-income Americans than among those with greater wealth.[2] And as we saw in Chapter 8, the turnout rate of college-age Americans, though it rose in 2004 and 2008, remains substantially lower than the turnout rate of adults over 65. It should come as no surprise, then, that Social Security and Medicare are much more frequent campaign issues than are college loans. Those who participate are more likely to be heard.

Political Institutions and Rules

The second cluster of environmental influences on the parties includes the nation's basic framework of political institutions: whether the government is federal or unitary, whether it is parliamentary or has separated powers, and how its positions of power are structured. Then there are the laws that regulate the parties, ranging from the secret ballot and state laws governing the makeup of party committees to federal laws regulating campaign spending.

In many ways, the American electoral environment differs from that of most other democracies.[3] Most other democratic nations do not divide governmental powers so insistently among different branches and levels of government. Few other democracies choose most of their leaders in single-member districts with plurality rules for electing officials, or stagger the terms of different types of officials. The direct primary limits the party organization's role in the selection of candidates to a degree unknown in most other democracies. The American parties are regulated more heavily than are parties in other nations, and American state laws defining the party organizations have no parallel in the democratic world. The effect of this regulation—and in most cases its aim—is to restrict the development of the party organizations. An unintended effect is to boost the power of the party in government relative to that of the party organization.

As a result, the major American parties differ in some important ways from parties in most other democracies. In particular, the parties are more candidate-centered. Party leaders have fewer effective tools to keep party legislators and other elected officials acting in accord with the party's stands. The American parties and their candidates raise much larger sums of money from private interests and spend much more on campaigns than do parties in other democracies. With the important exceptions of the direct primary and the secret ballot, however, these rules have probably changed less dramatically over time than has the nature of the electorate.

Societal Forces

A third set of environmental influences refers to events and trends in the larger society that affect politics at a particular time. The horrors of the September 11 attacks, the relocation of American industries to Mexico and China, and the changes in women's roles and family structures have had powerful effects on the nation's agenda. Thus, they have become part of the parties' agenda as well and affect the parties' platforms, campaign appeals, and supporting coalitions.

Other societal forces include the number and character of organized interests in the nation, the types and behavior of the media, and other means of representing interests. If individuals find alternative ways to pursue their political goals that seem more effective than the parties, they will use them. If the "hot line" of a local newspaper is better able to track down a reader's Social Security check or if an interest group is more vocal in opposing abortion, then why should the individual try to achieve her political aims through a party? The nature of the parties at any given time, then, depends in part on the available alternatives to parties and the competition among them.

All these elements of their environment have contributed to the unique character of the American parties. Thus, as we summarize the dramatic changes that have occurred in the parties' structure, supporting coalitions, and strength during the past four decades, we will pay special attention to the effects of their environment and especially to changes in the electorate.

PARTY DECLINE IN THE 1960s AND 1970s

A basic feature of the American parties is that the three party sectors are bound together only loosely. The party organization has not been able to involve large numbers of party identifiers in its structure and activities, nor has it been able to direct the campaigns or the policy making of the party in government. The party decline that was becoming apparent in the 1960s affected the three sectors very differently.

The Parties in the Electorate

During a time of upheaval in many of aspects of American life, voters' loyalty to the parties weakened noticeably in the late 1960s and 1970s. More people began to think of themselves as independents rather than as strong party identifiers. Those who remained attached to a party no longer took their party's advice in elections as much as they once did. The parties, then, found themselves with smaller numbers of less loyal identifiers.

One result was a surge in ticket splitting. By 1968, almost half of the respondents in national surveys said they had voted for more than one party's candidates in state or local elections, and by 1974 that figure topped out at 61 percent. At the aggregate level, the number of congressional districts selecting a presidential candidate of one party and a congressional candidate of the other party exceeded 30 percent for the first time in history in 1964 and reached 44 percent early in the next decade.[4]

As education levels increased, some voters became more responsive to the issue-oriented candidacies of the time. The campaigns of Barry Goldwater in 1964, Eugene McCarthy and George Wallace in 1968, and George McGovern in 1972 spurred many people's awareness of political issues. As television came to be used more widely in campaigns, others were drawn to candidates' media images. The attractive faces and ready smiles that television screens convey evoked some of the support that party symbols once commanded.

To a greater extent than they had in the 1950s, then, voters became more inclined to respond to candidates as individuals than as members of a party. Independent candidates for president and governor gained some success. Because candidates and issues change far more often than parties, the result was a less stable pattern of voting.

Party Organizations

The last of the great party machines were fading by the 1960s and 1970s. The famous Daley machine in Chicago was ripped apart in a series of tumultuous struggles. Party organizations could no longer depend on the patronage and preferments that once were so vital in recruiting party activists. Instead, more people were being drawn into party activism because of their commitment to particular issues. These were better-educated people, and they demanded greater participation in the party's decisions. Some of these new activists felt that compromise was a dirty word; to them, standing on principle was more important than winning an election. If their party did not satisfy their ideological goals, they stood ready to leave it for other groups—candidates' campaigns and single-issue organizations—that were more narrowly targeted to meet their needs.

Other aspects of the party organization were under stress as well. As the direct primary came to dominate presidential nominations, party organizations gave up their control over nominations to whoever voted in the primary. By the time a primary season had ended, the party's presidential nominee had been determined, so its nominating convention no longer had much of an independent role. As grassroots activists came to expect a bigger say within the party organization, its own internal decision making was no longer under the party leaders' control. This was particularly true of the Democrats, who in 1972 and 1976 nominated presidential candidates who were well outside the mainstream of their own party.

In addition to their declining influence over nominations, by the 1960s and 1970s the party organizations had lost their central role in campaigns more generally. To run in primaries, candidates now had to build their own campaign organizations, raise their own campaign money, and choose how to spend it. The campaign assets that they once received from their local party organizations—fund-raising, volunteers, information about public opinion—could now be obtained directly from pollsters, issue-oriented activists, or campaign consulting firms that were, in effect, "rent-a-party" agencies. Campaign finance reforms gave candidates an incentive to try to raise nonparty money at a time when the technologies for doing so were becoming more effective and widely available.

In fact, the campaign skills that local party organizations could offer their candidates were fairly primitive at that time, especially in comparison with the skills of many independent consultants. The national parties began to develop expertise in newer campaign technologies during the 1970s and to share their resources with state and local parties, but consultants had already established a beachhead. Even in the face of new vigor in the national committees, the party organizations in the 1970s remained more decentralized than did life and politics in the United States. Voters were looking more and more to national political leaders and symbols, but the party organizations still tended to be collections of state and local activists.

The Party in Government

In the 1960s and 1970s, elected officials came to depend more than ever on direct appeals to voters. Officeholders had been freed from reliance on the party organization by the direct primary, their direct access to the media, and the money and volunteers they could attract independent of the party's efforts. Because of split-ticket voting, candidates didn't even need to rely on party identification. Through personal style, personal appeals, and personal funds, they developed a "personal vote" independent of party.[5]

It became harder than ever to unseat an incumbent, especially in Congress. The cycle perpetuated itself; because there was not as much chance of beating an elected official, serious challengers did not appear as frequently. When they did, party organizations were not vigorous enough to provide challengers with the campaign resources they so desperately needed. Holding public office became more of a profession—a lifetime career—even at the state and local levels, where political professionals had formerly been rare.

As incumbents became more secure electorally, even though many did not feel that way, congressional parties gained greater freedom from the party organizations. Legislative party leaders found it harder to marshal their members on behalf of the legislative party's bills or the programs of the party's president. The Democratic Party in Congress was especially diverse, divided between southern conservatives and northern moderates and liberals. Thus, congressional Democrats were reluctant to grant much power to their legislative party leaders; neither the southern nor the northern Democrats could trust that leaders selected from the other group would act to serve the needs of all members of the congressional party. Senate and House Republicans were a varied group as well. So party-line voting in Congress fell to an all-time low at this time. However, it was a perverse kind of freedom. Protected from the demands of party leaders, legislators were thus more exposed to other pressures, mainly from large numbers of interest groups.

With the legislative parties less cohesive and strong, presidents and governors could exercise greater leadership. Presidents did not depend on their party organizations for much; in fact, with the help of federal campaign money after 1974, presidential candidates were able to run their campaigns free of obligation to the party organization at any level. By that time, however, divided government had become the norm. That undercut executives' power by permitting the opposition party to block their initiatives.

Shifting Power Centers within the Parties

These changes had produced a major shift of power within the parties. The party organizations had lost power not only to the individual members of the party in government but also to other political intermediaries, especially interest groups and the mass media. Party organizations and their leaders became even more vulnerable to suspicions that they were run by bosses plotting in smoke-filled rooms. Visions of "boss rule" were as much alive at party conventions in the 1960s and 1970s as they were in the early 1900s, even though, ironically, the resources that the party organizations had in the early 1900s, which could have justified the charge of boss rule at that time, were largely eroded by the 1960s.

The result was a peculiar kind of political party. A party organization is the only sector of the party whose interests go beyond winning individual elections. It is the party organization that sustains the party when its candidates lose their races. It is the organization that links the party's officeholders and office seekers; it can call them to collective action of the type that parties were created to achieve. Without it, party candidates are individual entrepreneurs seeking individual goals in a political system that requires collective decisions. The decline of the party organizations was a major force in the decline of the parties more generally.

PARTY RENEWAL

This marked decline was not the end of the story, however. The American parties responded to these challenges, just as they have adapted to changing circumstances at other times in the past. The steady decay of the parties was stopped and reversed, but some of the changes that took place in the 1960s and 1970s continue to leave their imprint even now. The parties have had to adjust to new roles in American politics.

Change in the Parties' Electoral Coalitions

The slow, steady change in the parties' supporting coalitions (see Chapter 7) has led to recurring speculation that a party realignment has taken place—that the two parties' coalitions have changed in significant enough ways to alter the nature of the party system. The symptoms that normally precede a major coalitional change began to be present in the mid-1960s: lower voter turnout, more ticket splitting, greater support for third-party or independent candidates, and divided government.

When Republicans won both the presidency and the Senate in 1980 and gained control of the House in 1994—the first time since 1954 that there was a Republican majority in both Houses of Congress—some concluded that the long-awaited realignment had occurred. They pointed out that in addition to the new Republican strength, the party coalitions had clearly changed from those of the New Deal. Black Americans are now steadfastly Democratic, white southerners have moved into the Republican Party, and religious conservatives, southern and nonsouthern, have become a major force within the GOP.

FIGURE 16.1   Eroding Democratic Strength in the South, U.S. House and Senate Seats, 1955–2009.

Note: Data points are the percentage of U.S. senators and House members from the 13 southern states (Ala., Ark., Fla., Ga., Ky., La., Miss., N.C., Okla., S.C., Tenn., Texas, Va.) who are Democrats.

Sources: Data for 1955–1995 from *Congressional Quarterly Weekly Report*, November 12, 1994: 3231. Data for 2005 from *CQ Weekly*, November 6, 2004, pp. 2664–2666, and December 11, 2004, p. 2931. Data for 2009 compiled by the author.

Other demographic categories such as marital status and sexual identity have taken on a partisan tinge, as unmarried people (especially women) and gay people have come to identify preponderantly as Democrats. The most striking feature of this new alignment has been the decline of Democratic strength in the South (see Figure 16.1), which reached a modern low in 2005. As a result, in the 1990s and for a time in the early 2000s, Republicans came closer to parity with the Democrats in both party ID and election results than they had since the 1930s.

A Return to Democratic Party Dominance?

As Chapter 7 showed, however, there's an argument that this Republican resurgence has passed its peak. In the 2004, 2006, and 2008 elections, Democratic candidates at the state and federal levels regained their footing. Even in the South, Barack Obama won many suburban counties in North Carolina and Virginia, where educational levels are rising and high-technology jobs make up an increasing share of the economy. It was in the less prosperous, more rural southern counties where Republican John McCain found his greatest support. The ability of Democratic candidates to increase their margins among more educated and upper-income voters in all regions and to attract large majorities of the fastest-growing segments of the electorate—young people and Latinos in particular—may have put a choke hold on the idea of a Republican realignment.[6]

These changes led to a feverish debate among Republicans as to what went wrong. Conservative Republicans argued that voters had not rejected conservative principles; instead, the problem was that once Republicans gained power, they sacrificed these principles (small government, in particular) and pandered to voters' short-term interest in tangible benefits in order to win a lasting Republican majority.

The declining number of moderate Republicans disagreed. Many warned that the party's hard-line stands on social issues, dear to the hearts of white evangelical Christians, were limiting the party's attractiveness to independents. As one Republican strategist put it, "appealing to a shrinking base may not be the best election strategy."[7] Adding to the base would require tolerating alternative viewpoints and finding ways to enlist the support of young people, Latinos, and suburbanites. That is the plan the Democrats followed in 2006 and 2008 to regain strength; although the Democratic revival was due in part to Republican missteps, it was led by more centrist Democratic candidates who were promoted by the party in moderate and conservative congressional districts.

The risk for the Republicans is that a more inclusive, "big tent" appeal could alienate the remaining Republican base. There are alternatives. In the short run, the party was able to win several races in 2009 by stimulating independents' fears about Obama's programs. A longer-term strategy would be for the party to shift its emphasis rather than its stands: to focus more on broadly shared priorities such as economic growth and less on such hot-button issues as same-sex marriage and abortion. This debate has important implications for the parties. If both parties return to a more inclusive strategy, backing moderate candidates in closely contested districts, then the clarity of the parties' stands would decline. If we accept the conditional party government theory (see Chapter 13), the change could weaken the parties' leadership in Congress.

Even if Democratic dominance has returned, however, there is good evidence that we are now in a different party system from that of the New Deal. This sixth party system has emerged differently from the New Deal party system. In contrast with the tumultuous changes that followed the Depression of the 1930s, the more recent changes in party coalitions have developed over a period of decades and continue to evolve. Election results have been mercurial. Republican House candidates went from great success in 1994 to panic in 1998, success in 2002, and desperation in 2006 and 2008. The proportion of people calling themselves independents remains high. Independent candidates have aroused public interest. Polls do not reveal any great public enthusiasm for the major parties or, for that matter, many other aspects of American politics. Even a full-fledged realignment of the parties' coalitions, in a world of primaries, would not give back the party organizations' power to nominate their candidates. Lasting change in the parties' coalitions could not guarantee an end to the more candidate-centered electoral world that has resulted.

Thus, the events of the 1960s and 1970s resulted in a continuing challenge to party loyalties. Large numbers of voters now rely on sources other than the parties, such as cable TV, blogs, and single-issue groups, for their political information. Sometimes these sources reinforce partisan views; in other cases, they don't.[8] Even with this formidable competition, however, parties remain important landmarks on most people's political maps. Levels of party identification rebounded in the 1990s, and partisanship is at least as strong an influence on people's voting now as it was before the 1960s.[9] Split-ticket voting, especially as measured by the number of districts voting for a presidential candidate of one party and a congressional candidate of the other, hit a 50-year low in 2004.[10]

The Rise of More Cohesive Parties in Government

Well before the current revival of partisanship among voters—and a possible cause of it—the parties in government had begun a revival of their own. By the mid-1970s, the long decline in party unity in Congress had stopped and the organizational seeds had been sown for greater party strength. By the 1980s, the congressional parties had become more cohesive than they had been in a century. Their cohesion was enhanced by the coalitional changes within the party electorates. The slow, steady movement from the Democratic "solid South" to a largely Republican South left both congressional parties more homogeneous, which in turn made it easier for each party to offer clear alternatives on big issues. In many states, as well, legislative parties were becoming more unified and taking clearer positions on issues.

Parties also took on greater importance in the executive branch. The Reagan administration came into office in 1981 as the most ideologically committed and the most partisan in decades. Reagan's leadership placed conservative principles at the top of the GOP's agenda and solidified the hold of his brand of conservatives on the party. The Democrats became more unified in response. By the mid-1990s, there was intense partisan conflict between a programmatically committed, Republican-led Congress and an activist Clinton White House. The battles have continued, resulting in a level of incivility that can threaten congressional effectiveness. Consider one House member's recollection of a new member orientation program in which a Democratic leadership staff member suggested the importance of getting to know Republican legislators. One of the new Democrats replied, "Why would we want to do that?"[11]

The New "Service Parties"

The party organizations have revived just as dramatically. Facing an environment of candidate-centered campaigns, both parties retooled their national organizations to provide services to the party's candidates. They have used their increased funding and staffing to help state and local parties, recruit candidates, offer them more resources, and thus step up their role in campaigns, compared with the 1960s and 1970s.

The new service party, however, differs a great deal from the grassroots organizations of earlier years. Because its main role is to support candidates, it is not very visible to voters, nor can it always make a major impact on campaigns. In the big-spending world of campaign finance, party organizations do not often bring enough money to the table to be able to dominate political campaigning or at times even to be heard very clearly. The service party is one of many forces trying to win the attention of candidates, influence elected officials, and mobilize citizens.

The party organizations, in short, are more vigorous now than they have been in years. There is a greater balance of power between the national and state and local parties now than ever existed before. Party organizations have adapted to new conditions by taking on a new form: that of the service party. However, as service parties, the party organizations are no longer as distinctive as they used to be in the sense of providing campaign resources that no other group could deliver.

THE FUTURE OF PARTY POLITICS IN AMERICA

These trends are vital to us because political parties are vital to us. Parties have the potential to do a great deal of good for a democracy. They can enable political leaders to work together in achieving shared interests over time. They can provide cues that permit voters to make decisions on candidates and issues with relatively little effort. Parties can bring voters to the polls, which helps to legitimize a democracy. Perhaps most important, parties organize majorities, which are necessary for governing. Interest groups can effectively represent intense minorities, but there are not many alternatives to the parties for organizing lasting and predictable majorities.

A Changing Intermediary Role

Elections require voters to make large numbers of choices, even though most voters have little information. Parties serve as efficient guides. The value of the party label in elections is probably greatest when a mass electorate has just begun to develop and has serious need for information. As the electorate matures, its needs change. One explanation for American voters' decreased reliance on party loyalties in the 1960s and 1970s was that voters had become better educated than was the case in the early 1900s and could sift through a broader range of political messages without the need for party labels as a guide.[12]

It is interesting, then, that although education levels have continued to increase since the 1960s, party identification has reasserted itself as an influence on many voters' choices. Why should partisanship help citizens who have so many other sources of information about candidates and issues? Perhaps *because* they are exposed to so much information. Without this simple guide, the blizzard of political communication could serve as more of a deterrent than a tool. At the same time, the fact that the two major parties have drawn farther apart from one another on important issues lends even more meaning to the party labels for politically engaged citizens. Added to the heightened party competition in the 2000s and the resulting intensity of campaign advertising, changes in the political environment can make an individual's partisanship even more meaningful to him or her.

Granted, the parties' traditional dominance in politics has been eroded by competition from organized interests and the media. A century ago, someone concerned about environmental quality would probably have had to pursue his or her goals through a political party; not many groups focused specifically on resource conservation or pollution control. Now, however, along with the growing reach of government into most aspects of private life, a huge array of organized interests has developed that permit individuals to establish a "designer link" with the political system. If someone prefers to see politics entirely from the perspective of environmental rights or property rights, several groups exist to make that possible. There is no need to compromise or to support a coalition of other groups' needs and a range of candidates, as a party loyalty would encourage.

In this fractured political world, parties become even more important as a means of broadening individuals' perspectives and improving their ability to hold elected officials accountable. The parties have long struggled with hostile environmental forces, from a system of separated powers that is inhospitable to strong parties to a political culture suspicious of all parties. However, as we have seen throughout this book, the parties are adaptable. They are not the intermediaries they were in 1900 or 1950, but for large numbers of Americans and for the policy-making process, the major parties remain the most important intermediaries.

The Need for Strong Parties

Although we need parties, we don't like them. We don't even like to admit that they influence us. Most of us claim that issues and candidates' personal qualities have the biggest impact on our votes. Yet it's clear that partisanship is closely related to our attitudes toward issues and candidates and is the source of much of their influence.[13]

Democracy is unworkable without parties.[14] The United States has probably come closer to testing that principle than any other democracy; much of American local politics has been, at least officially, nonpartisan for some time. But when parties are reduced to playing a smaller role in politics, the quality of democracy is weakened.

Consider the role strong parties can play in Congress and state legislatures. As a representative body, Congress is structured to permit legislators to give their constituents what they want: short-term, tangible benefits such as disaster relief, expanded Medicare benefits, and jobs on pork-barrel projects. Legislators facing reelection seek the Holy Grail of constituent service: a project such as a new dam or highway that provides tangible benefits to their own constituents but whose costs are paid by taxpayers all over the country. But if the individual voter and the individual legislator are motivated to pay close attention to the benefits they can get for their district, who is motivated to pay attention to the collective cost? Very few voters support the idea of raising their own taxes in order to pay for benefits to others, or even to pay for benefits to themselves.

Strong legislative parties have an incentive to take responsibility for the collective costs.[15] Some legislative party members can gain personal career advantages by becoming leaders of their congressional party. When the party's members in Congress are elected from similar districts and hold similar views, they can afford to trust these legislative party leaders with greater power to structure the choices they will make. Members realize that although their own reelection needs are primary, they also need coordination within the legislature in order to pass bills and to help with the endless tasks of legislative life.

By using the carrots and sticks discussed in Chapter 13, legislative party leaders can induce their party colleagues to make truly national policy, not just "Christmas tree" legislation that consists of pork-barrel ornaments for each congressional district. By holding their legislators to this party program, they can create a favorable brand name for their party in elections, which voters can come to recognize and associate with their own district's candidate. In the absence of strong parties, it is difficult to imagine where this collective responsibility might come from. Without strong parties, individual members of Congress and state legislatures have every reason to behave in ways that conflict with their collective interest and that of their constituents.[16]

In a society dominated by interest groups and other intermediaries, most people would not be as well represented. Among the many links between citizens and government, only the parties have the incentive to create majorities in order to win a wide range of elections over a long period. In turn, that gives the parties, to a greater extent than interest groups or even elected officials, a reason to pay attention to those citizens who are not activists or big campaign contributors. As political scientist Walter Dean Burnham has written, parties are the only devices that can "generate countervailing collective power on behalf of the many individually powerless against the relatively few who are individually—or organizationally—powerful.[17]

It is the parties that can mobilize sheer numbers against the organized minorities who hold other political resources. The parties do so in the one political arena where sheer numbers count most heavily: elections. Because of that, parties traditionally have been the means by which newly enfranchised but otherwise powerless groups gained a foothold in American life. The old-style urban machines, for example, provided the instrument with which recent immigrants won control of their cities from the more established Anglo-Saxon Protestant elites.

In a less party-driven politics, well-organized minorities with critical resources—money, insider knowledge, and technological expertise—would probably have even greater advantages than they do now. As we have seen from research on nonpartisan elections, eliminating the party symbol often makes it tougher for citizens to hold their representatives responsible.[18] That may be one reason why participation has declined more sharply in recent decades among poorer and less-educated Americans; they may feel less represented by a politics in which the parties are no longer preeminent.[19]

Finally, weakened parties would rob the political system of an effective means of governing. Without at least moderately strong parties, it is harder to mobilize majorities in support of policies. Individual candidates, freed from party loyalties, would have to recreate majorities for every new legislative proposal. The result could be gridlock, in which legislatures splinter into conflicting and intransigent groups. Laws and policies could continue to be made only by shifting coalitions of elected officials, campaign contributors, and interest groups. Because these coalitions would be less permanent and less identifiable to the public, they would be much harder for citizens to hold accountable. The result could further undermine public confidence in democratic politics.

How to Make the Parties Stronger

Because parties bring so much value to American democracy, some analysts have considered ways to expand the parties' role in political life. The most potent solutions—abolishing the separation of powers, the direct primary, and the antiparty sentiment engrained into the political culture—are not on the table, of course. But there are less dramatic ways in which the parties might be strengthened.

A survey by Larry J. Sabato and Bruce Larson showed that most respondents would like the parties to be more active in helping people deal with government. Sabato and Larson propose, among other ideas, that party organizations could create "mobile units" to help citizens in areas where the U.S. (and perhaps the state) representative is from the other party. That would allow the party organization, not just members of the party in government, to perform constituent service. They note that this idea was especially attractive to respondents who described themselves as alienated from politics.[20]

By providing attractive nonpolitical benefits such as low-cost health insurance, as many interest groups do now, parties could help to build long-term loyalty among their volunteers.[21] Parties could also renew their connection with citizens by airing campaign ads promoting the party as a whole, rather than just individual candidates. To this point, the bulk of both parties' money goes to fund ads that do not mention the party itself. These ads could strengthen the meaning of party by stressing the link between the party's stands and individuals' daily lives.

CONCLUSION: THE PARTIES' PROSPECTS

The American parties have never lacked interesting challenges. The electorate has become more and more varied. Traditional group ties have broken down. New groups, from antiabortion to animal liberation, are tilling the ground that the major parties once owned. Most voters still identify with a party, but they also respond to candidates, issues, and national trends. The result is a more diverse, complicated politics that no single set of loyalties or political organizations can easily contain.

The parties can't meet every political need. They can't be pure in their issue stands while still making the compromises necessary to build coalitions and govern. They find it hard to offer policy alternatives in campaigns without engaging in the partisan conflict that many Americans find so distasteful. It is difficult for parties to unite their officeholders and office seekers on a single agenda while giving candidates the independence to choose their own appeals and meet their own districts' needs. Parties can't provide party accountability to an electorate that wants to choose candidates individually.

We will continue to challenge the parties with these conflicting expectations and criticisms. The parties' distinctive character has sustained them longer than any other tool of democratic politics. For the sake of representation, effective policy making, and accountability in governance, even the most independent-minded citizens have a stake in sustaining vigorous party politics in the United States.

Appendix

TABLE A.1 Party "Hard Money" Receipts, 1975–1976 to 2007–2008 (in millions)

	National	Senate	House	State/Local	Total
Democratic Committees					
1975–1976	$13.1	1.0	0.9	0.0	15.0
1977–1978	$11.3	0.3	2.8	8.7	26.4
1979–1980	$15.1	1.7	2.1	11.7	37.2
1981–1982	$16.4	5.6	6.5	10.6	39.3
1983–1984	$46.6	8.9	10.4	18.5	98.5
1985–1986	$17.2	13.4	12.3	14.1	64.8
1987–1988	$52.3	16.3	12.5	44.7	113.8
1989–1990	$14.5	17.5	9.1	44.7	78.5
1991–1992	$65.8	25.5	12.8	73.7	163.3
1993–1994	$41.8	26.4	19.4	55.6	132.8
1995–1996	$108.4	30.8	26.6	93.2	221.6
1997–1998	$64.8	35.6	25.2	63.4	160.0
1999–2000	$124.0	40.5	48.4	149.3	275.2
2001–2002	$67.5	48.4	46.4	114.2	217.2
2003–2004	$404.4	88.7	93.2	171.2	688.8
2005–2006	$130.8	121.4	139.9	161.9	483.1
2007–2008	$260.1	162.8	176.2	287.4	763.3
Republican Committees					
1975–1976	$29.1	12.2	1.8	0.0	43.1
1977–1978	$34.2	10.9	14.1	20.9	84.5
1979–1980	$76.2	23.3	28.6	33.8	169.5
1981–1982	$83.5	48.9	58.0	24.0	215.0
1983–1984	$105.9	81.7	58.3	43.1	297.9
1985–1986	$83.8	84.4	39.8	47.2	255.2
1987–1988	$91.0	65.9	34.7	66.0	251.3
1989–1990	$68.7	65.1	33.2	39.3	202.0
1991–1992	$85.4	73.8	35.3	72.8	264.9
1993–1994	$87.4	65.3	26.7	75.0	244.1
1995–1996	$193.0	64.5	74.2	128.4	416.5
1997–1998	$104.0	53.4	72.7	89.4	285.0
1999–2000	$212.8	51.5	97.3	176.6	465.8
2001–2002	$170.1	59.2	123.6	132.5	424.1
2003–2004	$392.4	79.0	185.7	182.9	782.4
2005–2006	$243.0	88.8	176.3	157.5	599.0
2007–2008	$427.6	94.4	118.3	222.3	792.9

Note: Beginning with 1987–1988, total receipts do not include monies transferred among the listed committees.

Source: Federal Election Commission, at www.fec.gov/press/press2009/05282009Party/20090528Party.shtml (accessed May 29, 2009) and www.opensecrets.org/parties/index.php (accessed March 27, 2009)

TABLE A.2 Party Identification, 1952–2008

	1952	1956	1960	1964	1968	1972	1976	1980	1984	1988	1992	1996	2000	2004	2008
Strong Democrats	22%	21%	20%	27%	20%	15%	15%	18%	17%	17%	18%	18%	19%	17%	19%
Weak Democrats	25	23	25	25	25	26	25	23	20	18	18	19	15	16	15
Independent Democrats	10	6	6	9	10	11	12	11	11	12	14	14	15	17	16
"Pure" Independents	6	9	10	8	11	13	15	13	11	11	12	9	12	10	11
Independent Republicans	7	8	7	6	9	10	10	10	12	13	12	12	13	12	12
Weak Republicans	14	14	14	14	15	13	14	14	15	14	14	15	12	12	13
Strong Republicans	14	15	16	11	10	10	9	9	12	14	11	12	12	16	13
Others	3	4	2	1	1	1	1	2	2	2	1	1	1	0	1
%	101	100	100	101	101	99	101	100	100	101	100	100	99	100	100
Cases	1,793	1,762	1,928	1,571	1,556	2,707	2,864	1,614	2,236	2,033	2,478	1,714	1,785	1,197	2,258

Note: Based on surveys of the national electorate conducted immediately before each presidential election in recent years as part of the American National Election Studies program at the University of Michigan. Due to rounding, percentages do not always add up to 100 percent.

Source: Data made available by the Inter-University Consortium for Political and Social Research.

TABLE A.3 Percent of Party Identifiers Voting for Their Party's Presidential Candidates, 1952–2008

	1952	1956	1960	1964	1968	1972	1976	1980	1984	1988	1992	1996	2000	2004	2008
Strong Democrats	84%	85%	90%	95%	85%	73%	91%	86%	87%	93%	93%	96%	97%	97%	94%
Weak Democrats	62	62	72	82	58	48	74	60	67	70	69	82	89	83	84
Independents, closer to Democrats	60	68	88	90	52	60	72	45	79	88	71	76	72	84	89
Independents	—	—	—	—	—	—	—	—	—	—	—	—	—	—	—
Independents, closer to Republicans	93	94	87	75	82	86	83	76	92	84	62	68	79	83	79
Weak Republicans	94	93	87	56	82	90	77	86	93	83	60	70	85	89	88
Strong Republicans	98	100	98	90	96	97	96	92	96	98	87	94	97	98	96

Note: The table entries are the percentages of each category of partisans who reported a vote for their party's candidate for president. To find the percentage voting for the opposing party's candidate or some other candidate, subtract the entry from 100 percent. Individuals who did not vote for president are excluded from the table.

Source: American National Election Studies, University of Michigan; data made available by the Inter-University Consortium for Political and Social Research.

TABLE A.4 Percent of Party Identifiers Voting for Their Party's Congressional Candidates, 1952–2008

	1952	1956	1960	1964	1968	1972	1976	1980	1984	1988	1992	1996	2000	2004	2008
Strong Democrats	89%	94%	93%	94%	88%	91%	89%	85%	89%	88%	86%	88%	87%	91%	87%
Weak Democrats	77	86	86	84	73	80	78	69	70	82	82	71	73	86	78
Independents, closer to Democrats	64	83	84	79	63	80	76	70	78	87	74	69	70	80	76
Independents	—	—	—	—	—	—	—	—	—	—	—	—	—	—	—
Independents, closer to Republicans	81	83	74	72	81	73	65	68	61	64	65	79	67	68	72
Weak Republicans	90	88	84	64	78	75	66	74	66	70	63	79	79	81	75
Strong Republicans	95	95	90	92	91	85	83	77	85	77	82	97	86	88	90

Note: The table entries are the percentages of each category of partisans who reported a vote for their party's candidate for Congress. To find the percentage voting for the opposing party's candidate or some other candidate, subtract the entry from 100 percent. Individuals who did not vote or did not vote for Congress are excluded from the table.

Source: American National Election Studies, University of Michigan; data made available by the Inter-University Consortium for Political and Social Research.

Notes

PART ONE: PARTIES AND PARTY SYSTEMS

1. This is the title of Harold Lasswell's pioneering book, *Politics: Who Gets What, When, How* (New York: McGraw-Hill, 1936).
2. See Regina Smyth, *Candidate Strategies and Electoral Competition in the Russian Federation* (Cambridge: Cambridge University Press, 2006), and Henry E. Hale, *Why Not Parties in Russia?* (Cambridge: Cambridge University Press, 2006).
3. E. E. Schattschneider, *Party Government* (New York: Rinehart, 1942), p. 1.
4. Austin Ranney, *Curing the Mischiefs of Faction* (Berkeley: University of California Press, 1975).

CHAPTER 1: WHAT ARE POLITICAL PARTIES?

1. In *The Party Decides* (Chicago: University of Chicago Press, 2008), Marty Cohen, David Karol, Hans Noel, and John Zaller argue that these interest groups and other social groups are part of the party coalition itself. Many other scholars see these groups as external to parties but a vital part of their environment.
2. These definitions come from Edmund Burke, "Thoughts on the Cause of the Present Discontents" (1770) in *The Works of Edmund Burke* (Boston: Little, Brown, 1839), vol. I, pp. 425–426; Anthony Downs, *An Economic Theory of Democracy* (New York: Harper & Row, 1957), p. 24; William Nisbet Chambers, "Party Development and the American Mainstream," in William Nisbet Chambers and Walter Dean Burnham, eds., *The American Party Systems* (New York: Oxford University Press, 1967), p. 5; John H. Aldrich, *Why Parties?* (Chicago: University of Chicago Press, 1995), pp. 283–284; and V. O. Key, Jr., *Politics, Parties, and Pressure Groups* (New York: Crowell, 1958), pp. 180–182.
3. V. O. Key, Jr., used this "tripartite" conception to organize his classic text, *Politics, Parties, and Pressure Groups*. Key attributed the concept of party in the electorate to Ralph M. Goldman, *Party Chairmen and Party Factions, 1789–1900* (Ph.D. diss., University of Chicago, 1951).
4. See Denise L. Baer and David A. Bositis, *Elite Cadres and Party Coalitions* (Westport, CT: Greenwood Press, 1988), pp. 21–50.
5. See Joseph A. Schlesinger, "The Primary Goals of Political Parties," *American Political Science Review* 69 (1975): 840–849.
6. This image is Joseph A. Schlesinger's in "The New American Political Party," *American Political Science Review* 79 (1985): 1152–1169.
7. State legislative elections in Nebraska are nonpartisan, although the candidates' partisan ties are obvious to many voters, and statewide officials (such as the governor and attorney general) are elected on a partisan ballot.
8. See William N. Chambers, *Political Parties in a New Nation* (New York: Oxford University Press, 1963); A. James Reichley, *The Life of the Parties* (Lanham, MD: Rowman & Littlefield, 2000); and Aldrich, *Why Parties?*
9. Quoted in David Von Drehle, "Origin of the Species," *Washington Post*, July 25, 2004, p. W12.
10. See John H. Aldrich and Ruth W. Grant, "The Antifederalists, the First Congress, and the First Parties," *Journal of Politics* 55 (1993): 295–326.
11. Chilton Williamson, *American Suffrage* (Princeton: Princeton University Press, 1960).
12. Neal R. Peirce and Lawrence D. Longley, *The People's President* (New Haven: Yale University Press, 1981).
13. See Aldrich, *Why Parties?* Chapter 4, and Reichley, *The Life of the Parties*, Chapter 5.
14. See Reichley, *The Life of the Parties*, Chapters 6–11.
15. See Moisei Ostrogorski, *Democracy and the Organization of Political Parties, Volume II: The United States* (Garden City, NY: Anchor Books, 1964, originally published in 1902).

16. On party reform, see Austin Ranney, *Curing the Mischiefs of Faction* (Berkeley: University of California Press, 1975); and Richard Hofstadter, *The Age of Reform* (New York: Vintage Books, 1955).

17. See Mark A. Smith, *The Right Talk* (Princeton: Princeton University Press, 2000).

18. Frank Newport, "On Economy, Republicans Trust Business; Dems Trust Gov't," March 12, 2009, at http://www.gallup.com/poll/116599/Economy-Republicans-Trust-Business-Dems-Trust-Gov.aspx (accessed May 8, 2009).

19. See Leon Epstein, *Political Parties in the American Mold* (Madison: University of Wisconsin Press, 1986), pp. 155–199.

20. Data from the 2008 National Election Study, University of Michigan; data made available by the Inter-University Consortium for Political and Social Research. Distrust of parties is common in other nations as well; see Ingrid van Biezen and Michael Saward, "Democratic Theorists and Party Scholars," *Perspectives on Politics* 6 (2008): 21–35.

CHAPTER 2 THE AMERICAN TWO-PARTY SYSTEM

1. Arend Lijphart, *Electoral Systems and Party Systems* (New York: Oxford University Press, 1994).

2. See John F. Bibby and L. Sandy Maisel, *Two Parties—Or More?* 2nd ed. (Boulder, CO: Westview, 2003), p. 46.

3. Charles S. Bullock III, "It's a Sonny Day in Georgia," in Larry J. Sabato, ed., *Midterm Madness* (Lanham, MD: Rowman & Littlefield, 2003), p. 177.

4. Interparty competition refers to competition between the parties, as opposed to competition within a particular party ("intra-party"). The index was first presented in Austin Ranney, "Parties in State Politics," in Herbert Jacob and Kenneth Vines, eds., *Politics in the American States* (Boston: Little, Brown, 1965), p. 65. For alternative indices, see Thomas M. Holbrook and Emily Van Dunk, "Electoral Competition in the American States," *American Political Science Review* 87 (1993): 955–962, and James W. Ceaser and Robert P. Saldin, "A New Measure of Party Strength," *Political Research Quarterly* 58 (2005): 245–256.

5. See Peverill Squire, "Uncontested Seats in State Legislative Elections," *Legislative Studies Quarterly* 25 (2000): 131–146, and data from the National Council of State Legislatures, at http://www.ncsl.org/programs/press/2004/unopposed_2004.htm (accessed March 31, 2007).

6. Data from *CQ Weekly* postelection figures. On the influence of incumbency on elections, see Gary C. Jacobson, *The Politics of Congressional Elections*, 7th ed. (New York: Longman, 2008), Chapter 3; Stephen Ansolabehere, James M. Snyder, Jr., and Charles Stewart III, "Old Voters, New Voters, and the Personal Vote," *American Journal of Political Science* 44 (2000): 17–34; and Scott W. Desposato and John R. Petrocik, "The Variable Incumbency Advantage," *American Journal of Political Science* 47 (2003): 18–32.

7. John M. Carey, Richard G. Niemi, and Lynda W. Powell, "Incumbency and the Probability of Reelection in State Legislative Elections," *Journal of Politics* 62 (2000): 671–700.

8. Stephen Ansolabehere and James M. Snyder, Jr., "The Incumbency Advantage in U.S. Elections," *Election Law Journal* 1 (2002): 315–338.

9. John R. Alford and David W. Brady, "Personal and Partisan Advantage in U.S. Congressional Elections, 1846-1990," in Lawrence C. Dodd and Bruce I. Oppenheimer, eds., *Congress Reconsidered*, 5th ed. (Washington, DC: CQ Press, 1993), p. 147.

10. Gary C. Jacobson, "The Congress: The Structural Basis of Republican Success," in Michael Nelson, ed., *The Elections of 2004* (Washington, DC: CQ Press, 2005), pp. 166–167.

11. Bruce I. Oppenheimer, "Deep Red and Blue Congressional Districts," in Dodd and Oppenheimer, eds., *Congress Reconsidered*, 8th ed. (Washington, DC: CQ Press, 2005), pp. 135–157.

12. Bill Bishop with Robert G. Cushing, *The Big Sort* (New York: Houghton Mifflin, 2008).

13. Alan I. Abramowitz, Brad Alexander, and Matthew Gunning, "Incumbency, Redistricting, and the Decline of Competition in U.S. House Elections," *Journal of Politics* 68 (2006): 75–88.

14. See Robert S. Erikson and Gerald C. Wright, "Voters, Candidates, and Issues in Congressional Elections," in Dodd and Oppenheimer, eds., *Congress Reconsidered*, 9th ed. (Washington, DC: CQ Press, 2009), p. 83.

15. Maurice Duverger, *Political Parties* (New York: Wiley, 1954). See also Octavio Amorim Neto and Gary W. Cox, "Electoral Institutions, Cleavage Structures, and the Number of Parties," *American Journal of Political Science* 41 (1997): 149–174.

16. This used to be a frequent occurrence in the United States. In 1955, 58 percent of all state legislative districts were multimember; this number had declined to 10 percent by the 1980s. See Richard Niemi, Simon Jackman, and Laura Winsky, "Candidates and Competitiveness in Multimember Districts," *Legislative Studies Quarterly* 16 (1991): 91–109.
17. Other minorities are affected as well; James D. King, in "Single-Member Districts and the Representation of Women in American State Legislatures," *State Politics and Policy Quarterly* 2 (2002): 161–175, found that a change from multimember to single-member districts decreases the representation of women in state legislatures.
18. See A. James Reichley, *The Life of the Parties* (Lanham, MD: Rowman & Littlefield, 2002), p. 4.
19. Leon Epstein, *Political Parties in the American Mold* (Madison: University of Wisconsin Press, 1986), pp. 129–132.
20. V. O. Key, Jr., *Politics, Parties, and Pressure Groups*, 5th ed. (New York: Crowell, 1964), pp. 229ff.
21. See Louis Hartz, *The Liberal Tradition in America* (New York: Harcourt, Brace and World, 1955). However, the "consensus" varies depending on the level of abstraction being discussed; see Stanley Feldman and John Zaller, "The Political Culture of Ambivalence," *American Journal of Political Science* 36 (1992): 268–307.
22. Marjorie Randon Hershey, "Third Parties," in Matthew J. Streb, ed., *Law and Election Politics* (Boulder, CO: Lynne Rienner, 2005), pp. 23–42.
23. See Ronald B. Rapoport and Walter J. Stone, *Three's a Crowd* (Ann Arbor: University of Michigan Press, 2005), on Republican successes in appealing to Ross Perot supporters in 1994 and 1996, and Shigeo Hirano and James M. Snyder, Jr., "The Decline of Third Party Voting in the U.S.," *Journal of Politics* 69 (2007): 1–16.
24. Brian F. Schaffner, Matthew J. Streb, and Gerald C. Wright, "A New Look at the Republican Advantage in Nonpartisan Elections," *Political Research Quarterly* 60 (2007): 240–249.
25. Brian F. Schaffner, Matthew J. Streb, and Gerald C. Wright, "Teams without Uniforms," *Political Research Quarterly* 54 (2001): 7–30.
26. Gerald C. Wright and Brian F. Schaffner, "The Influence of Party," *American Political Science Review* 96 (2002): 367–379.
27. J. David Gillespie, *Politics at the Periphery* (Columbia: University of South Carolina Press, 1993).
28. Holly A. Heyser, "Minnesota Governor," in Sabato, ed., *Midterm Madness*, pp. 233–245.
29. Among the best books on American third parties are Steven J. Rosenstone, Roy L. Behr, and Edward H. Lazarus, *Third Parties in America*, 2nd ed. (Princeton: Princeton University Press, 1996); Paul S. Herrnson and John C. Green, *Multiparty Politics in America*, 2nd ed. (Lanham, MD: Rowman & Littlefield, 2002); Bibby and Maisel, *Two Parties—Or More?*, and Rapoport and Stone, *Three's a Crowd.*
30. Joseph M. Hazlett II, *The Libertarian Party* (Jefferson, NC: McFarland and Company, 1992).
31. As evidence, almost all third-party presidential candidates since 1900 have received less support on Election Day than they did in preelection polls; see Rosenstone, Behr, and Lazarus, *Third Parties in America*, p. 41.
32. Rosenstone, Behr, and Lazarus, *Third Parties in America*, p. 162.
33. See Paul R. Abramson, John H. Aldrich, and David W. Rohde, *Change and Continuity in the 1992 Elections* (Washington, DC: CQ Press, 1994).
34. This is called "fusion." See Howard A. Scarrow, *Parties, Elections, and Representation in the State of New York* (New York: New York University Press, 1983).
35. See Lee Epstein and Charles D. Hadley, "On the Treatment of Political Parties in the U.S. Supreme Court, 1900–1986," *Journal of Politics* 52 (1990): 413–432; Richard Winger's *Ballot Access News*, at http://www.ballot-access.org, and issues of the *Election Law Journal.*
36. Orit Kedar, "When Moderate Voters Prefer Extreme Parties," *American Political Science Review* 99 (2005): 185–199.
37. James E. Campbell, "The 2002 Midterm Election," *PS* 36 (2003): 203–207.

PART TWO: THE POLITICAL PARTY AS AN ORGANIZATION

1. See Alan Ware, ed., *Political Parties* (New York: Basil Blackwell, 1987).

CHAPTER 3: THE STATE AND LOCAL PARTY ORGANIZATIONS

1. Andrew M. Appleton and Daniel S. Ward, *State Party Profiles* (Washington, DC: CQ Press, 1997), Appendix.
2. A public utility is a government-regulated provider of services, such as a gas or a water company. Leon Epstein, *Political Parties in the American Mold* (Madison: University of Wisconsin Press, 1986), pp. 155–199.
3. The cases are *Tashjian v. Republican Party of Connecticut* (1986), *Eu v. San Francisco County Democratic Central Committee et al.* (1989), and *California Democratic Party v. Jones* (2000). See David K. Ryden, " 'The Good, the Bad, and the Ugly,' " in John C. Green and Daniel M. Shea, eds., *The State of the Parties*, 3rd ed. (Lanham, MD: Rowman & Littlefield, 1999), pp. 50–65.
4. V. O. Key, Jr., *Politics, Parties and Pressure Groups* (New York: Crowell, 1964), p. 316.
5. Samuel J. Eldersveld, *Political Parties: A Behavioral Analysis* (Chicago: Rand McNally, 1964).
6. The organization of American political parties differs from what Robert Michels calls the "iron law of oligarchy"—that organizations are inevitably controlled from the top. See Robert Michels, *Political Parties* (Glencoe, IL: Free Press, 1949).
7. M. Craig Brown and Charles N. Halaby, "Machine Politics in America, 1870–1945," *Journal of Interdisciplinary History* 17 (1987): 587–612.
8. See David Mayhew, *Placing Parties in American Politics* (Princeton: Princeton University Press, 1986), pp. 19–21.
9. See Kenneth Finegold, *Experts and Politicians* (Princeton, NJ: Princeton University Press, 1995).
10. Steven P. Erie, *Rainbow's End* (Berkeley: University of California Press, 1988); but see John F. Bibby, "Party Organizations 1946–1996," in Byron E. Shafer, ed., *Partisan Approaches to Postwar American Politics* (New York: Chatham House, 1998), pp. 142–185.
11. Anne Freedman, *Patronage: An American Tradition* (Chicago: Nelson-Hall, 1994), Chapter 5.
12. Kenneth R. Mladenka, "The Urban Bureaucracy and the Chicago Political Machine," *American Political Science Review* 74 (1980): 991–998.
13. Michael Johnston, "Patrons and Clients, Jobs and Machines," *American Political Science Review* 73 (1979): 385–398.
14. James L. Gibson, Cornelius P. Cotter, John F. Bibby, and Robert J. Huckshorn, "Whither the Local Parties?" *American Journal of Political Science* 29 (1985): 139–160.
15. Cornelius P. Cotter, James L. Gibson, John F. Bibby, and Robert J. Huckshorn, *Party Organization in American Politics* (New York: Praeger, 1984), pp. 49–53
16. See Cotter et al., *Party Organization in American Politics*, p. 54, for 1964–1980. On 1984: James L. Gibson, John P. Frendreis, and Laura L. Vertz, "Party Dynamics in the 1980s," *American Journal of Political Science* 33 (1989): 67–90. On 1988: Charles E. Smith, Jr., "Changes in Party Organizational Strength and Activity 1979–1988," unpublished manuscript, Ohio State University, 1989. See also Samuel J. Eldersveld, "The Party Activist in Detroit and Los Angeles," in William J. Crotty, ed., *Political Parties in Local Areas* (Knoxville: University of Tennessee Press, 1986), pp. 89–119.
17. Daniel M. Shea and John C. Green, "Local Parties and Mobilizing the Vote," in John C. Green and Daniel J. Coffey, eds., *The State of the Parties*, 5th ed. (Lanham, MD: Rowman & Littlefield, 2007), pp. 217–228. See also John Frendreis and Alan R. Gitelson, "Local Parties in the 1990s," in Green and Shea, eds., *The State of the Parties*, 3rd ed., pp. 135–153.
18. Shea and Green, "Local Parties and Mobilizing the Vote," pp. 222 and 224.
19. Carol S. Weissert, "Michigan," in Appleton and Ward, eds., *State Party Profiles*, pp. 153–160.
20. On county party leaders' efforts to recruit women candidates, see Melody Crowder-Meyer, "Party Strength and Activity and Women's Representation at the Local Level," Paper presented at the 2009 Midwest Political Science Association.
21. L. Sandy Maisel, "American Political Parties: Still Central to a Functioning Democracy?" in Jeffrey E. Cohen, Richard Fleisher, and Paul Kantor, eds., *American Political Parties: Decline or Resurgence?* (Washington, DC: CQ Press, 2001), pp. 112–114.
22. Gary F. Moncrief, Peverill Squire, and Malcolm E. Jewell, *Who Runs for the Legislature?* (Upper Saddle River, NJ: Prentice Hall, 2001).
23. John J. Coleman, "The Resurgence of Party Organization?" in Shea and Green, eds., *The State of the Parties* (Lanham, MD: Rowman & Littlefield, 1994), pp. 282–298.

24. A. James Reichley, *The Life of the Parties* (Lanham, MD: Rowman & Littlefield, 2000), pp. 129–130.

25. Malcolm E. Jewell and Sarah M. Morehouse, *Political Parties and Elections in American States*, 4th ed. (Washington, DC: CQ Press, 2001), p. 4.

26. Jewell and Morehouse, *Political Parties and Elections*, p. 1.

27. See James L. Gibson, Cornelius P. Cotter, John F. Bibby, and Robert J. Huckshorn, "Assessing Party Organizational Strength," *American Journal of Political Science* 27 (1983): 193–222.

28. Jewell and Morehouse, *Political Parties and Elections*, p. 52; John H. Aldrich, "Southern Parties in State and Nation," *Journal of Politics* 62 (2000): 655–659.

29. Jewell and Morehouse, *Political Parties and Elections*, p. 211.

30. Anthony Gierzynski, *Legislative Party Campaign Committees in the American States* (Lexington: University Press of Kentucky, 1992).

31. Robert E. Hogan, "Candidate Perceptions of Political Party Campaign Activity in State Legislative Elections," *State Politics and Policy Quarterly* 2 (2002): 66–85.

32. Raymond J. La Raja, "State Parties and Soft Money," in John C. Green and Rick Farmer, eds., *The State of the Parties*, 4th ed. (Lanham, MD: Rowman & Littlefield, 2003), pp. 132–150.

33. Anthony Corrado, "Political Party Finance under BCRA: An Initial Assessment," Brookings Institution paper, 2004, at www.brookings.edu/views/papers/corrado20040311_paper.pdf (accessed May 31, 2005).

34. Sarah M. Morehouse and Malcolm E. Jewell, "State Parties," in Green and Farmer, eds., *The State of the Parties*, p. 151. The budget estimates come from Robert J. Huckshorn and John F. Bibby, "State Parties in an Era of Political Change," in Joel L. Fleishman, ed., *The Future of American Political Parties* (Englewood Cliffs, NJ: Prentice-Hall, 1982), pp. 70–100, and Aldrich, "Southern Parties," p. 656.

35. Derek Willis, "State Parties Adjust to McCain-Feingold," Center for Public Integrity press release, Washington, DC, August 26, 2004.

36. See Aldrich, "Southern Parties," pp. 656–657.

37. Aldrich, "Southern Parties," Table 7, pp. 656–657.

38. See Ari Berman, "The Prophet," *The Nation*, January 5, 2009, at www.thenation.com/doc/20090105/berman (accessed July 22, 2009).

39. Kimberly H. Conger, *The Christian Right and Republican State Politics* (New York: Palgrave MacMillan, 2009).

40. See Marty Cohen, David Karol, Hans Noel, and John Zaller, *The Party Decides* (Chicago: University of Chicago Press, 2008), and Jonathan Bernstein and Casey B. K. Dominguez, "Candidates and Candidacies in the Expanded Party," *PS* 36 (2003): 165–169.

41. John H. Kessel, "Ray Bliss and the Development of the Ohio Republican Party During the 1950s," in John C. Green, ed., *Politics, Professionalism, and Power* (Lanham, MD: University Press of America, 1994), pp. 48–61.

42. See Jewell and Morehouse, *Political Parties and Elections*, p. 36. See also Edward G. Carmines and James A. Stimson, *Issue Evolution* (Princeton: Princeton University Press, 1989), and Joseph A. Aistrup, *The Southern Strategy Revisited* (Lexington: University Press of Kentucky, 1996).

43. Charles Prysby, "North Carolina," and Anne E. Kelley, "Florida," in Appleton and Ward, eds., *State Party Profiles*, pp. 234–243 and 62–64.

44. See the articles in John A. Clark and Charles Prysby, eds., "Grassroots Party Activists in Southern Politics, 1991–2001," *American Review of Politics* 24 (Spring and Summer, 2001), pp. 1–223.

45. Aldrich, "Southern Parties," p. 655.

46. Walter Dean Burnham, *Critical Elections and the Mainsprings of American Politics* (New York: Norton, 1970), p. 72.

47. Alan Ware, *The Breakdown of the Democratic Party Organization 1940–80* (Oxford, England: Oxford University Press, 1985).

CHAPTER 4: THE PARTIES' NATIONAL ORGANIZATIONS

1. Cornelius P. Cotter and Bernard C. Hennessy, *Politics without Power: The National Party Committees* (New York: Atherton, 1964).

2. See Philip A. Klinkner, *The Losing Parties: Out-Party National Committees, 1956–1993* (New Haven: Yale University Press, 1994).

3. James W. Ceaser, "Political Parties—Declining, Stabilizing, or Resurging," in Anthony King, ed., *The New American Political System* (Washington, DC: American Enterprise Institute, 1990), p. 115. See also Sidney M. Milkis, *The President and the Parties* (New York: Oxford University Press, 1993).

4. Jo Freeman, *A Room at a Time* (Lanham, MD: Rowman & Littlefield, 2000).

5. John C. Green, ed., *Politics, Professionalism, and Power: Modern Party Organization and the Legacy of Ray C. Bliss* (Lanham, MD: University Press of America, 1994).

6. See Austin Ranney, *Curing the Mischiefs of Faction* (Berkeley: University of California Press, 1975); William J. Crotty, *Decisions for the Democrats* (Baltimore: Johns Hopkins University Press, 1978); and Byron E. Shafer, *The Quiet Revolution* (New York: Russell Sage Foundation, 1983).

7. John F. Bibby, "Party Renewal in the Republican National Party," in Gerald M. Pomper, ed., *Party Renewal in America* (New York: Praeger, 1981), pp. 102–115.

8. See Paul S. Herrnson, "The Revitalization of National Party Organizations," in L. Sandy Maisel, ed., *The Parties Respond*, 2nd ed. (Boulder, CO: Westview, 1994), pp. 45–68.

9. Federal Election Commission, at www.fec.gov/press/20030320party/20030103party.html (accessed June 11, 2003). Unless otherwise noted, the remaining data in this chapter come from the FEC.

10. See Marian Currinder, *Money in the House* (Boulder: Westview, 2009), pp. 34–39.

11. Emily Cadei, "Incumbents Feed the Party Coffers," *CQ Weekly*, October 6, 2008, p. 2642.

12. Gary C. Jacobson, "Congress: The Second Democratic Wave," in Michael Nelson, ed., *The Elections of 2008* (Washington, DC: CQ Press, 2009), pp. 107–108.

13. See Paul S. Herrnson, *Party Campaigning in the 1980s* (Cambridge, MA: Harvard University Press, 1988), p. 47.

14. See David B. Magleby and J. Quin Monson, eds., *The Last Hurrah?* (Provo, UT: Center for the Study of Elections and Democracy, 2003).

15. Daniel A. Smith, "Strings Attached," in Magleby and Monson, eds., *The Last Hurrah?* p. 194.

16. David A. Dulio and Candice J. Nelson, *Vital Signs* (Washington, DC: Brookings, 2005), p. 39.

17. Jacobson, "Congress: The Second Democratic Wave," p. 107.

18. Elaine C. Kamarck, "Assessing Howard Dean's Fifty State Strategy and the 2006 Midterm Elections," *The Forum* 4 (2006), at www.bepress.com/forum/vol4/iss3/art5 (accessed April 13, 2007).

19. Ari Berman, "The Prophet," *The Nation*, January 5, 2009, at www.thenation.com/doc/20090105/berman (accessed December 19, 2008).

20. Adam Nagourney, "Dean Seeks Some Respect (and Credit) for Obama's Victory," *New York Times*, November 11, 2008, at www.nytimes.com/2008/11/12/us/politics/12web-nagourney.html (accessed April 11, 2009).

21. Howard Fineman, "How Bush Did It," *Newsweek*, November 18, 2002, pp. 32 and 34.

22. Richard L. Berke, "GOP Mobilizes to Help Hopefuls in Primary Races," *New York Times*, March 3, 2002, p. 26.

23. James W. Ceaser, Andrew E. Busch, and John J. Pitney, Jr., *Epic Journey* (Lanham, MD: Rowman & Littlefield, 2009), p. 46.

24. Timothy P. Nokken, "Ideological Congruence Versus Electoral Success," *American Politics Research* 31 (2003): 3–26. The campaigns were those of Don Cazayoux in Louisiana and Travis Childers in Mississippi.

25. Leon D. Epstein, *Political Parties in the American Mold* (Madison: University of Wisconsin Press, 1986), p. 200.

26. John J. Coleman, "The Resurgence of Party Organization?" in Daniel M. Shea and John C. Green, eds., *The State of the Parties* (Lanham, MD: Rowman & Littlefield, 1994), pp. 311–328.

CHAPTER 5: PARTY ACTIVISTS

1. Peter B. Clark and James Q. Wilson, "Incentive Systems: A Theory of Organizations," *Administrative Science Quarterly* 6 (1961): 129–166.

2. See A. James Reichley, *The Life of the Parties* (Lanham, MD: Rowman & Littlefield, 2000), pp. 72 and 118, 128–130, 174–176; and Martin Shefter, *Political Parties and the State* (Princeton, NJ: Princeton University Press, 1994).

3. The 1976 case is *Elrod v. Burns*; the 1980 case is *Branti v. Finkel*; and the 1990 case is *Rutan v. Republican Party of Illinois*.

4. On the case for patronage, see the dissenting opinions to the Supreme Court's *Elrod*, *Branti*, and *Rutan* decisions. The case against patronage is well put in Anne Freedman, *Patronage: An American Tradition* (Chicago: Nelson-Hall, 1994), Chapter 5.

5. Cornelius P. Cotter, James L. Gibson, John F. Bibby, and Robert J. Huckshorn, *Party Organizations in American Politics* (New York: Praeger, 1984), p. 42; and Robert J. Huckshorn, *Party Leadership in the States* (Amherst: University of Massachusetts Press, 1976), p. 37.

6. See Sidney Verba, Kay Lehman Schlozman, and Henry E. Brady, *Voice and Equality* (Cambridge, MA: Harvard University Press, 1995), pp. 112–121.

7. John C. Green, John S. Jackson, and Nancy L. Clayton, "Issue Networks and Party Elites in 1996," in John C. Green and Daniel M. Shea, eds., *The State of the Parties*, 3rd ed. (Lanham, MD: Rowman & Littlefield, 1999).

8. Samuel J. Eldersveld, "The Party Activist in Detroit and Los Angeles," in William Crotty, ed., *Political Parties in Local Areas* (Knoxville: University of Tennessee Press, 1986), Chapter 4.

9. John A. Clark, John M. Bruce, John H. Kessel, and William Jacoby, "I'd Rather Switch than Fight," *American Journal of Political Science* 35 (1991): 577–597; Mary Grisez Kweit, "Ideological Congruence of Party Switchers and Nonswitchers," *American Journal of Political Science* 30 (1986): 184–196; and Dorothy Davidson Nesbit, "Changing Partisanship among Southern Party Activists," *Journal of Politics* 50 (1988): 322–334.

10. Verba, Schlozman, and Brady, *Voice and Equality*, p. 121.

11. See M. Margaret Conway, *Political Participation in the United States*, 2nd ed. (Washington, DC: CQ Press, 1991), p. 61.

12. See Clark and Wilson, "Incentive Systems." Note that the term "professional," as used here, does not necessarily refer to someone who is paid for party work.

13. See Marty Cohen, David Karol, Hans Noel, and John Zaller, *The Party Decides* (Chicago: University of Chicago Press, 2008), pp. 88–91 and 178 (quote on p. 89).

14. Michael A. Maggiotto and Ronald E. Weber, "The Impact of Organizational Incentives on County Party Chairpersons," *American Politics Quarterly* 14 (1986): 201–218.

15. Robert D. Putnam, *Bowling Alone* (New York: Simon & Schuster, 2000).

16. Verba, Schlozman, and Brady, *Voice and Equality*, Chapter 3.

17. American National Election Studies, University of Michigan; data made available by the Inter-University Consortium for Political and Social Research.

18. See Paul Allen Beck and M. Kent Jennings, "Updating Political Periods and Political Participation," *American Political Science Review* 78 (1984): 198–201; and Steven E. Finkel and Gregory Trevor, "Reassessing Ideological Bias in Campaign Participation," *Political Behavior* 8 (1986): 374–390.

19. See Verba, Schlozman, and Brady, *Voice and Equality*, pp. 15–16 and Chapters 9–14.

20. Henry E. Brady, Kay Lehman Schlozman, and Sidney Verba, "Prospecting for Participants," *American Political Science Review* 93 (1999): 153–168.

21. Verba, Schlozman, and Brady, *Voice and Equality*, pp. 135 and 139–144.

22. See, for example, Patrick R. Cotter, Samuel H. Fisher III, and Patrick Fuller, "Alabama: Maturing Party Competition," *American Review of Politics* 24 (2003): 26.

23. See Verba, Schlozman, and Brady, *Voice and Equality*, p. 190, Chapters 7 and 12, for campaign activists; Kyle L. Saunders and Alan I. Abramowitz, "Ideological Realignment and Active Partisans in the American Electorate," *American Politics Research* 32 (2004): 285–309, for party activists more generally; Ronald B. Rapoport, Alan I. Abramowitz, and John McGlennon, *The Life of the Parties* (Lexington: University of Kentucky Press, 1986), Chapter 3, for state convention delegates; Samuel J. Best and Brian S. Krueger, "Analyzing the Representativeness of Internet Political Participation," *Political Behavior* 24 (2005), pp. 183–216, for online activists; Chapter 10 of this book for national convention delegates, and American Political Science Association Task Force, "American Democracy in an Age of Rising Inequality," *Perspectives on Politics* 2 (2004): 655, on protest activity.

24. See Michael Margolis and Raymond E. Owen, "From Organization to Personalism," *Polity* 18 (1985): 313–328.

25. Malcolm E. Jewell and Sarah M. Morehouse, *Political Parties and Elections in American States*, 4th ed. (Washington, DC: CQ Press, 2001), p. 86.

26. Verba, Schlozman, and Brady, *Voice and Equality*, pp. 84–91.

27. Ibid., pp. 220–225.

28. Edward G. Carmines and James Woods, "The Role of Party Activists in the Evolution of the Abortion Issue," *Political Behavior* 24 (2002): 361–377.

29. See, for example, Cotter, Fisher, and Fuller, "Alabama: Maturing Party Competition," pp. 27–29; and Charles Prysby and John A. Clark, "Conclusion," *American Review of Politics* 24 (2003): 214–215.

30. Saunders and Abramowitz, "Ideological Realignment and Active Partisans in the American Electorate."

PART THREE: THE POLITICAL PARTY IN THE ELECTORATE

1. See Angus Campbell, Philip E. Converse, Warren E. Miller, and Donald E. Stokes, *The American Voter* (New York: Wiley, 1960), Chapter 6.

2. Steven E. Finkel and Howard A. Scarrow, "Party Identification and Party Enrollment," *Journal of Politics* 47 (1985): 620–642.

CHAPTER 6: PARTY IDENTIFICATION

1. Party identification is developing in newer democracies such as Russia and the Ukraine as well, even in the face of overwhelmingly negative attitudes toward political parties. See Arthur H. Miller and Thomas F. Klobucar, "The Development of Party Identification in Post-Soviet Societies," *American Journal of Political Science* 44 (2000): 667–685; and Ted Brader and Joshua A. Tucker, "The Emergence of Mass Partisanship in Russia, 1993–1996," *American Journal of Political Science* 45 (2001): 69–83.

2. For a summary of these approaches, with an argument for party identification as social identity, see Donald Green, Bradley Palmquist, and Eric Schickler, *Partisan Hearts and Minds* (New Haven: Yale University Press, 2002), Chapter 5. See also Thomas M. Carsey and Geoffrey C. Layman, "Changing Sides or Changing Minds?" *American Journal of Political Science* 50 (2006): 464–477.

3. John R. Petrocik, "An Analysis of the Intransitivities in the Index of Party Identification," *Political Methodology* 1 (1974): 31–47; and Herbert F. Weisberg, "A Multidimensional Conceptualization of Party Identification," *Political Behavior* 2 (1980): 33–60. See also Green, Palmquist, and Schickler, *Partisan Hearts and Minds*, Chapter 2.

4. Jeremy Zilber, *Why Mommy Is a Democrat* (Madison, WI: Jeremy Zilber, 2006), and Katharine DeBrecht, *Help! Mom! There Are Liberals Under My Bed!* (Los Angeles: World Ahead Publishing, 2005).

5. Paul Allen Beck and M. Kent Jennings, "Family Traditions, Political Periods, and the Development of Partisan Orientations," *Journal of Politics* 53 (1991): 742–763.

6. Paul Allen Beck, Russell J. Dalton, Steven Greene, and Robert Huckfeldt, "The Social Calculus of Voting," *American Political Science Review* 96 (2002): 57–73.

7. Richard G. Niemi and M. Kent Jennings, "Issues and Inheritance in the Formation of Party Identification," *American Journal of Political Science* 35 (1991): 970–988.

8. Green, Palmquist, and Schickler, *Partisan Hearts and Minds*, pp. 7–8.

9. Duane F. Alwin and Jon A. Krosnick, "Aging, Cohorts, and the Stability of Sociopolitical Orientations over the Life Cycle," *American Journal of Sociology* 97 (1991): 185–187.

10. See William Clagett, "Partisan Acquisition vs. Partisan Intensity," *American Journal of Political Science* 25 (1981): 193–214.

11. James E. Campbell, "Sources of the New Deal Realignment," *Western Political Quarterly* 38 (1985): 357–376; and Warren E. Miller, "Generational Changes and Party Identification," *Political Behavior* 14 (1992): 333–352.

12. The seminal report of these studies is Angus Campbell, Philip E. Converse, Warren E. Miller, and Donald E. Stokes, *The American Voter* (New York: Wiley, 1960).

13. See Paul Allen Beck, "The Dealignment Era in America," in Russell J. Dalton, Scott C. Flanagan, and Paul Allen Beck, eds., *Electoral Change in Advanced Industrial Democracies* (Princeton, NJ: Princeton University Press, 1984), pp. 244–246.

14. Philip E. Converse and Gregory B. Markus, "Plus ça change . . . : The New CPS Election Study Panel," *American Political Science Review* 73 (1979): 32–49. See also Donald Philip Green and Bradley Palmquist, "How Stable Is Party Identification?" *Political Behavior* 16 (1994): 437–466, and Paul Goren, "Party Identification and Core Political Values," *American Journal of Political Science* 49 (2005): 881–896.

15. Russell Dalton, "The Decline of Party Identification," in Russell J. Dalton and Martin P. Wattenberg, eds., *Parties without Partisans* (Oxford, UK: Oxford University Press, 2000), pp. 19–36. On split-ticket voting, see Barry C. Burden and David C. Kimball, *Why Americans Split Their Tickets* (Ann Arbor: University of Michigan Press, 2002).

16. Martin P. Wattenberg, *The Decline of American Political Parties, 1952–1994* (Cambridge, MA.: Harvard University Press, 1996), p. ix.

17. See James H. Kuklinski, Paul J. Quirk, Jennifer Jerit, and Robert F. Rich, "The Political Environment and Citizen Competence," *American Journal of Political Science* 45 (2001): 410–424.

18. David G. Lawrence, "On the Resurgence of Party Identification in the 1990s," in Jeffrey E. Cohen, Richard Fleisher, and Paul Kantor, eds., *American Political Parties: Decline or Resurgence?* (Washington, DC: CQ Press, 2001), pp. 30–54.

19. James W. Ceaser and Andrew E. Busch, *Red Over Blue* (Lanham, MD: Rowman & Littlefield, 2005), p. 136.

20. See John R. Petrocik, "Party Identification: Leaners Are NOT Independents," Conference on The American Voter Revisited, University of Iowa, May 2008.

21. Pew Research Center for the People and the Press, "Dems' Favorability Advantage Widens," January 29, 2009, at www.pewresearch.org/pubs/1098/democratic-favorability-advantage-widens (accessed May 1, 2009). See also Gary C. Jacobson, "Congress: The Second Democratic Wave," in Michael Nelson, ed., *The Elections of 2008* (Washington, DC: CQ Press, 2009), p. 104.

22. David Madland and Ruy Teixeira, "New Progressive America: The Millennial Generation," at www.americanprogress.org/issues/2009/05/millennial_generation.html (accessed July 25, 2009).

23. See, for example, Robert Huckfeldt, Paul E. Johnson, and John Sprague, *Political Disagreement* (New York: Cambridge University Press, 2004), p. 74.

24. Jeffrey M. Jones, "Liberals' Confidence in Obama Remains High," January 2, 2009, at www.gallup.com/poll/113602/Liberals-Confidence-Obama-Remains-High.aspx (accessed May 8, 2009).

25. The poll data are from Green, Palmquist, and Schickler, *Partisan Hearts and Minds*, p. 127. They see these poll results, however, as evidence that the two groups of partisans are using different standards of evaluation rather than as an indicator of perceptual bias.

26. See Wendy M. Rahn, "The Role of Partisan Stereotypes in Information Processing about Political Candidates," *American Journal of Political Science* 37 (1993): 472–496, and Michael W. Wagner, "Think of It This Way," Ph.D. dissertation, Indiana University, 2006.

27. Andy Baker, Barry Ames, and Lucio R. Renno, "Social Context and Campaign Volatility in New Democracies," *American Journal of Political Science* 50 (2006): 382–399.

28. See, for example, Larry M. Bartels, "Partisanship and Voting Behavior, 1952–1996," *American Journal of Political Science* 44 (2000): 35–50.

29. Paul Allen Beck, Lawrence Baum, Aage R. Clausen, and Charles E. Smith, Jr., "Patterns and Sources of Ticket Splitting in Subpresidential Voting," *American Political Science Review* 86 (1992): 916–928.

30. See Barry C. Burden and David C. Kimball, "A New Approach to the Study of Ticket-Splitting," *American Political Science Review* 92 (1998): 533–544.

31. Kyle L. Saunders, Alan I. Abramowitz, and Jonathan Williamson, "A New Kind of Balancing Act," *Political Research Quarterly* 58 (2005): 69–78.

32. Burden and Kimball, "A New Approach."

33. Scott Basinger and Howard Lavine, "Ambivalence, Information, and Electoral Choice," *American Political Science Review* 99 (2005): 169–184.

34. See Morris P. Fiorina, *Retrospective Voting in American National Elections* (New Haven: Yale University Press, 1981); and Michael B. MacKuen, Robert S. Erikson, and James A. Stimson, "Macropartisanship," *American Political Science Review* 83 (1989): 1125–1142.

35. And on which the individual sees differences between the parties, see Carsey and Layman, "Changing Sides or Changing Minds?"

36. Paul R. Abramson, John H. Aldrich, and David W. Rohde, *Change and Continuity in the 2004 and 2006 Elections* (Washington, DC: CQ Press, 2007), Chapter 6.

37. These figures are much higher than those presented in Chapter 8 because respondents to the 2008 American National Election studies often over-report their levels of voter turnout.
38. Sidney Verba and Norman H. Nie, *Participation in America* (Chicago: University of Chicago Press, 1987), Chapter 12.
39. See Bruce E. Keith, David B. Magleby, Candice J. Nelson, Elizabeth Orr, Mark Westlye, and Raymond E. Wolfinger, *The Myth of the Independent Voter* (Berkeley: University of California Press, 1992), and Abramson, Aldrich, and Rohde, *Change and Continuity*, pp. 97–99.
40. V. O. Key, Jr. (with Milton C. Cummings), *The Responsible Electorate* (Cambridge, MA: Harvard University Press, 1966).
41. See David Nather, "Courting the Independents," *CQ Weekly,* June 16, 2008, p. 1610.
42. Todd Donovan, "A Goal for Reform," *PS: Political Science and Politics* 40 (2007): 683.
43. See Paul R. Abramson, John H. Aldrich, and David W. Rohde, *Change and Continuity in the 1992 Elections* (Washington, DC: CQ Press, 1995), p. 245.
44. See Martin P. Wattenberg, *The Rise of Candidate-Centered Politics* (Cambridge, MA: Harvard University Press, 1991).
45. Exit poll data (excluding independent leaners) from www.cnn.com/ELECTION/2006/pages/results/states/US/H/00/epolls.0.html (accessed April 22, 2007).
46. Exit poll data (excluding independent leaners) from www.cnn.com/ELECTION/2008/results/polls/#USP00p1 (accessed May 10, 2009).

CHAPTER 7: PARTY COALITIONS AND PARTY CHANGE

1. See Edward G. Carmines and James A. Stimson, *Issue Evolution* (Princeton: Princeton University Press, 1989); and Paul M. Sniderman and Thomas Piazza, *The Scar of Race* (Cambridge: Harvard University Press, 1995).
2. See, for example, Jerome M. Clubb, William H. Flanigan, and Nancy H. Zingale, *Partisan Realignment* (Beverly Hills, CA: Sage, 1980), Chapter 3.
3. See John H. Aldrich, *Why Parties?* (Chicago: University of Chicago Press, 1995).
4. See V. O. Key, Jr., "A Theory of Critical Elections," *Journal of Politics* 17 (1955): 3–18; Walter Dean Burnham, *Critical Elections and the Mainsprings of American Politics* (New York: Norton, 1970); and James L. Sundquist, *Dynamics of the Party System* (Washington, DC: Brookings Institution, 1973).
5. These events typically unfold over a period of time, but for convenience, the beginning of each party system is located in the year in which the new majority party coalition first took office.
6. Michael Holt, *The Rise and Fall of the American Whig Party* (New York: Oxford University Press, 2003).
7. The third party system actually contained two distinct periods. From the end of the Civil War in 1865 through 1876, Democratic voting strength in the South was held in check by the occupying Union army and various Reconstruction policies and laws. So to reflect the true party balance during this time, it is helpful to differentiate between 1861–1876 and the 1877–1896 period.
8. A. James Reichley, *The Life of the Parties* (Lanham, MD: Rowman & Littlefield, 2000), p. 104.
9. Jeff Manza and Clem Brooks, *Social Cleavages and Political Change* (Oxford: Oxford University Press, 1999).
10. James Madison, *The Federalist No. 10*, November 22, 1787.
11. See Larry Bartels, *Unequal Democracy* (Princeton: Princeton University Press, 2008).
12. See Paul R. Abramson, John H. Aldrich, and David W. Rohde, *Change and Continuity in the 2004 and 2006 Elections* (Washington, DC: CQ Press, 2007), pp. 188–190.
13. Jeffrey M. Stonecash, *Class and Party in American Politics* (Boulder, CO: Westview Press, 2000), pp. 13 and 139, and Chapter 4.
14. On the change in upper-income people's attitudes toward the Republican Party, see Mark D. Brewer, *Party Images in the American Electorate* (New York: Routledge, 2009), pp. 25–26.
15. See Russell J. Dalton, Scott C. Flanagan, and Paul Allen Beck, eds., *Electoral Change in Advanced Industrial Democracies* (Princeton, NJ: Princeton University Press, 1984).

16. Henry E. Brady, "Trust the People: Political Party Coalitions and the 2000 Election," in Jack N. Rakove, ed., *The Unfinished Election of 2000* (New York: Basic Books, 2001), p. 55.

17. See Frank Newport, "Democrats Do Best Among Generation Y and Baby Boomers," May 8, 2009, at www.gallup.com/poll/118285/Democrats-Best-Among-Generation-Baby-Boomers.aspx?CSTS=alert (accessed May 9, 2009).

18. Steven M. Cohen and Charles S. Liebman, "American Jewish Liberalism," *Public Opinion Quarterly* 61 (1997): 405–430. See also L. Sandy Maisel and Ira N. Forman, eds., *Jews in American Politics* (Lanham, MD: Rowman & Littlefield, 2003).

19. CNN exit poll data, at www.cnn.com/ELECTION/2008/results/polls/#val=USP00p2 (accessed May 12, 2009).

20. See David C. Leege and Lyman A. Kellstedt, eds., *Rediscovering the Religious Factor in American Politics* (Armonk, NY: M. E. Sharpe, 1993).

21. Frank Newport, "Blacks as Conservative as Republicans on Some Moral Issues," Gallup Poll, December 3, 2008, at www.gallup.com/poll/112807/Blacks-Conservative-Republicans-Some-Moral-Issues.aspx (accessed May 8, 2009).

22. This was also the result of anti-immigrant ballot propositions sponsored by California Republicans in the 1990s; see Shaun Bowler, Stephen P. Nicholson, and Gary M. Segura, "Earthquakes and Aftershocks," *American Journal of Political Science* 50 (2006): 146–157.

23. CNN exit poll data, at www.cnn.com/ELECTION/2008/results/polls/#USP00p1 (accessed May 12, 2009).

24. See Torben Iversen and Frances Rosenbluth, "The Political Economy of Gender," *American Journal of Political Science* 50 (2006): 1–19.

25. Janet M. Box-Steffensmeier, Suzanna De Boef, and Tse-Min Lin, "The Dynamics of the Partisan Gender Gap," *American Political Science Review* 98 (2004): 515–528; and Karen M. Kaufman and John R. Petrocik, "The Changing Politics of American Men," *American Journal of Political Science* 43 (1999): 864–887.

26. Kira Sanbonmatsu, *Democrats, Republicans, and the Politics of Women's Place* (Ann Arbor: University of Michigan Press, 2002), Chapter 3; see also Christina Wolbrecht, *The Politics of Women's Rights* (Princeton: Princeton University Press, 2000); and Brian Schaffner, "Priming Gender," *American Journal of Political Science* 49 (2005): 803–817.

27. Calculated from *CQ Weekly*'s profiles of House freshmen in 2008 and 2009 issues.

28. Calculated from www.cnn.com/ELECTION/2008/results/polls/#val=USP00p3 (accessed May 12, 2009).

29. Greg D. Adams, "Abortion: Evidence of an Issue Evolution," *American Journal of Political Science* 41 (1997): 718–737.

30. David O. Sears, Richard R. Lau, Tom R. Tyler, and Harris M. Allen, Jr., "Self-Interest vs. Symbolic Politics in Policy Attitudes and Presidential Voting," *American Political Science Review* 74 (1980): 670–684.

31. Quoted in Thomas B. Edsall, "Political Party Is No Longer Dictated By Class Status," *Washington Post*, November 9, 2000, p. A37.

32. See Geoffrey C. Layman, *The Great Divide* (New York: Columbia University Press, 2001).

33. Nicholas A. Valentino and David O. Sears, "Old Times There Are Not Forgotten," *American Journal of Political Science* 49 (2005): 673.

34. Jeffrey M. Stonecash, *Political Parties Matter* (Boulder: Lynne Rienner, 2006), Chapter 4.

35. Merle Black, "The Transformation of the Southern Democratic Party," *Journal of Politics* 66 (2004): 1001–1017.

36. Valentino and Sears, "Old Times There Are Not Forgotten," p. 676. See also Earl Black and Merle Black, *Divided America* (New York: Simon & Schuster, 2007), pp. 32–39 and 74–91.

37. Gary Miller and Norman Schofield, "The Transformation of the Republican and Democratic Party Coalitions in the U.S.," *Perspectives on Politics* 6 (2008): 433–450.

38. John R. Petrocik, "Party Coalitions in the American Public," in John C. Green and Daniel J. Coffey, eds., *The State of the Parties*, 5th ed. (Lanham, MD: Rowman & Littlefield, 2007), p. 285.

39. Martin P. Wattenberg, *The Decline of American Political Parties 1952–96* (Cambridge, MA: Harvard University Press, 1998).

40. Donald Green, Bradley Palmquist, and Eric Schickler, *Partisan Hearts and Minds* (New Haven: Yale University Press, 2002), pp. 141 and 158.

41. Helmut Norpoth, "Under Way and Here to Stay: Party Realignment in the 1980s?" *Public Opinion Quarterly* 51 (1987): 376–391; and Warren E. Miller, "Party Identification, Realignment, and Party Voting," *American Political Science Review* 85 (1991): 557–570.

42. Ronald Brownstein, "GOP Has Lock on South, and Democrats Can't Find Key," *Los Angeles Times*, December 15, 2004, p. A1.
43. See Earl Black and Merle Black, *The Rise of Southern Republicans* (Cambridge, MA: Harvard University Press, 2002); Michael F. Meffert, Helmut Norpoth, and Anirudh V. S. Ruhil, "Realignment and Macropartisanship," *American Political Science Review* 95 (2001): 953–962; and Paul Frymer, "The 1994 Electoral Aftershock," in Philip A. Klinkner, ed., *Midterm* (Boulder: Westview, 1996), pp. 99–113.
44. Alan Cooperman and Thomas B. Edsall, "Evangelicals Say They Led Charge for the GOP," *Washington Post*, November 8, 2004, p. A1.
45. See Alan I. Abramowitz, "The Incredible Shrinking Republican Base," Sabato's Crystal Ball, 6 (May 1, 2009).
46. David R. Mayhew, *Electoral Realignments* (New Haven: Yale University Press, 2002); see also Carmines and Stimson, *Issue Evolution*; Byron E. Shafer, ed., *The End of Realignment?* (Madison: University of Wisconsin Press, 1991); and Samuel Merrill III, Bernard Grofman, and Thomas L. Brunell, "Cycles in American National Electoral Politics, 1854–2006," *American Political Science Review* 102 (2008): 1–17.
47. See Paul Allen Beck, "A Tale of Two Electorates," in John C. Green and Rick Farmer, eds., *The State of the Parties*, 4th ed. (Lanham, MD: Rowman & Littlefield, 2003), pp. 38–53.

CHAPTER 8: PARTIES AND VOTER TURNOUT

1. See Pippa Norris, *Electoral Engineering* (Cambridge: Cambridge University Press, 2004).
2. The term "suffrage" means the right to vote. See Alexander Keyssar, *The Right to Vote* (Boulder, CO: Basic Books, 2009).
3. The Supreme Court case overturning the poll tax was *Harper v. Virginia State Board of Elections* (1966).
4. Jerrold G. Rusk, "The Effect of the Australian Ballot Reform on Split Ticket Voting: 1876–1908," *American Political Science Review* 64 (1970): 1220–1238.
5. Stephen M. Nichols and Gregory A. Strizek, "Electronic Voting Machines and Ballot Roll-off," *American Politics Quarterly* 23 (1995): 300–318.
6. Paul Kleppner, *Continuity and Change in Electoral Politics, 1893–1928* (Westport, CT: Greenwood, 1987), pp. 165–166.
7. Peverill Squire, Raymond E. Wolfinger, and David P. Glass, "Residential Mobility and Voter Turnout," *American Political Science Review* 81 (1987): 45–65.
8. Walter Dean Burnham, "Theory and Voting Research," *American Political Science Review* 68 (1974): 1002–1023.
9. The Supreme Court finally ended the white primary in *Smith v. Allwright* (1944).
10. See V. O. Key, Jr., *Southern Politics in State and Nation* (New York: Knopf, 1949).
11. Chandler Davidson and Bernard Grofman, eds., *Quiet Revolution in the South* (Princeton, NJ: Princeton University Press, 1994).
12. The landmark Supreme Court cases are *Baker v. Carr* (1962); *Reynolds v. Sims* (1964); and *Wesberry v. Sanders* (1964).
13. The Supreme Court declined to ban partisan gerrymandering most recently in the case of *Vieth v. Jubelirer* (2004).
14. Thomas B. Edsall, "Parties Play Voting Rights Role Reversal," *Washington Post*, February 25, 2001, p. A1. See also Kevin A. Hill, "Does the Creation of Majority Black Districts Aid Republicans?" *Journal of Politics* 57 (1995): 384–401.
15. The cases are *Miller v. Johnson* (1995) and *Easley v. Cromartie* (2001), respectively. On majority–minority districts, see David T. Canon, *Race, Redistricting, and Representation* (Chicago: University of Chicago Press, 1999).
16. See Jeff Manza and Christopher Uggen, "Punishment and Democracy," *Perspectives on Politics* 2 (2004): 491–505.
17. See Robert L. Dudley and Alan R. Gitelson, *American Elections: The Rules Matter* (New York: Longman, 2002), pp. 7–15.
18. See Benjamin Highton and Raymond E. Wolfinger, "Estimating the Effects of the National Voter Registration Act of 1993," *Political Behavior* 20 (1998): 79–104.
19. Ruy A. Teixiera, *The Disappearing American Voter* (Washington, DC: Brookings, 1992), Chapter 4; and Glenn E. Mitchell and Christopher Wlezien, "The Impact of Legal Constraints on Voter

Registration, Turnout, and the Composition of the American Electorate," *Political Behavior* 17 (1995): 179–202.

20. Nathaniel Persily, testimony before the U.S. Senate Committee on Rules and Administration, March 11, 2009, at www.rules.senate.gov/public/index.cfm?FuseAction=InNews.MajorityNews&ContentRecord_id= f72bc608-5056-8059-76f6-97bcc0202f3d (accessed May 13, 2009).

21. Raymond E. Wolfinger and Jonathan Hoffman, "Registering and Voting with Motor Voter," *PS: Political Science and Politics* 34 (2001): 85–92; and Michael D. Martinez and David Hill, "Did Motor Voter Work?" *American Politics Quarterly* 27 (1999): 296–315.

22. See the symposium "Voter Identification," *PS: Political Science & Politics* 42 (2009): 81–130. The case is *Crawford v. Marion County Election Board* (2008).

23. Michael R. Alvarez, Stephen Ansolabehere, Adam Berinsky, Thad Hall, Gabriel Lenz, and Charles Stewart III, "2008 Survey of the Performance of American Elections," May 5, 2008, p. 17.

24. See Justin Buchler, Matthew Jarvis, and John E. McNulty, "Punch Card Technology and the Racial Gap in Residual Votes," *Perspectives on Politics* 2 (2004): 517–524.

25. See Michael Tomz and Robert P. Van Houweling, "How Does Voting Equipment Affect the Racial Gap in Voided Ballots?" *American Journal of Political Science* 47 (2003): 46–60.

26. Abby Goodnough, "Lost Record of Vote in '02 Florida Race Raises '04 Concern," *New York Times*, July 28, 2004, p. 1.

27. Ian Urbina, "Hurdles to Voting Persisted in 2008," *New York Times*, March 11, 2009, at www.nytimes.com/2009/03/11/us/politics/11vote.html (accessed May 13, 2009).

28. Because of the difficulties in estimating American turnout, many "official" turnout figures *underestimate* it. The percentages here and in Figure 8.3 correct for this underestimation. Their denominator is an effort to estimate the *eligible* population: the voting-age population minus the number of noncitizens living in the United States. The numerator of the turnout fraction is the number of voters who cast a vote for president or for the office with the highest vote in midterm elections. See Walter Dean Burnham, "The Turnout Problem," in A. James Reichley, ed., *Elections American Style* (Washington, DC: Brookings, 1987), pp. 97–133, and Michael McDonald, "Voter Turnout," at www.elections.gmu.edu/voter_turnout.htm (accessed May 17, 2009).

29. Unless otherwise indicated, turnout figures are those of the U.S. Census Bureau.

30. Exit poll data from www.elections.nytimes.com/2008/results/president/national-exit-polls.html (accessed May 15, 2009).

31. Walter Dean Burnham, "The Changing Shape of the American Political Universe," *American Political Science Review* 59 (1965): 7–28.

32. Richard A. Brody, "The Puzzle of Participation in America," in Anthony King, ed., *The New American Political System* (Washington, DC: American Enterprise Institute, 1978), pp. 287–324.

33. See John H. Aldrich, "Rational Choice and Turnout," *American Journal of Political Science* 37 (1993): 246–278.

34. Paul R. Abramson, John H. Aldrich, and David W. Rohde, *Change and Continuity in the 2004 and 2006 Elections* (Washington, DC: CQ Press, 2007), p. 90; and Robert A. Jackson, "Clarifying the Relationship between Education and Turnout," *American Politics Quarterly* 23 (1995): 279–299.

35. See Rebecca B. Morton, *Analyzing Elections* (New York: Norton, 2006), pp. 53–55.

36. See Sidney Verba, Norman H. Nie, and Jae-On Kim, *Participation and Political Equality* (Cambridge: Cambridge University Press, 1978).

37. Cliff Zukin, Scott Keeter, Molly Andolina, Krista Jenkins and Michael X. Delli Carpini, *A New Engagement?* (Oxford: Oxford University Press, 2006).

38. Karl T. Kurz, Alan Rosenthal, and Cliff Zukin, "A Challenge for All Generations," National Conference of State Legislatures report, 2003.

39. See Daniel M. Shea and John C. Green, *The Fountain of Youth* (Allegheny College: Center for Political Participation, 2004).

40. See Zukin et al., *A New Engagement?* Chapter 6.

41. Lawrence Bobo and Franklin D. Gilliam, Jr., "Race, Sociopolitical Participation, and Black Empowerment," *American Political Science Review* 84 (1990): 377–393.

42. Scott D. McClurg, "The Electoral Relevance of Political Talk," *American Journal of Political Science* 50 (2006): 737–754.

43. Nancy Burns, Kay Lehman Schlozman, and Sidney Verba, "The Public Consequences of Private Inequality," *American Political Science Review* 91 (1997): 373–389.

44. See Steven J. Rosenstone and John Mark Hansen, *Mobilization, Participation, and Democracy in America* (New York: Longman, 2003), pp. 141–156.
45. Lyn Ragsdale and Jerrold G. Rusk, "Who Are Nonvoters?" *American Journal of Political Science* 37 (1993): 721–746.
46. Abramson, Aldrich, and Rohde, *Change and Continuity*, p. 97.
47. Robert A. Jackson, "The Mobilization of U.S. State Electorates in the 1988 and 1990 Elections," *Journal of Politics* 59 (1997): 520–537.
48. David K. Levine and Thomas R. Palfrey, "The Paradox of Voter Participation?" *American Political Science Review* 101 (2007): 143–158.
49. Gerald M. Pomper, "The Presidential Election," in Michael Nelson, ed., *The Elections of 2008* (Washington, DC: CQ Press, 2009), p. 47. See also Michael P. McDonald, "The Return of the Voter," *The Forum* 6 (2008), at www.bepress.com/forum/vol6/iss4/art4 (accessed May 14, 2009).
50. See Donald P. Green and Alan S. Gerber, *Get Out the Vote!* (Washington, DC: Brookings Institution, 2004), and Kevin Arceneaux and David W. Nickerson, "Who Is Mobilized to Vote?" *American Journal of Political Science* 53 (2009): 1–16.
51. Thomas Patterson, press release from the Vanishing Voter Project, John F. Kennedy School of Government, Harvard University, November 11, 2004.
52. McDonald, "The Return of the Voter."
53. Brad T. Gomez, Thomas G. Hansford, and George A. Krause, "The Republicans Should Pray for Rain," *Journal of Politics* 69 (2007): 649–663.
54. Jack Citrin, Eric Schickler, and John Sides, "What If Everyone Voted?" *American Journal of Political Science* 47 (2003): 75–90.
55. See, for example, Andrea Louise Campbell, "Parties, Electoral Participation, and Shifting Voting Blocs," in Paul Pierson and Theda Skocpol, eds., *The Transformation of American Politics* (Princeton: Princeton University Press, 2007), pp. 68–102.
56. Adriel Bettelheim, "Youth's Long-Term Role in Politics," *CQ Weekly*, November 10, 2008, p. 2973.
57. APSA Task Force Report, "American Democracy in an Age of Rising Inequality," *Perspectives on Politics* 2 (2004): 658.
58. Paul S. Martin, "Voting's Rewards," *American Journal of Political Science* 47 (2003): 110–127.

CHAPTER 9: HOW PARTIES CHOOSE CANDIDATES

1. See Alan Ware, *The American Direct Primary* (Cambridge: Cambridge University Press, 2002). On the spread of the primary to other democracies, see John M. Carey and John Polga-Hecimovich, "Primary Elections and Candidate Strength in Latin America," *Journal of Politics* 68 (2006): 530–543.
2. Stephen J. Wayne, *The Road to the White House 2008* (Belmont, CA: Wadsworth, 2008), pp. 6–8.
3. Charles E. Merriam and Louise Overacker, *Primary Elections* (Chicago: University of Chicago Press, 1928).
4. Robert M. La Follette, *La Follette's Autobiography* (Madison, WI: R. M. La Follette, 1913), pp. 197–198.
5. Some states allow third parties to nominate their candidates through conventions.
6. Federal Election Commission *Record, Party Guide Supplement* 31 (May 2005).
7. See Craig L. Carr and Gary L. Scott, "The Logic of State Primary Classification Schemes," *American Politics Quarterly* 12 (1984): 465–476; and Steven E. Finkel and Howard A. Scarrow, "Party Identification and Party Enrollment," *Journal of Politics* 47 (1985): 620–652.
8. See Thomas M. Holbrook and Raymond J. La Raja, "Parties and Elections," in Virginia Gray and Russell L. Hanson, eds., *Politics in the American States*, 9th ed. (Washington, DC: CQ Press, 2008), Table 3-3. Note that experts disagree on these definitions and on the dividing line between an "open" and a "closed" primary.
9. A 1986 Supreme Court decision (*Tashjian v. Republican Party of Connecticut*) upheld the Connecticut party's efforts to establish an open primary by overriding the state's closed primary law. This decision affirmed the authority of the party, rather than the state, to control its own nomination process. However, most state parties would prefer a closed primary to an open one.
10. The case was *California Democratic Party v. Jones* (2000). On blanket primaries, see Bruce E. Cain and Elisabeth R. Gerber, eds., *Voting at the Political Fault Line* (Berkeley: University of California Press, 2002).

11. Lynn Vavreck, "The Reasoning Voter Meets the Strategic Candidate," *American Politics Research* 29 (2001): 507–529, and Philip Paolino and Daron R. Shaw, "Lifting the Hood on the Straight-Talk Express," *American Politics Research* 29 (2001): 483–506.

12. Gary D. Wekkin, "Why Crossover Voters Are Not 'Mischievous' Voters," *American Politics Quarterly* 19 (1991): 229–247.

13. See the monthly newsletter *Ballot Access News*, at www.ballot-access.org.

14. See, for instance, Thomas A. Reitz and Rebecca B. Morton, "Majority Requirements and Minority Representation," *NYU Annual Survey of American Law* 63 (2008): 691–725.

15. V. O. Key, Jr., *American State Politics: An Introduction* (New York: Knopf, 1956), p. 195.

16. John G. Geer and Mark E. Shere, "Party Competition and the Prisoner's Dilemma," *Journal of Politics* 54 (1992): 741–761.

17. See, for example, Malcolm E. Jewell and Sarah M. Morehouse, *Political Parties and Elections in American States*, 4th ed. (Washington, DC: CQ Press, 2001), p. 123.

18. Marjorie Randon Hershey, "The Media: Coloring the News," in Michael Nelson, ed., *The Elections of 2008* (Washington, DC: CQ Press, 2009), pp. 128–129.

19. Paige L. Schneider, "Factionalism in the Southern Republican Party," *American Review of Politics* 19 (1998): 129–148.

20. Matt Bai, "Fight Club," *New York Times Magazine*, August 10, 2003, pp. 24–27.

21. Gary F. Moncrief, Peverill Squire, and Malcolm E. Jewell, *Who Runs for the Legislature?* (Upper Saddle River, NJ: Prentice Hall, 2001), p. 39.

22. Sarah McCally Morehouse, *The Governor as Party Leader* (Ann Arbor: University of Michigan Press, 1998), pp. 22–23.

23. Jewell and Morehouse, *Political Parties and Elections in American States*, pp. 109–110.

24. L. Sandy Maisel, Linda L. Fowler, Ruth S. Jones, and Walter J. Stone, "Nomination Politics," in L. Sandy Maisel, ed., *The Parties Respond* (Boulder, CO: Westview, 1994), pp. 155–156.

25. See Jewell and Morehouse, *Political Parties and Elections in American States*, pp. 118–120, and Jay Goodliffe and David B. Magleby, "Campaign Finance in U.S. House Primary and General Elections," in Peter F. Galderisi, Marni Ezra, and Michael Lyons, eds., *Congressional Primaries and the Politics of Representation* (Lanham, MD: Rowman & Littlefield, 2001), pp. 62–76.

26. Malcolm E. Jewell, "Northern State Gubernatorial Primary Elections: Explaining Voting Turnout," *American Politics Quarterly* 12 (1984): 101–116.

27. Jewell and Morehouse, *Political Parties and Elections in American States*, pp. 124–125.

28. John G. Geer, "Assessing the Representativeness of Electorates in Presidential Primaries," *American Journal of Political Science* 32 (1988): 929–945. For more recent data showing minimal differences, see Alan Abramowitz, "Don't Blame Primary Voters for Polarization," *The Forum* 5 (2008), at www.bepress.com/forum/vol5/iss4/art4 (accessed July 11, 2009).

29. Karen M. Kaufmann, James G. Gimpel, and Adam H. Hoffman, "A Promise Fulfilled?" *Journal of Politics* 65 (2003): 457–476.

30. James Adams and Samuel Merrill III, "Candidate and Party Strategies in Two-Stage Elections Beginning with a Primary," *American Journal of Political Science* 52 (2008): 344–359.

CHAPTER 10: CHOOSING THE PRESIDENTIAL NOMINEES

1. See John S. Jackson III and William J. Crotty, *The Politics of Presidential Selection*, 2nd ed. (New York: Longman, 2001), Chapters 3 and 4.

2. See Larry M. Bartels, *Presidential Primaries and the Dynamics of Public Choice* (Princeton, NJ: Princeton University Press, 1988), pp. 17–21.

3. Marty Cohen, David Karol, Hans Noel, and John Zaller, *The Party Decides* (Chicago: University of Chicago Press, 2008), p. 168.

4. Byron E. Shafer, *Bifurcated Politics* (Cambridge, MA: Harvard University Press, 1988), pp. 181–184.

5. William G. Mayer and Andrew E. Busch, *The Front-Loading Problem in Presidential Nominations* (Washington, DC: Brookings Institution Press, 2004), pp. 24–25.

6. James W. Ceaser, Andrew E. Busch, and John J. Pitney, Jr., *Epic Journey* (Lanham, MD: Rowman & Littlefield, 2009), p. 22.

7. Marjorie Randon Hershey, "Shedding Light on the Invisible Primary," in Larry J. Sabato, ed., *Get in the Booth! The Presidential Election of 2004* (New York: Longman, 2004), pp. 27–47.

8. See John H. Aldrich, *Before the Convention* (Chicago: University of Chicago Press, 1980); and Paul-Henri Gurian and Audrey A. Haynes, "Campaign Strategy in Presidential Primaries," *American Journal of Political Science* 37 (1993): 335–341.

9. John M. Broder, "Show Me the Delegate Rules and I'll Show You the Party," *New York Times*, February 17, 2008, Week in Review, p. 1.

10. Proportional representation doesn't always slow down the Democratic nomination race; if one candidate gains early momentum, as has happened in most recent Democratic races, then the party can settle on a nominee quickly. But when the leading candidates are closely matched in support, PR can prolong their competition.

11. For an interesting analysis, see Jonathan Weisman, Shailagh Murray, and Peter Slevin, "Strategy Was Based on Winning Delegates, Not Battlegrounds," *Washington Post*, June 4, 2008, p. A1.

12. Justin M. Sizemore, "How Obama Did It," *Sabato's Crystal Ball* 6, June 5, 2008.

13. Ibid.

14. See Richard Herrera, "Are 'Superdelegates' Super?" *Political Behavior* 16 (1994): 79–92. The Republicans send a smaller number of unpledged delegates, including state party chairs, to their national convention.

15. See Patrick J. Kenney and Tom W. Rice, "Voter Turnout in Presidential Primaries," *Political Behavior* 7 (1985): 101–112; and Barbara Norrander and Gregg W. Smith, "Type of Contest, Candidate Strategy, and Turnout in Presidential Primaries," *American Politics Quarterly* 13 (1985): 28–50.

16. Bartels, *Presidential Primaries and the Dynamics of Public Choice*, pp. 140–148.

17. Mark J. Wattier and Raymond Tatalovich, "Gods, Generals, and the Confederate Flag," The Citadel Symposium on Southern Politics, Charleston, 2004.

18. See Scott Keeter and Cliff Zukin, *Uninformed Choice* (New York: Praeger, 1983); and John G. Geer, *Nominating Presidents* (New York: Greenwood Press, 1989).

19. Samuel L. Popkin, *The Reasoning Voter* (Chicago: University of Chicago Press, 1991), Chapters 6–8.

20. Bartels, *Presidential Primaries and the Dynamics of Public Choice*, Chapter 4.

21. Paul R. Abramson, John H. Aldrich, Phil Paolino, and David W. Rohde, " 'Sophisticated' Voting in the 1988 Presidential Primaries," *American Political Science Review* 86 (1992): 55–69.

22. See Walter J. Stone, Ronald B. Rapoport, and Alan I. Abramowitz, "Candidate Support in Presidential Nomination Campaigns," *Journal of Politics* 54 (1992): 1074–1097.

23. Michael G. Hagen and William G. Mayer, "The Modern Politics of Presidential Selection," in William G. Mayer, ed., *In Pursuit of the White House 2000* (New York: Chatham House, 2000), pp. 17–21.

24. Mark J. Wattier, "Platform Pledges and Campaign Communications," *Southeastern Political Review* 19 (1991): 170–192.

25. L. Sandy Maisel, "The Platform-Writing Process," *Political Science Quarterly* 108 (1993–1994): 671–699.

26. Gerald M. Pomper, "Party Responsibility and the Future of American Democracy," in Jeffrey E. Cohen, Richard Fleisher, and Paul Kantor, eds., *American Political Parties: Decline or Resurgence?* (Washington, DC: CQ Press, 2001), pp. 170–172.

27. See Lee Sigelman and Paul J. Wahlbeck, "The 'Veepstakes,'" *American Political Science Review* 91 (1997): 855–864.

28. These data and those cited in the rest of the chapter come from the *New York Times*/CBS News polls of Democratic and Republican National Convention delegates.

29. See John S. Jackson III, Barbara L. Brown, and David Bositis, "Herbert McClosky and Friends Revisited," *American Politics Quarterly* 10 (1982): 158–180; and Warren E. Miller and M. Kent Jennings, *Parties in Transition* (New York: Russell Sage Foundation, 1986), Chapters 7–9.

30. See John W. Soule and Wilma E. McGrath, "A Comparative Study of Presidential Nomination Conventions," *American Journal of Political Science* 19 (1975): 501–517.

31. Denise L. Baer and David A. Bositis, *Elite Cadres and Party Coalitions* (New York: Greenwood Press, 1988), Chapter 7.

32. Shafer, *Bifurcated Politics*, Chapter 8, and Costas Panagopoulos, ed., *Rewiring Politics* (Baton Rouge: Louisiana State University Press, 2007).

33. See Emmett H. Buell, Jr., "The Changing Face of the New Hampshire Primary," in William G. Mayer, ed., *In Pursuit of the White House 2000* (New York: Chatham House, 2000), pp. 87–144.

34. Nelson W. Polsby, *The Consequences of Party Reform* (Oxford: Oxford University Press, 1983).

35. See Barbara Norrander, *Can Presidential Primaries Be Reformed?* (New York: Routledge, 2009), and Caroline Tolbert and Peverill Squire, eds., "Reforming the Presidential Nominating Process," *PS: Political Science and Politics* 42 (2009): 27–79.

CHAPTER 11: THE GENERAL ELECTION

1. See Paul S. Herrnson, *Congressional Elections*, 5th ed. (Washington, DC: CQ Press, 2008), and Marjorie Randon Hershey, *Running for Office* (Chatham, NJ: Chatham House, 1984).

2. See Gary C. Jacobson, *The Politics of Congressional Elections*, 7th ed. (New York: Longman, 2009).

3. Edward I. Sidlow, *Challenging the Incumbent* (Washington, DC: CQ Press, 2003).

4. See Herrnson, *Congressional Elections*, pp. 221–244.

5. John R. Petrocik, William L. Benoit, and Glenn J. Hansen, "Issue Ownership and Presidential Campaigning, 1952–2000," *Political Science Quarterly* 118 (2003): 599–626.

6. See, for example, David A. Dulio, *For Better or Worse* (Albany, NY: SUNY Press, 2004).

7. James A. Thurber and Candice J. Nelson, eds., *Campaign Warriors* (Washington, DC: Brookings, 2000).

8. See Darrell M. West, *Air Wars*, 5th ed. (Washington, DC: CQ Press, 2009).

9. Jeff Valenzuela, "Midwest Local TV Newscasts Devote 2.5 Times as Much Air Time to Political Ads as Election Coverage," press release, Joyce Foundation, November 21, 2006.

10. Markus Prior, "News vs. Entertainment," *American Journal of Political Science* 49 (2005): 577–592.

11. See Doris A. Graber, *Mass Media and American Politics,* 8th ed. (Washington, DC: CQ Press, 2009), Chapter 4.

12. Dave Barry, "Scandal Sheep," *Boston Globe Magazine*, March 15, 1998, pp. 12–13.

13. See Stephen E. Frantzich, "E-Politics and the 2008 Presidential Campaign," in William J. Crotty, ed., *Winning the Presidency 2008* (Boulder: Paradigm, 2009), p. 146.

14. Aaron Smith, "The Internet's Role in Campaign 2008," at www.pewresearch.org/pubs/1192/internet-politics-campaign-2008 (accessed April 15, 2009).

15. Richard J. Semiatin, *Campaigns in the 21st Century* (Boston: McGraw Hill, 2005), p. 178.

16. Exit poll data, at www.cnn.com/ELECTION/2008/results/polls/#val=USP00p2 (accessed June 6, 2009).

17. See David B. Magleby and J. Quin Monson, *The Last Hurrah?* (Provo, UT: Center for the Study of Elections and Democracy, 2003), Chapters 1 and 12.

18. See Richard R. Lau and Gerald M. Pomper, "Effectiveness of Negative Campaigning in U.S. Senate Elections," *American Journal of Political Science* 46 (2002): 47–66; and John G. Geer, *In Defense of Negativity* (Chicago: University of Chicago Press, 2006). On its use by challengers, see James N. Druckman, Martin J. Kifer, and Michael Parkin, "Campaign Communications in U.S. Congressional Elections," *American Political Science Review* 103 (2009): 343–366.

19. Yanna Krupnikov, "Who Votes? How and When Negative Campaign Advertisements Affect Voter Turnout," Ph.D. Dissertation, University of Michigan, 2009.

20. Paul R. Abramson, John H. Aldrich, and David W. Rohde, *Change and Continuity in the 2000 and 2002 Elections* (Washington, DC: CQ Press, 2003), pp. 261–262.

21. Gerald M. Pomper, "The Presidential Election," in Michael Nelson, ed., *The Elections of 2004* (Washington, DC: CQ Press, 2005), pp. 57 and 61.

22. Alan Abramowitz, "Terrorism, Gay Marriage, and Incumbency," *The Forum* 2 (2004), at www.bepress.com/forum.

23. See Robert Huckfeldt and John Sprague, "Political Parties and Electoral Mobilization," *American Political Science Review* 86 (1992): 70–86; Peter W. Wielhouwer, "The Mobilization of Campaign Activists by the Party Canvass," *American Politics Quarterly* 27 (1999): 177–200; and Steven J. Rosenstone and John Mark Hansen, *Mobilization, Participation, and Democracy in America* (New York: Longman, 2003), Chapter 6.

24. Donald P. Green and Alan S. Gerber, *Get Out the Vote!* (Washington, DC: Brookings Institution Press, 2004), pp. 92–93.

25. David W. Nickerson, "Quality Is Job One," *American Journal of Political Science* 51 (2007): 269–282.

26. John P. Frendreis, James L. Gibson, and Laura L. Vertz, "The Electoral Relevance of Local Party Organizations," *American Political Science Review* 84 (1990): 225–235.

27. Daron R. Shaw, "The Effect of TV Ads and Candidate Appearances on Statewide Presidential Votes, 1988–96," *American Political Science Review* 93 (1999): 345–61.

28. Daron R. Shaw, "A Study of Presidential Campaign Effects from 1952-1992," *Journal of Politics* 61 (1999): 387–422; and Adam Simon, *The Winning Message* (Cambridge: Cambridge University Press, 2002).

29. See Paul Freedman, Michael Franz, and Kenneth Goldstein, "Campaign Advertising and Democratic Citizenship," *American Journal of Political Science* 48 (2004): 723–741. For a different view, see Gregory A. Huber and Kevin Arceneaux, "Identifying the Persuasive Effects of Presidential Advertising," *American Journal of Political Science* 51 (2007): 957–977.

30. D. Sunshine Hillygus and Simon Jackman, "Voter Decision Making in Election 2000," *American Journal of Political Science* 47 (2003): 583–596; Matthew A. Baum, "Talking the Vote," *American Journal of Political Science* 49 (2005): 213–234

31. Shanto Iyengar and John R. Petrocik, " 'Basic Rule' Voting," in James A. Thurber, Candice J. Nelson, and David A. Dulio, eds., *Crowded Airwaves* (Washington, DC: Brookings, 2000), p. 142.

32. David A. M. Peterson, "Campaign Learning and Vote Determinants," *American Journal of Political Science* 53 (2009): 445–460.

33. On priming, see Joanne M. Miller and Jon A. Krosnick, "News Media Impact on the Ingredients of Presidential Evaluations," *American Journal of Political Science* 44 (2000): 295–309; and Shanto Iyengar and Donald Kinder, *News That Matters* (Chicago: University of Chicago Press, 1987).

34. Russell J. Dalton, Paul A. Beck, and Robert Huckfeldt, "Partisan Cues and the Media," *American Political Science Review* 92 (1998): 111–126.

35. See Robert Huckfeldt and John Sprague, "Networks in Context," *American Political Science Review* 81 (1987): 1197–1216; and Paul Allen Beck, "Voters' Intermediation Environments in the 1988 Presidential Contest," *Public Opinion Quarterly* 55 (1991): 371–394.

36. The classic is Paul Lazarsfeld, Bernard Berelson, and Hazel Gaudet, *The People's Choice* (New York: Columbia University Press, 1948).

37. See Thomas M. Holbrook and Scott D. McClurg, "The Mobilization of Core Supporters," *American Journal of Political Science* 49 (2005): 689–703.

38. See Paul S. Herrnson and Diana Dwyre, "Party Issue Advocacy in Congressional Election Campaigns," in John C. Green and Daniel M. Shea, eds., *The State of the Parties*, 3rd ed. (Lanham, MD: Rowman & Littlefield, 1999), pp. 86–104.

CHAPTER 12: FINANCING THE CAMPAIGNS

1. Unless otherwise noted, all figures cited in this chapter come from Federal Election Commission reports. For excellent analyses of campaign finance, see Michael J. Malbin, ed., *The Election after Reform* (Lanham, MD: Rowman & Littlefield, 2006); and Marian Currinder, *Money in the House* (Boulder, CO: Westview, 2009).

2. "Congressional Candidates Raised $1.42 Billion in 2007–2008," December 29, 2009.

3. Data from the New Jersey Election Law Enforcement Commission, at www.elec.state.nj.us/ELECReport/EntityListingDetailView.aspx?Report=NonPac&Type=G&Year=2007&Office=1 (accessed June 24, 2009).

4. Data from the National Institute on Money and State Politics; Linda Casey, "High Court Contests," April 28, 2009, at www.followthemoney.org/press/ReportView.phtml?r=390 (accessed June 14, 2009). See also James L. Gibson, "Challenges to the Impartiality of State Supreme Courts," *American Political Science Review* 102 (2008): 59–75.

5. See John J. Coleman and Paul F. Manna, "Congressional Campaign Spending and the Quality of Democracy," *Journal of Politics* 62 (2000): 757–789.

6. Gary C. Jacobson, *The Politics of Congressional Elections*, 7th ed. (New York: Pearson-Longman, 2009), p. 45.

7. See these articles in the *American Journal of Political Science:* Donald Philip Green and Jonathan S. Krasno, "Salvation for the Spendthrift Incumbent," 32 (1988): 884–907; Gary C. Jacobson, "The Effects of Campaign Spending in House Elections," 34 (1990): 334–362; and Kenneth Benoit and Michael Marsh, "The Campaign Value of Incumbency," 52 (2008): 874–890.

8. On state elections, see Michael J. Malbin and Thomas L. Gais, *The Day after Reform* (Albany, NY: Rockefeller Institute, 1998).

9. Peter Francia, John C. Green, Paul S. Herrnson, Lynda W. Powell, and Clyde Wilcox, *The Financiers of Congressional Elections* (New York: Columbia University Press, 2003).

10. Jose Antonio Vargas, "Obama Raised Half a Billion Online," *Washington Post*, at voices.washington-post.com/44/2008/11/20/obama_raised_half_a_billion_on.html (accessed June 25, 2009).

11. Frank J. Sorauf, *Inside Campaign Finance* (New Haven, CT: Yale University Press, 1992), Chapter 4.

12. Gregory Wawro, "A Panel Probit Analysis of Campaign Contributions and Roll-Call Votes," *American Journal of Political Science* 45 (2001): 563–579.

13. See Richard L. Hall and Frank W. Wayman, "Buying Time," *American Political Science Review* 84 (1990): 797–820.

14. FEC, "2009 Coordinated Party Expenditure Limits," at www.fec.gov/info/charts_441ad.shtml (accessed June 25, 2009).

15. On public funding, see Michael J. Malbin, "Small Donors, Large Donors and the Internet," at www.cfinst.org/president/pdf/PresidentialWorkingPaper_April09.pdf (accessed June 7, 2009).

16. The case was decided in 1976. See Thomas E. Mann, "Linking Knowledge and Action," *Perspectives on Politics* 1 (2003): 69–83.

17. The cases are *Colorado Republican Federal Campaign Committee v. Federal Election Commission* (1996), known as "Colorado I," and *McConnell v. Federal Election Commission* (2003).

18. From the record in *McConnell v. Federal Election Commission*, quoted in Adam Cohen, "Buying a High-Priced Upgrade on the Political Back-Scratching Circuit," *New York Times*, September 15, 2003, p. A22.

19. See Anthony Corrado, Sarah Barclay, and Heitor Gouvea, "The Parties Take the Lead," in John C. Green and Rick Farmer, eds., *The State of the Parties*, 4th ed. (Lanham, MD: Rowman & Littlefield, 2003), pp. 97–114.

20. For a different view of the partisan impact of soft money, see Raymond J. La Raja, *Small Change* (Ann Arbor: University of Michigan Press, 2008).

21. John Kenneth White and Daniel M. Shea, *New Party Politics* (Belmont, CA: Wadsworth, 2004), p. 258.

22. John Solomon and Matthew Mosk, "Nonprofits Become a Force in Primaries," *Washington Post*, December 5, 2007, p. A1.

23. Federal Election Commission memo, October 20, 2008, at saos.nictusa.com/aodocs/1003774.pdf (accessed June 14, 2009).

24. Paul S. Herrnson, "The Congressional Elections," in Gerald M. Pomper, ed., *The Election of 2000* (New York: Chatham House, 2001), p. 170.

25. Mark J. Rozell, Clyde Wilcox, and David Madland, *Interest Groups in American Campaigns*, 2nd ed. (Washington, DC: CQ Press, 2005), pp. 146–147.

26. IRS data as of October 3, 2007, reported at www.opensecrets.org/overview/527cmtes.asp?level=C& cycle=2006 (accessed November 10, 2007).

27. Steve Weissman, "Soft Money Political Spending by 501(c) Nonprofits Tripled in 2008 Election," February 25, 2009, at www.cfinst.org/pr/prRelease.aspx?ReleaseID=221 (accessed June 13, 2009).

28. Michael J. Malbin, "Political Parties Under the Post-*McConnell* Bipartisan Campaign Reform Act," *Election Law Journal* 3 (2004): 183.

29. Karen Foerstal and Peter Wallsten, "Campaign Overhaul Mired in Money and Loopholes," *CQ Weekly*, May 13, 2000, p. 1084.

30. Raymond J. La Raja, "State Parties and Soft Money," in Green and Farmer, eds., *The State of the Parties*, 4th ed., pp. 132–150.

31. Jonathan Krasno and Kenneth Goldstein, "The Facts About Television Advertising and the McCain-Feingold Bill," *PS Political Science & Politics* 35 (2002): 210.

32. Richard Morin and Claudia Deane, "Exit Polls in Doubt for Nov. Elections," *Washington Post,* August 16, 2002, p. A1.

33. Raymond J. La Raja, "State and Local Political Parties," in Malbin, ed., *The Election after Reform*, Chapter 4.

34. Michael M. Franz, Joel Rivlin, and Kenneth Goldstein, "Much More of the Same," in Malbin, ed., *The Election after Reform*, Chapter 7.
35. Michael Malbin, "Analysis: Obama Small Donor % About Same as Bush; Large Donors 80% More Than Small," news release, Campaign Finance Institute, November 24, 2008.
36. President George W. Bush's propensity to give many of his biggest contributors appointments to high-level government jobs was not matched by President Obama, but even so, several big Obama bundlers were nominated for ambassadorships in 2009.
37. See Robert C. Boatright, "Fundraising—Present and Future," in Richard J. Semiatin, ed., *Campaigns on the Cutting Edge* (Washington, DC: CQ Press, 2008), pp. 10–26.
38. Joseph E. Sandler and Neil P. Reiff, "State and Local Parties Must Tread Carefully Through the Campaign Finance Minefield," *Campaigns & Elections* 25 (2004), pp. 50–51; and La Raja, "State and Local Political Parties."
39. Raymond J. La Raja, "From Bad to Worse," *The Forum*, 6 (2008), at www.bepress.com/forum/vol6/iss1/art2 (accessed June 14, 2009).
40. Data from National Conference of State Legislatures, at www.ncsl.org/programs/legismgt/about/ContribLimits.htm (accessed June 27, 2009).
41. See Michael Miller, "Gaming Arizona," *PS: Political Science and Politics* 61 (2008): 527–532.

PART FIVE: THE PARTY IN GOVERNMENT

1. See the report of the Committee on Responsible Parties of the American Political Science Association, *Toward a More Responsible Two-Party System* (New York: Rinehart, 1950).
2. Associated Press, "AP: GOP Changed Spending of Billions," *New York Times on the Web*, August 5, 2002.

CHAPTER 13: PARTIES IN CONGRESS AND STATE LEGISLATURES

1. Ruth Marcus, *Washington Post*, February 18, 2009, p. A13, quoting Politico.com.
2. Keith Krehbiel, "Where's the Party?" *British Journal of Political Science* 23 (1993): 225–266.
3. Gary W. Cox and Keith T. Poole, "On Measuring Partisanship in Roll-Call Voting," *American Journal of Political Science* 46 (2002): 477–489; and Gerald C. Wright and Brian F. Schaffner, "The Influence of Party," *American Political Science Review* 96 (2002): 367–379.
4. Steven S. Smith, *Party Influence in Congress* (Cambridge: Cambridge University Press, 2007).
5. D. Roderick Kiewiet and Mathew D. McCubbins, *The Logic of Delegation* (Chicago: University of Chicago Press, 1991).
6. Even Cannon faced limits, however; see Eric D. Lawrence, Forrest Maltzman, and Paul J. Wahlbeck, "The Politics of Speaker Cannon's Committee Assignments," *American Journal of Political Science* 45 (2001): 551–562.
7. Steven S. Smith and Gerald Gamm, "The Dynamics of Party Government in Congress," in Lawrence C. Dodd and Bruce I. Oppenheimer, eds., *Congress Reconsidered*, 9th ed. (Washington, DC: CQ Press, 2009), p. 149.
8. Gary W. Cox and Mathew W. McCubbins, *Legislative Leviathan*, 2nd ed. (Berkeley: University of California Press, 1993), pp. 279–282.
9. Barbara Sinclair, "Evolution or Revolution?" in L. Sandy Maisel, ed., *The Parties Respond*, 3rd ed. (Boulder, CO: Westview, 1998).
10. Barbara Sinclair, *Unorthodox Lawmaking*, 2nd ed. (Washington, DC: CQ Press, 2000), pp. 103–106.
11. C. Lawrence Evans and Walter J. Oleszek, *Congress Under Fire* (Boston: Houghton Mifflin, 1997); and Lawrence C. Dodd and Bruce I. Oppenheimer, "A Decade of Republican Control," in Dodd and Oppenheimer, eds., *Congress Reconsidered*, 8th ed. (Washington, DC: CQ Press, 2005), Chapter 2.
12. Mike Allen, "GOP Leaders Tighten Their Grip on House," *Washington Post*, January 9. 2005, p. A5.
13. Marian Currinder, *Money in the House* (Boulder, CO: Westview, 2009), chapter 2 and p. 203.
14. David W. Rohde, *Parties and Leaders in the Postreform House* (Chicago: University of Chicago Press, 1991). See also Barbara Sinclair, *Legislators, Leaders, and Lawmaking* (Baltimore: Johns Hopkins University Press, 1995).

15. See, for example, William T. Bianco and Itai Sened, "Uncovering Evidence of Conditional Party Government," *American Political Science Review* 99 (2005): 361–371.

16. See John H. Aldrich and David W. Rohde, "The Consequences of Party Organization in the House," in Jon R. Bond and Richard Fleisher, eds., *Polarized Politics* (Washington, DC: CQ Press, 2000), pp. 31–72.

17. Smith, *Party Influence in Congress*, Chapter 5.

18. Barbara Sinclair, "The New World of U.S. Senators," in Dodd and Oppenheimer, eds., *Congress Reconsidered*, 9th ed. (Washington, DC: CQ Press, 2009), pp. 1–22.

19. Smith and Gamm, "The Dynamics of Party Government in Congress," pp. 141–164.

20. See Nathan W. Monroe, Jason M. Roberts, and David W. Rohde, eds., *Why Not Parties?* (Chicago: University of Chicago Press, 2008).

21. The exceptions are some southern states and Nebraska, which is nominally nonpartisan. See Malcolm E. Jewell and Sarah M. Morehouse, *Political Parties and Elections in American States*, 4th ed. (Washington, DC: CQ Press, 2001), Chapter 8.

22. Jewell and Morehouse, *Political Parties and Elections*, pp. 236–238.

23. Keith E. Hamm and Robert Harmel, "Legislative Party Development and the Speaker System," *Journal of Politics* 55 (1993): 1140–1151; and Malcolm E. Jewell and Marcia Lynn Whicker, *Legislative Leadership in the American States* (Ann Arbor, MI: University of Michigan Press, 1994).

24. Paul S. Herrnson, *Congressional Elections*, 5th ed. (Washington, DC: CQ Press, 2008); and Kathryn Pearson, "Congressional Party Discipline," paper delivered at the 2002 Annual Meeting of the Midwest Political Science Association.

25. Thomas Stratmann, "Congressional Voting over Legislative Careers," *American Political Science Review* 94 (2000): 665–676.

26. Juliet Eilperin, "House GOP Practices Art of One-Vote Victories," *Washington Post*, October 14, 2003, p. A1.

27. See Gary W. Cox and Mathew D. McCubbins, *Setting the Agenda* (Cambridge: Cambridge University Press, 2005).

28. Barbara Sinclair, "Orchestrators of Unorthodox Lawmaking," *The Forum*, 6 (2008), at www.bepress.com/forum/vol6/iss3/art4 (accessed June 29, 2009).

29. Julius Turner, *Party and Constituency*, rev. ed., Edward V. Schneier, ed. (Baltimore: Johns Hopkins University Press, 1970), pp. 16–17.

30. Gregory L. Giroux, "GOP's Effectiveness Shows in Party Unity Votes," *CQ Weekly*, April 19, 2003, p. 923.

31. Jason M. Roberts and Steven S. Smith, "Procedural Contexts, Party Strategy, and Conditional Party Voting in the U.S. House of Representatives, 1971–2000," *American Journal of Political Science* 47 (2003): 305–317.

32. Nelson W. Polsby, "The Institutionalization of the United States House of Representatives," *American Political Science Review* 62 (1968): 144–168, and Walter Dean Burnham, *Critical Elections and the Mainsprings of American Politics* (New York: Norton, 1970), pp. 91–134.

33. Jewell and Morehouse, *Political Parties and Elections*, p. 251.

34. Rohde, *Parties and Leaders in the Postreform House*, Chapter 3. See also M. V. Hood III, Quentin Kidd, and Irwin L. Morris, "Of Byrd[s] and Bumpers," *American Journal of Political Science* 43 (1999): 465–487; and Stanley P. Berard, *Southern Democrats in the U.S. House of Representatives* (Norman: University of Oklahoma Press, 2001).

35. Roberts and Smith, "Procedural Contexts."

36. On Pelosi's Speakership, see Kathryn Pearson and Eric Schickler, "The Transition to Democratic Leadership in a Polarized House," in Dodd and Oppenheimer, eds., *Congress Reconsidered*, 9th ed., pp. 165–188.

37. *ADA Today*, Spring, 2009, Vol. 64, p. 1, at www.adaction.org/media/votingrecords/2008.pdf (accessed June 27, 2009).

38. Barry Burden, "Candidate Positioning in U.S. Congressional Elections," *British Journal of Political Science* 34 (2004): 211–227.

39. Thanks to Rachel Bloom and John Cranford for these data.

40. Mark A. Peterson, *Legislating Together* (Cambridge, MA: Harvard University Press, 1990); and Cary R. Covington, J. Mark Wrighton, and Rhonda Kinney, "A 'Presidency-Augmented' Model of Presidential Success on House Roll Call Votes," *American Journal of Political Science* 39 (November 1995): 1001–1024.

41. Gary C. Jacobson, *The Politics of Congressional Elections*, 7th ed. (New York: Pearson-Longman, 2009), p. 255.
42. C. Lawrence Evans and Claire E. Grandy, "The Whip Systems of Congress," in Dodd and Oppenheimer, eds., *Congress Reconsidered*, 9th ed., p. 210.
43. James M. Snyder, Jr., and Tim Groseclose, "Estimating Party Influence in Congressional Roll-Call Voting," *American Journal of Political Science* 44 (2000): 187–205.
44. Gerald C. Wright, Tracy Osborn, and Jonathan Winburn, "Parties and Representation in the American Legislatures." Paper presented at the 2004 Annual Meeting of the Midwest Political Science Association, p. 14.
45. Jewell and Morehouse, *Political Parties and Elections*, p. 244.
46. Wright, Osborn, and Winburn, "Parties and Representation in the American Legislatures."
47. David Denemark, "Partisan Pork Barrel in Parliamentary Systems," *Journal of Politics* 62 (2000): 896–915.
48. Anthony Gierzynski, *Legislative Party Campaign Committees in the American States* (Lexington: University of Kentucky Press, 1992); and Daniel M. Shea, *Transforming Democracy* (Albany: State University of New York Press, 1995).
49. Cox and McCubbins, *Legislative Leviathan*.
50. See Gary Cox, *The Efficient Secret* (New York: Cambridge University Press, 1987).

CHAPTER 14: THE PARTY IN THE EXECUTIVE AND THE COURTS

1. Quoted in Adam Clymer, "Not So Fast," *New York Times*, April 1, 2001, sec. 4, p. 1.
2. Elizabeth Benjamin, "At Obama's Request, Steve Israel Stands Down," www.nydailynews.com/blogs/dailypolitics/2009/05/at-obamas-request-steve-israel.html (accessed November 15, 2009).
3. Libby Copeland, "Campaign Gone South," *Washington Post*, October 31, 2006, p. C1.
4. James E. Campbell, "Predicting Seat Gains from Presidential Coattails," *American Journal of Political Science* 30 (1986): 164–183.
5. See Bruce Cain, John Ferejohn, and Morris Fiorina, *The Personal Vote* (Cambridge, MA: Harvard University Press, 1987).
6. Paul R. Abramson, John H. Aldrich, and David W. Rohde, *Change and Continuity in the 2004 and 2006 Elections* (Washington, DC: CQ Press, 2007), pp. 261–263; but see Ray C. Fair, "Presidential and Congressional Vote-Share Equations," *American Journal of Political Science* 53 (2009): 55–72.
7. See, for instance, Paul S. Herrnson, *Congressional Elections*, 5th ed. (Washington, DC: CQ Press, 2008), p. 24.
8. See James E. Campbell, "Presidential Coattails and Midterm Losses in State Legislative Elections," *American Political Science Review* 80 (1986): 45–63.
9. Robin F. Marra and Charles W. Ostrom, Jr., "Explaining Seat Change in the U.S. House of Representatives, 1950–86," *American Journal of Political Science* 33 (1989): 541–569.
10. Chris Cillizza, "No Surprise," *Washington Post*, March 17, 2006, at www.blog.washingtonpost.com/thefix/2006/03/a_philosophical_divide_in_hous.html (accessed July 12, 2007).
11. The classic statement is Angus Campbell, "Surge and Decline: A Study of Electoral Change," in Campbell, Philip E. Converse, Warren E. Miller, and Donald E. Stokes, eds., *Elections and the Political Order* (New York: Wiley, 1966), pp. 40–62.
12. See Gary C. Jacobson and Samuel Kernell, *Strategy and Choice in Congressional Elections*, 2nd ed. (New Haven: Yale University Press, 1983).
13. Richard Born, "Surge and Decline, Negative Voting, and the Midterm Loss Phenomenon," *American Journal of Political Science* 34 (1990): 615–645.
14. See Abramson, Aldrich, and Rohde, *Change and Continuity*, p. 196.
15. David Baumann, "At the Top of His Game," *CQ Weekly*, May 18, 2009, p. 1142–1143.
16. Hugh Heclo, "Issue Networks and the Executive Establishment," in Anthony King, ed., *The New American Political System* (Washington, DC: American Enterprise Institute, 1979), pp. 87–124.
17. Hugh Heclo, *A Government of Strangers* (Washington, DC: Brookings Institution, 1977).

18. Joel Aberbach and Bert A. Rockman, "Clashing Beliefs Within the Executive Branch," *American Political Science Review* 70 (1976): 456–468.

19. Joel D. Aberbach and Bert A. Rockman, "The Political Views of U.S. Senior Federal Executives, 1970–1992," *Journal of Politics* 57 (1995): 838–852.

20. See Carrie Johnson, "Holder Begins Justice Revamp," *Washington Post*, April 9, 2009, p. A1.

21. Robert A. Carp and Ronald Stidham, *Judicial Process in America* (Washington, DC: CQ Press, 2001), p. 292.

22. Stuart S. Nagel, "Political Party Affiliations and Judges' Decisions," *American Political Science Review* 55 (1961): 843–850. See also Jeffrey A. Segal and Harold J. Spaeth, *The Supreme Court and the Attitudinal Model* (Cambridge: Cambridge University Press, 1993).

23. Juliet Eilperin, "Environmental Group Cites Partisanship in the Judiciary," *Washington Post*, October 9, 2004, p. A2.

24. See Randall D. Lloyd, "Separating Partisanship from Party in Judicial Research," *American Political Science Review* 89 (1995): 413–420.

25. See Robert Barnes, "Partisan Fissures Over Voter ID," *Washington Post*, December 25, 2007, p. A1.

26. Elisha Carol Savchak, Thomas G. Hansford, Donald R. Songer, Kenneth L. Manning, and Robert A Carp, "Taking It to the Next Level," *American Journal of Political Science* 50 (2006): 485–486.

27. See Amy Goldstein and Dan Eggen, "Immigration Judges Often Picked Based on GOP Ties," *Washington Post*, June 11, 2007, p. A1.

28. Sheldon Goldman, "The Bush Imprint on the Judiciary," *Judicature* 74 (1991), 294–306.

29. Sheldon Goldman, Elliot Slotnick, Gerard Gryski, and Gary Zuk, "Clinton's Judges," *Judicature* 84 (2001): 244, 249.

30. R. Jeffrey Smith, "The Politics of the Federal Bench," *Washington Post*, December 8, 2008, p. A1.

31. Daniel J. Parks, "Senate Judicial Nominations Spat Again Frustrates Appropriators," *CQ Weekly*, October 20, 2001, pp. 2470–2471. See also Sarah A. Binder and Forrest Maltzman, "Senatorial Delay in Confirming Federal Judges, 1947–1998," *American Journal of Political Science* 46 (2002): 190–199.

32. See Melinda Gann Hall, "State Supreme Courts in American Democracy," *American Political Science Review* 95 (2001): 315–330.

CHAPTER 15: THE SEMI-RESPONSIBLE PARTIES

1. E. E. Schattschneider, *Party Government* (New York: Rinehart, 1942), pp. 131–132.

2. Committee on Political Parties of the American Political Science Association, *Toward a More Responsible Two-Party System* (New York: Rinehart, 1950).

3. Jeffrey M. Jones, "More Americans See Democratic Party as 'Too Liberal," at www.gallup.com/poll/121307/more-americans-see-democratic-party-too-liberal.aspx (accessed November 16, 2009).

4. See Austin Ranney, *The Doctrine of Responsible Party Government* (Urbana: University of Illinois Press, 1964), Chapters 1 and 2.

5. Schattschneider, *Party Government*, p. 208.

6. E. E. Schattschneider, *The Semi-Sovereign People* (New York: Holt, Rinehart, and Winston, 1960).

7. See John Kenneth White and Jerome M. Mileur, eds., *Challenges to Party Government* (Carbondale: Southern Illinois University Press, 1992).

8. See Malcolm E. Jewell and Sarah M. Morehouse, *Political Parties and Elections in American States*, 4th ed. (Washington, DC: CQ Press, 2001), p. 222; and Morris Fiorina, *Divided Government* (New York: MacMillan, 1992), Chapter 3.

9. John J. Coleman, "Unified Government, Divided Government, and Party Responsiveness," *American Political Science Review* 93 (1999): 821–835, and David R. Mayhew, *Divided We Govern*, 2nd ed. (New Haven, CT: Yale University Press, 2005).

10. Richard Born, "Split-Ticket Voters, Divided Government, and Fiorina's Policy-Balancing Model," *Legislative Studies Quarterly* 19 (1994): 95–115.

11. A. James Reichley, *The Life of the Parties* (Lanham, MD: Rowman & Littlefield, 2000), Chapter 6.

12. David E. Rosenbaum, "Bush to Return to 'Ownership Society' Theme in Push for Social Security Changes," *New York Times*, January 16, 2005, p. 20.

13. Edward G. Carmines and James A. Stimson, *Issue Evolution* (Princeton, NJ: Princeton University Press, 1989); see also Geoffrey C. Layman and Thomas M. Carsey, "Party Polarization and 'Conflict Extension' in the American Electorate," *American Journal of Political Science* 46 (2002): 786–802.

14. Jason M. Roberts and Steven S. Smith, "Procedural Contexts, Party Strategy, and Conditional Party Voting in the U.S. House of Representatives, 1971–2000," *American Journal of Political Science* 47 (2003): 305–317. See also Barbara Sinclair, *Party Wars* (Norman: University of Oklahoma Press, 2006).

15. Charles Barrilleaux, Thomas Holbrook, and Laura Langer, "Electoral Competition, Legislative Balance, and American State Welfare Policy," *American Journal of Political Science* 46 (2002): 415–427.

16. Sheryl Gay Stolberg, "The Revolution That Wasn't," *New York Times*, February 13, 2005, section 4, p. 1. Data are from the National Taxpayers Union.

17. Robin Kolodny, "Moderate Party Factions in the U.S. House of Representatives," in John C. Green and Daniel M. Shea, eds., *The State of the Parties*, 3rd ed. (Lanham, MD: Rowman & Littlefield, 1999), pp. 271–285.

18. Nicol C. Rae, "Party Factionalism, 1946–1996," in Byron E. Shafer, ed., *Partisan Approaches to Postwar American Politics* (New York: Chatham House, 1998), pp. 41–74.

19. Stephanie L. Witt, "Idaho," in Andrew M. Appleton and Daniel S. Ward, eds., *State Party Profiles* (Washington, DC: CQ Press, 1997), pp. 82–88.

20. The seminal study is Philip E. Converse, "The Nature of Belief Systems in Mass Publics," in David Apter, ed., *Ideology and Discontent* (New York: Free Press, 1964), pp. 206–261.

21. John Zaller and Stanley Feldman, "A Simple Theory of the Survey Response," *American Journal of Political Science* 36 (1992): 579–616.

22. Kathleen A. Frankovic and Monika L. McDermott, "Public Opinion in the 2000 Election," in Gerald M. Pomper, ed., *The Election of 2000* (New York: Chatham House, 2001), pp. 76–78 and 88–89.

23. Paul R. Abramson, John H. Aldrich, and David W. Rohde, *Change and Continuity in the 1984 Elections* (Washington, DC: CQ Press, 1986), Chapter 6.

24. Alan Abramowitz, "Don't Blame Primary Voters for Polarization," *The Forum* 5 (2008), at www.bepress.com/forum/vol5/iss4/art3 (accessed July 11, 2009).

25. Kyle L. Saunders and Alan I. Abramowitz, "Ideological Realignment and Active Partisans in the American Electorate," *American Politics Research* 32 (2004): 293.

26. Jacob S. Hacker and Paul Pierson, "Abandoning the Middle," *Perspectives on Politics* 3 (2005): 33–53.

27. Marc J. Hetherington, "Resurgent Mass Partisanship," *American Political Science Review* 95 (2001): 619–631.

28. Gerald M. Pomper and Marc D. Weiner, "Toward a More Responsible Two-Party Voter," in John C. Green and Paul S. Herrnson, eds., *Responsible Partisanship?* (Lawrence: University Press of Kansas, 2002), pp. 181–200. See also David R. Jones and Monika L. McDermott, "The Responsible Party Government Model in House and Senate Elections," *American Journal of Political Science* 48 (2004): 1–12.

29. Paul Allen Beck, "A Tale of Two Electorates," in John C. Green and Rick Farmer, eds., *The State of the Parties*, 4th ed. (Lanham, MD: Rowman & Littlefield, 2003), pp. 38–53.

30. See Seth E. Masket, "It Takes an Outsider," *American Journal of Political Science* 51 (2007): 482–497.

31. See Brandice Canes-Wrone, David W. Brady, and John F. Cogan, "Out of Step, Out of Office," *American Political Science Review* 96 (2002): 127–140.

32. John R. Hibbing and Elizabeth Theiss-Morse, "Process Preferences and American Politics," *American Political Science Review* 95 (2001): 145–153.

33. David C. King, "The Polarization of American Political Parties and Mistrust of Government," in Joseph S. Nye, Philip Zelikow, and David C. King, eds., *Why People Don't Trust Government* (Cambridge: Harvard University Press, 1997), pp. 155–178.

34. David Von Drehle, "Political Split Is Pervasive," *Washington Post*, April 25, 2004, p. A1.

35. Leon D. Epstein, "What Happened to the British Party Model?" *American Political Science Review* 74 (1980): 9–22.

36. Jerome M. Clubb, William H. Flanigan, and Nancy H. Zingale, *Partisan Realignment* (Beverly Hills, CA: Sage, 1980), pp. 155–188.

CHAPTER 16: THE PLACE OF PARTIES IN AMERICAN POLITICS

1. See Robert Harmel and Kenneth Janda, *Parties and Their Environments* (New York: Longman, 1982).
2. See Ruy A. Teixeira, *The Disappearing American Voter* (Washington, DC: Brookings Institution, 1992), Chapter 3
3. See Stephen K. Medvic, *Campaigns and Elections* (Boston: Wadsworth, 2010), pp. 312–314.
4. Harold W. Stanley and Richard G. Niemi, *Vital Statistics on American Politics 1999–2000* (Washington, DC: CQ Press, 2000), pp. 44 and 133.
5. Bruce E. Cain, John Ferejohn, and Morris P. Fiorina, *The Personal Vote* (Cambridge, MA: Harvard University Press, 1987).
6. Philip A. Klinkner and Thomas Schaller, "LBJ's Revenge," *The Forum* 6 (2008), at www.bepress.com/forum/vol16/iss4/art9 (accessed July 17, 2009).
7. Joe Gaylord, quoted in David Nather, "The 'Big Tent' Collapses," *CQ Weekly*, November 17, 2008, p. 3082.
8. See Robert Huckfeldt and Paul Allen Beck, "Contexts, Intermediaries, and Political Activity," in Lawrence C. Dodd and Calvin Jillson, eds., *The Dynamics of American Politics* (Boulder, CO: Westview Press, 1994), Chapter 11. On the other hand, organized interests have become more polarized by party since the Reagan years; see Jack L. Walker, Jr., *Mobilizing Interest Groups in America* (Ann Arbor: University of Michigan Press, 1991), Chapter 8, and media coverage frequently refers to party; see Marjorie Randon Hershey, "If 'The Party's in Decline,' Then What's That Filling the News Columns?" in Nelson W. Polsby and Raymond E. Wolfinger, eds., *On Parties* (Berkeley: Institute of Governmental Studies, 1999), pp. 257–278.
9. Larry M. Bartels, "Partisanship and Voting Behavior, 1952–1996," *American Journal of Political Science* 44 (2000): 35–50.
10. Gary C. Jacobson, *The Politics of Congressional Elections*, 7th ed. (New York: Longman, 2004), p. 163.
11. Rep. Daniel Lipinski, "Navigating Congressional Policy Processes," in Lawrence C. Dodd and Bruce I. Oppenheimer, eds., *Congress Reconsidered*, 9th ed. (Washington, DC: CQ Press, 2009), p. 344.
12. See Ronald Inglehart, *Culture Shift* (Princeton, NJ: Princeton University Press, 1990), Chapters 10 and 11.
13. Larry J. Sabato and Bruce Larson, *The Party's Just Begun* (New York: Longman, 2002), pp. 2–4.
14. John H. Aldrich, *Why Parties?* (Chicago: University of Chicago Press, 1995), p. 3.
15. David R. Mayhew, *Congress: The Electoral Connection* (New Haven: Yale University Press, 1974), especially pp. 141–149.
16. See Marjorie Randon Hershey, "Political Parties as Mechanisms of Social Choice," in Richard S. Katz and William Crotty, eds., *Handbook of Party Politics* (London: Sage, 2005), pp. 75–88.
17. Walter Dean Burnham, *Critical Elections and the Mainsprings of American Politics* (New York: Norton, 1970), p. 133.
18. See Gerald C. Wright and Brian F. Schaffner, "The Influence of Party," *American Political Science Review* 96 (2002): 367–379.
19. See Steven J. Rosenstone and John Mark Hansen, *Mobilization, Participation, and Democracy in America* (New York: Macmillan, 1993), Chapter 8.
20. Sabato and Larson, *The Party's Just Begun*, pp. 156–157.
21. Ibid., pp. 159–160.

Index